G.F. Watts *Victorian Visionary*

G. F. Watts *Victorian Visionary*

HIGHLIGHTS FROM THE WATTS GALLERY COLLECTION

Mark Bills and Barbara Bryant

with contributions by

Stephanie Brown, Michael Wheeler and

Julia Dudkiewicz

Yale University Press New Haven and London
in association with
Watts Gallery Compton

© Watts Gallery, 2008

First published by Yale University Press in association with Watts Gallery
on the occasion of the exhibition at Guildhall Art Gallery, City of London,
and the Mercer Art Gallery, Harrogate Museums and Arts

Printed in Italy by Conti Tipocolor SrL, Florence
Designed by Catherine Bowe and Sally Salvesen

Library of Congress Cataloging-in-Publication Data

Bills, Mark.
  G.F. Watts : Victorian visionary : highlights from the Watts Gallery
collection / Mark Bills and Barbara Bryant ; with contributions by
Stephanie Brown, Michael Wheeler and Julia Dudkiewicz.
      p. cm.
  Includes bibliographical references and index.
  ISBN 978-0-300-14257-0 (cloth : alk. paper)
  ISBN 978-0-300-15294-4 (paper : alk. paper)
  1. Watts, George Frederic, 1817–1904 – Criticism and interpretation.
2. Watts Gallery. I. Bryant, Barbara II. Watts, George Frederic,
1817–1904. III. Title. IV. Title: GF Watts.

ND497.W3B54 2008
759.2--dc22

                                            2008019045

Cover illustrations
Front: *Endymion* (detail, cat.81)
Back: *A Dedication* (detail, cat.77)

Frontispiece: *Progress* (detail, cat.79)

Contents

Foreword

As a collector of nineteenth-century paintings and owner of some of Watts's masterpieces, I am delighted to celebrate the first tour of the Watts Gallery collection in one hundred years.

It is true to say that out of darkness comes light! The Watts Gallery building has been seriously at risk for over ten years, and the collection has been under threat. Thanks to the wonderful generosity of our bene-factors, and as Patron of the Watts Gallery Hope Appeal, I am very glad that we are able to restore and conserve some of our paintings so that during the much needed restoration of the Gallery, the Watts Gallery collection can reach new audiences and engage fresh admirers. The last time there was such a tour, was when Mary Seton Watts refurbished and developed the Gallery in 1905 following Watts's death in 1904.

G.F. Watts is an enigma. It is sometimes difficult, in the wealth of his output and the breadth of his artistic genres, to find the man. I am so pleased that the Curator of Watts Gallery, Mark Bills, with the help of experts such as Barbara Bryant, Michael Wheeler and Stephanie Brown, has persevered in his diligence to find the 'real Watts' and bring to light fresh findings on these, his masterpieces. In the foreword to Veronica Franklin Gould's book *G.F. Watts – The Last Great Victorian*, the former curator Richard Jefferies wrote: 'what emerges across the gulf that now separates us from the Victorian age, despite Watts's small stature, is a kindly, gentle giant'. We must remember that Watts was the most famous artist in England at the time of his death. Now, just over one hundred years on, I am delighted that we can celebrate this heroic artist and social philanthropist, whose art and its message are still so powerful today.

Isabel Goldsmith
Collector of nineteenth-century paintings and
Patron and Trustee of the Watts Gallery Hope Project
May 2008

Acknowledgements

The work of a catalogue of this scale needs the help of a great many people. Watts Gallery is deeply grateful to all its benefactors and major donors and would especially like to thank:

Heritage Lottery Fund
Esmée Fairbairn Foundation
The Deborah Loeb Brice Foundation
Garfield Weston Foundation
The John Ellerman Foundation
The Wolfson Foundation
Guildford Borough Council
The George John and Sheilah Livanos Charitable Trust
Richard Ormond CBE
Professor Rob Dickins CBE
Christopher Forbes
Peter Harrison Foundation
The Robert Gavron Charitable Trust
An Anonymous Donor
David Pike
The Pilgrim Trust
The Isabel Goldsmith Patino Foundation
The Art Fund
J Paul Getty Jnr Charitable Trust
The Rothschild Foundation
The Linbury Trust
Finnis Scott Foundation
The Foyle Foundation
The Foundation for Sport and the Arts
The Ingram Trust
English Heritage
Hamish Dewar Ltd
Man Group PLC Charitable Trust
The Mercers' Company
Billmeir Charitable Trust
The Michael Marks Charitable Trust
KPMG Foundation
The Henry Moore Foundation
Prince of Wales Foundation
and many other donors, patrons, adopters and friends

Watts Gallery would particularly like to thank the following for their support of this exhibition: Hamish Dewar Conservation, David Pike and Robert Napier as well as the Patrons, Friends, volunteers and stewards of Watts Gallery without whom none of this would have been possible. Further thanks are due to Adlib, The City of London Guides, Blackwell Green (part of the Heath Lambert Group), Christie's Images, Bridgeman Art Library, the National Portrait Gallery, St Bride Library, Corporation of London Libraries, Nevill Keating Pictures, Leighton House Museum and Neville Rolt and Richard Harris from BAS Printers.

The authors would like to thank Vivien Knight, Curator at the Guildhall Art Gallery, where the exhibition opens, who has supported this project from the outset. Malcolm Warner and Amy Meyers also offered early encouragement. Thanks are also due to those who helped and assisted in various ways: Brian Allen, Martin Beisly, Sally Bills, Heather Birchall, Julius Bryant, Max Bryant, Alan Cowie, Mary Cowling, Melva Croal, Sue Demetriadi, Professor Rob Dickins, Richard Dorment, Louise Drover, Edwina Ehrman, Gabrielle Elfer, Susanna Fergusson, the late John George, Pam Gomer, Veronica Franklin Gould, Gillian Hardy, Richard Harris, Julian Hartnoll, James Hervey-Bathurst, Patricia Jackson, Christopher Jordan, Elizabeth Klaiber, David and Barbara Knight, Graham Larkin, Brandon Lindberg, Seamus McKenna, Elizabeth Milton, Sandy Nairne, Lady Angela Nevill, Richard and Leonee Ormond, Terry Parker, Annette Peach, Ben Pearce, Amy Plewis, Jennifer Ramkalawon, Aileen Ribeiro, Daniel Robbins, Neville Rolt, Alison Smith, The Hon. Mrs. Charlotte Thompson, Barbara Thompson, Hilary Underwood, Melanie Unwin, Emma Verey, Alex Werner, Nigel Wilkins and Joseph Wisdom. Special thanks go to Dr Desna Greenhow for her research in the Watts Gallery Archive and to Colin Grant for editing the catalogue. At Yale University Press we are indebted to Sally Salvesen and Catherine Bowe.

Adopt a Watts

A special mention and thanks must go to those who have directly sponsored the conservation of specific artworks for this exhibition through our Adopt a Watts Scheme; Mr & Mrs John Vardon (*After the Deluge*); Sir Christopher and Lady Laidlaw, in memory of Helen Violet Prichard (*End of the Day*); Mrs Hazel Watson (*A Lamplight Study: Herr Joachim*); Mr Robert Napier (*John Stuart Mill*); Mr David Pike (*Found Drowned* and *Miss May Prinsep*); The Friends of the British Antique Association Trust & Emma Verey (*Paolo and Francesca*); Mr Philip Martyn (*Progress*); Mr Mark Jones (*Study of a Hand*); HK Associates (UK) Limited, A Development and Cultural Planning Consultancy, Roger & Heather Kerswell (*A Dedication*); Mrs Anthea Vernell (*The Sower of the Systems*).

Introduction

The atmosphere of Watts and Victorian idealism: an atmosphere so completely vanished from the world of art in which we now live, that the somewhat long introduction is really needed to make it vivid or human to us. These three elements may legitimately be predicated of it as its main characteristics: first, the sceptical idealism, the belief that abstract verities remained the chief affairs of men when theology left them; second, the didactic simplicity, the claim to teach other men and to assume one's own value and rectitude; third, the cosmic utilitarianism, the consideration of any such thing as art or philosophy perpetually with reference to a general good. They may be right or wrong, they may be returning or gone for ever; theories and fashions may change the face of humanity again and yet again, but at least in that one old man at Limnerlease, burn, and will burn until death, these convictions, like three lamps in an old pagan temple of stoicism. (Chesterton 1904)

Apart from his prolific output of work, which includes the monumental sculpture of *Physical Energy* that stands in both Kensington Gardens in London and at the Rhodes Memorial in South Africa, over fifty masterpieces at Tate Britain in London and his 'Hall of Fame' series in the National Portrait Gallery in London, the other great tangible legacy of G.F. Watts, OM, RA (1817–1904), is the Watts Gallery, lying just south of London in the green Surrey hills. Watts Gallery is unique. Unique is an overused word, but in this case it is correct. Watts Gallery is the only purpose-built art gallery for a single professional artist's collection that exists in the United Kingdom. Not only is the building situated in a village where Watts lived and worked, it also houses a collection of international importance. The listed Arts & Crafts building, which opened in 1904, was also constructed to house apprentice potters who worked in the pottery founded by Mary Watts in 1898, following the success of community involvement in creating the cemetery chapel for Compton a hundred yards from the Gallery in 1897. Watts Gallery offers visitors the opportunity to see the heart of the artist's endeavours, the environment that inspired him, and the symbols of his beliefs in terms of the buildings he and his second wife Mary Seton Watts created; and through the range of his work and the archival material, given Watts's long life, the Gallery and its collection provide a unique glimpse into a rich period of British history. The chapel, the pottery, Watts's home Limnerslease, the Gallery, and the apprentice potters' accommodation, which now houses the Curator and Assistant Curator, reveal the essence of Arts & Crafts values.

But all this would not be unique if it was not for the driving force that lay behind the buildings, place, collection and experience – G.F. Watts, the artist himself. At the time of his death in 1904 Watts was one of the most famous artists of his generation. There were obituaries in newspapers across the world. Today Watts provokes a mixed reaction and, for many, his name remains unknown. Why did his star decline? Some would say that his work was too dark, too challenging. Some would say that his standards were not

G.F. Watts at Limnerslease,
Compton (cat. 90)

consistent. But for those who take the time to discover the range, breadth and inspiration of his work, Watts provides a most satisfying, rich and surprising journey of enjoyment and understanding.

As Chesterton wrote in his book on Watts, the artist lived in a 'world in which painters were trying to be novelists, and novelists, trying to be historians, and musicians doing the work of schoolmasters, and sculptors doing the work of curates'. Watts used art as a form of communication. Antony Gormley, the leading British sculptor, describes Watts as 'the first real international – his wish for universalism marks him out as a pioneer of the modernists who believed in the creation of art that transcended race, creed and language'. His social history paintings, *Found Drowned* (cat.14), *Under a Dry Arch* (cat.15), *The Irish Famine* (cat.16) and *The Seamstress* (c.1849–50; Watts Gallery), are strong statements about the darker side of the great industrial revolution unfolding in Britain at that time. His allegorical paintings carry a strong message about such issues as gluttony, greed, death, progress and prostitution. Watts was inspired by the idea of painting vast frescoes in public places to capture famous moments in history or to communicate the great themes of life. Although we have the fresco at Lincoln's Inn in London and some remaining frescoes hanging in Malvern School, Gloucestershire, it is a shame that he was not given more free reign to leave us paintings at such places as Euston Station!

Looking for the essence of Watts is about looking at his work and life from all angles. This catalogue will hopefully provide a refreshing and thorough insight into the impulses and demons that drove his prolific and magnificent output. However, if you wish to commune even more directly with this elusive character who has left us such a monumental legacy, a visit to Postman's Park, just tucked away behind St Paul's Cathedral in the heart of the City of London, is the place to go. There so simply, so quietly, Watts has left the stamp of his personal credo – that ordinary citizens achieve extraordinary acts. 'The utmost for the highest' is no trivial, joking mantra for Watts and Mary Seton Watts. It was the driving rhythm of their lives.

The Watts Gallery Trustees are delighted that Watts's studio collection, now just over a hundred years on, can once again be enjoyed by visitors. In 1905, when Mary Seton Watts began building extensions to the Gallery following Watts's death, the collection was sent out on tour to London and other parts. Then, as now, the collection going on tour will enable some vital restoration of the Watts Gallery. The Arts & Crafts Grade II*-listed building is deemed 'at risk'. Rain is coming in through the roof, the collection is damaged by the extreme conditions and some of the galleries are not accessible to disabled people. At times like this one is faced with hard choices and challenging decisions. The Watts Gallery Trustees have needed to assess the real importance of the Gallery and Watts. After careful thought and consultation the Trustees chose the centenary of Watts's death and the founding of the Gallery in 2004 to launch the Watts Gallery *Hope* Project. Inspired by Watts's poignant and iconic painting of a blindfolded girl astride the globe playing a single-stringed instrument and yet making music (cat.59), the Watts Gallery *Hope* Project has six aims. It seeks to save the building, rescue and conserve the collection, develop audiences, increase income, strengthen the role of the Gallery locally, nationally and internationally, and establish Watts Gallery as a centre for exploring Victorian art, social history and craft. Thankfully, this £10m project is now well advanced with support from the Heritage Lottery Fund and other generous donors listed in the acknowledgements. However, to ensure the future of the Gallery for another hundred years, the Watts Gallery Trustees are seeking further gifts of support to increase its financial reserves and to ensure that the collection is maintained to national standards.

I would like to make special mention of Veronica Franklin Gould, biographer of *G.F. Watts: The Last Great Victorian* and curator of *The Vision of G.F. Watts*, a centenary exhibition in 2004 at Watts Gallery. Veronica has maintained her interest in and passion for Watts when his profile was hidden from view; her commitment and leadership has enabled us to rebuild awareness of Watts and celebrate the artist's great achievements. We are most grateful.

Watts reputedly said: 'I may not be recognised in the first hundred years after my death, and not even the second hundred.' In taking his prime collection on tour a hundred years on from its last outing, and in re-seizing the three tenets of his convictions, truth, education and the good of others, it seems timely and apt that we secure through this exhibition the deserved and long-awaited recognition for this great artist, as well as preserve his legacy and selfless contribution to our national heritage by saving Watts Gallery.

Perdita Hunt
Director

1. Watts Gallery, Compton

Watts Gallery: A Temple of Art in Rural England

Mark Bills

Besides the charm of its environment, the gallery is well lighted, the pictures are well arranged, and the collection contained within its walls is thoroughly representative of the late painter's life-work … A more serious atmosphere than is generally found in a picture-gallery.[1]

When the Watts Gallery reopened in 1906, shortly after a new gallery extension had been completed, it swam in a sea of ecstatic and complimentary national publicity. 'The money value of the pictures alone', wrote the influential dealer and critic David Croal Thomson, 'is immense, so that the proposed gift will be one of the greatest in artistic annals.'[2] Its trustees included leading figures from the art world such as Sir Charles Holroyd, the director of the Tate Gallery (then the National Gallery of British Art) and later the National Gallery, who curated its 1906 rehang. Given the national importance of the gallery's collection, the nature of the gallery, 'a simple and rural type of building',[3] and its location in the heart of rural Surrey may at first have appeared surprising. Yet G.F. Watts's reputation was such that in 1906 the Watts Gallery became a place of pilgrimage and a model for other galleries. 'I find that visitors', wrote Mary Watts, 'experience an added pleasure in passing from a collection of art into the beauty and peace of nature.'[4]

The purpose-built gallery that was constructed in 1903 to continuously house and publicly display the works of G.F. Watts has survived over a hundred years of the artist's fluctuating reputation and the tyranny of changing opinion. Its aim was to be timeless, built for future generations as a living memorial to the artist. 'Its universality', declared a journalist on its opening, 'is its most striking feature. It stands unique in this respect: that so much of it will appeal as powerfully to future generations as to the present, unless human thought and feeling undergo a transformation so great as to be inconceivable.'[5] More than a century later, human thought and feeling may not be radically different, but cultural changes have meant that a contemporary audience can find the messages of Watts's paintings less instantaneously universal. The works themselves continue to fascinate visitors, and the ethos that art should be open to all persists in the continued work of the gallery. As Watts himself expressed, 'I can testify after the experience of some years to the humanizing and even encouraging effects works of art can have upon those whose lives are a round of dulnesses [*sic*], lacking the ordinary enjoyment known to the more fortunate.'[6]

The idea of having a public gallery devoted to the work of G.F. Watts was by no means new when building work began on the Watts Gallery. Little Holland House, Watts's studio house in Kensington, had a gallery attached, which was designed by George Aitchison in 1881. In many ways this antecedent provided much of the outline for the Watts Gallery itself. In 1901 the *Windsor Magazine* advertised:

> To the picture gallery at Little Holland House the public are admitted on Saturdays and Sundays, from two till six – a privilege largely taken advantage of by all sorts and conditions of people. It should be remembered that some fine examples of Mr Watts' paintings can here be carefully and quietly studied by the aid of descriptions prepared by the artist.[7]

In the Watts Gallery the opening hours of two to six were retained (but extended to include every day except Thursday), the majority of the collection at Compton was from the Little Holland House Gallery, and the rich red that decorated

2. Watts Gallery, 1906

3. Painting Gallery, Little Holland House, photograph by Charles Dixon

the London gallery was also adopted in Surrey. Another similarity between the two was that they both began life, in part, as an open picture store for the ever growing collection of the artist's work, as Mrs Barrington noted of the Little Holland House Gallery, saying that it served 'to hold all the pictures, finished and unfinished, which were piled up in the studio, one upon another'.[8] Ronald Chapman, a relative of the Wattses' adopted daughter, recalled that the Watts Gallery was initially 'simply used as a storehouse, but afterwards like a gallery at Little Holland House' and 'opened to the public'.[9] The inclusion of unfinished work and sketches cheek by jowl with finished pictures was common to both galleries. The *Chronicle* wrote that works, 'in their incomplete state, are now shown in the hope of his profiting by public criticism', but also that 'surely Mr. Watts cannot pretend to care one atom what the public or the critics say!'[10]

The clear desire to make all of his work available to anyone and everyone is at the root of the

Watts Gallery's foundation. Watts wished his art to be seen by a wide audience, and he promoted and encouraged the view that he was a servant of the nation, a tireless commentator who painted for the public alone. His aim that 'art may speak … with the solemn and majestic ring in which the Hebrew prophet spoke to the Jews of old, demanding noble aspirations, condemning … prevalent vices' may sound archaic to contemporary ears.[11] In the late nineteenth century, when art was seen as having a role akin to religion, Watts was a high priest. The gallery was a temple, as Watts expressed in a letter to *The Times*: 'Art and music, which should enter the gallery scheme, would be found powerful auxiliaries of the pulpit, which cannot now give its utterances the weight possessed by the Hebrew Prophets or the Church of the Middle Ages.'[12] The didactic messages and ideas that Watts wished to continue into the future was a clear motivation for the construction of a purpose-built gallery, but there was also the question of preserving his own genius for perpetuity, a far less discussed motive. His gifts to the Tate, the National Portrait Gallery and many other galleries roused a commentator in the 1890s to question 'his taste in publicly, in his lifetime, offering these pictures to the nation'. Furthermore,

> without wishing to offend Mr. Watts, we must ask if it is judicious on his part, if it is just to his fellow artists, to propose to take up so much space in the National Gallery [now Tate], if that is where the pictures are to go, when such a course inevitably must mean the utter exclusion of the work of some of his fellows?[13]

Yet Watts's views on art galleries were far from straightforward. In a lengthy letter to T.C. Horsfall in Manchester, which *The Times* published in 1890, Watts explicitly expressed his opinions on galleries. His general principles were those of the enlightened of the era, a belief that art galleries were of 'vital importance to every one interested in the general improvement of the population'.[14] The difficulty he saw was that picture galleries served only those with a highly developed sense of art and that the main aim of such galleries is edification, not the training of

4. G.F. Watts, photograph by E.H. Mills

5. Picture Gallery, Little Holland House, photograph by Charles Dixon

6. G.F. and Mary Watts at Little Holland House

7. C.H. Turnor in his car 'Aegidia', 1902, Turnor family archive, thanks to Rosemary McCorquodale

8. 'Berthorpe', Christopher Hatton Turnor's house in Compton, *c*.1906, Turnor family archive, thanks to Rosemary McCorquodale

new artists, for 'artists, like poets, are born, not made'.[15] He believed that education was the way in which a populace unused to art galleries could be sensitised to enjoy paintings, through increased observation of 'the wonders and beauty of some of the common objects around'. An educational gallery, such as those that he supported in the most deprived areas of London, should contain copies and good examples, be essentially didactic in nature and encourage teaching and copying around them. Watts wrote:

> The Rev. S. Barnett, of St. Jude's, Whitechapel, borrows and exhibits in holiday times a few pictures, and crowds of the very lowest from the squalid slums in the district throng to see them. There is always someone to point out and explain. The result has been found to be most satisfactory.

The creation of his own picture gallery in Compton, in a sense, embraced both aims. On the one hand it permitted free entry at certain times to everyone and included his own written interpretation serving his educational aims, while its rural setting surrounded by nature stimulated its audience to appreciate beauty and art. On the other, he was creating a contemplative 'high' art space – a space where, David Croal Thomson pointed out in 1906, 'actual copying is not permitted in the gallery'.[16]

How this was best served in the village in Compton was due in part to circumstance, the Arts and Crafts movement and the fact that he was extremely well represented as an artist in the Tate Gallery and the National Portrait Gallery. As David Croal Thomson expressed it:

> Sufficient for the moment to know that the gallery is so arranged as to give a comprehensive idea of the magnitude of the work the artist produced, and with the collections of his pictures in the Gallery of British Art [Tate], and in the National Portrait Gallery, to render this knowledge practically complete.[17]

The initial move to Compton had been elicited by the need to have a winter retreat from London, and visits to friends there led to the building of

Limnerslease, a grand house and studio designed by Ernest George in 1890. Compton became a cause, particularly for Mary, Watts's second wife, whose involvement with the Home Arts and Industries Association led to the development of a pottery in the village, and the building of a cemetery chapel and village hall. The Wattses took over Compton as both 'lord and lady' of the manor, but importantly with a great sense of civic duty, which led to Mary's work and ultimately to the creation of the Watts Gallery. Mary recalled how winter visits became a permanent move:

> Now that he required summer weather for the work on the Tennyson statue at Limnerslease, we went less and less to London. He therefore decided to build a small picture gallery there. For this purpose he bought some three acres of ground, that the building might not be attached to the house, though easily reached by five minutes walk through our garden. Mr Christopher Turnor, who had become a neighbour of ours, with whom Signor liked very much to exchange thoughts upon the many and wide subjects they had in common undertook to design a picture gallery, as well as a hostel for the young fellows who came to work at the gallery.[18]

Their neighbour, Mr Christopher Turnor (1873–1940), had been living in Compton with his parents in the first house he had designed, which was built in 1901 and named 'Berthorpe' after his aunt Bertha Turnor. This grand house, rather eclectic in design, showed the influence of his first teachers, Sir Edwin Lutyens (1869–1944) and Robert Weir Shultz (1860–1951), with whom he worked in the late 1890s, as well as being reminiscent of interiors of grand artist-studio houses. While Turnor was resident in Compton he struck up a strong relationship with Watts, whom the young man deeply admired. Turnor, in his late twenties when he first met Watts, was essentially an amateur architect who later became renowned as an agriculturalist and land reformer. Why Watts had selected him as the architect is not certain, although one might speculate that he was, in being local, fulfilling part of the Home Arts and Industries ethos but, more particularly,

that a bright young architect in awe of the old master might make the perfect malleable and dynamic creator of his projected gallery. There is little doubt that Watts would have a greater say with Turnor than an established architect. In her diaries Mary makes it clear that Turnor's visits to Limnerslease were frequent, in 1902 recalling how they were a 'great pleasure to Signor now, the visits of Mr. C Turner' and in 1903 quoting Watts that 'contact with a young fellow like that does me good'.[19]

'During those years at Compton', Turnor was later to recall, 'it was my privilege to see a good deal of G.F. Watts ("Signor") one of the greatest men I ever met, not only as a painter but as a thinker far in advance of his times on many subjects.'[20] Through the architect's recollections in his journal and his memorial book to Watts, it is clear the extent of his admiration of the painter. 'Dear old Signor asked me to build the picture gallery at Compton', he wrote, '& to keep it a simple & rural type of building, my difficulty was that he would never tell me how many pictures it was to house, and I had to double it soon after completing it.'[21] In terms of the exterior, the building showed all the charm of Arts and Crafts

9. Christopher Hatton Turnor's monogram, Turnor family archive, thanks to Rosemary McCorquodale

10. Laying the foundation stone of the Watts Gallery, 23 February 1903, G.F. Watts's 86th birthday

style, which clearly Watts had wanted, rendered in concrete and Surrey tiles. On 23 February 1903 foundation stones for the gallery and its flanking hostels for potters were laid by Watts himself on his eighty-sixth birthday, 'corner stones of a little building at Compton, to which has been given the name of The Hostel'.[22] Photographs survive of the event, which took place on a cold winter day. Symbolically and perhaps not uncharacteristically, Watts wrote an enigmatic note that was 'buried in the corner stone' of the hostel:

> How much more potent are the evil works of man to produce effects while he lives, how much more potent to produce good effects are his good deeds after his death; his evil deeds while he lives may cause individual misery, family distress, disruption of states; his good deeds, in discoveries, in elevating poetry, in noble art, for ever after his death, go on accumulating benefits to humanity.[23]

The building was completed shortly afterwards, sometime in the summer of 1903. It was an eventful year for the architect: the completion of the Watts Gallery and the death of his uncle Edmund Turnor, which meant an inheritance that included Stoke Rochford Hall and a further 24,000 acres of family estates in Lincolnshire. Despite this, his close connection with the Wattses meant a continued working relationship with Mary Watts after Signor's death with the extension of the Watts Gallery and Mary's designs for the reredos at Stoke Rochford. On 30 September 1903 Mary recalls in her diaries: 'Our pictures come from L.H.H. [Little Holland House] Gallery.' It was at this time, less than a year from his death and suffering bouts of ill health, that Watts wrote to Mrs Barrington showing his frustration when the works were moved from the London to the Compton gallery: 'everything must be crowded here,' adding that 'I am sick of the whole thing!'[24] Such dissatisfaction was not with how the gallery looked when it opened in the following spring, but rather with the arrival of the paintings at the gallery, clearly too many for the new gallery to accommodate. Many had to be stored in his Limnerslease studio and Watts must have faced difficulties having to choose which he would display. As quoted above, Turnor later gave an architect's excuse, that the client 'would never tell me how many pictures it was to house'. Why the gallery didn't open until April 1904, some six months later, further testifies to the careful consideration of the hang that Watts oversaw. In the case of *The Good Samaritan*, for example, Mary recalls that 'the canvas was framed and hung in the then newly built gallery by his direction'.[25] The hostel itself, the accommodation for potters, was already occupied, and on 11 January 1904 Mary records in her diary that 'Signor enjoyed the play, by the children – at the Hostel'.

The Watts Gallery opened its doors on the afternoon of Good Friday, 1 April 1904, and as *The Times* Court Circular recorded, 'the privilege of inspecting the artist's work at first hand was taken advantage of by hundreds of visitors'.[26] The gallery was essentially a rectangular C-shaped box with lighting provided by a series of semi-circular windows placed above the hanging rail, a wonderful detail made of glazed green ceramic tiles. The ceiling was covered in leaf (possibly silver) and gold lacquer, which allowed light to be reflected down onto the paintings. The building provided the optimum wall space of three corridors of paintings hung from picture rail to the skirting. The first gallery catalogue, from 1904, lists 105 paintings, the bust of Clytie (presumably the bronze) and two casts in plaster

12. The Red Gallery, Watts Gallery, 1906

13. The Red Gallery, with the Main or Green Gallery visible through the three arches, 1906

from the 'Elgin marbles' from Little Holland House. The wall coverings were particularly important to Watts as the background and surround to his paintings. The artist had always favoured deep red as the perfect colour to show his paintings to advantage and the Watts Gallery was to be no exception. In the Tate Gallery archive a letter from Watts illustrates his favour of the colour and how his works on display there can be 'made magnificent in itself by means of a splendid colour say the deepest and warmest red that can be got! … The general effect on entering the room would be that of a grand strain of music.'[27] The Watts rooms at the Tate were painted this colour, despite and perhaps because of the fact that all the others were dull green. The gallery walls of Little Holland House also adopted the colour scheme. The Watts Gallery was no exception to this and the walls shone with a deep rich crimson. The richness of the colour was heightened by the fact that it was in fact

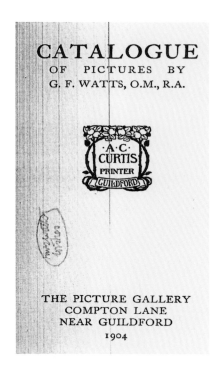

CATALOGUE
OF PICTURES BY
G. F. WATTS, O.M., R.A.

·A·C·
CURTIS
PRINTER
GUILDFORD

THE PICTURE GALLERY
COMPTON LANE
NEAR GUILDFORD
1904

15. A piece of the original 'Venetian Design' Tynecastle wall covering chosen by Watts for the gallery at Compton

embossed, as Mrs Steuart Erskine described it in *The Studio*, 'dark crimson hand-made linen in a raised design'.[28] The paper was produced by Tynecastle, a branch of the Morton and Co. furniture company begun in 1870 by William Scott Morton (1840–1903) with his brother John.[29] Appropriately, given his admiration for Titian and Tintoretto, the pattern selected by Watts was 'The "Venetian" Design. T1', an intricate floral motif that provided an ideal backdrop for his paintings. In many of his works Watts applied a ground coat of yellow paint in the belief that it would shine through to the surface of the painting. On a surviving piece of the embossed wall covering can be seen an undercoat of yellow, which was painted to give a richer glow to its red finish.

The hanging of the gallery must have provided a great opportunity for Watts, for he would have not have been able to assert the same control at other galleries. There is little doubt that the works were quite densely hung: 105 paintings, many on a large scale, must have been placed cheek by jowl. The basis of the arrangement of the works themselves is difficult to ascertain as no images of the hang survive, although the catalogue gives some indication of the order of display. The grouping of the paintings appears not to be determined by date, genres or finished state, but by themes, aesthetics and practical restrictions. Pendant pictures are hung together, but any chronological account or groupings of portraits and landscapes seem to have been studiously avoided. Portraits were exhibited alongside landscapes, other portraits, allegorical and social subjects: no distinction was made between them, just as sixty years divided canvases that sidled together on the crimson wall. What seems to emerge is that the artist ensured that each wall was evenly balanced, with a finished work alongside smaller versions and studies. In the subsequent hang of 1906 care was taken to continue this principle, as David Croal Thomson commented: 'In the gallery at Compton care is taken not to emphasise any branch of Mr Watts's work too greatly; while there are examples, and these almost all of the first quality, of every character of subject which appealed to him – portraits, allegorical pieces, and landscapes.'[30] Such hanging allowed each painting to be seen more clearly and individually, rather than as a large homogeneous group. The aim was to have a whole wall of paintings, with no gap between frames, and, like in the music of Wagner,[31] to show recurrent motives or themes undergoing transformations within different contexts, in this case within different paintings. The wall of colour and symmetry and choice of subjects served to emphasise the musical analogy.

Yet such a way of presenting paintings, as Watts himself was aware, was not without its difficulties. If the whole benefited from the musical strain, it also meant that individual works might be sacrificed, so information to lead the visitor became an important element of the display of Watts's art. In a dense hang works can compete, and Watts acknowledged that some help was needed, so he provided labels as he had for his gallery at Little Holland House. Words were a starting point for visitors, as the *Surrey Advertiser* reviewer wrote just after its opening:

> There are altogether more than a hundred canvases in the gallery … A little plan has been adopted which should prove very helpful to those desirous of getting at the real meaning of the pictures … Below or by the side of many of the paintings is placed a slip of paper, upon which is written a short description of the theme, and in many cases a suggestion of the idea underlying them. These little helps to understanding must not be taken as a complete explanation of the pictures … But the suggestions are decidedly helpful.[32]

A later catalogue of 1904 also provided such explanations, which could be basic descriptions, as for *The First Oyster*, 'no.72 B.C. A prehistoric experiment; tasting the first oyster', or lengthier and more suggestive interpretations, similar to those produced for his exhibition at the Peoples Palace at the Mile End Road:

> No.12 *The Slumber of the Ages*, All such pictures are symbolic, they do not represent fact, but are forms used to suggest ideas, as notes in music or as the gestures of an actor. In this picture the great stretches of time, since the earth ceased to be a formless mass, are represented as a mighty mother, with man, the child upon her lap, growing to conscious knowledge of himself and of his place in the scheme of creation. Painted in 1901.[33]

The death of Watts on 1 July 1904 turned the Watts Gallery into a shrine. The household name, the artist and genius, embodiment of the religious spirit of the Victorian period had died. He had risen with the nineteenth century and his death was at the twilight of its beliefs, values and aesthetics. At some point shortly afterwards the gallery closed to allow for its enlargement; as Turnor recalled, 'I had to double it soon after completing it.' Many of the paintings were still stored at Limnerslease and Mary wanted to see these on public display in the gallery. The closure of the building also provided the gallery with the opportunity to tour its core collection, and in the wake of Signor's death a memorial exhibition was timely. The exhibition opened at the Royal Academy early in 1905, and although it included a large number of loans, at its heart were eighty paintings from the Watts Gallery. The vast exhibition, with minor changes at each of its venues travelled to Edinburgh, Manchester and Newcastle,

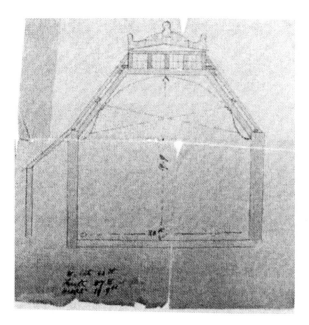

ending in Dublin in 1906. While the collection was touring to critical acclaim, Turnor had designed and was building a new, even larger gallery extension to accommodate more works. Importantly, a large central gallery also afforded visitors the luxury of being able to view larger works from a distance, making it comparable in scale to the Watts gallery at the Tate.

The entrance to the new gallery was created with three arches cut through the back wall, each of which was gilded. The gallery's sloping ceiling, following the simple rural style of the existing building, was also gilded and lacquered with gold, and the walls were painted with a green distemper. It reflected the original C-shaped gallery, yet was less elaborate in its wall coverings and its picture rails were wooden rather than ceramic. To distinguish between the two galleries, the new guidebooks simply called them by their colour, the Red and Green Galleries. The new gallery was lit by a large lantern that ran along the full length of the ridge of the roof. The *Tribune* described the gallery and explained the success of the colour scheme and lighting:

> The gallery is a plain building, admirably designed for its purpose. The walls of one part of it are coloured red and of the other green, with an effect of quiet richness which

enhances the rich colour of the pictures. The ceiling, where it slopes towards the top lights, is covered with soft gilding, so that the light reflected from it on to the pictures below is not harsh or glaring as it would be if reflected off a whitewashed ceiling, but warm and rich like sunlight, even on the most sunless days. This is a point that deserves notice of the directors of other picture galleries.[34]

The gallery was completed in early 1906, and around this time a sculpture gallery was added to house Watts's great *gesso grosso* models of *Tennyson* and *Physical Energy*. This further addition was not available to the visiting public until a temporary corridor was added, which in time became a permanent feature. With Watts's death came the problem of how to rehang the new gallery. Signor had been able to oversee the 1904 hang and Mary did not feel she was the right person for this important task. Instead, she chose Sir Charles Holroyd (1861–1917), and it is a reflection of the high regard that Watts was held within the art world that Holroyd consented. His admiration for Watts as both curator and fellow artist was expressed in the space given to Watts at the Tate Gallery, as well as in the fine portrait of G.F. Watts at the Tate given by Mrs Holroyd in 1919. He was appointed Director of the National

Gallery in May 1906, and in 1911 he redecorated and rehung their galleries, whose decoration, interestingly, was remarkably similar to that at the Watts Gallery. Red and green were very much the traditional colours of galleries, but the review of the National Gallery in *The Times* in 1911 sounds very like the *Tribune*'s review of the Watts Gallery in 1906:

> It will be found that a rich Cordova red has been used in the central room … and green in the surrounding ones opening on to it … Dull gold has been used in the large western gallery, and even before the pictures were in gave the effect that was rich, subdued, and majestic in the warm glow of a London winter afternoon. In summer the effect of this splendid gallery should be finer still.[35]

According to Mary's diary, on 30 April 1906 'the last pictures went into their right place this morning'. Forty-five paintings were displayed in the new Green Gallery, and ninety-two in the original Red Gallery. Given that the latter had lost three arches of wall space and had originally shown 105 paintings, this indicated a similarly dense hang. The reopening shortly afterwards elicited a national wave of enthusiasm, and in contrast to the relatively low-key first opening in April 1904, it was reviewed in all the leading journals of the period. 'Now Compton is the object of pilgrimage to many people coming from all parts of the earth,' David Croal Thomson wrote.[36] Mrs Steuart Erskine from *The Studio* proclaimed 'a more serious atmosphere than is generally found in a picture-gallery'.[37] Hilda Haking in her article, 'The Shrine of George Frederick Watts, RA', declared: 'The colourings of the inside walls, chosen by Mrs Watts, is of gorgeous hues of alternate green and gold and crimson, a fit setting to the warmth and colouring of this magnificent collection of paintings, all by the same great master's hand, and arranged by Sir Charles Holroyd.'[38]

After the reopening it became clear to Mary that a professional curator was required to manage the gallery (a caretaker had been used in Watts's lifetime). An eminent curator had overseen the hang, but for the running and care of the gallery a full-time curator was needed. Mrs Watts officially appointed Charles H. Thompson in early 1907 as curator and secretary, and he remained in the position until 1931.[39] He was an artist by training, and as *The Times* noted of one of his leading portraits, he was 'a friend and disciple of G F Watts, traces of whose influences can be seen in the work'.[40] The first meeting of the Trustees of the Watts Gallery, at which Thompson was confirmed in position, was held on 20 February 1907 and included Mrs G.F. Watts, Lord Balcarres, Sir Charles Holroyd and Mr Herbert A. Powell. The presence of eminent figures on the board, such as Sir Robert Witt and the Earl of Ilchester, has continued throughout

18. Mary Watts at the entrance to the Watts Gallery, *c*.1914

19 and 20. Two views of the Sunken Gallery, 1930s, annotated with Rowland Alston's analysis of the lighting

the gallery's history, for part of the Watts Gallery bequest is that the trustees have a representative from the National Gallery and the National Portrait Gallery. They also reflected how the reputation of Watts and the Watts Gallery was fiercely guarded and promoted by Mary Watts. She remained a tireless supporter of her late husband, ensuring his display in many galleries and making the Watts Gallery a centre for art by, for example, securing a visit from the International Art Congress in August 1908, members of which travelled to Limnerslease on 'a special train' which 'left Waterloo at 1 50pm'.[41]

The early years of the Watts Gallery, before the First World War, was a golden period. It was a centre of pilgrimage for those who revered the dead artist and who revered an art that was in its twilight, before the world was changed forever in 1914. In a long report by Charles Thompson in 1915 the curator reported to the trustees about the first decade of its existence. One of the most interesting parts of the document, aside from the extra security measures taken by the gallery due to a fear of suffragettes slashing the paintings, were the observations about visitors to Compton. Thompson reported:

> Quite recently, a visit from about thirty-six Members and Associates of the Royal Academy of Arts. I am glad to be able to report that the latter were profuse in their expression of admiration, not only for the works of Art contained in the Collection, but also for the arrangement of the Exhibits, the decorations, and lighting, of the Galleries; which is the most gratifying tribute to be received from so eminent a body of artists.[42]

While the artistic establishment greatly approved, there were also 'indications of a steadily growing interest in the collection on the part of the general public … A particularly pleasant feature is the number of working people who come to see it', including 'a party of German Working men who were travelling in England'. The educational aspect of the gallery and the belief that art should reach out to all was enshrined in the gallery's ethos. But more telling of the times was the appearance of Roger Fry, who, according to Thompson in 1909, 'gave a short address on the work of G.F. Watts'. Fry, despite his later rejection of Victorian art, initially felt an admiration for Watts and believed that the portraits of Joachim, Garibaldi and the Countess Somers 'take rank with the finest achievements of English art for all times'.[43]

After the First World War two things became increasingly clear to Mary: the rural location meant that visitors needed to make a special effort to get to the gallery; and Watts's reputation in the wake of Modernism was on the decline. In a notebook dating from 1924 she wrote her thoughts on the gallery, and although she is as positive and determined as ever, a defensive note can be detected:

> Since his death I have come to regard the Gallery as in a great part built & endowed to his memory, thinking that in all probability it is the only form of memorial he would have been pleased to know of.
>
> As to the objection of its distance from London the real lovers who <u>really</u> matter, will manage in the end to get here by rail & (now) by bus to Compton from Guildford – as by the many means from cars to bicycles that now reduce distance and therefore time to a min.
>
> And so far I find that visitors experience an added pleasure in passing from a collection of art into the beauty & peace of nature … Then also in many regard to the crowds now visiting the National galleries, we may remember this little gallery, inconspicuous from the air, was here open to the public when the great art galleries in London had to be closed.[44]

Despite changing opinion towards Watts and all things Victorian, Mary continued her struggle: the room dedicated to Watts at the Tate Gallery remained and the Watts Gallery was essentially an expanding memorial gallery. In the 1920s a few changes were made, the most major of these being the addition of a sunken gallery designed by Laurence Powell, a local architect, around 1925.[45] It allowed more space to exhibit works, and although it clearly displayed a more modern design, a lower ceiling and art deco-style steps, its use of natural lighting, parquet flooring and floor-to-ceiling hanging showed that it was

21. 'Hall of Fame' corridor, 1920s

essentially an extension of the gallery. The addition of a temporary corridor allowed the sculpture gallery to open to the public; the grand studio doors originally from Little Holland House were also opened and *Physical Energy* could be wheeled out on its railway track on sunny days. On a visit in 1920 a journalist reported that these were 'wide open to the air, and beyond them, backed by trees' and that the corridor was filled with Hollyer's photographs of portraits, 'a national portrait gallery of those whom the artist knew and painted'.[46] The main gallery remained essentially the same as it had since the gallery opened, a contemplative space in which to absorb

22. The Red Gallery, 1930s (including the curator's sketched plan for a new gallery wall)

23. The Main Gallery (Green Gallery), Watts Gallery, 1940s, with the Tate loan, *Story from Boccaccio* (1844–7) on the left

the major works of Watts on display there, the principle change being the addition of seating to encourage longer and more relaxed viewing.

As the century progressed, Modernism looked with less favour on Watts, and new art and design no longer saw the Watts Gallery as a paradigm for exhibition and display. G.K. Chesterton, who greatly admired Watts, noted as early as 1904 how a preceding period of history can suddenly become unintelligible and wrote: 'They saw it not as splendid, not as disastrous, not as fruitful, not as good or bad, but simply as ugly.'[47] Mary Watts, who remained an unceasing advocate of her late husband's work, lived until 1938, her pottery surviving until the 1950s; yet keeping Watts alive in an increasingly dismissive cultural climate was a difficult task.

In 1931 Charles Thompson was replaced as curator by Rowland Alston. Alston had also trained as an artist following his release from a German prisoner-of-war camp after being severely wounded at the battle of the Somme. He trained at the Slade and then the Royal College and was invited by Mrs Watts to be curator: 'in

spite of the great disparity in age,' *The Times* wrote, 'Mrs Watts became devoted to him and relied on his help.' Alston, born in 1896, was a different generation to Thompson and Mary Watts and was far more modern, but Mary put her trust in him, allowing him ultimately to modernise the gallery, which experienced its most dramatic changes under his curatorship. His obituary summed up these achievements:

> As curator Alston was conscientious and whole-hearted in his care for the fabric of the gallery and of its contents, and, not in the least, for the amenities of its delightful rural setting. From a somewhat ramshackle affair he developed it by degrees into a model little gallery, arranged with taste and admirably lighted on principles of which he made a special study in Holland.[48]

It is indicative of Alston's times that the Watts Gallery had been seen as ramshackle. To modern sensibilities floor-to-ceiling hanging and rich dark colours were simply ugly and claustrophobic, but it was only in the last year of Mary's life and after her death that Alston was able to make the changes that he wanted. The year of Mary's death, 1938, was a key turning point in the history of the Watts Gallery and indeed within the history of Watts's national reputation. Alston, as his obituary noted, had made a study of modern museum lighting, particularly in Holland. It is perhaps no surprise to find in the Watts Gallery Archives a series of articles on 'Modern Museum Lighting' by Dr Hannema, Director of the Boymans Museum, Rotterdam, and Mr A. van der Steur, Rotterdam City Architect, dating from 1931. The principles outlined in the article were adopted particularly in the Sunken Gallery at the Watts Gallery.

The most radical changes were made to the gallery in 1938, as the trustees agreed to redecorate and rehang. The minutes read: 'The curator was instructed to continue redecorating the Gallery and to put up partitions in the red gallery. The trustees were unanimous.' Light had been a problem, or more particularly glare from the high semicircular windows, and Alston wished to solve this. Yet it was not simply a question of lighting:

the whole aesthetic of the hang was brought into question. Watts's colour and hanging preferences were overturned in favour of modern neutrality. This was the period for such changes, and, sadly this time, *The Times* saw the Watts Gallery as a paradigm of how to improve and modernise the gallery on a small budget. It was simply forgotten

24. 'Signor', photograph by C. H. Turnor, Turnor family archive, thanks to Rosemary McCorquodale

how the design and hang had originally been so widely admired. The article, 'Improvements in Compton', published in April 1938, is worth quoting at length:

> At that time [1904–6] the functional requirements of a picture gallery were imperfectly considered; it was looked upon as a place to house rather than display pictures; and beyond external seemliness, plenty of wall space and top lighting of a sort little else was attempted. What is being done resolves itself into the internal reorganization … the primary object of enabling the pictures to be better seen. This involves two principle factors: improved lighting and more suitable decorations for the walls … For the colouring of the walls, which, as originally applied, is rather 'fierce', a neutral tint has been adopted of a tone corresponding to the average middle-tone of the pictures, giving value to their light and darks.[49]

What happened was that the original wall covering was painted a kind of beige, two internal walls were added and a new, much lower picture rail was added. Paintings were hung more thematically and in a far more modern and aesthetic manner, the Sunken Gallery becoming a portrait gallery. In effect, there was an attempt to homogenise the whole of the gallery. A new ethos had arrived, a new kind of professionalism to which the gallery did not seem suited. The gallery became an institutional member of the Museums Association, it reduced its entry price from one shilling to sixpence on the three days it charged, Mary Watts died and Limnerslease was put up for sale.

Alison Smith has written insightfully on Watts and the National Gallery of British Art and she notes the impact of 1938: 'The death of Mary Watts in 1938 effectively signaled the dismantling of the bequest. Even before this time, the artist's hegemonic position was being challenged within the institution itself, Holroyd and MacColl in particular having campaigned for a more inclusive representation of the British school.'[50] Watts's reputation was at a low ebb and the Watts Gallery had lost its former importance. During the following years other changes were made,

including a major loan from the Tate of the monumental *Story from Boccaccio* (1844–7; see fig.23), which was indicative of Watts's changing position at the London gallery. In 1949 the elaborately constructed lantern that directed light onto the gilded ceiling was replaced with 'a new skylight … put in the main gallery for £220'.[51]

Wilfrid Blunt, a drawing master from Eton and brother of Anthony Blunt, became curator after Alston's death in 1959 and up until 1985 quietly maintained the gallery while writing a large number of books on a variety of subjects including *England's Michelangelo* about the life and works of G.F. Watts.[52] Despite his often wicked humour about Watts and the prevailing opinion about the artist, Blunt was a supporter of Watts and defended him against his critics, including in debates at the Oxford Union. In 1985, after Blunt suffered terminal ill health, his assistant Richard Jefferies became curator. Jefferies railed against the modernisation instigated by Alston and heroically kept the gallery going for over two decades. This meant preserving and amending it on a shoestring. The addition of furniture, plants and the curator's eccentric charm imparted a rambling Victorian allure to the gallery, preserving the sense that nothing had ever changed.

The greatest change in the gallery's history since 1906 has come as a result of the deterioration of the fabric of the building, but the immediate future of the Watts Gallery has been secured by the *Hope* Project, funded by the Heritage Lottery Fund, Trusts and inspired individuals. The challenge is that those who shape the future vision of the gallery do not lose sight of its past, and that they understand its original ethos and how it has been expressed in the gallery. The danger is that they forget what it is exactly that makes the gallery unique: a building and a collection, and their intimate connection. Its picture hanging and its displays must be sensitive to this or it will be lost in a sea of less than unique galleries that abound in this country. It must not lose this vision. As visitors enter and leave the gallery, they can see the motto of G.F. Watts emblazoned in Arts and Crafts style, an ambitious statement of what the gallery needs to live up to: 'The Utmost to the Highest'.

1. Erskine 1906, p.189.
2. David Croal Thomson, 'The New Watts Gallery at Compton', *Art Journal*, November 1906, p.321.
3. Christopher Hatton Turnor, handwritten memoirs, p.221, private archive.
4. Mary Seton Watts, notebook dated 7 May 1924, Watts Gallery Archive.
5. *Surrey Advertiser*, 2 April 1904, clipping in Watts Gallery Archive.
6. G.F. Watts, letter to *The Times*, 13 April 1897, published 16 April 1897, p.6.
7. Charles T. Bateman, 'Mr. G F Watts and his art', *Windsor Magazine*, June 1901, p.15.
8. Barrington 1905, p.89.
9. Ronald Chapman, *The Laurel and the Thorn*, London 1945, p.137.
10. *Chronicle*, 29 December 1896, clipping in Watts Gallery Archive.
11. *Review of Reviews*, June 1902, clipping in Watts Gallery Archive.
12. G.F. Watts, letter to *The Times*, 16 April 1897, p.6.
13. *Chronicle*, 29 December 1896, clipping in Watts Gallery Archive.
14. *The Times*, September 22, 1890, p.6.
15. Ibid.
16. David Croal Thomson, 'The New Watts Gallery at Compton', *Art Journal*, November 1906, p.323.
17. Ibid.
18. Watts 1912, II, p.305.
19. 9 January 1902 and 4 January 1903, transcribed from the original manuscript (private collection) by David Stewart.
20. Christopher Hatton Turnor, handwritten memoirs, p.219, private archive.
21. Ibid., p.221.
22. *Surrey Advertiser*, 2 April 1904, clipping in Watts Gallery Archive.
23. Christopher Hatton Turnor, photographic journal of his buildings with his own annotations, unnumbered, private archive.
24. Barrington 1905, p.148.
25. Watts Catalogue, I, p.65.
26. *The Times*, 2 April 1904, p.7.
27. Letter from Watts to the Tate Gallery 1897, quoted in Alison Smith, 'Watts and the National Gallery of British Art', in Trodd and Brown 2004, p.159.
28. Erskine 1906, p.190.
29. In the 1870s the firm began to make wallpaper and became renowned for their invention of Tynecastle Tapestry, a canvas wall covering inspired by fifteenth- to sixteenth-century Spanish and Italian embossed-leather wall hangings. The 3-D nature of the canvas and the revolutionary way in which it was made meant that it was a more economic, lighter, yet durable alternative to plasterwork.
30. David Croal Thomson, 'The New Watts Gallery at Compton', *Art Journal*, November 1906, p.323.
31. See Watts 1912, I, p.258.
32. *Surrey Advertiser*, 1904, April, clipping in Watts Gallery Archive.
33. Watts Gallery, *Catalogue of Pictures*, 1904, Watts Gallery Archive.
34. A. Clutton Brock, 'A Surrey Shrine', *Tribune*, 4 June 1906.
35. *The Times*, 4 January 1911, p.11.
36. David Croal Thomson, 'The New Watts Gallery at Compton', *Art Journal*, November 1906, p.321.
37. Erskine 1906, p.189.
38. Hilda Haking, 'The Shrine of George Frederick Watts, RA', *Lady's Realm*, November 1906.
39. 'The appointment of Mr Charles H. Thompson as secretary to the trustees, and the confirmation of his appointment as curator of the pictures, was proposed by Sir Charles Holroyd, seconded by Mr Powell, and carried' (Minutes of the Trustees of Watts Gallery, 20 February 1907, Watts Gallery Archive).
40. *The Times*, 11 January 1939, p.10.
41. 'The International Art Congress', *The Times*, 3 August 1908, p.11.
42. 'Watts Picture Gallery, Curator's Report, Period from February 18th 1908 to November 15th 1915', Watts Gallery Archive.
43. Roger Fry, quoted in Virginia Woolf, *Roger Fry: A Biography*, London 1940, p.107.
44. Mary Seton Watts, notebook dated 19 March 1925, Watts Gallery Archive.
45. The 1957 Watts Gallery catalogue notes it being built in 1925 and Mary mentions it being built in her notebook dated 19 March 1925, Watts Gallery Archive.
46. *The Times*, 18 August 1920, p.13.
47. Chesterton 1904, p.4.
48. *The Times*, 22 December 1958, p.11.
49. 'Watts Picture Gallery, Improvements at Compton', from our art critic, *The Times*, 5 April 1938, p.14.
50. Alison Smith, 'Watts and the National Gallery of British Art', in Trodd and Brown 2004, p.165.
51. Minutes of the Meeting of Trustees of the Watts Gallery, 28 October 1949 ('It was reported that a new sky light had been put in the main gallery for £220 and that it was satisfactory').
52. There have only been five curators in the Watts Gallery's 104-year history: Charles H. Thompson (1907–31), Rowland Wright Alston (1931–58), Wilfrid Blunt (1959–85), Richard Jefferies (1985–2006) and Mark Stephen Bills (2006–).

Invention and Reinvention: The Art and Life of G.F. Watts   *Barbara Bryant*

On 28 April 1837 a brilliantly sunny day set the stage for a landmark event in the London art world. Crowds thronged Trafalgar Square; a military band struck up at 1 p.m. as King William IV arrived to open the new home of the Royal Academy of Arts (fig.26). Housed in a new building by William Wilkins, the Academy took the eastern side, while the western side was to be occupied by the National Gallery.[1] The King ascended the stairs of the grand portico (still one of most splendid features of the London cityscape) and here, in a brief ceremony, the President of the Academy, Sir Martin Archer Shee, presented William IV with the keys to the building. Monarch and President then set off on a private tour of the sixty-ninth exhibition of the Royal Academy prior to the public opening. Royal portraits, such as David Wilkie's *Portrait of His Majesty King William IV*[2] and Shee's *Portrait of the Queen* (Royal Collection), took pride of place in the finest gallery, the East Room, near St Martin's Lane. Here the royal entourage also admired William Etty's massive scene from classical mythology, *The Sirens and Ulysses* (Manchester City Galleries), as well as works by the most eminent Academicians. On display in 1837 were Edwin Landseer's *The Old Shepherd's Chief Mourner* (V&A), among others by this popular artist, along with J.M.W. Turner's *The Parting of Hero and Leander* (Tate Britain, on loan by Trustees of the National Gallery) and *The Story of Apollo and Daphne* (Tate Britain), and the posthumously exhibited *Arundel Mill and Castle* (Toledo Museum of Art) by Academy stalwart, John Constable.

As King William and the President passed through the Middle Room, they might have glimpsed *A Wounded Heron* (fig.27; cat.3) by a first-time exhibitor named George Frederic Watts.

This modest study, as well as two portraits, probably went unnoticed. Some years earlier, Shee had pronounced to Watts's father, 'I can see no reason why your son should take up the profession of art',[3] haunting words that became a stimulus for the young artist, rather than a deterrent. With some sense of triumph, for Watts as well as for the institution of the Royal Academy, that day in April proved a defining moment. Aged twenty, Watts received his first official recognition, with his work on view at the premier exhibition venue in London. Here is where his career began. It lasted until the twentieth century and his death in 1904, sixty-seven years later. In that time Watts repeatedly reinvented himself as an artist. This essay will consider his career through successive shifts of direction in his art, as well as his own personal reinventions, best seen in portrayals of him and in his own self-portraits (figs 25, 28, 34, 45; cats 1, 12, 51).

By the end of his life Watts had become one of the most famous artists in the world, possessor of honorary degrees, accolades of foreign academies of art and most notably, in 1902, the newly instituted Order of Merit, which he received as the only artist in an inaugural group of twelve. His considerable output has yet to be catalogued definitively but he painted over 800 paintings and produced countless drawings, in addition to sculpture. Widely recognised in his lifetime and still today as one of the great portrait painters of the Victorian era, he sought in his imaginative and symbolical paintings to speak of deeper ideas and truths in a visual language of astonishing originality. His variety is celebrated in this catalogue – portraits, subject paintings, drawings, sculpture are all represented. Indeed, his whole career can be explored and enjoyed through the collections of the Watts Gallery.

25. *Self Portrait ('The Venetian Senator')* (detail, p.122)

Artistic education in London in the 1830s and 1840s

The roots of Watts's distinctive persona can be identified in his early life and career, a mixture of difficult circumstances and artistic awareness.[4] Born in 1817 as the eldest son of a second marriage, young George was a sickly infant. His father (cat.2), who made musical instruments, was a sensitive man, if unsuccessful in business. The name 'George Frederic' was probably intended to invoke the musical world of his father by alluding to Handel, the anniversary of whose birth fell on the same day, 23 February, as the new baby's birth. The deaths of two younger brothers in 1823, and then the severe blow of his mother's death in 1826 when he was only nine, meant that death dominated his early life and was to be an obsession for him ever after. His father's struggle to raise his young family in reduced circumstances made his upbringing serious and sometimes sad.[5] Into adulthood Watts recalled the constraints of the strictly evangelical religious observations, especially on Sundays, turning him against organised religion in all forms. Not surprisingly, he knew the Bible well, adding to it his personal preferences of Homer's *Iliad* and the works of Sir Walter Scott. Although poor health prevented him from attending school regularly, he did show talent for drawing. Encouraged in this pursuit, Watts drew from an early age and many examples are preserved (cat.6), reflecting his youthful reading interests and his precocious facility as a draughtsman.

Born and raised a Londoner, Watts lived with his father and half-sisters at various addresses in the metropolis. As the family's fortunes declined around 1826, they moved to Star Street, Paddington, then on the outskirts of the urban centre. George Watts senior, through professional connections with another family of pianoforte makers, arranged for his son to enter the studio of sculptor William Behnes (1794–1864) in Soho. In 1827, aged ten, the youngster began informal attendance at the busy sculpture studio on Dean Street. One of the more remarkable characters of late Regency London, Behnes enjoyed success at this stage in his career, with commissions for public monuments and portrait busts flowing in.[6] Watts learned by drawing from plaster casts (cat.6) in the accepted academic fashion; more importantly, he encountered the antique for the first time. As a sculptor, Behnes and his assistants carved and worked with marble, but the studio also provided Watts with access to plaster casts of the Elgin marbles which he soon discovered in the original only a short walk away at the British Museum in Bloomsbury. Newly installed from 1832, these works became the touchstones for Watts's entire artistic career, as he later commented: 'The Elgin Marbles were my teachers. It was from them alone that I learned.'[7] Benjamin Robert Haydon (1786–1846), the great propagandist for these masterpieces, visited Behnes's studio in the mid-1830s and, according to one source,[8] encouraged Watts to continue studying the marbles, inviting the young artist to visit his own studio, an encounter alas left unrecorded.

Watts admired Behnes's other talent as an accomplished portrait draughtsman and turned himself to producing small portrait drawings in coloured chalks and pencil as a way to earn a living. Around 1830 he also experimented with oils, especially once the sculptor's studio moved to Osnaburgh Street near Regent's Park. Here Charles Behnes, William's younger brother, introduced Watts to wider literary horizons and arranged tuition in oils. His oil copies, including one after Peter Lely and another after Anthony Van Dyck, smoked to appear old, started Watts towards more formal training as a painter. Another copy, a small colour study after Van Dyck's *George Gage with Two Attendants* (then thought to portray Rubens; fig.30), reveals his attentiveness to the past masters of portraiture available at the National Gallery. The time spent in Behnes's studio had another considerable influence, as the young artist followed the progress of portrait busts of noted individuals in London, such as the architect John Nash and the politicians Lord Eldon and Lord Brougham. He observed that portraying eminence was well within the reach of the skilled portraitist, a lesson not lost on the young artist and one that much later saw realisation in his own gallery of worthies.

By the age of sixteen Watts had his own studio on Upper Norton Street near Fitzroy Square and supported himself as a portrait draughtsman, but he had grander aspirations. Seeking out the highest exemplars of the past, he drew an approximate

27. *A Wounded Heron* (cat.3)

28. *Self-Portrait, c.*1835–40, oil on copper, 12.7 × 10.2 cm (5 × 4 in), COMWG184

29. Copy after Raphael?, *Paul Preaching at Athens*, late 1830s, black, white and red chalk, 19.5 × 27 cm (7¾ × 10¾ in), COMWG207.240b

30. Copy after Van Dyck, *Portrait of George Gage with Two Attendants*, late 1830s, watercolour on paper, 14 × 13.5 cm (5½ × 5¼ in), COMWG2007.197

school. The routine of copying, when he already had developed this facility on his own, was stultifying. His oils had also advanced to a degree of fluency in both technique and study of character, as in portraits of himself in 1834 (cat.1) and his father (cat.2). Experimentation in these years also shows him painting a small self-portrait on copper (fig.28), revealing seriousness in self-presentation. With the lack of actual teaching in the Schools, based as it was on a system of rotating visiting Academicians, Watts became disenchanted; however, it did not stop his ambitions. He matured as an artist during the 1830s when the ideal of history painting was still very much alive and he inherited a belief in 'high art', as epitomised in the work of the old masters, the great artists of the recent past such as Joshua Reynolds, and living history painters such as William Hilton, the Keeper in the Royal Academy. Hilton had in fact praised Watts's drawings,[10] but discouraged him from attempting original compositions even though the young artist felt ready to move forward. Recorded on the Royal Academy Schools's books for two years, he attended intermittently, but did make his debut, as discussed earlier, at the Academy exhibition of 1837, possibly in part thanks to time served in the Schools and his contacts there.

Portraiture occupied Watts's energies and enabled him to acquire new studio premises on Clipstone Street in the artists' district north of Oxford Street. Producing portraits in the spirit of the recent guiding light of British portraiture, Thomas Lawrence (1769–1830), he gained some aristocratic patronage, but essentially he received commissions from London's middle classes for modestly sized oils, precise in their execution. Not noticeably political, Watts painted the portrait of the radical MP and Benthamite, John Arthur Roebuck (1802–79), which led to a curious commission to paint the late Jeremy Bentham from a wax effigy.[11] Watts did not neglect leisure activities, enjoying choral singing and cricket with his friend Nicolas Wanostrocht (1804–76), whose pen name was Nicolas Felix. For him, in about 1837, the young artist produced a series of fluent drawings illustrating cricket positions, later lithographed as illustrations to a popular book, *Felix on the Bat* (1845).

rendition of *Paul Preaching at Athens* (fig.29),[9] one of the cartoons by Raphael then at Hampton Court Palace, as a way to learn how to organise a large multi-figure composition. Watts's techniques developed sufficiently for him to enter the Royal Academy Schools at Somerset House on 30 April 1835, aged eighteen, studying first in the antique

The real turning point for Watts's fortunes occurred indirectly as a result of that momentous Academy exhibition of 1837. Here the portrait of an émigré Greek shipping merchant, Constantine Ionides (1775–1852), commissioned from the artist Samuel Lane, hung near some of Watts's own works. Ionides's son, Alexander Constantine (1810–90), desired a copy of this portrait and through an acquaintance he offered Watts the sum of £10 for the job. This oft-cited episode in the artist's early life proved decisive, for, as the copy was preferred,[12] the original by Lane was sent to Greece, while the family kept Watts's portrait. This incident marked the beginning of a friendly relationship that lasted for more than half a century. Ionides immediately commissioned further works, including two vivid family groups, one known by a drawing (cat.5) and the other, a grand family portrait (cat.4), which was acquired in 2004 by the Watts Gallery. Portraying these transplanted Greeks and their extended family, often in native costume, indirectly fuelled Watts's appreciation of ancient Greek art. It was also an economic lifeline for him while still at the early age of twenty.

With some secure patronage, Watts attempted subject paintings in oils, first modestly sized works from classical mythology, Shakespeare and romantic literature.[13] *Blondel* (fig.31) depicts the late twelfth-century troubadour, a real historical figure, singing outside the prison where Richard Coeur de Lion is held. Probably a study for the larger work sent to the British Institution in 1843, this gentle scene from the medieval past also shows a convincingly realised figural pose. In increasingly more ambitious works Watts drew on the traditional subjects for history painting. He was ready to act when in April 1842 the Fine Arts Commission announced a competition to decorate the new Palace of Westminster, built by Charles Barry and A.W.N. Pugin, with the aim of promoting historical painting. Artists were to submit cartoons (large drawings) with life-sized figures illustrating scenes from British history and the native poets, Shakespeare, Milton and Spenser. With a larger studio on Robert Street, off Hampstead Road, Watts prepared his own entry from the *Annals* of Tacitus: *Caractacus Led in Triumph through the Streets of Rome* (V&A, originally

15 ft/4.6 m across, now in three fragments). Noteworthy for correct draughtsmanship, the large composition required many studies. One surviving study (fig.33) clearly shows the same model as in the cartoon with the head gazing upwards rather than outwards.[14] This man, very much of 1840s London rather than ancient Rome, is unidealised both in the drawing and the cartoon. Such drawings, this one comparatively large in size, tested variations in pose, but for Watts these head studies were an extension of his portrait work and a way of humanising the scene. The overall composition of Caractacus, now

31. *Blondel*, c.1843, oil on canvas, 29.7 × 24.7 cm (11½ × 9¾ in), COMWG.NC.13

32. *Caractacus Led in Triumph through the Streets of Rome*, lithograph after the cartoon of 1843, 37.5 × 57 cm (14¾ × 22½ in), from *The Prize Cartoons*, St Bride Library, London

33. Study related to *Caractacus Led in Triumph*, c.1842–3, black chalk on grey paper, 44.6 × 36.3 cm (17½ × 14¼ in), © The Trustees of the British Museum

known by a much reduced drawing and lithograph (fig.32), displays a skilful Raphaelesque arrangement, marshalling the many figures into readable groupings and also injecting a note of humanity into what could have been a coldly academic exercise. The exhibition of 140 entries opened in June 1843 in Westminster Hall. The judges, who included the 3rd Marquess of Lansdowne, Sir Robert Peel and William Etty, awarded Watts one of the three top prizes (premiums) of £300. With this money he planned a belated artistic 'grand tour' to study the techniques of fresco painting in Italy. Less than a month later he embarked on a journey that dramatically changed his life.

In 1843, aged twenty-six, Watts set off for Europe.
After six weeks in Paris staying in the Quartier
Latin with fellow artist Edward Armitage, he
travelled on to Chalon-sur-Saône, down the
Rhône to Avignon, on to Marseilles, then to Italy
via Leghorn (Livorno) and Pisa. He ended his
journey in Florence in the early autumn of 1843
where he intended to study fresco painting and its
techniques. Urged to visit the 4th Baron Holland,
the English minister, and his wife, Watts arrived
at their palatial town house, the Casa Feroni on
the via dei Serragli. As his host later noted, he
'came for a few days, and stayed several years'.[15]
During this period he visited the art collections in
Florence at the Uffizi and in palazzi and
churches. His high ideals consolidated, as he
began to see himself as part of the great traditions of old master painting, evident in his self-
portrait (fig.34). Far removed from the harsher
existence of his life in London, Watts reinvented
himself in this highly romanticised self-image.
During a fancy dress party at the Casa Feroni in
February 1845 he donned a suit of armour
discarded by another guest, and then painted
himself in the spirit of Renaissance prototypes.
The landscape with fading sun lends a serious
tone to the image, enhanced by the young artist's
guarded expression. Freed from the day-to-day
need to earn a living by residing with his patrons,
the Hollands, Watts devoted himself to his art
fully for the first time in his life.

The young artist enjoyed a close friendship
with Lord Holland and particularly with his wife
Mary Augusta (cat.7), daughter of the 8th Earl of
Coventry and close in age to Watts. The Hollands
often escaped to the hills outside Florence and
their villa at Careggi. Here and in town Watts
spent much of his time painting and drawing his
hosts and a circle of fascinating and eccentric
friends, including members of the Italian nobility,
wealthy expatriates and collectors. He became a
sensitive portrait draughtsman, studying faces to
gain an understanding of character and personality. As a way of thanking his hosts, he drew some
forty portraits of the Hollands' friends, a unique
series that remains together.[16] Other works in oil,
such as grand manner portraits, reflected the

34. *Self-Portrait*, 1845, oil on
canvas, 86.4 × 66 cm (34 ×
26 in), private collection

35. *The Drowning of the Doctor of Lorenzo de' Medici*, c.1844–5, the fresco *in situ* (photo: The Conway Library, Courtauld Institute of Art, London)

36. *Petraia* (detail, cat.9.1)

traditions associated with his sitters and their families, some echoing Joshua Reynolds and others the old masters. Yet he also assimilated a suave continental mode for his Italian sitters, revealing versatility in his stylistic choices.

Watts studied fresco techniques and painted one full-scale fresco (fig.35; see cat.10) during these four years. His social life also flourished; he frequented the Café Doney, a coffeehouse where an international set of artists met and enjoyed a lifestyle totally unlike his previous life in London. He relaxed by painting landscapes in the area around the Medici villa at Careggi (see cat.9). A view of the Villa Petraia (fig.36) reveals changes in his palette and colour coming to the fore along with a new lightness of touch. With Lord Holland, he toured the Riviera coast to Marseilles. In Italy they visited Milan, Rome, Perugia and Naples. Seeing Pompeii and climbing up Vesuvius, as well as the experience of Rome, further encouraged his love of the antique.

In 1846, once the Hollands departed, Watts stayed on at Careggi and made new friends among high-born English families who rented the villa, such as the Duff Gordons. There he used a converted orangery for more ambitious large-scale paintings, which occupied the latter portion of his stay. Italian literature and history, including tales by Boccaccio and Boiardo, inspired an early version of *Paolo and Francesca* (see cat.49), from Dante's *Inferno*, and *The Origin of the Quarrel between the Guelph and Ghibelline Families* (fig.37), an episode from thirteenth-century Florentine history.[17] The latter story also received dramatic treatment in Dante's *Inferno* (XVIII, 107) and *Paradiso* (XVI, 65, 140), and, more readily for Watts, in Samuel Rogers's *Italy*, an immensely popular collection of verse tales published in the 1820s. Buondelmonte, a young Guelph nobleman who has promised to marry a woman of the Ghibelline clan, is tricked into falling in love with a beauty of the Donati family. The painting shows the young man riding through Florence; he sees the Donati girl after her malicious mother raises her daughter's veil

and instantly falls in love. This sets off a chain of events that alienates the Ghibelline faction, war ensues, and Buondelmonte is murdered. Watts shows the moment of falling in love, but suggests the violence to come with the fighting dogs and vagrants in the foreground. The immediate impulse for the painting, especially its rich colour and the baroque panoply of its composition, can be found in the artist's new environment in Italy, but its roots were still present in English literature.

Fired with enthusiasm for painting large ambitious works, Watts kept in touch with his patron Alexander Constantine Ionides, hoping that the Greek would offer a commission.[18] His letters to this friend reveal his interests for the first time; he impressed on Ionides that 'it has always been my ambition to tread in the steps of the old masters'.[19] Various projects for paintings in 1846–7 eventually proved abortive. The letters also dwell at length on Watts's identification with Greek art and culture, especially the fifth-century BC Athenian sculptor Pheidias, who became a personal hero for Watts. When news arrived of further competitions for the decoration of the new Palace of Westminster, he planned and submitted a patriotic subject of England's first naval victory, *Alfred Inciting the Saxons to Prevent the Landing of the Danes by Encountering Them at Sea* (see cat.11); once again he enriched energetic figure groups with an intense palette. His second, and more unusual, submission from English poetry, *Echo* (Tate Britain, on loan to Watts Gallery), which was derived from Keats's poem, forecast his later poetic inclinations. Watts packed all these extremely large works and others for his trip to London in late spring 1847. On arriving back, aged thirty, he found the art world much changed and his place in it no longer so assured.

Return to London and the crisis of 1850

In June 1847 the exhibition of entries for the fourth competition for the Houses of Parliament decorative scheme opened at Westminster Hall, and *Alfred* appeared with a quotation from an unnamed history of England. Winning another first class premium of £500 confirmed Watts's status as a history painter, and shortly afterwards

37. *The Origin of the Quarrel between the Guelph and Ghibelline Families, c.*1844–6, oil on canvas, 320 × 259.1 cm (126 × 102 in), COMWG.45

38. *Self-Portrait, c.*1848–50, reproduced in Watts 1912, I, opp. p.106 (drawing now lost)

39. *Time and Oblivion, c.*1848–50, oil on canvas, 195.5 × 321.5 cm (77 × 126½ in), Eastnor Castle Collection, Herefordshire

the government purchased *Alfred* for £200. Yet he received no actual commissions to paint murals in the new Palace of Westminster. Some of his contemporaries such as Charles West Cope and John Calcott Horsley, who had participated in the second and third competitions in 1844 and 1846, were now at work on commissions. After an absence of four years Watts had lost ground, yet expectations were still high. Some sections of the art world expected him to take the lead as the history painter of his generation, but in the wake of Haydon's tragic suicide exactly a year before in June 1846, this genre was discredited. Didactic subjects from classical history were seen as old-fashioned; large-scale works were also out of favour. In William Thackeray's *Our Street* (first published in December 1847) the author, under the pseudonym 'Michel Angelo Titmarsh', scoffs at outsized history paintings and misguided artistic aspirations, and the book includes a thinly disguised Watts as the artist George Rumbold.[20]

Watts turned his attention to executing works on his own behalf, using rooms provided by Robert Holford (1808–92) at the palatial Dorchester House, then under construction on Park Lane. Watts had met the wealthy Holford, who had amassed a notable collection of old master paintings, in Italy. But the two men had very different tastes: Watts 'prosed away about Phidias in my usual style', while Holford extolled Giorgione.[21] At Dorchester House Watts worked on some unusual large works, including *Satan* (cat.13), which was bold in style and visionary in its conception, and *Time and Oblivion* (fig.39), one of his most abstruse subjects, which was part allegory and part his own invention. In the latter work two figures in classical drapery represent universal types. The scythe identifies Time, but otherwise the treatment does not rely on tradition. The simplified handling with strong flat colours derives from fresco and mural painting. He did not send the massive canvas to exhibition at this time, realising it was out of step with contemporary tastes, yet John Ruskin (1819–1900), a new friend, admired and borrowed it. Ruskin, who called Watts 'the only real painter of history or thought we have in England',[22] tried to guide his work, without success. Shortly after, Ruskin became preoccupied with his young Pre-Raphaelite protégés.

Yet he and Watts often discussed the aims of art, and almost as if referring to *Time and Oblivion*, Watts wrote to him: 'My own views are too visionary and the qualities I aim at are too abstract to be attained, or perhaps to produce any effect if attained.'[23]

To further his career, Watts relied on annual exhibitions and on his influential friends. He turned to portraiture for his income, producing both oils and drawings. His connections with the Ionides clan and the Hollands meant that he did not have to look far for work. But, when he exhibited an unusual full-length portrait of Lady Holland in the manner of contemporary French art at the Royal Academy in 1848,[24] the critics reacted strongly: 'Such works will not maintain the position or justify the notice assigned to the artist elsewhere.'[25] He could not find patrons for the history paintings that he had planned and personally he was not happy. The change in surroundings from the beauties of Italy and life with the Hollands, where he was removed from mundane day-to-day responsibilities, to London, where he had to fend for himself, plunged him into moodiness, melancholy and ultimately ill-health. In this spirit he conceived a series of social realist canvases depicting the problems of mid-century Victorian society: *Found Drowned* (cat.14), *The Irish Famine* (cat.16), *Under a Dry Arch* (cat.15) and *The Seamstress* (c.1849–50; Watts Gallery). Drained of colour, these works reflected his own state of mind. Such modern-life subjects did not go to public exhibitions, but they had an impact, as some were on view to his own circle of friends in his new studio on Charles Street in Mayfair.

Aristides and the Shepherd (fig.40), worked on from 1848 until 1850, also encapsulates the changes in Watts's thinking during this phase of re-evaluation. The subject had antecedents: one of Haydon's last works depicted Aristides, as did one of Watts's planned history paintings,[26] but on returning to London, he reframed the subject as a two-figure composition. Drawn from Plutarch's *Life of Aristides* and the episode on his ostracism, or exile, from Athens, the work shows the main character standing next to a seated shepherd who is about to cast his vote. The shepherd, weary of hearing about 'Aristides the Just', decides to vote in favour of the ostracism, but as he cannot write,

40. *Aristides and the Shepherd* (*The Ostracism of Aristides*), 1848–52, oil on canvas, 305 × 213 cm (120 × 84 in), COMWG33

41. *The Good Samaritan*,
c.1850–2, oil on canvas, 254.7
× 189.2 cm (100¼ × 74½ in),
© Manchester City Galleries

he asks Aristides to inscribe his vote, failing to
realise that the man he has asked is the intended
victim of the ostracism. Stoically resigned to his
fate, Aristides does as requested. Watts no longer
treats the subject in heroic or even narrative
terms: it now has a more reflective quality as the
story of individual emotions. The two colossal,
powerfully modelled figures lend universality to
the theme. But Watts was unsure of this work and
sent it to a minor exhibition venue, not the Royal
Academy.

A turning point in Watts's professional career
occurred at the Royal Academy of 1850 when he
exhibited an over-life-size painting, *The Good
Samaritan* (fig.41). In the catalogue he commented
that it was 'painted as an expression of the artist's
admiration and respect for the noble philan-
thropy of Thomas Wright of Manchester', citing
further an article from *Chambers's Edinburgh Journal*
on Wright's work to help former prisoners get
back on their feet and 'turn felons into citizens'.[27]
This painting had a message for its audience,
almost as if Watts had camouflaged the thinking
behind social realist paintings with a biblical tale
that his audience could readily identify with. But
its uncompromising style, with powerful figures
based on sculpture and simplified handling as in
Time and Oblivion, made no concessions to popular
taste. Furthermore, when the Academy's hanging
committee placed the painting in a poor position
in the galleries, Watts took it as an insult. For the
next eight years he stopped sending in his major
paintings and submitted nothing at all between
1853 and 1857.

Living by now near Berkeley Square, Watts
shared his studio with Charles Couzens, who
portrayed him in a large miniature-type portrait
(cat.12). He stands alongside a cast of the
Parthenon frieze, gazing downwards at one of his
own drawings after these antique masterpieces.
His personal life again shifted in direction when
he befriended neighbours Sara and her husband
Thoby Prinsep (cat.41), an official of the East
India Company recently returned from the subcontinent to sit on the Council of India. In 1849
he became infatuated with Sara's sister Virginia
Pattle, one of seven extraordinary sisters, many
of whom featured in Watts's work.[28] Virginia's
marriage in October 1850 to Charles, Viscount

42. *Justice: A Hemicycle of
Lawgivers*, engraving,
The Illustrated London News,
4 February 1860, reproduced
with the permission of the
Guildhall Library, City of
London

Eastnor (later 3rd Earl Somers), devastated the
artist, but he remained close to the Prinseps and
Pattles. Later that year he was able to intercede
with Lady Holland to grant the Prinseps a lease
for the dower house on the Holland House estate
in Kensington, where he moved in as well.

Watts stood at a personal and professional
crossroads in 1850. He knew that he was not
going to succeed in the forum of the Royal
Academy. It was only thirteen years on from his
debut in 1837, but he now realised that he would
have to make his name without the institutional
support of the Academy.

The 1850s: Watts in the private and public sphere

Mirroring his experiences in Florence, Watts
moved into Little Holland House with the
Prinseps as resident artistic luminary for Sara's
bohemian salon, prompting her remark (like the
Hollands' before): 'He came to stay three days;
he stayed thirty years.'[29] Living there during this
decade, he had the security of a home and a studio, as well as a family atmosphere. The Pattle sisters and their children acted as ready models for
drawings and subject paintings, as well as sitting
for his experimental portraits. A whole social
world came to gatherings at the Prinseps, including musicians, beautiful women, writers like
Tennyson, the young Pre-Raphaelites and
Frederic Leighton (1830–96); Watts enjoyed such
interesting company. By the second half of the

43. *The Triumph of the
Red Cross Knight (St George
Overcoming the Dragon)*, c.1852–3,
fresco, 246.5 × 175.3 cm
(97 × 69 in), Upper Waiting
Hall, House of Lords,
© Palace of Westminster,
London

1850s he acquired a reputation as an artist following a distinctive path within the extended circles
of Little Holland House.

Watts also made important connections
through an elite group of cultivated politicians,
writers and artists in the newly formed
Cosmopolitan Club. His former studio on
Charles Street became the meeting place for the
Club, which also served as a semi-public display
space for his paintings including *Echo* and his
social realist series. As his own intellectual ambitions grew in such company, he conceived some
grand schemes, such as his own personal project
to paint portraits of the eminent men of the day,
now known as 'The Hall of Fame', which became
a preoccupation for his entire career. His friend,
the writer and dramatist Tom Taylor (1817–80),
invited Watts, as a noted advocate of 'high art', to
contribute to a life of Haydon, published in 1853.
This allowed him a forum to expound his ideas
on 'awakening a national sense of Art'.[30] He promoted the idea of large-scale wall paintings in
fresco to adorn public buildings, ideally with the
sponsorship of the government. Although this did
not seem such a far-fetched idea in 1853 with the
Westminster project in full swing, ultimately it
was not the way forward for British art. As an
advocate for the public role of art, Watts
attracted the attention of individuals such as
Ruskin, Austen Henry Layard and Henry Acland
of Oxford, who promoted his work and helped
with various ventures. His commission to paint a
mural for Lincoln's Inn doubtless came about
through his contacts. In this fresco, *Justice: A
Hemicycle of Lawgivers* (fig.42), designed in the mid-
1850s, Watts gathered together a cast of characters from history, yet instilled a contemporary
spirit into the work by having his friends pose for
the lawgivers. The success of this project elevated
his public profile considerably.

Watts's plan to paint 'The Progress of Cosmos'
for Euston Station foundered, but the scheme
inspired his grand conception to paint a series of
murals he considered as a 'history of the world',
eventually termed by later commentators 'The
House of Life'. In November 1852, when Watts
finally received a commission to paint one of the
frescoes in the new Palace of Westminster, he had
a chance to put his beliefs into practice. The Poets'

Hall, more formally known as the Upper Waiting Hall of the House of Lords, contained upright panels over 10 feet high by various artists, including Cope, John Callcott Horsley and Watts's friend, Edward Armitage, showing scenes from the works of native poets.[31] Assigned Edmund Spenser, Watts painted *The Triumph of the Red Cross Knight* (fig.43; see also cat.18), which could be read as a tale of a knight as conqueror or as an allegory of the Anglican Church with the main character as St George protecting the virgin Una, herself emblematic of truth and the one true religion. The composition focuses on the main characters as romantic lovers united after the lengthy battle that culminates in the knight slaying the dragon. As Spenser wrote in *The Faerie Queene* (book I, canto XI):

> So down he fell, that the earth him underneath
> Did groan, as feeble so great load to lift …
> So down he fell, and like an heaped mountain
> lay.

The heroic figure of the knight stands triumphant, gazing heavenwards, and places his foot on the dead dragon with his gaping mouth. Although the technique of fresco was ill suited to the English climate, this mural, situated in the seat of government, put Watts's work into the public sphere, seen by lawmakers and opinion-formers on a daily basis. The murals painted for the Prinseps at Little Holland House, for Virginia, now Lady Somers, and her husband, the 3rd Earl Somers, at Carlton House Terrace, and for the 3rd Marquess of Lansdowne at Bowood in Wiltshire also had audiences of the literary and intellectual elite and helped to make Watts's name as an artist on an unconventional and individual path.

Patronage for Watts's portraiture in this decade grew out of his connections with the powerful and well connected in London society. Sensitive, large-scale portrait drawings were the only works he sent to the Royal Academy for a few years after 1850 and these were much admired. Close study of the growing collection of old masters in the National Gallery, especially by Venetian artists, influenced his practice of portraiture as the decade progressed, as did his knowledge of the noted collections of his friends Henry Layard,

Henry Danby Seymour and George Cavendish Bentinck. In 1853 he toured Italy, visiting Genoa, Pisa, Florence and Bologna, as well as Venice for the first time, and even acquiring an old master portrait for his own collection.[32] In 1855–6 a visit to Paris at the behest of the Hollands resulted in a group of portraits of their friends, such as Prince Jérôme Bonaparte and the Princess Lieven, in which Watts essayed an appropriately French style in the manner of Ingres and his followers. Contemplating and copying old master portraits at the Louvre also informed his overall re-evaluation of this genre.[33]

Prompted by the establishment of the National Portrait Gallery, which opened in 1856, Watts embraced portraiture with new enthusiasm. Traditionally, it did not occupy the same elevated station as history painting, but it now had a higher profile in society. By the later 1850s Watts declared his intention to renew his engagement with portrait painting by endeavouring to 'produce pictures that shall be valuable in all times both as faithful records and as works of art'.[34] With some of these new works, modern grand-manner portraits such as *Jeanie Nassau Senior* (Wightwick Manor), Watts re-entered the arena of the Royal Academy in 1858, although he signalled his ambiguous attitude to the institution by using a pseudonym. His portrayals of the Poet Laureate Tennyson, who became a close friend, began in 1857 and forged new avenues in portraiture, with mood and introspection conveying more than an ordinary portrait.[35] Watts became the painter of poets and by extension a poet in paint. The 'Moonlight Portrait' of Tennyson (Eastnor Castle Collection), exhibited at Colnaghi's in 1859, exemplified his new, more poetic interpretation of his sitters in a style inspired by Venetian art. Most importantly, and no doubt spurred on by the recent bequest to the nation of J.M.W. Turner (finally settled in 1856), Watts decided to form his own collection of portraits of eminent individuals. Widely known and referred to in the press, this plan set Watts apart as an artist of high ideals, if somewhat unorthodox commercial practice.

Travel further afield to Asia Minor on Charles Newton's expedition to excavate ancient Halicarnassus proved a defining experience for

with their original colouring. On exposure to the air, the colour swiftly faded. This direct experience of such transitory effects fuelled his later reinterpretation of classical subjects. The environment of the Greek islands inspired a range of works, including *The Genius of Greek Poetry* (cat.48) as well as pure landscapes (cat.20.1).

At the end of the decade Watts, by now in his early forties, had returned to the Royal Academy and enjoyed public accolades at the unveiling of his mural at Lincoln's Inn. Commissions for portraits, mainly for the more artistically aware, were steady. He had developed a distinctive following but had abandoned any idea of a career in traditional history painting and instead cultivated his vein of poetic portraits and subject paintings.

The 1860s: new directions in portraiture and the poetic impulse

In this decade Watts established himself as a portraitist of distinction, gained new patronage and conceived some of his most important subjects. He continued to paint his friends, but as his reputation expanded beyond the circles of Little Holland House, he received a series of important commissions for ambitious portraits from patrons well versed in the arts and also took these works to the Royal Academy. *Prudence Penelope Cavendish Bentinck and her Children* (RA 1860; fig.44) and *Lady Margaret Beaumont and her Daughter* (RA 1862; private collection) fuse the great traditions in portraiture with a more modern approach, both in the presentation of the sitters and in a refinement of handling.

Watts pursued his personal goal of painting eminent individuals yet he aimed to go beyond the portrayal of fame. Inspired with a notion of modern beauty, he produced a series of poetic images of young women, such as *Miss Alice Prinsep* (RA 1861; private collection), which effectively formed a parallel collection. In seeking out appropriate sitters, Watts met the rising actress Kate Terry and her younger sister Ellen, an event that had a major impact on his personal life.[37] Tom Taylor brought the actresses to Little Holland House where Watts painted *The Sisters* (1862–3; Eastnor Castle Collection), an image of poetic beauty that went beyond the boundaries

44. *Prudence Penelope Cavendish Bentinck and her Children*, c.1857–60, oil on canvas, 127 × 101.6 cm (50 × 40 in), © Tate, London, 2008; presented by W.G.F. Cavendish-Bentinck, 1948

Watts. Newton had earlier encouraged him to visit his consular post in Mytilene to 'see the landscape which Homer saw'.[36] Now organising his own excavations, he urged Watts to come with him. Away for six months from October 1856 to the spring of 1857, Watts again removed himself from the London art scene, visiting Constantinople, sailing in the Mediterranean and staying at Bodrum (cat.20). Here at the site of the Mausoleum of Halicarnassus, one of the seven wonders of the ancient world, the artist witnessed ancient sculptures as they were unearthed, still

of portraiture.[38] Although Kate was the theatrical star of the moment, Watts focused on Ellen. Motivated to 'remove an impulsive girl from the dangers and temptations of the stage', Watts married her in February 1864; he was about to turn forty-seven and she seventeen. They separated within a year, but during their brief time together she inspired some of his most beautiful paintings, including *Choosing* (RA 1864; NPG) and *Ophelia* (cat.30).

In 1865 Julia Margaret Cameron made and exhibited a portrait photograph of the artist, entitled *The Whisper of the Muse* (fig.45), which reveals his reinvention of himself as a poet-artist. As one of the Pattle sisters, Cameron knew Watts well by the time that she took this photograph of him while he visited Tennyson on the Isle of Wight. Music and poetry combined in an image that shows Watts removed from the day-to-day concerns of the working artist; indeed, he is not even shown with a palette, but appears as one who is open to other avenues of inspiration. This conjunction of poet and painter epitomised Watts's new persona.

Critical praise in the 1860s, from commentators such as Tom Taylor, F.G. Stephens (1828–1907)

and William Michael Rossetti (1829–1919), confirmed Watts's unique status in the contemporary art world. A younger generation of artists in the circle of Dante Gabriel Rossetti (1828–82) paid close attention to his work, especially as he ventured into new types of subject matter. He exploited exhibition venues other than the Royal Academy that had sprung up to cater for more innovative art. One of these was the French Gallery, a commercial gallery on Pall Mall,[39] where in 1865 Watts exhibited *A Study with the Peacock's Feathers* (fig.47).[40] This luxurious image pays homage to the Venetian Renaissance, but the

45. Julia Margaret Cameron, *The Whisper of the Muse* (Portrait of G.F. Watts), later copy after the original photograph of 1865, 13 × 10 cm (5½ × 4 in), Watts Gallery Archive

46. *Alfred Tennyson*, c.1863–4, oil on canvas, 62.3 × 50.7 cm (24½ × 20 in), private collection, © Christie's Images

known for his sympathetic treatment of artists with eye disorders.[41] The relationship between patron and artist took on a unique character; they were 'kindred spirits'. In 1863 Bowman visited Watts's studio and, seeing some unfinished works, he requested that Watts complete his self-portrait (c.1862–4; Tate Britain) along with 'the head of the great poet' for his collection in Hampstead, sending a cheque for one hundred guineas. In Bowman's thinking these two, 'painter and painted', would be like 'a pair of nobles answering one to the other on my walls'.[42] That these works functioned in such an imaginative way was a tribute to Watts's unconventional approach to the portrait. The portrait of Tennyson (fig.46) followed on from two earlier portrayals of the poet.[43] His new image situated the poet in a starkly frontal view tightly focused on the face and opening out to a mysterious seashore setting. Cloaked in black, with a burst of laurel, emblematic of the poet, behind his head, this view of Tennyson, his face and eyes especially, has a hypnotic power. Chesterton considered the background 'the mere materialising of the poet's own spirit in the eternal laurels and the eternal seas'.[44] Two versions of the portrait were painted in parallel. One the artist kept for his own collection at the Little Holland House Gallery, later probably reworking it,[45] and then bequeathed it to the National Portrait Gallery in 1895. The other (fig.46), acquired by Bowman, one of Watts's most appreciative patrons, is characteristic of his handling of the 1860s. This canonical image of Tennyson, a visualisation of the interior life of a poet, possesses a resonance that could only derive from Watts's insight into his close friend's character.

In 1865 Watts first met his most steadfast patron, Charles Rickards, a well-to-do businessman-turned-philanthropist from Manchester; a portrait (Manchester City Galleries) resulted and then Rickards began to buy steadily until the late 1870s (cats 37, 41, 46, 51). The new sources of income available to Watts (not to mention his comfortable lifestyle with the Prinseps at Little Holland House) allowed him to innovate without necessarily expecting to sell his experimental works. He planned several major compositions, first by painting small designs and sometimes even exhibiting

47. *A Study with the Peacock's Feathers*, c.1862–5, oil on panel, 66 × 56 cm (26 × 22 in), Pre-Raphaelite Inc. by courtesy of Julian Hartnoll (photo: The Bridgeman Art Library)

title emphasises that it is the product of an artist's studio and, as a study of a nude model, it is a modern exercise in the painting of the beautiful. From the later 1850s onwards Watts had explored this avenue in decorative portrayals of young women, ostensibly portraits, but *A Study* took on a distinctly modern slant. The appreciative review by F.G. Stephens focused on the purely painterly values of the work, bringing it to the attention of an audience attuned to aestheticising values.

Such works appealed to the new type of collector, individuals such as William Bowman, a young but already renowned ophthalmologist in London

them, as he did at the Royal Academy in 1865 with *Design for a Larger Picture* (Memorial Art Gallery, Rochester), a study on panel showing a youth led down a thorny path by Eros.[46] Critics admired this work for its 'exquisite qualities of colour and design',[47] as F.G. Stephens commented. Its status as a 'design' not only indicated the future plan to enlarge the composition but also reflected an interest in works of art as the products of an artist's studio and as evidence of the working process, an idea that was new in the 1860s.

Watts's re-engagement with sculpture in this decade also had some intriguing repercussions. While actively working on *Clytie* (fig.74), his own reinterpretation of the spirit of Pheidian art, Watts turned to the antique again, specifically to the 'Oxford Bust'. He had initially been inspired by the actual antique bust discovered by himself and Newton around 1850 during an earlier phase of Pheidias worship, and by the 1860s he had a plaster cast of it in his studio (cat.40.1).[48] Using it as a model, he painted *The Wife of Pygmalion: A Translation from the Greek* (fig.48; see also cat.40) for the same Academy exhibition in 1868 at which *Clytie* was exhibited. Watts never saw any contradiction in associating the painting with a sculptor, since to him 'Phidias was eminently pictorial'.[49] While seemingly breathing life into the bust, he painted a character from the story of Pygmalion and Galatea. His earlier adoration of Pheidias as a guiding light for his work is here rendered into a modern context. Its rapturous reception by the poet Algernon Swinburne among others brought Watts's work into the avant-garde.[50]

With his return to the forum of the Royal Academy, questions arose as to why Watts was not yet an official member of this institution. In fact, he had long refused to comply with the initial step of putting himself forward for election, finding that to be objectionable and self-serving. And he had also created his career for much of the 1850s outside the realm of the Academy. His exclusion, and that of other artists, coincided with growing dissatisfaction both within and outside its ranks, culminating in a government inquiry led by a select committee in 1863, at which Watts and others such as William Holman Hunt and Edward Armitage testified. Here he offered some of his firm beliefs on art, on the importance of

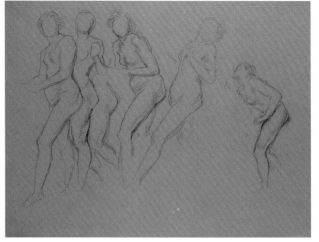

48. *The Wife of Pygmalion: A Translation from the Greek*, c.1868, oil on canvas, 66 × 53.3 cm (26 × 21 in), The Faringdon Collection Trust, Buscot Park, Oxfordshire

49. Studies of 'Long Mary', late 1860s, black chalk on buff paper, 37.5 × 53 cm (14¾ × 20¾ in), COMWG2007.639

Watts's reputation grew as his friends, such as Frederic Leighton (who had been staunchly pro-Royal Academy from the time of his election as Associate in 1864), promoted him to the Academy. Such moves encouraged a revision in the rules so that Watts's name could be put forward by the members, not himself, for election. Elected Associate of the Royal Academy on 31 January 1867, aged fifty, he was quickly elevated to full membership on 18 December of the same year, an event unique in the Academy's history and a testament to the esteem in which he was held by his fellow artists.

The 1870s: the Academy, the Grosvenor and the great compositions

In an apt echo of his debut at the inaugural exhibition of the Royal Academy in Trafalgar Square in 1837, Watts's initial task as an Academician was to serve on the hanging committee for the very first exhibition at the new premises at Burlington House in 1869. He entered somewhat reluctantly into the life of the institution, exhibiting his important works at the Academy, at least for a few years, then mainly sending portraits. Contact with the Academy and his colleagues prompted a group of portraits of artists such as Edward Burne-Jones (RA 1870; City Art Gallery, Birmingham), John Everett Millais (RA 1871; National Portrait Gallery) and Leighton (fig.50), some destined for his gallery of eminent men, others bestowed as gifts of friendship. The portrait of Leighton, a close friend and Kensington neighbour, shows the extent to which such naturalistic and informal portrayals conveyed a genuine sense of the person based on a personal connection the artist had with the sitters. Naturally, there were also some straightforward commissions with less leeway for interpretation, but at their best Watts's portraits conveyed qualities beyond mere likeness.

Watts also painted informal works for his own pleasure, such as the study of May Prinsep in the garden at Little Holland House (fig.51). May and Watts enjoyed a close relationship especially in the late 1860s when she posed for a range of works (cat.37). This landscape view went in 1870 to one of the minor exhibition venues, the Dudley Gallery, where it was exhibited as *From my Studio*

50. *Frederic Leighton*, c.1871, 66 × 53 cm (26 × 21 in), Leighton House Museum (purchased in 2004 with the support of the Heritage Lottery Fund, the Art Fund, the MLA/V&A Purchase Funds, the Friends of Leighton House Museum and Linley Sambourne House, and private donations)

mural painting and on life drawing from the human figure. He believed that such drawing should take place at an earlier stage for the student: 'I would demonstrate the action of the limbs and the use of the muscles, from the living model in combination with the antique.'[51] The model should be seen in motion, much as he worked with his own model 'Long Mary' (fig.49). Watts considered her even finer than a Pheidian type with 'more length of limb'.[52] Drawings of her carried out in the 1860s served as source material for his expressive use of the human figure for years to come.

Window. It shows the variety of his output, but it also has an element of autobiography. This seemingly simple study is a reminder that Watts's individuality was based partly on his life in the bucolic surroundings of Kensington removed from the fray in London. The image conveys personal information about the artist that has a wider relevance for Watts, who had been out of the mainstream for so long that he had acquired a romantic image. He exemplified an era when the art world was increasingly beginning to see itself as the subject, and the artist and his life in the studio were edging into public awareness.

For his subject paintings Watts formulated new goals. He began to consider his works as comprising groups, so that the individual components would benefit from being seen in conjunction with each other, like 'parts of an epic poem'.[53] Moreover, he decided, as he had already with his portraits, to accumulate a collection of his most highly regarded compositions, retaining works 'destined to become public property' until such time as he would present them to the nation.[54] Throughout the late 1860s and into the 1870s Watts conceived new imaginative subject paintings that embodied universal concepts. Known mainly by drawings (see cats 52–5) and oil studies, these now began to emerge as fully worked paintings on a large scale, as in the case of *Love and Death* (fig.52). In 1874 he explained it as follows:

> Love is not restraining Death for it could not do so. I wished to suggest the passionate though unavailing struggle to avert the inevitable. You know my great desire to use such talents as I may have and such experience in art as I have been able to acquire, with the object of proving that Art, like Poetry and music may suggest the noblest and tenderest thoughts, inspiring and awakening, if only for a time, the highest sensibilities of our nature.[55]

The work had been sparked by a personal drama, when Watts observed the lingering illness of his friend William Kerr, 8th Marquess of Lothian, who, despite the ministrations of his wife Constance and various doctors, died at a young age in 1870.[56] He channelled this painful experience into an allegorising design in which the

51. *From my Studio Window*, c.1870, oil on panel, 45.7 × 27.9 cm (18 × 11 in), COMWG160

youthful Love is unable to resist the majestically powerful female figure of Death. The private stimulus behind this work lent the imagery of death an even greater resonance. The actual design, first seen publicly in 1870, developed in several versions that increased in size, as was his practice with other compositions. These versions were often over life-size and required bigger venues for their essential qualities and impact to be appreciated. Watts's preferred appellation for such works was 'symbolical'; he also considered *Love and Death*, along with other 'symbolical' works, to be 'poems painted on canvas'.[57]

Growing disenchanted with the Royal Academy as an arena for his work, Watts commented that it was 'no place for a grave, deliberate work of art'.[58] When the Grosvenor Gallery opened in May 1877, he found his ideal exhibition venue. His friends Sir Coutts and Blanche Lindsay financed and established this new exhibition gallery to showcase the work of artists who found the Royal Academy too populist and too crowded. Watts appeared in strength. Major portraits of Burne-Jones (1833–98) and the Aesthetic patron Madeline Wyndham (fig.61), as well as the Grosvenor's co-founder Blanche, Lady Lindsay (1877; private collection), introduced a cast of characters of the Aesthetic era. To the young poet Oscar Wilde the Grosvenor aided a 'revival of culture and love of beauty'; he singled out *Love and Death* as an encounter between a 'grey phantom' and the 'beautiful boy', a tribute to Watts's 'great originative and imaginative genius … in the startling vividness of his conceptions'.[59] The triumphant appearance of the prime version of *Love and Death* revealed for the first time Watts's 'symbolical' paintings to the elite of the art world. William Michael Rossetti hailed the work as 'a majestic one, in which the author's highest powers have been worthily exercised'.[60]

In 1877 Watts arrived at a personal turning point as well when he finally severed the ties of his still-legal marriage by divorcing Ellen. With his artistic ideals at long last beginning to be

52. *Love and Death*, c.1874–7, reworked until 1887, oil on canvas, 248.9 × 116.8 cm (98 × 46 in), Whitworth Art Gallery, University of Manchester

appreciated, Watts regarded the Grosvenor Gallery as his primary venue. During the next ten years he sent the gallery nearly sixty paintings, unveiling a series of major compositions, including *Time, Death and Judgement* (cat.68) and *Paolo and Francesca* (fig.53; cat.49),[61] which he had refined over a long period of time. Such works satisfied his ambitions to paint ideas on a grand scale and their exposure encouraged extensive critical reaction to Watts's aims. Regarding *Paolo and Francesca*, F.G. Stephens wrote that 'these designs are full of poetry', while another commentator recognised images 'full of poetry and passion'.[62] The painting depicts with a majestic compositional sweep and in deep rich tones a nether region associated with the dead. Like other works by Watts, it transcends narrative to create a gloomy world of doomed souls that foreshadowed Symbolist concerns. Indeed, in 1883 this painting and several others went to the Galerie Georges Petit in Paris, where it was seen by Joris-Karl Huysmans, who in the classic *fin de siècle* text, *À Rebours* (1884), characterised Watts as 'a dreamy scholarly Englishman afflicted with a predilection for hideous hues'.[63] Such works, and those Watts exhibited in Paris in 1878 and 1880, had a key influence on Symbolism in France;[64] by the time paintings like *Hope* (cat.59) and *Mammon* (1885, Tate Britain; see also cat.62), recognised by French critics as 'allégories poétiques',[65] appeared at the Exposition Universelle in 1889, he seemed an integral part of this continental movement.

Thanks to this international exposure, Watts was asked by the Uffizi Gallery in Florence, along with Leighton and Millais (1829–96), to paint a self-portrait for the gallery, a request to which he enthusiastically responded, portraying himself seated before his great composition of *Time, Death and Judgement*. His patron Charles Rickards, emboldened by Watts's successes, arranged for his own collection of over fifty paintings by the artist to be seen in a one-man show at the Manchester Institution in 1880. News of this event reached London, leading in turn to Sir Coutts Lindsay's exhibition at the Grosvenor Gallery of more than 200 paintings by Watts in the winter of 1881–2, the first time a living artist was accorded a full-scale retrospective during his lifetime. This forty-year body of work was considered by one critic to be

'unremittingly faithful to a high ideal in art'.[66] The exhibition brought about a change in the widespread view of Watts as chiefly a painter of portraits to one who had a more wide-ranging output, placing the artist at centre stage in the art world.

The 1880s: displays, styles and Symbolism

By now in his sixties, Watts took on the role of senior figure in the London art world, with his comments on art drawing attention. His article on 'The Present Conditions of Art' provided a forum for his complaints about the Royal Academy and its commercial spaces being

53. *Paolo and Francesca* (detail, cat.49)

54. The Gallery at Little Holland House, *The Building News*, 7 October 1881, reproduced with the permission of the Guildhall Library, City of London

unsuited to his 'poems painted on canvas'. His introduction to the catalogue of the retrospective at the Grosvenor identified his favoured term for his major compositions as 'symbolical', non-narrative works in a poetic spirit. With such discussions in the public domain, and his art increasingly on view at home and aboard, Watts became one of the first modern artists to be seen as a personality and public figure. In 1882 Oxford University awarded him the honorary degree of Doctor of Civil Law (DCL) and Cambridge followed suit with a Doctor of Laws (LLD) in 1883. His planned bequest to the nation took tangible form in 1883 when the first instalment of portraits went to the National Portrait Galley. In 1885 the Prime Minister, Gladstone, offered baronetcies to Watts and Millais. Despite this flattering overture, Watts declined for a variety of reasons, his lack of financial resources to live up to the accolade being one.[67] This was just prior to his marriage to Mary Fraser-Tytler, who after 1886 became involved in the management of the great artist. During the 1880s a steady stream of articles about him and his work appeared. Still later in the 1890s these focused on his life and lifestyle as Watts himself contributed to the cult of the artist as celebrity, a social phenomenon taken for granted today.

In this process of the artist becoming the agent of his own image, and as part of his growing belief in the public and educational role of art, Watts increasingly took control of the presentation of his work. He had recently moved into his newly built home, New Little Holland House, on Melbury Road in Kensington. Here he had two painting studios and, as if to underline his renewed interest in sculpture, a special studio for that medium, including a passageway for marble to be delivered. In 1881, in the aftermath of the two major one-man shows, he built a glass-roofed gallery onto his house (fig.54), dubbed the Little Holland House Gallery, which opened to the public on Saturday and Sunday afternoons. The gallery, of a substantial size and with a separate hexagonal seating area, formed a major feature in his home as well as in the Kensington area. With the publicity attendant on these ventures, Watts featured in a collection of articles illustrated with photographs called *Artists at Home*. In this he is shown in the gallery surrounded by the cream of his collection (fig.55), including portraits such as *Blanche, Lady Lindsay* and *Cardinal Manning* (Grosvenor Gallery 1882; National Portrait Gallery), and other major works such as *Paolo and Francesca* (cat.49) and *The Spirit of Christianity* (1873–5; Tate, see cat.56). In practical terms, having his own gallery also promoted the sale of his work in an art world where he competed with artists such as Millais to sell his work for top prices. Watts felt that he, too, should command prices on the level of Millais and Lawrence Alma-Tadema, a point often mentioned in his letters.

His display of paintings and sculpture at the Little Holland House Gallery took on the self-conscious role of presenting his life's work, as Watts even rediscovered earlier paintings such as *A Wounded Heron* (cat.3) and incorporated them. The site functioned as a place of pilgrimage for his audience in London and a range of foreign visitors. In 1884, with the encouragement and assistance of a young American admirer, Watts sent fifty of his works to New York's newly opened Metropolitan Museum of Art. This landmark in the display of the work of a British artist was also the first 'blockbuster' exhibition on record. Following it, he began to bestow his work on institutions and countries, with Canada receiving a version of *Time, Death and Judgement* in 1886 and the United States and France also eventually gaining major works. An important group of his paintings went on view at the South Kensington Museum, then housing the national collection of British art. In 1887 the critic M.H. Spielmann produced a catalogue of Watts's works for *The Pall Mall Gazette*, thereby confirming public interest and the status of his life's work up to the age of seventy.

This sustained exposure heralded a renewed burst of creativity for Watts with the production of some highly original compositions. *Hope* is perhaps the best known, but others include *Dweller in the Innermost* (Grosvenor Gallery 1886; Tate Britain),[68] a personification of conscience, and '*The All-Pervading*' (see cat.72), which belong to a distinctly British contribution to international Symbolism. A new more mystical way of thinking informed his work, due in part to his association with the Society for Psychical Research and his friendship with one of its founders, Frederic Myers.[69] Mrs Russell (Emilie) Barrington – writer, amateur artist and friend to artists – commented on the 'mystic indefinite feeling of poetic truth' in his work at this time.[70] Haziness, amorphous mists and strange shadows pervade his imagery in the 1880s.

In tandem with this new kind of imagery came some unusual stylistic departures.[71] The artist experimented with different grounds, such as silk and absorbent muslin.[72] In an effort to counteract the dark qualities in his paintings of the 1870s, Watts consciously sought more pronounced effects of colour and light in his paintings of the 1880s. Barrington, an habitué of Watts's studio at this time, noted that 'the love of colour … reasserted itself' with intricate and subtle effects of tone.[73] Turner's works in the National Gallery, especially *Ulysses Deriding Polyphemus*, provided renewed inspiration at this time. Watts experimented with pastel itself as a medium allowing for the application of pure colour and, as observed by Barrington, often used oil paint as one might use pastel, with the dry pigment put on with loose, free touches.[74] This change was vividly expressed in a bust-length nude, *Uldra* (fig.56), a spirit of the rainbow from northern European

folklore, who appears as the sunlight falls on the water spray.[75] With its riot of rainbow-tinted colours, light dissolves the outline of the figure, and atmospheric effects suffuse the image, creating a swirling play of light and colour over the surface of the painting. Similar effects occur in *Love and Life* (cat.60), *Dawn* (RA 1888; unlocated), in some of the landscapes of this period such as cat. 65, and in *Olympus on Ida* (1885; private collection). In the oil study for the last, Watts transformed an earlier composition, *The Three Goddesses* (c.1872; private collection),[76] by placing the figures in a hazy golden atmosphere surrounded by clouds. He left the oil study unfinished, as he was so pleased with 'a certain opalescent quality'.[77] Valuing these works for their colouristic effects, Watts exhibited them widely: *Uldra* at New York in 1884 and the final version of *Olympus on Ida* at the Exposition Universelle in Paris in 1889.[78] These paintings, overtly Symbolist exercises with ethereal figures in a cloud-like setting, epitomised a visionary quality that became uniquely identified with Watts's work.

Advanced critics discovered that Watts's increasingly visible *oeuvre* spoke to some of the

55. J. P. Mayall, 'Watts in the Gallery at Little Holland House', photograph in *Artists at Home*, 1884, Watts Gallery Archive, The Rob Dickins Collection

56. *Uldra*, *c*.1884, oil on canvas, 66 × 53.3 cm (26 × 21 in), COMWG.NC.21

current trends in European art. His work was widely seen abroad, not just in America (Chicago in 1893) and Paris, but also in Rome at the *In Arte Libertas* exhibition (1890), in Berlin at the International Exhibition of Fine Art (1891), in Munich at the Jahresausstellung (1893) showing twenty-three works (including cats 26, 30, 58), in Brusssels at La Libre Esthétique (1894) and at other exhibitions thereafter. Watts's commentators and admirers included French museum director Léonce Bénédite, who made purchases for the Luxembourg Museum, Paris. In 1893 Watts presented a large version of *Love and Life* (Musée d'Orsay; see cat.60) to this newly opened museum of contemporary art. French writer Robert de la Sizeranne, whose articles on English art appeared in *Revue des Deux Mondes* in 1894, gave a moving account of his experience of seeing Watts's 'symbolical' works. In 1894 the Belgian Symbolist Fernand Knopff wrote in *The Studio* in praise of Watts.[79] A younger generation of British writers with ties to artistic developments abroad also 'discovered' the octogenarian Watts. Arthur Symons, who visited the artist's studio shortly after he published *The Symbolist Movement in Literature* (1899), identified the 'great abstract tragedy' in *Love and Death*, evocatively commenting on '*The All-Pervading*' and *The Dweller in the Innermost* as displaying 'mesmeric dolls, like figures drawn by a medium in a state of a trance'.[80] He held the very strangeness of some of Watts's recent work up for scrutiny, including the 'ghostly flesh' of *Uldra*, but admitted that the artist 'rarely loses control of his own vision'.[81] Such comments, more widely shared once published in book form in 1906, exemplify how Watts's reinvention had crossed international boundaries and generational divides.

Later life and the late works: painting for posterity

To his contemporaries Watts occupied a unique place as a public figure; as an artist, his distinctive role is characterised by Spy's cartoon published in *Vanity Fair* on 26 December 1891: 'He paints portraits & ideas' (fig.57). As visualised in this mild caricature, the dapper external appearance of the artist, complete with his Titian-like skullcap, masks Watts, the deep thinker, but the tag line

57. *Vanity Fair* cartoon of Watts, 1891 (cat.97)

acknowledges that there was more to the artist than just being a successful establishment figure in the mould of Leighton or Millais. His later portraits, some already in the National Portrait Gallery,[82] plumb greater depths of character. Watts sought sitters specifically to enhance his self-created collection, in progress for decades and always intended to be left to the nation. He never painted as many scientists as he had hoped and greatly regretted that a plan to portray Charles Darwin shortly before his death in 1882 proved abortive.[83] Sitters from the realms of the arts, politics and academe came to the studio, although his attempt to paint royalty in the early 1880s, a commission for a full-length of the Prince of Wales, was a notable failure. Watts's unfinished portraits are as revealing as those he

completed. His incomplete *Richard Burton* (fig.58) is an intense record of a brief session of painting suffused with the simmering personality of the great explorer. Such works carried as much authenticity as more highly worked portrayals and as such took their place in the Little Holland House Gallery as integral to the multi-faceted display there.

Watts's social concerns fed into his art in the 1880s and 1890s, particularly through his association with Canon Samuel and Henrietta Barnett of St Jude's Church in Whitechapel, East London. The Barnetts staged art exhibitions to raise the spirits and aspirations of the poor, and from 1882 for a period of ten years Watts enthusiastically sent his works, as many as fourteen in 1886, to support their efforts. In 1888 he backed a similar project at the People's Palace for East London. His own commemoration of the heroic deeds of common people saw realisation in the Postman's Park at Aldersgate in the City of London. Essentially, Watts's life work was to be his legacy. Negotiations with the government, with the aid of friends like Frederic Leighton (by this time President of the Royal Academy), went on during the 1880s for his collection of 'symbolical' paintings to be given to the nation; it was agreed that his collection would go to the new Tate Gallery when it opened in 1897.

In 1896 another extensive retrospective of Watts's paintings took place at the New Gallery on Regent Street, London, the venue to which he sent many of his works from 1888 onwards. Here his life's work had its final cumulative presentation in the year of his eightieth birthday, itself a cause for special commemoration. His preface to the exhibition catalogue pointed out that this gathering was prior to the 'presentation to the Nation'. Even now, at the age of eighty, works were still unfinished, though completion was planned, especially for the last and largest version of *The Court of Death* (1870–1902; Tate Britain, see cat.67). Concluding the preface, he hoped that 'a bald and bare idea of the thread of thought connecting the whole together' could be seen; his object, he stated, had been 'to suggest, in the language of Art, Modern Thought in things ethical and spiritual'.[84] The exhibition itself fulfilled Watts's earlier unrealised project for a symbolic history of mankind, the so-called 'House of Life'.

The artist's reaction to his own collective achievement sparked off further innovations in the following few years, which were all the more remarkable for a man over eighty. Given his great age, Watts found mortality a powerful preoccupation. That he had lived into the new century made such thoughts all the more potent. He wrote around this time: 'Standing as one does at my age upon the brink of that dark abyss, deep, unmeasured, and unplumbed, the everyday becomes more and more attenuated in its interest.'[85] In the post-Darwinian world of the late Victorian era Watts, like his other contemporaries, sought new answers to questions of the beginning of life. A truly visionary work such as *The Sower of the Systems* (fig.59; cat.82) still has the power to astonish. G.K. Chesterton did not write specifically about *The Sower of the Systems* but does seem to allude to it when he imagines how, 'standing before a dark canvas upon some evening, he has made lines and something has happened'.[86] That something was the artist's own act of creation, a way of forestalling the closure of life by re-imagining its ultimate beginning.

If Watts gazed backwards before recorded time in *The Sower of the Systems*, he looked forwards in *Destiny* (fig.60), designed and largely painted in the last weeks of his life in 1904.[87] He had felt 'time's heavy hand' for some years,[88] but to start a work of over life-size (as he also did with *Progress*, cat.79) is nothing but life-affirming. Mysteriously poised just above the shore, the colossal Michelangelesque and sibyl-like figure of Destiny dominates the thoughtful putto below. The lapping waves at the sea's edge hint at time's passage, while the figure holds what must be the book of life, akin to the one in *The Court of Death*. The dark cape casting a shadow on the face of Destiny as she gazes downwards seems ominous, but the gloriously hot colours of the drapery inject a positive note. *Destiny*, a fateful vision of the future, along with *The Sower of the Systems* and *Progress*, embraced the concerns of the new century, allowing Watts to reinvent himself, yet again, this time for posterity.

60. *Destiny*, c.1904, oil on canvas, 213.4 × 104 cm (84 × 41 in), COMWG133

1. The National Gallery's rooms, on the western side of the building, were not yet ready and opened a month later; see W.T. Whitley, *Art in England: 1821–1837*, Cambridge, p.33. For the events surrounding the opening, see the *Literary Gazette*, 29 April 1837, p.272.

2. Possibly the version dated 1835 that went to the Examination Schools, Oxford, in 1838.

3. Watts 1912, I, p.22.

4. For fuller details on Watts's early life, see Bryant ODNB.

5. Watts 1912, I, p.31, noted 'much of his early life was not happy'.

6. However, Behnes's 'moral reputation' began to suffer at an early stage, according to his obituary in the *Art Journal*, 1864, p.83.

7. As Watts commented to John St Loe Strachey in 1895, quoted in Bryant ODNB.

8. Watts 1912, I, p.23; Barrington 1905, p.48.

9. This drawing, perhaps taken from an engraving or even a recollection of the original, may well date from any point between the mid-1830s to early 1840s; in composition it also relates to the engraving after William Hogarth's *Paul before Felix*, published in 1833.

10. Watts 1912, I, p.26.

11. Catherine Fuller (ed.), *The Old Radical: Representations of Jeremy Bentham*, exh. cat., Strang Print Room and Flaxman Gallery, University College, London, 1998, nos 32–3.

12. Watts 1912, I, pp.32–3; Basil Long, *Catalogue of the Constantine Alexander Ionides Collection, Volume I*, London, 1925, p.63.

13. For further information on the early works, see Bryant ODNB.

14. From the British Museum Print and Drawing Department accession number (1906.07-07.12) it is possible to identify this with the works given by Watts's executors to the museum, probably selected by the executors in consultation with British Museum staff for its very academic correctness and relation to one of Watts's key early works.

15. Ilchester 1937, pp.320–1.

16. For a selection of these drawings and discussion, see Bryant 2004, nos 9–12.

17. For a discussion of Samuel Rogers's poem and Watts's painting, see my entry on the oil study (now in a private collection) in *A Selection of Drawings and Oil Studies*, exh. cat., Julian Hartnoll's Gallery, London, 1986, no.7.

18. For further discussion of Watts in Italy, see Bryant ODNB and Gaja 1995.

19. Letter from Watts to Ionides, 15 June 1846, partly quoted in Watts 1912, I, p.76.

20. That Watts was aware of this caricature (Watts 1912, I, p.106) of himself as the artist just returned from Rome who 'used to talk about high art at the Caffe Greco' (*Our Street*, published in book form in 1848, p.14) must have brought home to him his anomalous position.

21. Letter to Georgiana Duff Gordon, 9 March 1847, partly quoted in Watts 1912, I, p.86.

22. Watts 1912, I, p.93.

23. Watts 1912, I, p.91.

61. Study for *Madeline Wyndham*, c.1865–70, oil on canvas, 53.3 × 27.9 cm (21 × 11 in), COMWG56

24. Discussed in Bryant 2004, pp.13, 74, along with his other painting seen that year, *M. Guizot* (private collection), also in a French manner.
25. *Athenaeum*, 27 May 1848, p.536.
26. I have discussed these developments in a forthcoming article on Watts's history paintings.
27. 'Occasional Notes: What Becomes of Discharged Prisoners?', *Chambers's Edinburgh Journal* XI (12 May 1849), pp.296–7. For a further discussion of the painting, see Staley 1978, pp.61, 63.
28. Bryant 2004, nos 19–21.
29. Watts 1912, I, p. 128.
30. Tom Taylor (ed.), *The Life of Benjamin Robert Haydon, Historical Painter*, London, 1853, III, p.372.
31. For a discussion of the murals (illustrated in colour), see Malcolm Hay and Jacqueline Riding, *Art in Parliament*, London, 1996, pp.94–7.
32. See Bryant 2004, p.16.
33. Bryant 2004, pp.16–19.
34. Bryant 2004, p.19, quoting Watts's letter to his friend and patron, George Cavendish Bentinck.
35. On Watts's portrayals of Tennyson, see Bryant 2004, no.34, p.110.
36. Watts 1912, I, p.142.
37. For a further discussion on the marriage of Watts and Ellen Terry, see Bryant ODNB; Loshak 1963, pp.476ff; Gould 2004, pp.67–76.
38. Bryant 2004, no.43.
39. Pamela M. Fletcher, 'Creating the French Gallery: Ernest Gambart and the Rise of the Commerical Art Gallery in Mid-Victorian London', *Nineteenth-Century Art Worldwide*, e-journal (www.19thc-artworldwide.org), VI (spring 2007).
40. Identified for the first time in my entry on this work in Watts Symbolism 1997 (Exhibitions), no.8, as the painting shown at the French Gallery in 1865. Watts Catalogue, I, p.115, called it the *Peacock Fan* with no exhibition history, a misidentification that still persists.
41. Bryant 2004, nos 48, 49.
42. Watts 1912, I, pp.217–18.
43. For the 'Moonlight Portrait', see Bryant 2004, no.34.
44. G.K. Chesterton, 'The Literary Portraits of G.F. Watts, R.A.', *The Bookman*, XIX (1900), p.81.
45. See Staley 1978, no.13.
46. See Bryant 1987–8 for a full discussion of this work, which evolved into the large composition, *Mischief* (National Gallery of Scotland). Watts gave this work to his friend Bowman.
47. F.G. Stephens, *Athenaeum*, 6 May 1865, p.627.
48. Watts 1912, I, p.238.
49. Watts 1912, I, p.147.
50. Rossetti and Swinburne 1868; discussed most recently in Elizabeth Prettejohn, *Art for Art's Sake: Aestheticism in Victorian Painting*, New Haven and London, 2007, pp.55, 58.
51. Watts 1912, I, p.213.
52. Barrington 1905, p.23.
53. Watts 1912, I, p.262.
54. Watts to Rickards, quoted in Watts 1912, I, p.262.
55. Watts to Rickards, 27 December 1874, quoted in Watts 1912, I, pp.283–4.
56. Bryant 1997, p.168; Bryant 2004, pp.32–3 and no.42. Watts also executed a tomb monument with the recumbent figure of Lothian, characterised by a powerful portrait of the deceased, for Blickling Church, Norfolk (a copy is at Jedburgh Abbey); see fig.73.
57. Watts in 'The Present Conditions of Art', *Nineteenth Century* (February 1880), p.250 (reprinted in Watts 1912, III, p.180), discussed further in Bryant 1996, pp.109ff.
58. Bryant 1996, p.109.
59. Oscar Wilde, 'The Grosvenor Gallery', *Dublin University Magazine*, July 1877, p.119.
60. *The Academy*, 16 June 1877, p.396.
61. Further discussed in Bryant 1997, no.48.
62. F.G. Stephens, *Athenaeum*, 10 May 1879; *Saturday Review*, 17 May 1879, p.619.
63. *À Rebours* (*Against Nature*), trans. Robert Baldick, London, 1959, p.136.
64. Discussed further in Bryant 1997, pp.65ff.
65. Quoted in Bryant 1997, p.76 (see also p.293 n.73), on a French critic's assessment of Watts's works in Paris in 1889.
66. Frederick Wedmore, *The Academy*, 14 January 1882, p.32.
67. Barrington 1905, pp.140–1, notes his tax problems, which exacerbated his chronic worries about money.
68. See Bryant 1997, no.75, pp.199–201.
69. Discussed further in Bryant 1997, pp.69, 71–5.
70. Barrington 1905, p.72.
71. For a further discussion, see Bryant 1997, pp.71ff.
72. Barrington 1905, p.66.
73. Barrington 1905, p.203; Cartwright 1896, pp.14–15, also discusses these atmospheric effects.
74. Barrington 1905, pp. 163, 204; she noted that some foreign critics even mistook some of Watts's paintings for pastels.
75. Watts Catalogue, I, p.151, identifies *Uldra* as a Scandinavian personification of the spirit of the waterfall.
76. Watts Symbolism 1997 (Exhibitions), no.14.
77. Watts Catalogue, I, p.109.
78. For the links with contemporary Post-Impressionism, see Bryant 1997, p.76.
79. For a further discussion see Bryant 1997, pp.76–81.
80. Arthur Symons, *Studies in the Seven Arts*, London, 1906 (originally published in 1900), pp.96–7.
81. Ibid., pp.104, 112.
82. Bryant 2004, p.23. The first three, *Lord Lyons*, *Lord Stratford de Redcliffe* and *Lord Lyndhurst* entered the NPG in 1883; a larger group followed in December 1895.
83. Watts 1912, II, p.142; also referred to in I, p.203.
84. Watts New Gallery 1896, pp.8–9.
85. Watts 1912, II, p.311.
86. Chesterton 1904, p.169. As one can tell from comments in his book, Chesterton met Watts (and had already published an article on his work in 1900; see note 44).
87. Watts Catalogue, I, p.39.
88. Barrington 1905, p.204. On Watts's thoughts in 1903 as the foundation stone was laid for the Watts Gallery, see p.6.

The Possibility of Watts: Religion and Spirituality in Victorian England

Michael Wheeler

At 6.30 in the morning, he asked [Mary] to read to him. She had no book near by, so she began to recite the opening verses of *In Memoriam*. Lily ran out to borrow a copy. Hunt lent his precious first edition:

Strong Son of God, immortal Love
  Whom we, that have not seen thy face,
  By faith, and faith alone, embrace,
Believing where we cannot prove …

The artist called the Messengers of Death to lead him away, crying again and again, 'Why, Why don't they come?' At 3.15 in the afternoon of Friday, 1 July 1904, he died.[1]

Deathbed scenes are a staple of Victorian biography, and none is more revealing than that of G.F. Watts, described here by Veronica Franklin Gould. The 'Signor' is attended by his loving second wife, who reads Tennyson to him; he cries out to the 'Messengers of Death' – for him not vague symbolic figures but present realities – and then the 'last great Victorian' is gone.

Many things 'made Watts possible', the most important being all those things that interest art historians. The subject of this chapter is religion, however, and here I want to look at some of the ways in which the religious mores of nineteenth-century England made Watts possible as a painter and sculptor of spiritual subjects who was recognized as great in his own time. And the deathbed scene I have quoted provides the first clues. Tennyson added the Prologue to *In Memoriam* in the so-called 'trial edition' of 1849, at the very end of the long gestation period of his sequence of lyrics, partly, it has been suggested, to assure his anxious fiancée, Emily Sellwood, that he could call himself a Christian.[2] Later, Tennyson felt that faith was 'too completely triumphant' in

the Prologue. How interesting, then, to find Mary Seton Watts reciting Tennyson at his most Christian to her dying husband, who, like the poet, longed for a wider, less dogmatic faith for England, explored other faiths and investigated alternative spiritual movements.

The friendship between Tennyson and Watts, memorialized in that powerful statue at Lincoln Cathedral (fig. 62) and in some of Watts's sub-Tennysonian verse, was sealed at Freshwater on the Isle of Wight, where they would walk and ride together in the early years of the poet's great fame, admiring the flora and discussing what Tennyson called the 'larger hope' for mankind.[3] The bohemian Tennyson, whose dirty collars and flowing clothes earned him the nickname of 'the gipsy' at Cambridge, became Poet Laureate on the death of Wordsworth in 1850 – the year of *In Memoriam* and of his marriage – and later accepted a baronetcy. Watts, a neater and indeed cleaner figure, was also bohemian in appearance and in spirit. He twice refused a baronetcy but did accept the newly created honour of the Order of Merit at the very end of his life. In Victorian and Edwardian England the visionary poet or artist could be at once bohemian outsider and garlanded insider, as the prophetic figure with a strong moral vision was regarded as a necessary presence.

In a moment I want to suggest that the Prologue to *In Memoriam* anticipates Watts in its appeal to divine wisdom, and I want to argue that it was the response of Victorian intellectuals to the biblical wisdom tradition that helped to make Watts possible. First, however, some thoughts about Tennyson and the Church of England in 1850, when the poet was forty-one and Watts thirty-three. Theologically, *In Memoriam A.H.H.* reflects the influence of both Arthur Hallam, Tennyson's brilliant Cambridge friend who had

62. *Monument to Lord Tennyson* (fig.77)

died young, and the leading Liberal Anglican, F.D. Maurice. But whereas Tennyson's virtual dismissal of hell as a place of everlasting punishment in the poem was widely welcomed by churchmen who had difficulties with the received doctrine on eternal punishment,[4] F.D. Maurice was dismissed from King's College London, where he was a professor, only three years later for expressing similar views. The poet, like the visionary painter, was freer than the preacher to explore ideas outside the establishment box. As F.W. Farrar put it – and he could have been writing of Watts here, rather than Tennyson and Browning – the 'intuitions of the poet like those of the saint, may contain more essential truth than the limitless inferences of theologians from dimly-apprehended metaphors'.[5] Ironically, then, the very dogmatism of Victorian Church teaching helped to make the visionary G.F. Watts possible. Many people who visited art galleries in the second half of the nineteenth century were crying out for something broader.

The fact is that in 1850 the Church of England was in deep difficulty, rather as it is today. Although the established Church had enormous power, wealth and presence in the nineteenth century, its history is that of internal disputes. In the 1840s religious conflict focused on, first, Newman's converting to Rome in 1845 and taking others with him; secondly, the Hampden case, concerning the appointment of a bishop whose beliefs were regarded as heterodox by Tractarians; and, thirdly, the notorious Gorham case, which turned on the doctrine of baptismal regeneration and precipitated an even greater crisis of authority in the Church of England. As the head of the newly restored Catholic hierarchy, Cardinal Wiseman, asked, what were Christians to make of an established Church of England whose clergy – High, Low and Broad – couldn't agree on what they believed about one of only two sacraments recognized by their tradition, namely that of baptism?[6]

So at the time of the publication of *In Memoriam* the Church of England had come close to breaking up. The first census of religious observance in England revealed the then shocking fact that only half the population attended services on Sundays. Meanwhile, Evangelical hostility towards both the 'papists', who seemed intent on reclaiming England for Rome, and the Tractarians, who continued to foster a lively Catholic revival within Anglicanism, intensified year by year. Then further disputes arose after the publication of three books: first, Darwin's epoch-making study, *The Origin of Species* (1859); secondly, the much more widely read collection of liberal Anglican *Essays and Reviews* (1860), which reflected the methods of German 'higher criticism' of the Bible; and, thirdly, Bishop John William Colenso's *The Pentateuch and the Book of Joshua Critically Examined* (1862–79), which showed that the first five books of the Bible contain contradictions and therefore cannot be regarded as true narratives of actual, historical matters of fact.

In the 1860s some educated lay people, particularly of the younger generation, such as Samuel Butler and Thomas Hardy, lost their faith and left off regular church attendance. As victory in the big battles over modern science and biblical criticism had already been claimed by the liberals, many traditionalists simply stuck to the old beliefs, including the literal truth of the Bible. Gradually, however, most Anglicans took a rather more liberal position on these matters. Nevertheless, *Lux Mundi*, a collection of essays edited by Charles Gore, who ventured to apply the word 'myth' to certain Old Testament narratives, raised a storm of protest as late as 1889, largely because its authors were devout Oxford High Churchmen, whereas the authors of *Essays and Reviews* had been regarded as marginal figures.

Where does Watts fit into all this? His own religious background was strictly Sabbatarian and, according to Gould, he lost his trust in narrow formalized religion when still a boy.[7] Later in life he was implacably opposed to Christian dogmatism and sectarianism, while recognizing the power and the beauty of Christ's teaching, which he, like some other intellectuals of his generation, attempted to harmonize with teachings from other faiths. His allegorical art works often embraced the very subjects that frightened conservative believers, such as evolution, progress and sexuality, but also offered a moral vision that was positively welcomed by some clergy, not only in his biblical paintings but also in his treatments of themes such as creation and transcendence.

The notorious vagueness of his cultural references – or should one say his syncretism? – allowed scope for selective interpretation, and this made him accessible to a wide range of people in his generation, if not necessarily in ours.

In certain respects his trajectory is similar to that of Ruskin, whose early private encouragement and later public celebration of Watts's art were very important to him. In 1847, when Ruskin told Watts that his painting *Satan* (fig.63; cat.13) was 'glorious',[8] the art critic was still a devout Evangelical. Later, his beliefs underwent many changes, susceptible as they were to his own sharpened critical awareness. What never left Ruskin, however, and what proved to be least open to the application of new critical tools by the scientists and biblical scholars of the day, was belief in divine wisdom and a God of peace. By the later 1860s he regarded the Bible as one among several important, divinely inspired but humanly produced wisdom texts. In the 1870s the creed that he wrote for the Guild of St George was explicitly designed to be accessible to Jews and 'Mahometans'. For the later Ruskin the 'Heavenly Wisdom' remained the 'creative spirit', mediating between the Creator and the creature, and witnessed not only in the Jewish and Christian traditions but also in Greek religion and Islam.[9] Much the same could be said of Watts, as indeed of Tennyson.[10] What all three of these 'great Victorians' shared was a belief in divine wisdom and in a 'larger hope' of some kind of universal salvation, and a longing for a broader understanding of religion and spirituality than the Church could offer.

Watts worked on his painting, *The Spirit of Religion*, for three or four years before it was exhibited at the Royal Academy as *Dedicated to All the Churches* in 1875. Later it was renamed *The Spirit of Christianity* (fig.64; cat.56.1) and a smaller version of it was referred to as *The Sacred Heart* by Rickards.[11] The changes of title reflect the indeterminacy of the picture itself, so characteristic of Watts in its scale (it is 9 feet high), its sense of transcendence (notice how Salvador Dalí learned from Watts's horizons) and its combination of specific cultural reference ('Suffer the little children to come unto me', Mark 10: 14) and a deliberate generalizing towards universality. This is

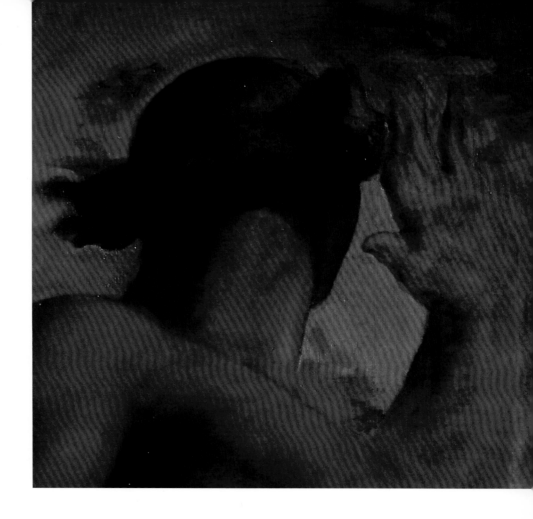

63. *Satan* (detail, cat.13)

and is not Jesus Christ, who is and is not masculine, whose robes are and are not priestly, and whose hair is and is not interwoven with a crown of thorns; these are and are not the seven churches of the Revelation; these are and are not the kind of clouds that are familiar in counter-Reformation paintings of the Ascension and the Assumption.

In *The Art of England*, his Oxford lectures of 1883, Ruskin says disappointingly little about Watts in 'Mythic Schools of Painting', but he says a good deal about William Holman Hunt's *The Triumph of the Innocents* (1883–4) in the previous lecture on 'Realistic Schools of Painting'. The contrast between Hunt's infant figures, drenched in symbolic detail evoking both the Herodian massacre in which they were killed and their new risen life in Christ, and Watts's more generalized infant figures is not made by Ruskin himself but nicely illustrates his distinction between 'realist' and 'mythic' schools of painting.

Watts's *Spirit of Christianity* did, however, receive the following notice from Ruskin in his *Academy Notes* for 1875:

> Here, at least, is one picture meant to teach; nor failing of its purpose, if we read it rightly. Very beautiful it might have been – and is, in no mean measure; but as years pass by, the artist concedes to himself, more and more, the privilege which none but the feeble should seek, of substituting the sublimity of mystery for that of absolute majesty of form. The relation between this grey and soft cloud of visionary power, and the perfectly substantial, bright, and near presence of the saints, angels, or Deities of early Christian art, involves questions of too subtle interest to be followed here; but in the essential force of it, belongs to the inevitable expression, in each period, of the character of its own faith. The Christ of the thirteenth century was vividly present to its thoughts, and dominant over its acts, as a God manifest in the flesh, well pleased in the people to whom He came; while ours is either forgotten, or seen by those who yet trust in Him, only as a mourning and departing Ghost.[12]

Not the *Holy* Ghost or Holy *Spirit* – the third person of a dynamically interacting Trinity – but a ghostly Christ, possibly something approximating to a Gnostic Christ, whom Ruskin reads as a cultural sign of the times, a product of the 'melancholy, long, withdrawing roar' of Matthew Arnold's 'Sea of Faith' in 'Dover Beach'. Again a contrast with Holman Hunt presents itself in Ruskin's earlier treatment of *The Light of the World* (1851–3), which he hugely admired as a study of the risen Christ *with us*, here in an England orchard, and which he described as 'true sacred art'.[13] So whereas Hunt produced realist and sacred art, Watts produced mythic and spiritual art.

Watts the poet-painter often shed most light on the principles behind his spiritual art in his

64. *The Spirit of Christianity* (cat.56.1)

comments on the work of his contemporaries, both artists and poets. He felt that Browning, for example, whose work he admired, lacked the 'strong poetic wing that should lift him above humanity, above creation', and he said this of the poet in 1887:

> He is occupied only with humanity – with a dissecting knife he lays the human heart open – but he never takes one, as the true prophet should to verses that show us a something beyond … or rather to heights … each takes its place among the stars, & the air of heavens infinity is blown upon our faces … For a great work of art, altitude & depth are absolutely necessary – but there is much needed besides.[14]

Hence, perhaps, in Watts's ambitious spiritual paintings the dramatic separation of the subject from the earth, and from the perspectives and parameters by which we perceive and locate ourselves in the here-and-now.

Watts sought in his visionary paintings to break out of temporal as well as spatial limits. Take, for example, *Time, Death and Judgement* (fig.65; cat.68). Signor explained to some visiting children his 'strong, young figure of Time, marching forward with a tread nothing could stop, not ruthless, but indifferent, which was why he had wide blank eyes'; in his hand he brought Death, always beautiful, pale and mysterious, with 'a veiled head and gentle bosom where we must all lay our heads at last'.[15] Watts substituted the young figure of Time for the traditional ancient figure of Old Father Time. More significantly, in terms of my current theme, Watts's three figures stand in place of the 'four last things' of Christian eschatology – death and judgment, but also heaven and hell – which preoccupied the preachers and theologians of Victorian England.

The picture is full of movement and creates a sense of sequence, and is yet, perforce, frozen in space and time. Remorseless *chronos*, or clock time, is fixed in the *kairos*, or meaningful moment or season, of the viewer's encounter with these three figures. Whereas Time faces us, full frontal, as he moves dynamically towards us and as if

beyond the picture plane, Death turns her face to one side, while Judgement's face is concealed, so that a sequence is set up through the eye's circular movement from Time to Death to Judgement. Such a sequence and such a movement are radically different from the narrative structures of Victorian Christian epics such as the Evangelical Edward Henry Bickersteth's *Yesterday, Today and For Ever* (1866), a poem that insists upon the implacable tread of divine judgement rather than of time.[16]

It is not difficult, then, to see why the Revd Samuel Barnett, the dynamic incumbent of St Jude's Church, Whitechapel, got into trouble when he used Watts for the purposes of religious education! The nobility of Watts's images and ideas, he persuaded his bishop, drew the attention of his poor parishioners away from other, less elevated sights on the streets. 'Never in my intercourse with my neighbours', he wrote, 'have I been so conscious of their souls and their souls' needs as when they hung around me listening to what I had to say of Watts's picture *Time, Death and Judgement*.'[17]

The obsession with eschatology in the Victorian Church, referred to above, turns on the difficult doctrine of divine judgment and the possibility of everlasting bliss or pain. Critics of the Church, including Tennyson, Ruskin and Watts, deplored teaching on judgment and hell, which engendered fear in believers, and called for what we might call a 'white' theology, with a stronger emphasis on the love that drives out fear. (Love was surely *the* subject for Watts.) As the world grew smaller, and the Victorians came to see that the majority of the earth's inhabitants were not Christian, the niceties of doctrinal disputes about hell within a divided Church of England became less engaging. The world also grew vastly older, as archaeologists and palaeontologists made their investigations. Thus even Judaism, the oldest of the great Abrahamic religions, began to seem recent in origin.

Watts was very sensitive to these developments, as we can see in this evocative passage from Gould's critical biography, where she draws on a wide range of published and unpublished material from the year 1893:

Inspired by their evening readings, the history of the Chaldeans, their beliefs, the discovery of the Library of Nineveh, he marvelled at the lofty, reasonable philosophy of the Brahmins. 'There is no study like this.' Samuel Laing's theories in *Human Origins* [1892] that spiritual civilization began not nineteen centuries ago, nor with Jewish belief or even Egyptian, but earlier still, impressed him: 'the soul of man … seeking its own science! as ours seek still.' These studies excited him, expanded his mind and soul. Riding along the Pilgrims Way, he talked of death, of letting go material things. 'The older I get the more I agree that the only reality is the spiritual.' Mary replied, 'You will soon ask for a paint-brush when you get to the new life.' He laughed. 'That I am sure I shall.'

Both were stimulated by Edward Carpenter's *Civilisation: Its Cause and Cure* [1889], the theory that in the fall of man is the development of self-consciousness, 'the dual self in conscious antagonism with each other – but will in time regain paradise by recognizing their *real unity*'.[18]

The interest expressed by all our three sages – Tennyson, Ruskin and Watts – in eastern religions is grounded in their longing for unity. Watts was particularly taken with Buddhism and took a close interest in the theosophical movement in England.[19]

Watts's huge contribution to the Symbolist movement was brought out by the exhibition *The Age of Rossetti, Burne-Jones & Watts: Symbolism in Britain, 1860–1910* at Tate Britain in 1997–8. In his brilliant introductory chapter to the catalogue, entitled 'Symbolism in Britain', Andrew Wilton focuses on psychology, to which many in the twentieth and twenty-first centuries turn for explanations, where formerly they might have turned to the Church. Wilton argues that the language of the 'unconscious' was being developed by artists and creative writers before Freud and Jung got to work, as Sir James Frazer showed in

65. *Time, Death and Judgement* (detail, cat.68)

The Golden Bough in the 1890s, and that the human psyche is the subject of Symbolism.[20]

Wilton goes on to explain that the Belgian 'idealist' painter, Jean Delville, 'admired both Watts and Burne-Jones, placing them in a modern pantheon with Moreau, Puvis and Wagner'; and Wilton finds in Delville's verse 'high-minded sentiments that echo the declared intention of many of Watt's pictures':

O God of Light in whom all worlds are one,
An atom from that fierce and fiery place
  Wherein men stray, behold before Thy Face
My soul, an eagle mounting to the sun.

O God, Who gazing on the perfect whole
Smiles at our loveliness of form or soul
  As gradually the prisoned self escapes,
Beyond all time, division, change, or death,
Thou art the immortal essence of all shapes.[21]

The opening line quoted here – 'O God of Light in whom all worlds are one' – could have been written by Tennyson and is one of Watts's main subjects. Watts's interest in theosophy, his eclectic spiritual symbolism and his openness to new channels of spiritual understanding suggest to me not only the beginnings of Symbolism but also ideas that anticipate today's New Age religion, which has no creed, no systematic theology and no imaginative or doctrinal boundaries. What made him possible in his own era, however, included developments in the very system within which he could not be contained, namely the Christian Church. And what made him so markedly Victorian, and so distant from our current situation, is the fact that he was a great moralist, whose imagination was stirred by the spirit as well as the mind.

1. Mary Watts's Diary, 1 July 1904, Watts Gallery Archive.
2. Tennyson 1982, pp.159–60.
3. Tennyson 1982, p.79.
4. Tennyson 1982, p.70.
5. Wheeler 1990, p.235.
6. Wheeler 2006, p.192.
7. Gould 2004, p.4.
8. Gould 2004, p.22.
9. Wheeler, 1999, pp.177, 226–32, 251.
10. Tennyson 1982, pp.36, 66, 128–9.
11. Gould 2004, p.392.
12. Cook and Wedderburn 1903–12, XIX, p.266.
13. Cook and Wedderburn 1903–12, XII, pp.329–30.
14. Gould 2004, p.219.
15. Gould 2004, p.121.
16. Wheeler 1990, pp.91–101.
17. Gould 2004, p.166.
18. Gould 2004, p.271.
19. Gould 2004, p.259.
20. Watts Symbolism 1997 (Exhibitions), p.12.
21. Watts Symbolism 1997 (Exhibitions), p.29.

Watts and Sculpture

Stephanie Brown

On his death in 1904 Watts was Britain's most revered artist. By the third quarter of the twentieth century, he was stranded on the margins of the revisionist decades that restored the Pre-Raphaelites and other Victorian artists to positions of critical respectability. A review of the 1978 *Victorian High Renaissance* exhibition, which comprised works by Frederic Leighton, Albert Moore (1841–93), Alfred Gilbert (1854–1934) and Watts, detected something of worth in the first three but concluded that, with minor exceptions, 'Watts is more or less unrevivable'.[1] Significantly, Watts's sculpture is not mentioned, although the exhibition included his celebrated bust of *Clytie*. It seems the pleasure of returning him to critical oblivion would have been forfeited, had any reference been made to Watts as a sculptor. Yet it is through his sculpture that Watts most clearly transcends his times, becoming not only eminently revivable but ultimately unclassifiable.

Watts only began pursuing sculptural ambitions in his fifties, having safely established his practice as a portraitist and subject painter. He was not dependent on success in sculptural competitions or in vying for commissions, and this partly accounts for his unrealistically grandiose proposals and adoption of idiosyncratic and technically questionable approaches that no professional sculptor could have risked. Watts had no practical training in sculpture, and though from an early age he drew from classical casts in the studio of the sculptor William Behnes, he claims to have received no instruction there, insisting that he 'learned in no school save that of Pheidias' and his 'only teachers were the Elgin Marbles'.[2] These assertions conveniently linked the untutored Watts with the most admired sculptor of classical Greece, and became a central plank on which he built his reputation. Inevitably, the understanding of Watts's Pheidianism has focused on the 'Elgin marbles', supported by their visible influence on his paintings. But Watts's sculpture demonstrates a much more complex response to Pheidias, as it evolves to incorporate different facets of Pheidian works.

The 'Elgin marbles', attributed at the time to Pheidias, were the pedimental sculptures, metopes and frieze taken from the Parthenon by Lord Elgin and deposited in the British Museum in 1816. They were admired for their elevated grandeur of form and for what was perceived as a remarkable, scientific naturalism in the treatment of anatomy. Watts was one of the first artists to study them closely, particularly the pedimental sculptures, which he drew throughout the 1830s and after, rendering them as strikingly naturalistic – closer to drawings from life than objective records of the fractured, fissured reality (fig. 67). He later engaged in imaginative completion of the marble fragments, most notably in his painting, *Ariadne in Naxos* (fig. 68), which restores the missing heads and limbs from the sculptures of Dione and Aphrodite, and places the figures in a landscape setting, further accentuating this naturalistic reading. *Ariadne* was an isolated example, however, and other paintings show a far less literal and descriptive treatment. In *The Genius of Greek Poetry* (cat.48) Watts imaginatively reconstructs the head and limbs missing from the Ilissos figure (one of the most influential pedimental sculptures) but fails to 'restore' the surface, so the rough impasto of the paint seems to consciously simulate the actual eroded texture of the marble. His awareness that the massive grandeur of the fragments actually resulted from anatomical exaggeration is apparent in *Evolution* (fig. 69) where the *figura quadrata* – the essentially squared torso characteristic of the male fragments – is conjured into a half-length female figure. The fictive development of the painted forms co-exists

66. *Physical Energy* (detail, cat.86)

67. Drawing of Theseus (now considered to be Dionysus) from the sculptures of the Parthenon ('Elgin marbles'), late 1840s–c.1850, 8.2 × 21.5 cm (3¼ × 8½ in), pencil on paper, from a sketchbook (COMWG2007.210)

68. *Ariadne in Naxos*, 1875, oil on canvas, 94 × 75 cm (19¼ × 29½ in), Guildhall Art Gallery, City of London

with a surface that, again, evokes the material condition of the marbles.

By the 1860s 'Pheidianism' had become synonymous with naturalistic treatment of the body in frequently eroticised, escapist representations of antiquity, validated by apparent archaeological accuracy in their detailed attention to costume and accessories. Watts's association with these aspects of the 'Victorian High Renaissance' was minimal, and despite his familiarity with the marbles, he stressed the elusive nature of Pheidian achievements: 'We know but half of the work of Pheidias, and we can judge of his greatness only by the fragments that remain, as nothing remains of that … mentioned in the very meagre written records.'[3] The 'fragments' was Watts's term for the pedimental sculptures and the 'nothing' referred to Pheidias's lost colossi – the huge chryselephantine (gold and ivory) statues of Zeus from Olympia and *Athena Parthenos* from the interior of the Parthenon, and the bronze *Athena Promachos* from the Acropolis.[4] The Athena statues, in particular, influenced Watts's proposals for public sculpture of commanding presence suitable for conveying serious moral messages.

Watts's understanding of Pheidias was unusual in focusing on 'fragments' and 'nothing' – on the damaged presence of the marbles and the absence of the colossi – which enabled him to create his own impression of their awesome appearance. He applied the very different materials and conditions of these works to his own sculpture, which shifts between reconfiguring original aspects of the marbles, reflecting their damaged state and attempting to fuse this with his response to the lost colossi. For Watts, Pheidian naturalism was of little interest compared to the didactic and imaginative potential of colossal and fragmented forms.

Significantly perhaps, Watts's earliest surviving sculpture represents an anatomical fragment, the *Head of Medusa* (fig. 70; cat.89), modelled in Florence in 1846. This also relates to imagery on Pheidias's *Athena Parthenos*, whose shield and aegis were embellished with the Medusa's head. Watts described his own work as 'not a relief nor can it be called a bust. It is in fact a head severed at the neck from the trunk, & lying on a slab'.[5] Despite this description, *Medusa* is not a sculpture in the round but in high relief. Although this may suggest the influence of two-dimensional sources, its closest affinities in form and treatment are with the *Medusa Rondanini* (second century AD; Glyptothek, Munich), the earliest work to present the Medusa as a beautiful woman, with wings in her hair and snakes encircling her face and neck. This is exactly how Watts shows her, and Mrs Watts stresses that: 'The face is that of a noble woman … she seems to have welcomed death.'[6] It thus differs both from the grotesque contortions of most Medusan imagery and from Symbolist and decadent interpretation, although the popularity of the subject in the later nineteenth century has attracted attention to the work because of problematic issues of dating.

The next evidence of Watts's practical interest in sculpture is both precisely dated and refers explicitly to Pheidias's colossi. In the catalogue for the 1864 Royal Academy exhibition, he describes a small oil sketch of *Time and Oblivion* as 'a design for sculpture, to be executed in divers materials after the manner of Pheidias'. This is curious because sculptural designs would usually be exhibited as maquettes not oil sketches, and *Time and Oblivion* (fig.39) was painted in 1848. But in the intervening years Watts had unsuccessfully attempted to introduce didactic fresco works to public buildings, and he turned to sculpture, 'the adaptation of painting to architecture being denied to him'.[7] The frescoes were related to his 'House of Life' scheme, at the centre of which *Time and Oblivion* was to convey 'a moral lesson'. The subject never materialised as sculpture, but two years later, in 1866, Watts wrote to his patron Charles Rickards soliciting support for 'a colossal bronze statue … a monument to the faithful who are not famous'.[8] Inspired by George Eliot's novel, *Felix Holt, the Radical*, this was an equally radical conception of a public sculpture where the subject was to be the public itself, celebrated in a monument to 'unknown worth'. Watts envisaged it as 'art of noble aim … necessary to a great nation … I think it would be a worthy thing to do I would give up all other work to be enabled to carry out such an idea.'[9] He would do this for expenses only, raising funds through public subscription if Rickards indemnified him against loss, but nothing came of this.

69. *Evolution*, 1898, oil on canvas, 167.6 × 134.6 cm (66 × 53 in), COMWG35

70. *Head of Medusa* (detail, cat.89)

71. *Design for a Statue for a Funerary Monument: Thomas Cholmondeley*, c.1866, chalk on paper, 22.5 × 6 cm (8¾ × 2¼ in), COMWG2006.17

By the mid-1860s, therefore, Watts had twice expressed ambitions to undertake self-generated public sculptures of didactic intent and colossal scale. His ideal was to update Pheidian works for modern purposes, but in actuality his sculpture from this period was quite different. His first large sculpture, the marble *Monument to Sir Thomas Cholmondeley* (1867; Church of St Mary and St Andrew, Condover, Shropshire), was commissioned by his friend Reginald Cholmondeley as a memorial to his brother, who had died in 1864. This is a competent effigy, whose kneeling pose adopts the retrospective style of nearby seventeenth-century monuments (see fig. 71). Watts then took on a succession of commissions for memorial works. *Lord Holland* (1869–70; Holland Park, London) belatedly commemorated the Third Baron Holland (d.1840), father of Watts's patron in Florence. Watts appears to have set out to imbue the seated figure with a life-like verisimilitude, and its informal and notably naturalistic appearance accords with its informal

parkland setting. His first open-air sculpture, *Lord Holland* is also the first work modelled by Watts for casting in bronze.

The Holland and Cholmondeley memorials, showing figures in contemporary dress, offered Watts little scope for ideal conceptions or for pursuing his interest in Pheidias. However, two other funerary commissions allowed explorations, not of the chryselephantine and bronze colossi discussed in relation to his personal projects, but of the drapery in the 'Elgin marbles'. Watts was already engaged in emulating this in *Ariadne in Naxos*, a pictorial transcription that embodied his understanding of the marbles as having 'the palpitations of colour, that seem to suggest all the elements of the picture, you unconsciously see it painted'.[10] It was, however, a different matter to transfer the effects of Pheidian drapery carving to sculpture itself as he did in the *Monument to Dr Lonsdale, Bishop of Lichfield* (1869–71; Lichfield Cathedral, see fig. 72) and the *Monument to Lord Lothian* (fig. 73). The vestments and robes of these figures presented an opportunity to introduce aspects of Pheidian carving into relatively mundane effigies. However, these recumbent tomb figures were somewhat ill suited to an approach intended to animate the 'kind of tremulous, palpitating beauty in every line of drapery' that Watts believed characterised a supreme achievement of Greek carving.

Watts carved the Lonsdale monument, not in marble but in the softer material of alabaster, which facilitated the introduction of intricate convolutions of drapery, although in parts this also appears rigidly linear. Mrs Watts reports: 'His treatment of the Bishop's lawn sleeves and robe was, he believed, at the time unique. It brings to mind his careful observation of Pheidian work.'[11] In the Lothian monument the results of this observation are actually more apparent and approach the organic variations that gave Pheidian drapery its 'palpitating beauty'. This was largely due to Watts undercutting the marble more deeply, intensifying the effects of light and shade and animating the shroud's complex interplay of sinuous folds and broader gathering. Watts used these monuments as exercises in accentuating aspects of the 'Elgin marbles' that he believed were undervalued:

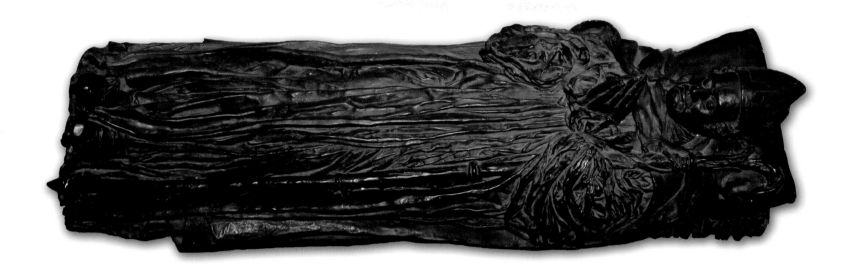

72. *Monument to Dr Lonsdale, Bishop of Lichfield*, 1869, plaster painted black, 71 × 261 × 109 cm (28 × 102¾ × 43 in), COMWG460

73. *Monument to Lord Lothian*, 1871–4, marble, life-size, St Andrew's Church, Blickling, Norfolk, Watts Gallery Archive

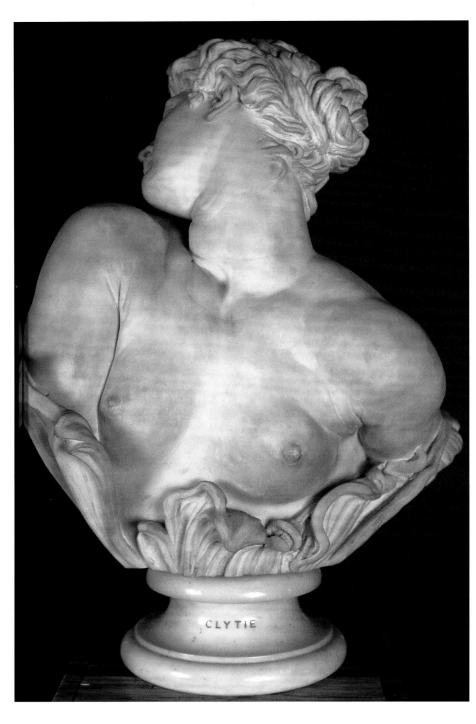

74. *Clytie*, *c.*1867–78, marble,
h. 71 cm (28 in), Guildhall Art
Gallery, City of London

No sculptor has seemed to consider that
[Pheidias] intentionally cut up his drapery …
By cutting up the drapery with innumerable
folds, he gave the idea of flexible material …
by many folds he took away the importance of
the mass, leaving the head and limbs free …
simple, massive and important.[12]

Watts disregarded the practical function of this
treatment – to intensify the definition of sculptures positioned in strong sunlight high up on
the pediments of the Parthenon and viewed
from below – applying it to horizontal figures
seen close to, in dim interiors. It is clear,
however, that he saw himself as introducing
something unique to contemporary sculpture,
something that distinguished him from more
conventional practitioners.

A work hitherto overlooked in Watts's group
of church monuments is the marble *Memorial to
Reverend John Armistead* (1876; Sandbach Church,
Cheshire). Made by Watts and his assistant
George Nelson, this high-relief carving shows
the subject half-length, behind a pulpit and
holding a Bible. Again, the most striking aspect
is the precise attention given to the behaviour of
the drapery, with the tight gathering of the
surplice offset by the looser folds of the sleeves.
The last of this group of works is Watts's contribution to the grave of Lady Waterford (1891;
Ford, Northumberland). Mary Watts designed
the Celtic cross that covers the grave itself,
while Watts's headstone design follows a more
conventional funerary idiom, with two kneeling
angels supporting a central wreath enclosing the
family crest.

Watts's tomb and memorial works indicate
something of his individual approach to sculpture, but it was only after completing the
Cholmondeley monument in 1867 that he began
a purely personal work, modelling a clay bust of
Clytie, which he carved in marble the following
year (fig. 74). Just as *Cholmondeley* looked to the
past, *Clytie* anticipated the future, introducing
values that became central to the New Sculpture
movement of the last quarter of the century.[13]
These values were evident in a new attention to
anatomical naturalism, and Watts was the first to
exercise this close sculptural imitation of the body

combined with a realistic impression of movement. *Clytie* was a subject inseparable from the idea of movement, and although Watts's early *Medusa* – accentuating stasis – was also an Ovidian subject, *Clytie* was his first ideal sculpture in the round. Ovid's *Metamorphoses* describes how Clytie, deserted by her lover Apollo, god of the sun, was changed into a sunflower or heliotrope, constantly turning to follow the sun's passage across the sky. Watts's bust shows Clytie morphing into a flower, her muscular arms and shoulders straining against the encroaching foliage that rises from the pedestal, leaving only her powerful neck free to move. Pinioned, and with the encircling leaves accentuating her breasts, *Clytie* appears markedly sensual, although there is little doubt that the subject provided an effective metaphor for Watts's belief in a constant human straining towards spiritual 'light'. He thus presents a form progressing upward 'from the vegetal, to the animal, to the intellect, to the spirit – the last of these, the space above *Clytie*'s head, deputizing for light – the immaterial force activating the whole heliotropic process'.[14]

Watts's idea for the bust and pedestal appears to have derived from the well-known *Clytie* in the Townley marbles collection in the British Museum.[15] However, the demure Townley bust emerges from a neat circlet of leaves, the head is lowered and there is no indication of movement. The energy and sensuality of Watts's *contrapposto* treatment have their origins elsewhere, in Michelangelo's *Dying Slave* (1513–16; Louvre, Paris). Furthermore, Watts's decision to show *Clytie* unfinished in the Royal Academy exhibition in 1868, while possibly indicating his first *sculptural* response to the surface of the 'Elgin marbles', may also have been vindicated by association with Michelangelo's *non finito* technique.[16] Along with these sculptural influences, *Clytie*'s convincing naturalism, the torsion of the neck and head, and the folds and creases of the flesh and skin show Watts's attention to the life model. According to Mrs Watts, he worked from three models: 'Long Mary', who regularly posed for him, for 'flexibility of movement … [and] magnificence of line'; Angelo Colorossi, 'a well-known Italian male model', for the muscles; and three-year-old Margaret Burne-Jones in her mother's arms,

presumably for the struggle against restraint.[17] Watts's interest in synthesizing these disparate elements into a convincing naturalistic physicality was motivated by his dislike for the prevailing neoclassical approach to ideal sculpture, the white, soapy-smooth surfaces and rigid poses, which he found 'bare and cold'. Writing to invite Gladstone to inspect *Clytie*, Watts explained his aim 'to get flexibility, impression of colour, and largeness of character, rather than purity and gravity'.[18]

Watts's reference to *Clytie*'s 'impression of colour' alludes to textural variations in chiselling to enliven the marble surface, a quality that he identifies with Pheidias. He believed that Pheidas used actual polychromy in his sculpture but that 'his method of suggesting difference of texture and colour (by means of his chisel alone) would certainly go far to render colour unnecessary'.[19] Watts's chiselling of *Clytie* was observed by Mrs Barrington, who refers to 'his subtle conception of different planes and delicate curves, worked in innumerable facets, which … would produce, he thought, a better effect of atmosphere and a more palpitating surface quality than chiselling the form with more direct touches'.[20] An unfinished example of Watts's carving technique can be seen in his marble bust of *Daphne* (*c*.1879–82; Tate), another Ovidian subject conceived as a companion to *Clytie* but never completed.

Clytie's expressive surface and unusually vigorous form attracted considerable praise when shown at the Royal Academy in 1868. The subject of eulogies by Swinburne and W.M. Rossetti, who drew attention to its Michelangelesque qualities, *Clytie* nevertheless revealed Watts as a sculptor with a wholly original approach.[21] This was reiterated by Edmund Gosse in 1894 when, in tracing the development of the New Sculpture, he cited *Clytie* as 'the true forerunner' of the movement, which was definitively launched with Leighton's *Athlete Strangling a Python* (RA 1877; Tate).[22] Leighton's *Athlete* extended the *contrapposto* and anatomical realism of *Clytie* into a full-length figure, as did Hamo Thornycroft's *Lot's Wife* (RA 1878; Leighton House), where the head, neck and shoulders are clearly indebted to Watts's bust.[23] Although his public debut as a sculptor was both widely acclaimed and influential in introducing

an unprecedented mimesis in sculptural representation of the body, Watts did nothing to develop these achievements or to consolidate his pioneering position within the New Sculpture. His only other major work demonstrating comparable values was executed under sufferance, and he subsequently made a complete volte-face in relation to sculptural verisimilitude.

If *Lord Holland* and *Clytie*, in very different ways, indicated Watts's interest in imparting life-like qualities to sculptural representation, his *Monument to Hugh Lupus* (fig. 75) developed this to an extreme degree. Though arguably one of the most impressive nineteenth-century British sculptures, *Hugh Lupus* has been consigned to virtual invisibility in Watts's *oeuvre*. Its location, on a private estate with no public access, has contributed to this critical neglect. More crucially, however, the subject confounds totalising views of Watts, whereby his

morally unimpeachable persona is indivisible from his works – characterised as 'noble imaginings' emanating from a mind committed to art's moral mission. The Watts literature either ignores *Hugh Lupus* or consists of brief allusions, generally recognising it as the prototype for *Physical Energy* and identifying Hugh Lupus as the first Norman Earl of Chester and ancestor of the Duke of Westminster.

In April 1870 the Duke (Hugh Lupus Grosvenor) asked Watts to make an equestrian bronze of heroic scale for the forecourt of Eaton Hall, Chester, which was being rebuilt in neo-Gothic style.[24] The proposed subject, his namesake Hugh Lupus, had followed the Conquest of 1066. Known as 'Lupus' (wolf), 'Gros Veneur' (fat huntsman) or simply 'Hugh the Fat', he reduced Cheshire to a wasteland, according to the records, was brutal and lecherous, loved hunting and eating, and became so obese that he couldn't walk and had to be hoisted onto his horse.[25] Surprisingly, the patron knew little about the subject, but by June 1870 he told Watts that he was reconsidering: 'In Ormerod's History of Cheshire, I find so <u>bad</u> an account of our hero … that I am rather shaken in my intention of erecting a statue in his honour.'[26] Instead, he proposed a statue of Oswald, medieval king and saint. Although Watts first gained recognition with a painting of a national hero intent on repelling foreign invasion, *Alfred Inciting the Saxons to Prevent the Landing of the Danes* (cat.11), he rejected this blameless alternative: 'I am sorry that your great ancestor's character will not bear investigation but … such a statue … with reference to the locality would be rather commemorative of an epoch than an individual.'[27] What he had in mind was a work 'with some suggestion of a time when violence and force were characteristic'.[28]

Watts considered Lupus's character and identity irrelevant to his idea for a symbolic work commemorating not an individual but an epoch, and his intention of representing a generalised figure is confirmed by preliminary wax and plaster sketches and the larger, more finished plaster of a nude figure on horseback, already constructed by November 1870. Watts was confident that this interpretation would be accepted as he had offered to undertake the work without payment, asking only for expenses – an extraordinary gesture given Westminster was England's wealthiest landowner. However, Watts apparently believed forgoing payment would buy him artistic autonomy: 'I should like to work for the dignity of art alone.' The opportunity to create his first major work, even in this private context, could potentially increase the prospects of support for ideal public sculpture, such as that proposed to Rickards. Watts even told Westminster that he hoped that the work might result in 'a great undertaking, worthy even of the nation', an unlikely expectation if the monument were to represent a singularly notorious Norman invader.[29] Watts, therefore, counted on his offer securing creative freedom, as his letters to Westminster imply. The latter, however, had different ideas.

Reassured that Hugh Lupus was an acceptable subject, Westminster subsequently insisted that the sculpture be very specifically individualised, sending Watts numerous historical details to incorporate in the work. In criticising Watts's small model, the Duke also reminded him that Lupus was so fat that the horse's position could not have supported his weight. When Watts eventually began the full-scale model in 1876, he changed the pose, and, until completed in 1883, the model underwent repeated modification and embellishment to accommodate the Duke's wish for historical accuracy. Had Watts used clay, as was usual for a full-scale model, this would have been impossible, but he constructed it from *gesso grosso* – a bulky mixture of plaster, glue size and chopped hemp or tow.[30] This could be modelled when soft and carved when cured, facilitating changes but encouraging a piecemeal approach to construction. By 1881 the model was almost finished when Watts, claiming that he had discovered a 'radical defect', decided to start again 'preferring to leave the thing undone than let it go less good than I could make it'.[31] Undoubtedly, he came to resent 'the thing' that monumentalised a fat, ignoble subject using a descriptive historical precision contrary to his intentions. In addition, the 'radical defect', almost certainly discovered by the Duke, not Watts, necessitated even more unpaid work.

The finished bronze of *Hugh Lupus*, erected in September 1884, was an extraordinary fusion of large, muscular forms and elaborate detail, with every variation of surface texture scrupulously observed. If *Clytie* was naturalistic, this was hyperrealistic. Watts, however, modified Lupus's legendary obesity, arranging the costume's complex folds and bindings to accentuate the sense of an underlying, straining bulk. He also introduced an extreme *contrapposto* with Lupus twisting to one side, and the horse to the other. This combination of closely observed action, precise detail and anatomical veracity in the treatment of the horse surpasses comparable works such as Carlo Marochetti's celebrated *Richard Coeur de Lion* (1860; Old Palace Yard, London), which appears bloated and mechanical in comparison. Nevertheless, *Hugh Lupus* signalled the end of Watts's engagement with naturalism and virtuoso execution, both of which he abandoned in his own practice and criticised in the practice of others.[32] He never accepted another sculptural commission and turned instead to an increasingly personal exploration of Pheidias.

Hugh Lupus does, however, appear to have reinforced Watts's determination to pursue 'art of noble aim' in public works. In 1887 he resurrected the proposal for a colossal bronze, first suggested in 1866 when he quoted from *Felix Holt* in alluding to the 'faithful who are not famous'. His revised idea, to commemorate the 'heroic' but obscure, was more precise and prosaic. Inspired by newspaper accounts of ordinary individuals who died attempting to rescue others, Watts proposed a monument that was, in turn, intended to save them from oblivion. Grandiose commemoration of ordinary individuals, however, was still too radical for the time, and it seems that Watts recognised this. In explaining his idea in a letter to *The Times* on 5 September 1887, he presented it as a national monument to coincide with Queen Victoria's Jubilee. He also produced a design showing a two-storeyed architectural structure surmounted by a gigantic *Britannia*, as a dual personification of Victoria and the common, heroic spirit of the nation. The proposal was ignored, and in 1900 Watts himself funded a modest version of the idea: the *Monument to Heroic Self-Sacrifice* (Postman's Park, Aldersgate, London), a low, covered cloister with the names of everyday heroes inscribed on glazed tiles along with a short account of their actions.[33]

Watts's 1887 proposal echoed John Flaxman's similarly unsuccessful one in 1799 for a 230-foot-high statue of *Britannia* intended to commemorate British naval victories. Flaxman's explanatory pamphlet referred to 'ancient colossal statues of Zeus and Athene by Phidias' (his *Britannia* design was based on the latter). He also stated his interest in 'distinguished public Monuments of antiquity to consider how far their designs might be applicable to the present purpose'.[34] Watts aspired to interpreting the Pheidian colossi for a modern public role as well, but rather than characterising them as 'distinguished', his descriptions emphasise their oddness, speculating that 'the chrys-elephantine sculptures would shock modern ideas, for it is certain no natural effects were imitated or recalled. It is not to be supposed the statue of Pallas Athene was very realistic.'[35] Writing in 1889, he suggests that: 'These statues,

could we see them, would probably surprise us very much by their archaic character: certainly they could in no sense have been realistic. Perhaps the Sphinx by the great pyramid, may afford some idea of what I mean … battered and ruined as it is.'[36] Such views were contrary to the vividly coloured, naturalistic treatment typifiying nineteenth-century re-creations of antique monuments. Watts insists on the colossi's 'archaic' character, likening them to the monochrome sphinx that he had seen and that, furthermore, was 'battered' like the 'Elgin marbles'. He imaginatively fused these Pheidian works to form an unusual synthesis suiting his personal aesthetic preferences, which he aimed to reveal in huge public works.

For Watts, sculpture was an art defined by its public role, and colossal monuments dominating accessible space exemplified its civic potential. For his contemporaries, sculpture became increasingly associated with the domestic sphere, through miniaturised versions for private appreciation in the drawing room. The cult of the statuette, accelerated by the New Sculpture, focused on small bronzes whose convincing anatomy and sensuous surfaces were notable for 'caressability'.[37] Watts repudiated such intimate values, linking his public projects with the awesome impact and distinctly un-homely qualities he imagined in the colossi. The *Athena Parthenos*, which he describes as 'probably most spiritual and exceedingly strange', directly influenced his *Aurora* (also referred to as *Dawn)*, begun in the 1870s and still being worked on months before his death.[38] He destroyed the first plaster version, and the second statue (fig. 76), of heroic proportions, was never completed. Despite its inconclusive status, *Aurora* clearly indicates Watts's transition from the organic naturalism of *Clytie* to an artificial archaicism. His original conception, a harmonious unveiling of the nude figure, was replaced in the second version by flattened planes and exaggerated linearity. Mrs Barrington remarks that Watts's imagination 'had been fired by the great Athena, the chryselephantine statue by Phidias … He hoped to carry out this figure of "Aurora" in gold and ivory (though) … perhaps celluloid might be used instead of real ivory.'[39] Watts never implemented this literal interpretation, concentrating instead on constantly reworking the forms to attain 'something far more archaic, straight and flat in line'.[40]

These effects were eventually incorporated in Watts's first completed colossal public work, the *Monument to Lord Tennyson* (figs 62, 77). After his friend, the Poet Laureate Alfred Tennyson, died in 1892, Watts was consulted about commissioning a statue and offered to make it himself, for expenses only. He began the *gesso grosso* model in 1898, using the base and armature for the first *Aurora*, a much smaller work.[41] A professional sculptor would not have made this mistake. *Tennyson* collapsed and Watts had to begin again. Although he had painted Tennyson's portrait several times, he worked from Thomas Woolner's 1876 bust of the poet and also sought advice on the treatment of the wolfhound.[42] Otherwise, the model was broadly generalised in its pyramidal form, with Tennyson's cloak allowing the introduction of significantly flattened planes and geometric linearity. When compared with *Hugh Lupus*, it is clear that Watts gave minimal attention to filing and carving the plaster into descriptive detail and realistic surface effects. Cast in 1903, the bronze retains the rough, pitted texture of unworked *gesso grosso*, analogous to the eroded surface of the 'Elgin marbles'.

Tennyson finally embodied Watts's ideal as a colossal monument of national and didactic significance, though, rather than being awesome and remote, it appears as an affectionate personal tribute. It was described as 'The Finest Statue in England' and 'A National Art Treasure', which nevertheless addressed the widest populace through its lack of bombast: 'No literary Apotheosis, the statue is just the figure of a thoughtful old man.'[43] The modernity of this conception is apparent. The contemporaneous *Monument to Victor Hugo* by Louis-Ernest Barrias (1902; Place Victor Hugo, Paris, destroyed 1942) also showed a national literary giant in pensive pose, but at the summit of an apotheosis festooned with allegorical excess. Watts's statue, evoking the most inconspicuous of Tennyson's verses, 'Flower in the Crannied Wall', depicted the poet's head bent, pondering over a tiny strand of toadflax.[44] Although this allowed the face to be seen at its great height (the bronze is 11 ft 8 in

76. *Aurora*, *c.*1876–1904, plaster, h. 223.5 cm (88 in), COMWG2007.957

and the marble base, 9 ft 6 in), the plant was hardly visible. Of more concern to one commentator, the statue had 'nothing in common in its somewhat impressionist vigour with the delicacy and finish of the Gothic Cathedral. It is too modern.'[45] Where the crisp medieval detail of *Hugh Lupus* had been an imposition, partly intended to complement the neo-Gothic architecture of Eaton Hall, *Tennyson* allowed Watts to exercise his idiosyncratic Pheidianism: 'The surface of the bronze is rough and modelled in a swift, sketchy style which conveys a sense of largeness and vigour like that of the "Physical Energy" at Burlington House.'[46]

The first bronze cast of *Physical Energy* had been displayed in the courtyard of the Royal Academy at Burlington House from April 1904 to September 1905, when it was sent to South Africa to be hauled up the Matopo Hills and sited at Cecil Rhodes's grave.[47] This proved impractical and the statue was finally installed in 1912 as part of the grandiose proto-fascistic Rhodes Memorial in Cape Town (fig. 78). The eventual connection with the arch-imperialist Rhodes has skewed

readings of this work and obscured Watts's original intention for the subject. This was simply to make the generalised equestrian statue that he had initially envisaged in 1870 for the *Monument to Hugh Lupus*, but that had been diverted into extreme naturalism and elaborate medieval detail. Once *Lupus* was completed, he returned to his original plaster sketch model and, with minor modifications, began constructing 'the work he was anxious to make as great as might be, the embodiment of physical energy' (fig. 79).[48] He aimed to create an ideal, universal work 'untrammelled by costume or period' and where the violence and force intended for *Lupus* were neutralised into 'energy'.[49] However, Watts was vague and inconsistent in explaining the work's meaning and, while referring to it as 'physical energy', also complained that commentators emphasised the physical at the expense of intellectual connotations, which were by no means evident.

Watts's explanations of *Physical Energy* encompassed apparently contradictory aspects of action and existence, ranging from the materialist to the cosmic. It was 'a symbol of that restless physical impulse to seek the still unachieved in the realm of material things … impelling man to undertake a new enterprise'.[50] It was also intended to suggest 'man as he ought to be – part of creation, of cosmos in fact, his great limbs to be akin to the rocks and to the roots, and his head to be as the sun'.[51] This description indicates Watts's aim to recreate the massive grandeur of the 'Elgin marbles' sculpture. He had approached *Physical Energy* with a view to translating one of the best-known figures, envisaging 'a sort of Theseus on horseback' but discovered that 'such a type was unsuited to action'.[52] He also stated: 'I do not wish my man to be like any model you could find anywhere; I do not wish my horse to be like a natural horse.'[53] Though aspects of massive Pheidian anatomy are apparent in the work, so is an emphatic linearity more directly attributable to the *écorchés* that Watts kept in his studio. These plaster casts of flayed human limbs and torsos, and a small *écorché* of a horse, reveal the underlying linear bundles of muscles, ligaments and tendons. They informed Watts's exaggeration of specific anatomical features in the horse and

78. *Physical Energy*, 1904, bronze cast, Rhodes Memorial, overlooking Cape Town, South Africa, photo Ann Laver

rider. Although the irregularity of surface and asymmetry of forms are more primitive than archaic, the result was totally anti-naturalistic – as Watts intended: 'I am careful to avoid any exhibition of [anatomical] knowledge in my work and this probably is not understood … I purposely avoid display of anatomical knowledge.'[54]

If inverting the anatomical verisimilitude of the dominant New Sculpture was not understood, Watts's seeming inability to complete the work also caused bafflement. The design originated in 1870; in 1884 he began the full-size *gesso grosso* model (Watts Gallery); in 1904 he was still making alterations to the model when he died (the first cast, for Africa, was made when the model was still 'in progress'). The hybrid nature of working with *gesso grosso* contributed to this, involving both additive and subtractive processes, which allowed endless adjustments of modelling and carving. Furthermore, an armature of metal bars topped with hooks and eyes, meant sections could easily

79. *Gesso grosso* model of *Physical Energy*, showing rider's arm and horse's lower jaw and foreleg removed. Though indistinct, this image records how Watts worked on disconnected parts of the model. Photograph from glass negative by unknown photographer, Watts Gallery Archive

80. *Physical Energy*,
Kensington Gardens,
London, photo The Conway
Library, Courtauld Institute
of Art

be dismantled and rearranged. Watts's vacillation regarding the meaning of *Physical Energy* thus matched his inability to settle on a definitive form. Mrs Watts observes that 'the difficulty of completion seemed to make the work endless … the limbs were removable and sometimes, without an arm or leg he seemed better satisfied; he thought that a piece of sculpture in fragments was more impressive than anything that had been completed could be.'[55] The importance that Watts placed on these fragmentary states of non-completion is evident in the number of photographs that he had taken, recording the work with different sections removed (fig.79). He very clearly used *Physical Energy* to explore the aesthetics of the sculptural fragment, reflecting ideas that originated in the eighteenth century, when the production of fragments was seen as a

metaphor for creative potential. The fragment as signalling an incomplete or 'unfinished' form also became central to the modernist rejection of the careful surface 'finish' characterised by the New Sculpture. In both senses this lack of 'finish' was built into *Physical Energy*, which effectively came together as an assemblage of fragments and whose rough, *gesso grosso* texture matched the eroded quality of the 'Elgin marbles' and also anticipated the expressive surface of modernist sculpture.

Although *Physical Energy* was an essentially private work, exploring Watts's personal response to Pheidias in fusing aspects of the colossi and the marbles, he saw no discrepancy between this subjectivism and the work's acceptability as a public monument. From the outset he planned it as 'a gift to the nation', envisaging a likely site on the

Embankment in London. That the first bronze cast ended up in Cape Town commemorating Cecil Rhodes resulted from contingencies initiated by others rather than Watts himself. The British government had already agreed to site the work in London, and after Watts's death in 1904 a second bronze cast was erected in 1907 in Kensington Gardens (fig.80). In 1959 a third cast was made for the British South Africa Company, originally founded by Rhodes. This was first erected in Lusaka, Northern Rhodesia, in 1960, but due to its association with the arch-imperialist Rhodes, when the black majority won independence in 1964, the statue was dismantled and sent to Salisbury, Southern Rhodesia, which was still under white rule. After this country gained independence in 1980, becoming Zimbabwe, *Physical Energy* was again removed to its current site at the back of the National Archives in Harare (formerly Salisbury).

The meaning of *Physical Energy* had been made synonymous with colonialism by those with very precise notions of how location could fix its meaning – unlike Watts whose ideas and intentions were generalised and vague. Recent literature on the sculpture of the period has also treated *Physical Energy* as sharing the connotations of imperialism and racial superiority detected in much of the New Sculpture – despite its antithetical formal characteristics. As for these formal characteristics, commentators have proposed irreconcilable interpretations of the work, identifying it as the last gasp of old-fashioned academicism, exhausted classicism and Victorian bombast, *and* as representing an anti-academic modernism driven by experimental subjectivity. Certainly, the latter evaluation accords with a consideration of the sculpture itself, uncoloured by associations with Rhodes or preconceptions conditioned by the biographical emphasis on Watts as 'the last great Victorian'. A closer attention to his diverse output indicates a series of departures from contemporary sculptural conventions, and a disregard for professional constraints in his self-generated projects for public monuments. *Physical Energy*, uncommissioned and made for no particular site, was the culmination of these ambitions and is a significantly early case of an idiosyncratically personal sculpture being sited in the public sphere. Its development also shows how sculptural process and the sculptural fragment gradually absorbed Watts more fully than sculpture as merely the completion of a pre-planned image. In this he anticipates twentieth-century sculptural practice rather more than the values associated with the 'Victorian High Renaissance'.

1. Keith Roberts, 'Victorian High Renaissance', *The Burlington Magazine*, CXX (1978), p.696.

2. These twin claims, made by Watts during his lifetime, became commonplaces of the Watts hagiography, including the earliest extended studies of his life and work: Macmillan 1903, Barrington 1905 and Watts 1912.

3. Watts 1912, I, p.73.

4. The Olympian Zeus was 13 metres (45 ft) high; the *Athena Parthenos* (depending on the source) was between 11 and 12½ metres (33–9 ft); and the *Athena Promachos* varies, according to source, from 7 to 16 metres (21–48 ft).

5. Watts Papers, Watts to Charles Rickards, 25 August 1871.

6. Watts 1912, I, pp.65–6.

7. Watts 1912, I, p.250.

8. Watts 1912, I, p.224.

9. Ibid.

10. Watts 1912, II, p.81.

11. Watts 1912, II, p.82

12. Ibid.

13. The New Sculpture was the most important tendency in British sculpture during the 1880s and 1890s, with some practitioners still working in this manner during the first decade of the twentieth century. The movement was notable for introducing a close attention to anatomical accuracy, naturalistic surface detail, carefully crafted finish and verisimilitude in recording the effects of movement on the body. Other leading proponents included Alfred Gilbert, Hamo Thornycroft, Gilbert Bayes and Albert Toft.

14. Trodd and Brown 2004, p.99.

15. Watts chose a subject already familiar in mass-produced form. The Townley bust was popular and widely circulated in commercial reductions. A version in Parian ware by Delpeche was issued by Copeland in 1855 and used as a prize by the Art Union after 1861. See also Alison Smith (ed.), *Exposed: The Victorian Nude*, exh. cat. Tate Britain, London, 2001, p.115.

16. Watts was unimpressed by Michelangelo's sculpture, considering the *David* 'a bad statue', though he admired the marble tondo of the Virgin and Child at the Royal Academy: 'It is quite lovely being left with a chiselled surface, for it is incomplete according to general apprehension, but in my opinion more perfect.' He also admired the spontaneity of Michelangelo's wax sketches. (Watts 1912, I, pp.73–4.)

17. Watts 1912, II, pp.44–5.

18. Watts 1912, I, p.237.

19. Watts 1912, I, p.149.

20. Barrington 1905, p.41 n.1. Mrs Barrington would only have observed Watts working on *Clytie* after 1876 when she became his neighbour. Commentators have consequently assumed that he was still working on the marble almost ten years after first exhibiting it. Even for Watts this seems unlikely, and plaster casts identical to the finished work were already circulating in early 1870. Rather, she probably observed Watts chiselling one of two subsequent marbles carved by Fabbrucci; see note 30.

21. Rossetti and Swinburne 1868, pp.27–8, 35–6.

22. Gosse 1894, p.139.

23. For David Getsy, 'The head and neck pose of *Lot's Wife* can be understood as a direct quote of the composition of Watts's bust. Gosse would later cite *Clytie* along with Leighton's *Athlete* as the inaugural work of the New Sculpture. Thornycroft fused these two prototypes into one for his first major ideal sculpture, paying homage to the new models sculptors now had before them.' (David Getsy, *Body Doubles: Sculpture in Britain, 1877–1905*, New Haven and London, 2004, p.55.)

24. In the interests of consistency the patron is referred to as the 'Duke' of Westminster, a title he was elevated to in 1874. In 1870, when the commission was proposed he was Marquess of Westminster. He had originally approached Landseer, whose colossal bronze lions were unveiled in Trafalgar Square in 1867, for this commission, but Landseer declined it.

25. The earliest account of Hugh Lupus is given in Ordericus Vitalis, *Historia Ecclesiastica* (1123–41), trans. Thomas Forester, *The Ecclesiastical History of England and Normandy* (4 vols), London, 1853–6, vol. II. Subsequent histories of Cheshire all give lurid accounts, including George Ormerod's, *The History of the County Palatine and City of Chester* (3 vols), London, 1816–19.

26. The underlined word appears thus in the letter from Westminster, 21 June 1870, National Portrait Gallery, Heinz Archive, Watts Correspondence, vol.4, p.33.

27. Letter from Watts, 22 June 1870, Grosvenor Papers, doc. ref. pp.13/160.

28. Watts 1912, I, p.256.

29. Letter from Watts, 15 June 1870, Grosvenor Papers, doc. ref. pp.13/159.

30. Modelling with clay gave Watts rheumatism. He abandoned it, having been introduced to *gesso grosso* by the Italian sculptor Aristide Fabbrucci, who also worked as his assistant. The adoption of this material, though unplanned, had a profound impact on Watts's attitude to surface and finish and to the importance of the model state itself. Rather than being an interim stage in the ultimate production of bronze casts, he viewed the plaster itself as the 'original' and arranged for a process that ensured it would not be destroyed during casting. In 1890 the Duke of Westminster presented the *gesso grosso* of *Hugh Lupus* to the Crystal Palace where it was destroyed by fire in 1936.

31. Watts 1912, II, p.10. Photographs by Frederick Hollyer of the first state of the model confirm that Watts did indeed start again. The original model shows a far lighter horse with nothing of the heavy muscularity of the second version, while the figure of Lupus is both slimmer and wearing costume differing in significant detail from the finished version.

32. Watts considered the academic practice of working from accurate anatomical observation, through drawing from the life model, to be an unnecessary display of knowledge and a prelude to essentially mechanical execution. Poynter and Leighton were cases in point and he thought the latter's approach to be as predictable as fretwork: 'There is never anything unexpected in it' (Watts Papers, 3 May 1893 and 1 October 1891).

33. For a full account see John Price, '"Heroism in Everyday Life": the Watts Memorial for Heroic Self Sacrifice', *History Workshop Journal*, 2007, 63 (1), pp.254–78.

34. John Flaxman, *A Letter to the Committee for Raising the Naval Pillar or Monument*, London, 1799. The statue was intended to stand on Greenwich Hill, London, as a conspicuous landmark.

35. Watts 1912, III, p.23.

36. Watts 1912, III, p.249.

37. Ezra Pound's term for the smooth verisimilitude of the New Sculpture. Rejecting this, he praised the sculptural modernism of Epstein, Gaudier-Brzeska and Gill, whose physical engagement with material and departure from mimetic surface was significantly anticipated by

Watts. Pound, 'The New Sculpture', *The Egoist*, I, no.4, 1914, and see David Getsy, *Body Doubles: Sculpture in Britain, 1877–1905*, New Haven and London, 2004, pp.181–2.

38. Watts 1912, II, p.316. An interview with Watts in *The Daily News* (11 September 1903) is titled '"The Dawn" Mr G.F. Watts's Great Work', and indicates the importance he placed on this. An article in the same paper in January 1904 reports him as 'at work on a colossal statue of "The Dawn"'. For further accounts of Watts's extended work on the subject, see Watts 1912, II, p.81, and note 39, below.

39. Barrington 1905, p.53.

40. Watts 1912, II, p.315.

41. Photographs by Frederick Hollyer taken when the first *Aurora* was in progress suggest that the statue was around 7 feet (2.1 metres) high.

42. A photograph taken by Christopher Turnor in August 1903 shows Watts working on the statue next to Woolner's distinctive bust of Tennyson (reproduced Watts 1912, II, opp. p.305). Woolner's bust was lent to Watts by Hallam Tennyson. See Terence R. Leach, 'Christopher Turnor, G.F. Watts and the Tennyson Statue', *Lincolnshire Past and Present*, no.8, Summer, 1992, p.16.

43. Headline from the *Lincolnshire Chronicle*, 21 July 1905; headline and description from the *Lincoln Leader*, 22 July 1905.

44. Watts had tried to embody 'how love and reverence should bind all creation. The dog loves his master, and looks up for guidance to the secret of the larger life – the man loves the flower, and looks down to the secret of the power that is beyond him' (*Lincolnshire Chronicle*, 21 July 1905). The conception was admired as a distillation of Tennyson's work and 'the sum and substance of all philosophy' (*Lincoln Leader*, 22 July 1905).

45. *Lincoln Leader*, 22 July 1905 ('Is the Statue out of Place').

46. Ibid.

47. For a detailed account of the complex history of *Physical Energy*, Watts's relationship with Rhodes and the different locations of the three bronze casts of the work, see Brown 2007.

48. Watts 1912, I, p.251.

49. Watts 1912, I, p.256.

50. Watts 1912, III, opp. p.270.

51. Watts 1912, II, p.265.

52. Ibid. The figure had been identified as Dionysus, god of wine and intoxication.

53. See note 50.

54. Watts Papers, 1 October 1891.

55. Watts 1912, II, p.236.

Note on the Catalogue Entries

For each entry the known provenance is given with gaps in ownership indicated. Contemporary exhibitions are cited along with relevant later exhibitions. If the catalogue cannot be traced, exhibition numbers are omitted. Many of the most important exhibitions of Watts's work are abbreviated, and full details of these can be found on p.306; other abbreviations used are NPG for the National Portrait Gallery, V&A for the Victoria and Albert Museum, and RA for the Royal Academy of Arts. Literature has been selected with an emphasis on primary sources; secondary sources have been cited if they present new material or original interpretations of Watts's work. Abbreviations for frequently cited sources can be found in the Bibliography on pp.304–5. Illustrations in the essays are referred to as figures, while illustrations in the entries are referred to as catalogue number followed by the number of the image within the entry. Authorship of the catalogue entries is indicated by following initials:

MB   Mark Bills
BB   Barbara Bryant
JD   Julia Dudkiewicz
SB   Stephanie Brown (on sculpture)

Found Drowned (detail, cat.14)

Early Life and Career

George Frederic Watts was born on 23 February 1817 at 52 Queen Street, Bryanston Square, London. His father George Watts (1775–1845) was a pianoforte maker and tuner. His mother Harriet Ann (1786/7–1826) was his father's second wife and died when Watts was just nine, his three younger brothers having died three years earlier in a measles epidemic. Watts himself suffered from ill health, which meant a strict religious home education augmented by the *Iliad* and the novels of Walter Scott. His early talent for drawing was encouraged by his father, and in 1827 he entered the studio of the sculptor William Behnes (1794–1864) in Dean Street, Soho. This gave Watts access to the 'Elgin marbles', works that would influence him throughout his career.

Watts entered the Royal Academy Schools on 30 April 1835 but found the relaxed attitude to teaching unhelpful, attending at first intermittently before ceasing to go at all. He first exhibited at the Royal Academy Summer Exhibition in 1837, when his works included *A Wounded Heron* (cat.3) and two portraits. Portraiture was both the bread and butter of a burgeoning artist and the opportunity to secure important patrons. His natural ability for portraiture ensured early patronage including many of those of the Ionides family (see cat.4).

In 1842 the Royal Fine Arts Commission announced a competition to decorate the new Palaces of Westminster through the submission of large-scale drawings (cartoons). The 140 entries were exhibited a year later and included Watts's *Caractacus Led in Triumph through the Streets of Rome* (fragments at the V&A; see fig.32), which won the artist the highest premium of £300.

MB

Portrait of the Painter at the Age of Seventeen
(detail, cat.1)

1. *Portrait of the Painter at the Age of Seventeen*, 1834

Oil on canvas, 53.3 × 38.1 cm (21 × 15 in)
Exhibition labels from the Royal Academy and
Manchester 1905 on reverse
COMWG10

PROVENANCE: collection of the artist (Little
Holland House by 1896); Lilian Mackintosh (Mrs
Michael Chapman) legal descendant of the artist,
given by her to the Watts Gallery in 1946 (no.47)

EXHIBITIONS: Watts New Gallery 1896, no.2;
Memorial Exhibitions, London 1905, no.1,
Edinburgh 1905, no.5, Manchester 1905, no.2,
Newcastle 1905, no.16, Dublin 1906, no.53A; Watts
London 1954, no.5; Watts Aldeburgh 1961, no.5;
Primitives to Picasso, Royal Academy 1962, no.189;
La Peinture Romantique Anglaise et les Préraphaélites,
Petit Palais, Paris 1972, no.318; Watts Whitechapel
1974, no.1

LITERATURE: Cartwright 1896, pp.2, 4; Sketchley
1904, pp.15–16; Watts Catalogue, II, p.168; Watts
1912, I, p.26; Chesterton 1904, pp.42–3; Blunt 1975,
p.6 (pl.1); Gould 2004, p.6 (fig.3)

In this half-length self-portrait the artist is staring directly out of the canvas at the viewer, its apparent simplicity and candour reflective of the looking-glass view that the artist has used. In the bottom left of the painting a small sketch of a seated-male nude can be discerned, giving the whole the sense of a study.[1] That it might be a painterly exercise is supported by Watts's comment:

> I paint myself constantly; that is to say, whenever I want to make an experiment in method or colour, and am not in the humour to make a design. So there are other portraits of me, and if I live there may be many more, but I should not like to display them to the public. I should feel a sort of absurdity attaching to such a proceeding.[2]

In fact, this portrait was made very public in Watts's own lifetime, being exhibited at the New Gallery in 1896–7 and prominently illustrated in Julia Cartwright's early monograph of the artist published in the same year. As he indicated, Watts painted a number of self-portraits throughout his life, which are more than just technical studies. They provide an insight into the artist's state of mind and the direction of his career, and reveal the changing artistic influences that affected him. The appearance of a study seems to be deliberate, even playful, rather than unconscious sketching.

In retrospect Watts believed that he had painted this work in 1834 when he was seventeen,[3] and Mary noted in her catalogue that it was only 'dragged out from obscurity in later years', considering the painting to be 'the earliest discovered so far'.[4] It had been painted immediately before Watts was admitted as a student to the Royal Academy Schools and sums up his early ambitions as an artist. Belonging to a period of pre-Victorian High Art, three years before Queen Victoria came to the throne, it presents the image of the artist as a Romantic. As Cartwright put it, 'the flowing locks and open collar complete the picture of a boy of genius'.[5] In the 1830s the loose artistic dress indicated a slightly faded bohemianism. Chesterton wrote whimsically: 'He belongs to that older race of Bohemians, of which even Thackeray only saw the sunset, the great old race of art and literature who were ragged because they were really poor, frank because they were really free, and untidy because they were really forgetful.'[6]

As an image of a Romantic genius, its similarity to the famous portrait of Percy Bysshe Shelley is marked.[7] Most striking, however, is its resemblance to Sir Joshua Reynolds's *Self-Portrait*, *c*.1747–8 (National Portrait Gallery), in which the young artist stares out of the canvas. In it Reynolds depicts himself head on, open collared and with free, loose hair. The major difference is that Reynolds's left hand is raised to shield the light and shadow his eyes, which explains Mary's catalogue note that 'at this date another study of the face, shadowed by the left hand, was painted and lost in early years'.[8] As a portrait, it is accomplished and precocious, produced with a deceptive ease and fluidity by an artist aware of his own genius and fully conscious of the image he wished to project.   MB

1   The New Gallery catalogue of 1896–7 calls it unfinished, whereas the Royal Academy 1905 Watts exhibition does not.
2   Watts 1912, I, p.245.
3   In Watts's own copy of *The New Gallery, Winter Exhibition MDCCCXCVI–VII, The Works of G F Watts* (Watts Gallery Archive), p.11, he has crossed out the age 18 and corrected it to 17, the date it bore for all subsequent exhibitions.
4   Watts Catalogue, II, p.169.
5   Cartwright 1896, p.4.
6   Chesterton 1904, pp.42–3.
7   *Percy Bysshe Shelley*, 1819, by Alfred Clint, after Amelia Curran and Edward Ellerker Williams, oil on canvas, National Portrait Gallery. Wilfrid Blunt in *England's Michelangelo* (p.6) also notes: 'It is Shelley as one might perhaps imagine him, rather than as he actually was.'
8   Watts Catalogue, II, p.169.

2. *George Watts, Father of the Artist,* 1834–6

Oil on canvas, 38 × 32 cm (15 × 13 in)
COMWG119

PROVENANCE: collection of the artist (Little Holland House Gallery); Lilian Mackintosh (Mrs Michael Chapman), legal descendant of the artist; given by her to the Watts Gallery in 1958

EXHIBITIONS: Watts London 1954, no.4

LITERATURE: Gould 2004, p.4

This life-size head study of George Watts (1774?–1845) in profile is one of two known portraits of the artist's father painted by his son while still in his teens. It is not listed in the Watts Catalogue, which just mentions the more finished bust-length portrait of George Watts facing the viewer (cat.2.1). The present profile study was only identified as another portrait of George Watts by Rowland Alston, Curator of Watts Gallery from 1931 to 1958.[1]

Watts was the oldest child from his father's second marriage, to Harriet, who died in 1826 when the boy was just nine. His father was chiefly responsible for the boy's upbringing and supported his artistic creativity from an early age. George (senior) was an unsuccessful cabinet-maker, pianoforte manufacturer and musical instrument inventor who struggled to support his family and outlived two wives. Watts

remembered his father as 'delicately minded, full of aspiration if not strong of purpose … he knew that the aim of his own life had not been attained; in the mouth there is something of petulant protest against circumstances that had proved too hard for his overcoming.'[2] Mary recalls that Watts was 'much attached to his father, the failure of whose life was a great pain to him … for the father was a man of peculiar refinement of mind, and I have been told of manner also.'[3] George died of bronchitis in 1845 during Watts's stay in Italy. Watts later wrote to a friend: 'My father's death has been a sad blow to me, nor have I yet recovered from the effects.'[4]

The more finished portrait of the artist's father was reputedly shown to the sculptor William Behnes for an assessment of the young Watts's painting ability. Mary records that Behnes was out at the time and that the picture was left for him. In old age George Frederic Watts 'could still remember the sound of the sculptor's footsteps, as he hurried around to congratulate the father on this the son's first portrait of marked success'.[5] Judging by the painting style and the appearance of the sitter, it is very likely that the two portraits were produced at the same time. Painted when the artist was just seventeen or eighteen, the two works provide an early insight into the development of Watts's treatment of portraiture as a genre.   JD

1   Watts London 1954, no.4.
2   Watts 1912, I, p.9.
3   Watts 1912, I, p.32.
4   Watts 1912, I, p.75.
5   Watts Catalogue, II, p.166.

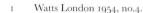

Cat. 2.1 *George Watts, Father of the Artist,* 1834, oil on canvas, 61 × 51 cm (24 × 20 in), COMWG3

3. *A Wounded Heron*, 1837

Oil on canvas, 91.4 × 71.1 cm (36 × 28 in)
Signed and dated lower right 'G F Watts 1837'
COMWG64

PROVENANCE: sold by the artist in 1837 or shortly
after; … with a dealer in Newcastle by 1888, when
purchased by Watts; Little Holland House Gallery;
part of the original Memorial Collection, 1905

EXHIBITIONS: Royal Academy 1837, no.328;
New Gallery 1889, no.1; Autumn Exhibition,
Manchester 1889; Leeds 1893; Art Museum,
Rugby School 1894; Watts New Gallery 1896, no.3;
Watts Gallery 1904, no.101; Memorial Exhibitions,
London 1905, no.38, Manchester 1905, no.4,
Newcastle 1905, no.182, Edinburgh 1905, no.27,
Dublin 1906, no.1; *The First Hundred Years of the
Royal Academy 1769–1868*, Royal Academy of Arts,
London, 1951–2, no.304; Watts London 1954, no.3;
Watts Aldeburgh 1961, no.12; *Royal Academy of Arts
Bicentenary Exhibition 1768–1968*, Royal Academy of
Arts, London, 1969, no.324; *La Peinture Romantique
Anglaise et les Préraphaélites*, Petit Palais, Paris, 1972,
no.319; Watts Whitechapel 1974, no.2; Watts
Compton 2004, no.1

LITERATURE: Spielmann 1886, p.32; Cartwright
1896, p.3; Sketchley 1903, pp.10–11; Macmillan
1903, p.16; Watts Gallery Catalogue 1904, no.101;
Chesterton 1904, pp.46–8; Barrington 1905, pp.113,
198; Watts Catalogue, I, p.71 (under *Heron, The
Wounded*); Watts 1912, I, pp.27–8, II, pp.145, 180;
Alston 1929, no.78; Blunt 1975, pp.8–10, 61

In 1837 Watts, aged twenty, had his own studio near Fitzroy Square in central London. He earned an adequate living as a painter of small oil portraits and drawings, yet he aspired to paint imaginative compositions and history paintings. One day he passed a poulterer's shop in his neighbourhood with a dead heron on display in the window. Later, he recounted that he was struck by the beauty of the dead bird, so he bought it and painted it 'as rapidly as the conditions required, but with the utmost care and painstaking'. His prominently placed signature,[1] easily readable on the lower right, conveys his pride in this work. The choice of subject may also be allied to his own life experience. An incident in his youth, when he accidentally crushed a pet bird, remained a powerful memory into later life. At this early stage his recollection of the experience must have been all the more immediate, exerting a magnetic pull towards a subject in which an injured bird featured.

In *A Wounded Heron* the dying creature is rendered in detail, and an adept handling of textures is combined with an ease and fluency of brushwork. It is essentially a still-life study with the bird filling the foreground space.[2] The intensity of the view, focused on the face of the dying heron, presses on the viewer the pathos of the scene. The addition of a landscape setting and a falconer on horseback brings the subject alive as a hawking scene, a theme that he had also essayed in another painting of about the same time showing a heron with outstretched wings (cat.3.1).[3]

Cat. 3.1 *Hawking* (also known as *The Falconer*), oil on
canvas, 25.4 × 20.3 cm (10 x 9 in), COMWG236

The work always had a special meaning to Watts as one of his first three paintings to appear at the Royal Academy's prestigious annual exhibition. He must also have remembered it as an early sale, a real encouragement for the young artist, but as a result it was lost to him until the late 1880s. In 1888, in conversation with artist friends Henry Holiday and his wife, he expressed regret that it was no longer in his possession; Kate Holiday suggested advertising to recover it. But there was no need for that, because coincidently, shortly after, a letter arrived from a dealer in Newcastle offering to sell it to the artist for a mere five pounds.[4] After its recovery Watts urged Mrs Barrington to come to the studio to see it, saying: 'you will see something which puts me to the greatest confusion!' She recorded that he 'deplored the loss of the power of completer finish which he possessed when he painted' this and other early works.[5]

Watts acquired *A Wounded Heron* with the intention that it could feature in the Little Holland House Gallery, but he also frequently sent it to exhibitions, beginning with the New Gallery in 1889, when he commented: 'The "Heron", for instance, they are now all praising, had no notice taken of it when it was first painted.'[6] A reviewer in *The Spectator* remarked on the curiosity of seeing Watts's first Academy painting, considering the wing well handled but the head ill drawn. Furthermore, he noted that 'one strongly feels the influence of the old Dutch dead game and bird painter, Hondekooter [*sic*]'.[7] Watts could not help commenting:

I see in the same paper a notice of the New Gallery; it is strange that one can never do anything in the way of painting without being supposed to be prompted by some old master. The critic finds the influence of Hondecoeter! I don't suppose at the time I painted 'The Heron' I had ever seen a picture by the Dutch painter, and even now I hardly recall anything of his. I think the criticism otherwise good enough! I daresay the head wants truth, for it was not studied from a living model, and cannot compare with Japanese birds.[8]

That Watts rejected the influence of Dutch art, albeit with the perspective of fifty years, is not surprising. A more likely exemplar for the young artist in the 1830s was the rising star of the British art world, Academician Edwin Landseer (1802–73), who specialised in depictions of animals, often incorporated in narrative or history paintings.[9] Watts could easily have seen Landseer's *Hawking in the Olden Time* (Iveagh Bequest, Kenwood, English Heritage),[10] exhibited at the Royal Academy five years before in 1832 and a year later at the British Institution. This large impressive work shows a heron in mid-air under attack from a falcon set loose by a hawking party. A low horizon line allows the drama to be played out against a magnificent skyscape. Watts surely recalled this work when he arranged his heron with its wingspan open and set a similar figure in medieval dress on a much smaller scale in the distance on the right-hand side. Indeed, the successful sale of *A Wounded Heron* may well have been due to it echoing a mode of painting associated with Landseer.

For Watts a long-held love of bird life and abhorrence of their mindless killing meant that these creatures reappeared in his art in allegorical form, as in *The Minotaur* (cat.71) of 1885 and in the later more suggestive *A Dedication* (cat.77). Whether the artist recognised these continuities is an interesting question, but certainly when the chance came to reclaim *A Wounded Heron*, he immediately acquired it for his own collection. He considered the array of his paintings on view at the Little Holland House Gallery to be a summation of his life's work. *A Wounded Heron* took its place as a key early example, along with the *Self-Portrait* (cat.1). BB

1 Early works such as this one show his signature in cursive style.
2 A highly detailed drawing of an open wing is in the collection of Watts's drawings at the Royal Academy of Arts, exhibited Watts London 1954, no.90.
3 Blunt 1975, p.8, considers that the hunter in the painting, *Hawking*, is Watts himself.
4 Cartwright 1896, p.9. Newcastle-upon-Tyne had some six art dealerships in *c*.1890: T.P. Barkas and Sons; Dodsworth; Hay and Son; Mawson, Swan and Morgan; O'Rowell and Robert Wood. Chesterton, however, imagines a variation on this story, that it was found in a 'dusty curiosity-shop', purchased by a friend and given to Watts.
5 Barrington 1905, p.198.
6 Watts 1912, II, p.145.
7 *The Spectator*, 18 May 1889, p.680.
8 Barrington 1905, p.113.
9 A reviewer in the *Daily News*, 2 May 1889, placed Watts's work in relation to that other noted animal painter James Ward (1769–1859), who exhibited regularly throughout the 1830s.
10 Richard Ormond, *Sir Edwin Landseer*, exh. cat., Philadelphia Museum of Art and the Tate Gallery, London, 1981–2, no.72, and Julius Bryant, *Kenwood: Paintings in the Iveagh Bequest*, New Haven and London, 2003, no.67, where Watts's work is discussed.

4. *Alexander Constantine Ionides and Euterpe Ionides with their Children,* 1840–1

Oil on canvas, 150 × 183 cm (59 × 72 in)
COMWGNC.26

PROVENANCE: painted on commission for Alexander Constantine Ionides and his wife; then by descent until sold; Sotheby's, London, 7 June 2005, no.6, when purchased for the Watts Gallery with the support of The Art Fund and the Heritage Lottery Fund

LITERATURE: Watts Catalogue, II, p.74; Basil Long, *Catalogue of the Constantine Alexander Ionides Collection* (V&A), vol.I, London, 1925, p.65; Ilchester 1937, pp.324–5; Blunt 1975, pp.12–13

This painting, the most ambitious portrait of Watts's early career, dates from late 1840–1. It shows the young family of up-and-coming textile merchant Alexander Constantine Ionides (1810–90). Of Greek descent, Ionides had recently acquired British citizenship. He commissioned this portrait to celebrate his growing status and his growing family. Part of the tightly knit Hellenic community in London, Ionides was public-spirited but also devoted to his family. Watts had already painted one group portrait for Ionides (see cats 5 and 5.1), and now his patron rewarded him with an even bigger commission. Watts probably painted an oil sketch now in the Victoria and Albert Museum on approval as a *modello*, or study, for the finished work.

After commissions in 1837 the Ionides family invited Watts to their comfortable villa in Tulse Hill, then a rural suburb south of London. Alexander had a wide circle of friends reflecting his interest in the art world[1] and also knew literary figures such as Thackeray. Alexander's wife Euterpe (1816–92), married at sixteen, already had four children by the age of twenty-four: Constantine the eldest (1833–1900), Aglaia (1834–1906), Luke (1837–1924) and the baby Alexander (called Alecco) (1840–98). In the portrait Euterpe, reclining on a divan, turns her head engagingly to look outwards. Each child is involved in individual movement: the little girl embraces her mother, the older boy strikes the pose of sailor, the child in the foreground proffers an apple, and the baby reaches outwards. A relaxed informality prevails because Watts already knew these individuals well. Interestingly, the father seems the most reticent, as he sits far to the left, somewhat in the shadows. The portrait was about the family, not intended for public exhibition but for display in their own home.

Euterpe had a special fondness for the artist. Her son later noted that Watts 'saddened his mother by saying how weak he was, and that he was soon going to die'.[2] Without much family of his own, the young artist, still aged in his early twenties, sought warmth and affection from others. Euterpe became the first welcoming motherly female in Watts's life and he was a frequent visitor to Tulse Hill.

For Watts the Ionides were more than just friends. He revered ancient Greek art, having studied the Elgin marbles in the British Museum from his youth. This connection with a modern Greek family had an added significance in placing him in touch with the classical past. Through them he gained an understanding of a country and culture that inspired him: they were the modern equivalent of classical Greeks. In the portrait the boys wear richly embroidered gold jackets and the white fustanella – the short white pleated skirt associated with the costume of the evzones, the ceremonial unit of the Greek presidential guard.[3] Apart from proclaiming the boys' origins, the costume lends an exotic touch. Indeed, this painting provides a glimpse into a multicultural Britain of the early 1840s. The portrait reflected the aspirations of the family and their success, yet it also revealed ties to their mother country that still held firm.

Watts aspired to history painting, but with few opportunities for such work he channelled his ambitions into this family group portrait, which developed into more than just a record of their likenesses. Painting a canvas some 5 feet across demonstrated Watts's early technical skills. The care taken in the construction of this fluent composition results in a work of real accomplishment. Warmer colours in the foreground contrast with the cool blues of the sky, while the landscape background adds to the grandeur of the image.

Ionides continued to be a supportive friend and patron to Watts. He commissioned a portrait (unlocated) of his two younger sisters Euphrosyne and Katerina, which also gave Watts the opportunity to try the grand manner. Family history records that he helped the young artist financially when he set off for Italy, and while Watts was abroad, they corresponded about a potential commission for a history painting. Immediately on Watts's return to London in 1847, he received commissions for portrait drawings and paintings from the Ionides and their many relations (see cat.27). Watts eventually painted five generations of the Ionides family by the 1890s. Many of these portraits are now in the Victoria and Albert Museum, as is the bequest by Alexander's son Constantine, the oldest boy in the portrait, who followed the family tradition of art collecting and patronage.[4]

Except to descendants of the sitters, this portrait was long known only by the oil study. In 2005 the Watts Gallery acquired the newly discovered large version, which so vividly documents an early chapter in Watts's life and career. BB

1   See Mark Evans, 'Blake, Calvert – and Palmer? The Album of Alexander Constantine Ionides', *Burlington Magazine*, CXLIV (2002), pp.539–49, and Dakers 1999, pp.7–9.
2   Ionides 1925, p.56.
3   The costumes survive at the Royal Museum of Scotland, Edinburgh (A1975.273, A–J).
4   On the family in general see Julia Ionides, 'The Greek Connection – The Ionides Family and Their Connections with Pre-Raphaelite and Victorian Art Circles', in *Pre-Raphaelite Art in its European Context*, ed. Susan Casteras and Alicia Craig Faxon, Madison and London, 1995, pp.160–74.

5. *Euterpe Ionides and her Children, c.1837*

Pencil on paper, 38 x 28 cm (15 x 11 in)
Inscribed (by a later hand) 'Ionides family'
COMWG 2007.186.b

PROVENANCE: collection of the artist; mounted in an album of drawings; Mary Watts; her legal descendant, Lilian Mackintosh (Mrs Michael Chapman); by descent until sold, Sotheby's, London, probably 10 July 1995, no.59 (an album of drawings); Jeffrey Cohen; Watts Gallery

LITERATURE (on the finished painting): Watts Catalogue, II, p.76; Watts 1912, I, pp.34–5; Ionides 1925, p.56; Julia Atkins, 'The Ionides Family', *Antique Collector*, 58 (1987), pp.86–94

This drawing is a study for a large oil portrait (now destroyed) of Alexander Constantine Ionides's wife Euterpe with their three oldest children: Constantine Alexander (1833–1900), Aglaia (1834–1906) and baby Luke, born in March 1837 (cat.5.1).[1] With the infant looking quite young, Watts probably executed the drawing at some point half-way through that year.

This commission may have followed shortly after Watts's first encounter with Ionides, when the latter engaged Watts to copy a portrait of his father by Samuel Lane (1780–1859), which was in the exhibition of the Royal Academy in 1837. As the famous account goes, he preferred the copy (now in the Victoria and Albert Museum) to the original. The unknown artist and the merchant developed a friendship. A further commission for a family group followed in 1840 (cat.4).

The drawing represents Watts's first idea for the upright composition of the mother and her children. Euterpe raises her hand to her lips, gesturing for silence from the two older offspring so as to prevent the infant from awakening.

Cat. 5.1 Frederick Hollyer, photograph of *Euterpe Ionides and Children*, Hollyer Album, Watts Gallery Archive

Executed on a fairly large sheet, the drawing is loosely handled yet thoroughly worked out. The oval format was a convention of portraiture in the 1830s, as was the swathe of drapery to add grandeur. Yet the overall idea was to turn the portrait into a scene of everyday life with a mother's gentle action animating what might have been a formal exercise. This drawing might well have been shown to Ionides for approval but somewhere between the drawing and finished oil (cat.5.1),[2] the composition and the conception changed. In the final version, no longer an oval in shape, the little girl is placed to the side of her mother,[3] the boy slightly lower, standing on the ground, and the baby more alert, looking outwards. Euterpe's gesture is modified, so that her hand is now just slightly raised.

The final portrait, a substantial painting on near life-size scale, hung at Tulse Hill and later on the staircase at 1 Holland Park, where Alexander Constantine Ionides moved in 1867. This home, reflecting his artistic friendships and interests, was decorated in fashionable Aesthetic style by Morris and Company. Luke, the baby in the portrait who later studied art in Paris with Whistler, liked to boast that he first knew Watts when 'I was a baby eight months old when he first painted me on my mother's knee'.[4] Watts kept the drawing, which was mounted in an album put together as a record of his early career. BB

1   The finished picture appears in a photograph by Hollyer of the staircase at Holland Park illustrating an article on the house in the *Art Journal* (1893); also reproduced in Dakers 1999, p.8; a small version, perhaps an oil study, is reproduced in Atkins 1987, p.86, possibly the same one that was on the art market in 2006.
2   An oil study is reproduced in Atkins 1987, p.86.
3   In preparation for the new arrangement, Watts painted a separate oil study of Aglaia's head looking outwards, illustrated in Watts Catalogue, II, p.75.
4   Ionides 1925, p.56.

6. *Study of a Hand, c.*1830–5

Black and white chalk on blue paper, 26.5 × 40.3 cm (10½ × 17 in)
COMWG2007.591

PROVENANCE: collection of the artist; mounted in an album of drawings; Mary Watts; her legal descendant, Lilian Mackintosh (Mrs Michael Chapman); by descent probably Sotheby's, London, 10 July 1995, no.59 (an album of drawings); Jeffrey Cohen; Watts Gallery

This large sheet, once mounted in an album of early drawings, is a study of a plaster cast of a female hand. One can see the hand rests on a base. Drawing from casts formed part of the basic training of all young artists, whether in the Schools of the Royal Academy or in private studios. It is a student work but not a mere copy, as it demonstrates some sensitivity in its realisation.

As a youngster, Watts first expressed his interest in art by drawing. When he showed talent as a draughtsman, his father recognised this and sought a way to develop it. Through a family introduction in around 1829 when he was aged about twelve, Watts entered the studio of the noted sculptor, William Behnes (1794–1864), in Soho. Here he encountered not only academic study pieces, such as the one in this drawing, but also casts after antique sculpture. It was but a short walk from Dean Street to the British Museum in Bloomsbury where Watts soon discovered real masterpieces of ancient Greek art, the Elgin marbles, which proved to be his life-long inspiration.

This drawing, one of a number of known academic studies by the young Watts, is so highly finished that it may well have been a presentation drawing, perhaps used to gain entry into the Royal Academy schools in 1835. Far from being a standard academic study, this work shows individuality in its unusual choice of viewpoint, looking downwards. The very fine shading indicates a range of tonal values. The shadow cast by the hand is created with a network of softly drawn, curved parallel lines. The skilful handling lends a life-like quality to a mere plaster cast. Its truncation at the wrist seems abrupt, as the drawing so clearly animates the hand. Indeed, it has a character all its own, easily identifiable as belonging to a plump, youthful female. One wonders why a cast existed of this particular hand, as it does not appear to be after the antique, but as Watts frequented Behnes's studio for a few years, it may well have been a working piece from there.

Interestingly, despite Watts's relocations around London and eventually to Surrey, he managed to retain many of his drawings. He had an entire album filled with drawings done, like this one, when he was a very young man. BB

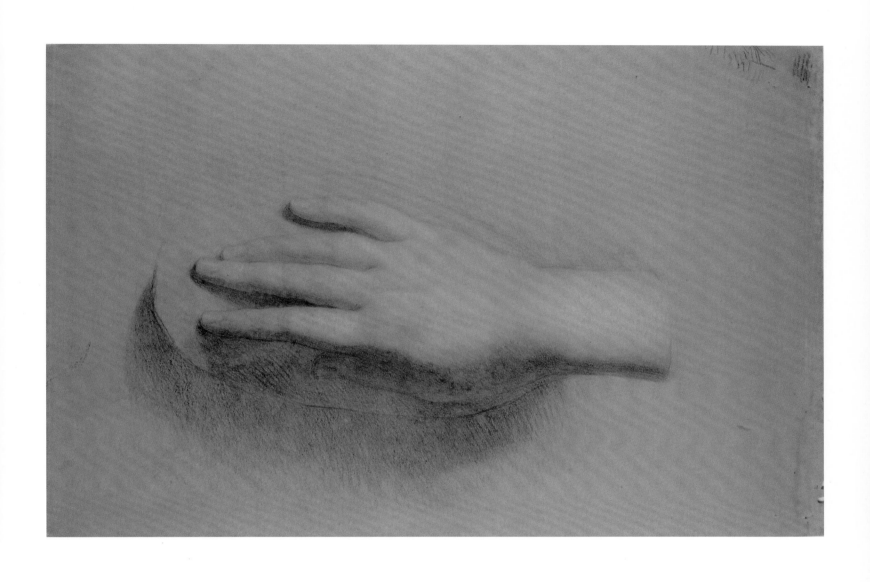

Travel and Italy 1843–7

In 1843, aged twenty-six, Watts set off for Europe with his prize money from the inaugural Houses of Parliament competition. He had never travelled abroad before. After six weeks in Paris he went on to Chalon-sur-Saône, down the Rhône to Avignon, onto Marseilles, then to Italy via Leghorn (Livorno) and Pisa. He ended his journey in Florence in the early autumn of 1843 where he intended to study fresco painting and its techniques. Urged to visit the 4th Baron Holland, the English minister, the young artist arrived at the Hollands' palatial town house, the Casa Feroni on the via dei Serragli, and shortly after moved in at their invitation.

Watts enjoyed a close friendship with Lord Holland and particularly with his wife Mary Augusta, the daughter of the 8th Earl of Coventry. The Hollands often retreated to their country villa at Careggi in the hills outside Florence. Here and in town Watts spent much of his time painting and drawing his hosts and their cosmopolitan circle of friends. His thriving social life included the Café Doney, a coffeehouse where an international set of artists met. He relaxed by painting landscapes in the area around the Medici villa at Careggi (see cat.9). With Lord Holland, he even made a quick visit back to London in 1845. They both toured the Riviera coast to Marseilles. In Italy they visited Milan, Rome, Perugia and Naples, where Augusta's family had the Villa Roccella. Seeing Pompeii and climbing up Vesuvius, as well as the experience of Rome, further encouraged his love of the antique. Steeped in Italian art and culture, he changed his outlook completely.

When the Hollands left Florence in 1846, Watts stayed on at Careggi. He encouraged his patron Alexander Ionides back in London to commission a historical painting on an ambitious scale. He planned to enter another competition for the decorations of the new Palace of Westminster. Watts's high ideals consolidated as he began to see himself as part of the great traditions of old master painting, evident in his self-portrait (opposite). BB

Self-Portrait (detail, fig.34)

7. *Mary Augusta, Lady Holland, c.1844*

Oil on canvas, 68.5 × 56 cm (27 × 22 in)
Inscribed (in another hand) 'M.A. Lady Holland by Watts'
COMWG55

PROVENANCE: painted for Lord and Lady Holland; displayed at Holland House, Kensington; probably passed to the Lilford branch of the family; … Ffrench family of Monivea Castle, Co. Galway; bought by the Earl of Ilchester from a sale at Monivea Castle in 1939; Christie's, London, 3 May 1940, no.103, bought Bell (or bought in); the Earl of Ilchester, by whom presented to the Watts Gallery, 1940

EXHIBITIONS: Watts Portraits 2004, no.4

LITERATURE: Watts Gallery Catalogue 1957, p.25, no.17; Bryant 2004, p.46;

Within a painted arch Augusta Lady Holland is seen before a freely sketched Italianate landscape with a low horizon opening up to an aquamarine sky. Although limited in colour to bluish greens, browns and greys, the vivacious handling of the thin oil paint freely applied in the loosest and most relaxed manner enlivens the portrait. The brushy treatment of the yellow-tinged cream colour of the dress, along with the cool tones of the landscape background, reveals the impact of Italy on Watts's palette. The whole image is further animated by the openly direct gaze of the sitter.

Lady Mary Augusta (1812–89), known as Augusta, spent much of her early life abroad. A noted linguist, she had also acquired a continental mode of behaviour somewhat at odds with conventional English manners. In 1833 she married the Hon. Henry Edward Fox (1802–59) in Florence. He succeeded as 4th Baron Holland in 1840 and continued to serve in the diplomatic service as Minister Plenipotentiary to the Court of the Grand Duke of Tuscany. Lord and Lady Holland lived grandly at the Casa Feroni, the base for the British Consulate, on the Via dei Serragli near the Pitti Palace. In 1843 Augusta was thirty-one; five years earlier she had suffered the stillbirth of a son and ill health continued to afflict her. One imagines that she found herself somewhat lonely amid the splendours of her surroundings. When the twenty-six-year-old Watts arrived on 3 October 1843, she and her husband took the young artist under their wing and their generous patronage; he moved into the Casa Feroni, living there and at their country villa on the outskirts of Florence for the next four years.

The many images, painted and drawn, of Lady Holland testify to the depth and intensity of the friendship that she shared with Watts. While he enjoyed the advantageous companionship of Henry Edward, he clearly spent most time with Augusta. Portrayals of her range from intimate pencil studies (see cat.8.1) and oil sketches (see cat.8) to formal oil portraits with references to Joshua Reynolds and the old masters, which were destined for the dynastic collections of Holland House in London.[1] The present portrait, though an oil, has an informal quality due to the extremely loose handling as well as showing Augusta at her toilette, as if looking into a mirror while she combs through her hair.

Although not considered a great beauty (her husband said as much),[2] she was noted for her auburn hair, usually elaborately braided, her large wide eyes and, not least, her famously tiny feet. In this portrait she appears to be untangling her braided hair as it cascades over her shoulders. As an image of a woman in her boudoir, *en déshabille*, it evokes depictions of Venus and courtesans in Venetian art of the late Renaissance or images of women at their toilette in the Rococo period. In both eras artists were admitted to the private realm of women showing them in openly tempting poses. In the 1840s this choice was unusual in British art, although one contemporary work affords a direct comparison. In 1843 Queen Victoria commissioned F.X. Winterhalter (1805–73) to portray her with loosened hair falling over her shoulder,[3] a work that she called her 'secret picture' and intended to be a birthday gift for Prince Albert that would remain in the private quarters. This unofficial type of art in which wives have themselves portrayed in alluring poses may explain the unusual qualities of Watts's work.

The trust that existed between Augusta and Watts comes across, as does a complicity that the two shared in the creation of painted and drawn images of her as a beautiful woman. This painting remained with the Hollands but left the collection at some point. Such a provocative image could never be shown in public spaces in Holland House in London, although the richly ornate Baroque Italianate frame links it with other portraits by Watts painted for his patrons in Italy. If it had been a personal treasure belonging to her husband, it might be that on his death in 1859 Augusta parted with the painting as harbouring too many memories. It entered the collections of the Watts Gallery in 1940, given, appropriately, by Lord Ilchester, a trustee and the successor to the collections of Holland House, who acquired it from a branch of the family in Ireland. BB

1   See my discussion of the portrayals of Lady Holland in Watts Portraits 2004, nos 1–4.
2   See Watts Portraits 2004, no.4.
3   Illustrated in Christopher Lloyd, *The Paintings in the Royal Collection: A Thematic Exploration*, London 1999 and 2003, p.71, fig.33.

8. *Lady Holland*, 1844

Oil on canvas, 38.1 × 45.7 cm (15 × 18 in)
Inscribed on the reverse in large decorative calligraphy, most probably by Lady Holland, 'This is to be given to my niece Carrie-M.A. Holland', and in the same hand 'Sketch by Watts of Lady Holland, Naples, 1844'
COMWG16

PROVENANCE: Lady Augusta Holland's collection; gift to her niece Carrie (?) … ; purchased in 1942 by Curator Rowland Alston for the Watts Gallery (according to Richard Jefferies, Alston purchased it from a bookshop for £15)

EXHIBITIONS: Watts London 1954, no.7; *Victorian Painting 1837–87*, Agnew's London, 1961; *Victorian Artists in England*, National Gallery of Canada, Ottawa 1965, no.154; Royal Academy of Arts, London, Bicentenary Exhibition 1968–9, no.323; Watts Whitechapel 1974, no.6; Tokyo, British Council 1975, no.61

LITERATURE: Chapman 1945, p.172; Blunt 1975, p.32; Bryant 2004, p.46; Gaja 1995, p.24

Cat. 8.1 *Study of Lady Holland*, c.1844, pencil on cream paper, 28.8 × 42.5 cm (11¼ × 16¾ in), COMWG2007.696

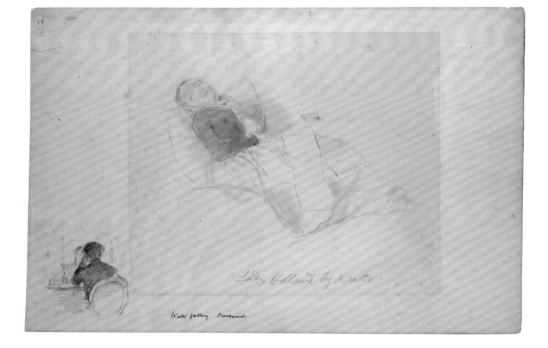

This oil sketch is a record of the influential patronage that Watts benefited from at the start of his career, as well as testimony to the affectionate friendship that the artist developed with Lady Augusta Holland. Watts met the Hollands during his first visit to Italy in 1843, where Baron Holland served as the British Minister at the Court of Tuscany from 1839 to 1846.[1] Within a month Watts had become an intimate of the Hollands' circle in Florence, where he stayed for almost four years. As a token of gratitude for their support and hospitality, Watts produced numerous likenesses of the Hollands including oil portraits and pencil studies, as well as the present picture. This informal portrayal records the intimate friendship between the young Watts and Lady Holland. Unlike the more formal half-length portraits of his patroness, this miniature oil sketch of Lady Augusta in bed was most probably produced on the spur of the moment without any preparations.

As Blunt pointed out, the picture came to be known as 'Lady Holland on a day-bed',[2] even though the subject clearly depicts Augusta in her sleeping attire within a curtained bed. Deep warm colours evoke candlelight. The present oil sketch is not listed in the Watts Catalogue, but inscribed on the back in distinctive calligraphy is written: 'Sketch by Watts of Lady Holland, Naples, 1844'. Watts was a guest at the Hollands' Casa Feroni in Florence and at Lady Holland's family home, Villa Rochella in Naples, where the present sketch was most probably produced, as suggested by the inscription.

At one of their last meetings Mary recalled that Watts and Augusta reminisced about the past and that he said: 'I tell her [Mary] you let me paint in every room in your house, and you did not let anyone else do that', she replied quickly, with a pretty little movement of her head, looking up with youth still in her eyes, "But you were not anybody else".'[3] Watts's freedom to enter all rooms in the house also extended to Lord Holland's bedroom, who expressed his annoyance about this, saying:

> Watts is becoming more maundering than ever and bores me to death by see-sawing from one leg to the other by my bed side when I receive the post and wish to have half a moment's peace to read my letters & newspapers–I am obliged to take measures to keep him out.[4]

This oil sketch of *Lady Holland* provides a unique insight into a friendship between Watts and Augusta that lasted until the end of her life. Further informal sketches of this type include a loose pen-and-ink sketch of a woman reclining in bed in the collection of the Watts Gallery, which appears to be Lady Holland (COMWG2007.465). There is also a detailed pencil drawing of the sleeping Augusta in day dress with sewing on her lap (cat.8.1). JD

1   Bryant 2004, p.40.
2   Blunt 1975, p.32.
3   Watts 1912, I, p.49.
4   Letter from Lord Holland to Augusta, 28 April 1845, quoted in Gaja 1995, pp.26–7, and partly quoted in Ilchester 1937, p.335 (Holland House Papers, British Museum, Add. MS 52032).

9. *Fiesole*, 1844–5

Oil on canvas, 66 × 86.4 cm (26 × 33 in)
COMWG12

PROVENANCE: collection of the artist; Mary Watts; on view at the Watts Gallery by 1920; Lilian Mackintosh (Mrs Michael Chapman), legal descendant of the artist; given by her to the Watts Gallery in 1946

EXHIBITIONS: Memorial Exhibitions, London 1905, no.172, Manchester 1905, no.42, Newcastle 1905, no.153, Edinburgh 1905, no.54, Dublin 1906, no.69; Watts London 1954, no.8; *Italian Art and Britain*, Royal Academy of Arts, London, 1960, no.233; Watts Aldeburgh 1961, no.7; *The Victorian Vision of Italy 1825–1875*, Leicester Museums and Art Gallery, Leicester, 1968, no.93; Watts Whitechapel 1974, no.5; Watts London and Compton 2006, no.3

LITERATURE: Watts Catalogue, I, p.55; Watts 1912, I, p.63; Watts Gallery Catalogue 1920, no.35, as *Fiesole from Careggi*; Alston 1929, no.80; Blunt 1975, p.40; Staley 1978, p.59; Gaja 1995, pp.31–2, 114; Staley and Underwood 2006, pp.15, 26

Although Fiesole is the title of the painting, the town itself appears on top of a hillside in the distance on the horizon and it might be more accurately known by its former title, *Fiesole from Careggi*. This landscape, like *Petraia* (cat.9.1),[1] depicts the area that surrounded Watts as he lived in the Hollands' villa on the outskirts of Florence. In *Fiesole* cultivated land in the foreground gives way in the middle distance to a range of distant hills and a remarkably freely painted sky with creamy yellow clouds soaring above. The muted palette of greens and browns lends a sombre character to the image. The architectural reference points consist of some characteristic Tuscan dwellings culminating in the hill town of Fiesole, whose famous architectural features are reduced to a few tiny white rectangles.

Watts painted the view from an overhanging open gallery, almost like a lookout point, under the projecting eaves of the villa at Careggi. In effect, it is an open-air sketch in the tradition of such views by foreign visitors to the south. Encompassed within the view are fields, orchards, olive trees and cypresses. Although there were some famous residences among the farmhouses in the area between Careggi and Fiesole, Watts downplays these features to give an expansive panorama of the valley of the Arno and the mountains towards Rome. He might well have made the trip to Fiesole, for it contained important Etruscan remains and commanded a superb view of Florence. But travel there was no easy matter as the town was set high on top of a steep hill, as one can see in the middle of the painting, and required a journey of several hours up a winding road. Murray's *Hand-Book for Travellers in Northern Italy* (1842) notes that only in recent years had a new road been built to ease the journey.

In the winter of 1844–5 Lord Holland commented that Watts became restless and 'more maundering than ever'. After completing the fresco at Careggi in May 1845 (fig.35; see cat.10), the artist apparently took 'a violent fancy for landscape'[2] or, in Lord Holland's exact words, he is 'now gone wild about landscape painting'.[3] At the same time, Lady Holland urged that he work 'for fame, riches and position'. But clearly the lure of the hills and the scenery surrounding him could not wait. Indeed, he featured landscapes in the backgrounds of his portraits right from his arrival, as seen in *Mary Augusta, Lady Holland* (1843; Royal Collection), showing Lady Holland in a Riviera hat, where the palette is lightened with colours that shine out under the blue Italian skies.[4] In his own *Self-Portrait* (fig.34) a sunset view shows the environs of Careggi. Landscape painting first engaged Watts during this time in Italy and it continued to feature in his work ever after. The artist retained this painting and *Petraia*, and although it is not known if they hung in the Little Holland House Gallery, they certainly served for Watts as a recollection of the defining years that he spent in Florence. BB

Cat. 9.1 *Petraia*, 1845, oil on canvas, 30.5 × 63.3 cm (12 × 25 in), COMWGNC22

1   Watts London and Compton 2006, no.1.
2   Ilchester 1937, pp.335–6.
3   As quoted in Gaja 1995, p.31.
4   Watts Portraits 2004, no.1.

10. Study for *The Drowning of the Doctor of Lorenzo de' Medici*, 1844

Oil on canvas, 20.3 × 25.4 cm (8 × 9½ in)
COMWG253

PROVENANCE: collection of the artist; Mary Watts; on view at the Watts Gallery by 1920; Lilian Mackintosh (Mrs Michael Chapman), legal descendant of the artist; given by her to the Watts Gallery in 1946

LITERATURE (on the fresco unless stated otherwise): Cosmo Monkhouse, 'George Frederick Watts, R.A.', *Scribner's Magazine*, XVI (1894), p.700 (on the oil sketch); Cartwright 1896, p.6; von Schleinitz 1904, p.10; Watts Catalogue, I, p.39 (on the oil sketch); Macmillan 1903, p.25; Sketchley 1904, p.20; Watts 1912, I, pp.61–3; Watts Gallery Catalogue 1920, no.49; Ilchester 1937, p.324; Blunt 1975, p.38, pl.4a; Nicholas Penny, 'The Activity of English Artists in Nineteenth Century Italy', *Giornale di viaggio in Italia: l'attivita dei pittori europei in Italia nell'800: occasioni e memorie*, Busto Arsizio, 1985, p.162 and illus.88; Gaja 1995, pp.64–6, 88, 124–5, p.113 (Appendix); Gaja 2005, pp.138–9

This animated oil sketch is an early idea for Watts's major fresco painting at the Villa Medicea di Careggi: *The Drowning of the Doctor of Lorenzo de' Medici* (fig.35).[1] The essentials of the composition and the colours are set out with great panache, with the thin oil medium allowing much energetic brushwork. Warm colours, relieved by confident touches of tiny white highlights, convey the tempestuous mood of the scene. As a working study, it served the specific purpose of orchestrating the movement of the figures involved in the violence.

Watts's original intention in going to Italy was to study fresco paintings and techniques, and Lord Holland, his host, held him to that plan. Initially, the young artist made some trials at the Casa Feroni in Florence, but then in the summer of 1844 he moved on to a bigger project, to decorate an open loggia at the Villa Medicea in Careggi outside the city. During the Renaissance the fabulously rich and powerful Medici were rulers of Florence from 1434. Cosimo de' Medici built Careggi, which in the era of his grandson Lorenzo Magnifico (*c*.1449–92) became the centre of a circle of intellectuals and philosophers. But Lorenzo, a great patron of the arts, died when relatively young under suspicious circumstances while at Careggi.

Enamoured of such tales from Italian history, Watts conceived several works relating to Lorenzo. For the subject of this fresco, perhaps with input from his friends the Hollands, he chose a supposed incident after Lorenzo's death that he could easily have found in William Roscoe's *Life of Lorenzo de' Medici*, first published in 1796 and in many editions thereafter. Lorenzo's death from fever could not be averted by his usual physician, 'the celebrated Pier Leoni of Spoleto', but as the disorder accelerated another doctor was called, to no avail. Roscoe noted that Pier Leoni left Careggi in a state of distraction and threw himself into a well, but a footnote explains, 'Whether Leoni died a voluntary death has been doubted', and one contemporary source recorded that Leoni feared for his life from the attendants of Lorenzo who, 'without just cause, suspect that he had occasioned his death by poison'.[2]

In Watts's oil sketch a combination of the two accounts results in a scene where two ruffians, the attendants of Lorenzo, wrestle Pier Leoni, dressed in black, back towards an open well; he grasps a rope, but a caped figure with a knife reaches up to cut it. To the lower right a startled dog rears backwards; to the far left an indifferent figure (possibly to be identified as Piero de' Medici) watches the proceedings. In the final painting more figures join the drama (and the dog departs). A priest rushes in from the right side to avert the murder.[3] The condemned doctor grimaces in fear as the head henchman wields his knife to cut the rope.

This complicated, large-scale composition, with over life-size figures executed in a medium unfamiliar to Watts, involved some trial and error in the working process. Lord Holland wrote:

> Watts's fresco is not quite flourishing as at first. It does not dry equally, and he is somewhat dispirited about it … He is really very busy. He and Peters are now drawing from a model for the back of the ruffian who is throwing the Doctor into the well. Watts means to make a study for each.[4]

The central group forms a densely interwoven unit, a tangle of flailing arms and legs, all studied from life. Various other studies for the composition[5] reveal developments beyond the initial oil sketch here, which has all the dynamism of the first idea for the subject. Watts's youthful interest in the more violent side of Renaissance Florence seems at odds with the balanced and idealised art of that period. But he took his inspiration from scenes of Medicean history and from the immediate surroundings at Careggi. The well, an actual feature of the villa, is clearly visible in the final fresco, which survives to this day (and was restored in 1998).[6] BB

1   Reproduced as early as 1904 in von Schleinitz 1904, p.10; also in Blunt 1975, pl.4a, and in colour in Gaja 1995, pl.V.
2   William Roscoe, *The Life of Lorenzo De'Medici*, London, 1846, 8th edn, p.550.
3   Gaja 2005, p.138, considers that this is Savonarola who is being restrained by Poliziano, another individual in the Medici circle.
4   Ilchester 1937, pp.324–5.
5   Watts Compton 2004, no.3.
6   Penny 1985 considers it 'certainly one of Watts's best works' in its clear and dynamic composition, which is well adapted to the architecture surrounding it.

11. Study for *Alfred Inciting the Saxons to Prevent the Landing of the Danes*, 1846

Pencil on paper, sheet folded, 21.5 × 35.5
(8½ × 14 in)
Inscribed (in another hand) 'Alfred inciting the
Saxons to put to sea'
COMWG2006.58

PROVENANCE: collection of the artist; mounted in
an album of drawings; Mary Watts; her legal
descendant, Lilian Mackintosh (Mrs Michael
Chapman); by descent until sold, Sotheby's,
London, 9 June 1994, no.213, to Spink; acquired by
the Watts Gallery

EXHIBITIONS: Watts Compton 2004, no.6

LITERATURE (on the subject): Cartwright 1896, p.6;
Sketchley 1904, pp.21–4; Watts Catalogue, I, p.2;
Watts 1912, I, pp.76, 78–80, 81, 87–9, 150; Roy
Strong, *And when did you last see your father?: The
Victorian Painter and British History*, London, 1978,
pp.114ff; McLean, Pelter and Shepherd 2003,
pp.35–8

This fine drawing is one of the surviving studies
for Watts's monumental painting *Alfred Inciting
the Saxons to Prevent the Landing of the Danes by
Encountering them at Sea* (cat.11.1). While at
Careggi in mid-1846, the artist was preparing
to paint a new work for entry in the fourth
competition to decorate the new Palace of
Westminster. The subject complied with one of
the categories, English history, required by the
Royal Fine Arts Commission. This scene of
England's first naval victory in the ninth
century AD was also calculated to appeal to the
nationalistic sympathies that motivated the
competitions.[1]

On a massive scale at nearly 20 feet across,
Alfred was Watts's most ambitious effort to date.
Alfred's reputation, as originator of England's
naval prowess, made him a traditional heroic fig-
ure, suitable for a history painting. The Anglo-
Saxon king harangues his subjects, exhorting

them to take to sea to defend England. The
notion of Alfred as a brave-hearted Englishman
came down to the Victorian era as part of the
cultural vocabulary. Watts's avowed model for
Alfred was the antique, yet there are also echoes
of old master traditions as well, especially
Raphael, whose works Watts had recently seen
in Rome.[2]

In the painting action is compressed into the
foreground space, apart from one small group in
the far distance who react to the Danish fleet
arriving on the horizon. Like *The Drowning of the
Doctor*, this energised composition relies on
strong, in some cases exaggerated, actions. The
sculptural figure of Alfred acts as the calm central point around which the dynamic movement
circles. In a letter to his friend Georgiana Duff
Gordon, who had seen the work in progress,
Watts wrote: 'Alfred stands, as you know, in the
centre of the picture, his foot upon the plank,

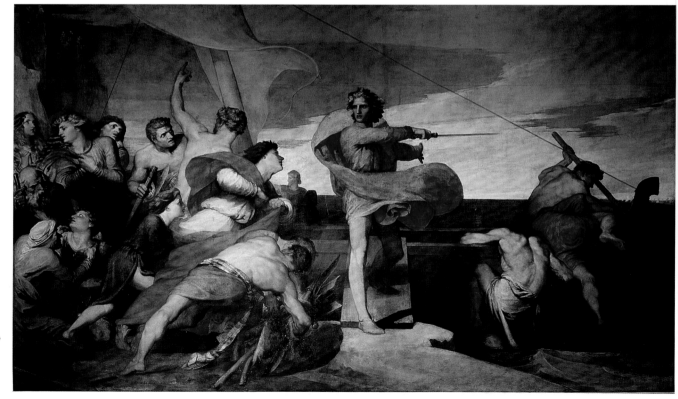

Cat. 11.1 *Alfred inciting
the Saxons to Prevent the
Landing of the Danes*,
c.1846–7, oil on canvas,
343 × 590 cm (135 ×
232¼ in), Houses of
Parliament, © Palace
of Westminster

about to spring into the boat. I have endeav-oured to give Him as much energy, dignity, and expression as possible, without exaggeration. Long-limbed and springy, he is about the size of the Apollo.'[3] He continues to describe an array of types among the tangle of individuals: an excited youth, a peasant, an older man with his wife and child, a maiden, a youth putting on armour, his old mother and father, a little boy clenching his fists, two men lifting weapons off the ground and, to the right side, two men rushing through water to climb on the vessel.

In the drawing some but not all of these characters can be identified. The main group to the left of Alfred is most fully worked; to his right two figures climbing into the boat are only loosely sketched in. Essentially, this study, with figures in the nude, establishes the actions for what is a fairly complicated arrangement. The artist certainly would have had recourse to models

for some of these poses, which seem intended as displays of anatomical proficiency. Watts's delin-eation of the nude figures with careful shading and attention to musculature attests to his early study in a sculptor's studio, where he mastered the skill to depict the human form.

Mary Watts recorded that the artist 'made numberless pencil drawings for this picture',[4] apparently about forty of them. Some are known:[5] one, a head study for Alfred, is clearly based on a type of antique head of Apollo, and another in an outline style lays out the whole composition. This moderately sized sheet, recently conserved, is an important record of Watts's process of working towards a major composition. On returning to London, and entering *Alfred* into the fourth competition, Watts won one of the first prizes, and the Commission purchased the painting, which has recently undergone conservation.[6] BB

1   Cartwright 1896 includes as part of its title 'the first naval victory of the English'.
2   Later Alfred also appears as a lawgiver in Watts's Raphaelesque mural at Lincoln's Inn (fig.42).
3   Watts 1912, I, p.79.
4   Watts 1912, I, p.81.
5   They are unlocated but exist in photographic prints from glass plate negatives; several are illustrated in Gaja 1995, pls 51 a–c.
6   On the conservation of the oil see McLean, Pelter and Shepherd 2003, pp.35–8.

Return to London and the Late 1840s

Watts returned to London from Italy in 1847 with his *Alfred Inciting the Saxons* (cat.11.1), which was awarded a first premium of £500 and purchased for a further £200 by the Royal Fine Arts Commission for the Palaces of Westminster. He lodged at the less than salubrious 48 Cambridge Street, off the Edgware Road, for two years and encountered a changed artistic climate. The great hero of history painting, B.R. Haydon, had committed suicide around the corner from Cambridge Street in 1846, and the press was becoming increasingly hostile towards the high art with which Watts was involved.

A move to the more fashionable 30 Charles Street, Berkeley Square, gave rise to new associations and a change in fortunes for the artist, who was facing a difficult time. Watts was also disturbed by the increasing poverty in London and Ireland, which he expressed in four paintings from this period, *Found Drowned* (cat.14), *The Seamstress* or *The Song of the Shirt* (*c.*1849–50; Watts Gallery), *The Irish Famine* (cat.16) and *Under a Dry Arch* (cat.15). These paintings were unique to this period, and *The Good Samaritan* (fig.41) was a turning point, as social concerns were expressed in a symbolic manner rather than through realism, which the artist later rejected.   MB

Charles Couzens, *G.F. Watts*, (detail, cat.12)

12. Charles Couzens (fl.1838–75), *G.F. Watts, c.*1849–50

Tempera on ivory, 41 × 21.4 cm (16 × 8 ½ in)
Signed in red paint: 'C Couzens'; handwritten in ink on a label: '...ature of Mr. G. F. Watts. ...y Charles Couzens ... nted about 1850.'
COMWG501

PROVENANCE: collection of the artist (Charles Street, Old and New Little Holland House Gallery); Lilian Mackintosh (Mrs Michael Chapman), legal descendant of the artist; given by her to the Watts Gallery in 1946 (no.48)

EXHIBITIONS: *The Rediscovery of Greece: Travellers and Romantics in the 19th Century*, Fine Art Society, London, June 1979, no.213

LITERATURE: Blunt 1975, pp.50, 56 (plate 5); Gould 2004, pp.27, 28

In June 1849 Watts moved from 48 Cambridge Street off Edgware Road to far more salubrious premises at 30 Charles Street, Berkeley Square. Its spacious central room was distinctive 'with a lofty ceiling and skylight'.[1] It had been previously used as commercial premises including exhibition and auction space; in 1847 'the great Room, 30, Charles Street' showed Duke Lante's collection of old master paintings and a decade later the tracings and drawings of Layard.[2] Such a fashionable position and large space for working on and exhibiting his large-scale works marked a change in fortune for the artist who had recently returned from Italy. The acquisition of a 'little piano' for this studio also indicates it was an ideal place for entertaining fellow artists and potential patrons.[3] Below the main studio

> was another he found himself able to lend to a miniature painter and copyist, called Charles Cozens [*sic*]. They had known each other as boys, and Cozens, being greatly influenced in his work by that of his friend, obtained commissions, and occasionally made copies of G.F. Watts's portraits, as these were frequently required by the Ionides.[4]

Mary also notes that Couzens made a copy of the watercolour of Caractacus for Watts.[5]

This painting of G.F. Watts by Charles Couzens dates from the time the artists shared 30 Charles Street. There is little recorded of Couzens, a miniaturist and copyist whom Watts used to make copies of his work. In this portrait Couzens employs a miniaturist's medium, tempera on ivory, to produce a fine full-length portrait of Watts around 1849 and 1850. How different the artist looks in this painting, compared to the self-portrait in armour painted while in Italy. Blunt writes:

It would appear that one of the first things that Watts did on his return to England was to get rid of his moustache and imperial [i.e. beard] ... the sacrifice effected a marked improvement in his appearance. We do not know how long he remained clean-shaven; but by 1853 a modest fringed beard had returned, and a year later ... he was sporting a lush growth that made so many of the great Victorians almost indistinguishable from one another and gave to their most trivial utterances the weight of major prophecy.[6]

Beneath the flippancy of Blunt's remarks is the observation that Watts was a supremely self-conscious and sensitive artist, whose appearance reflected his state of mind. The clean-shaven image of Watts in this painting is unique to the late 1840s, the period of the four social paintings. Dapper, stylish and perhaps even nervous, he is presented as a metropolitan and fashionable young man, an artist uncertain of his future but with his consistent inspiration represented in the background, a section of the Parthenon frieze by his beloved Pheidias. 'I am a pupil of the greatest sculptor of all, Pheidias',[7] he wrote and throughout his career referred to the ancient Greek sculptor as his master. In Little Holland House and in the Watts Gallery large plaster sections of the Parthenon frieze were on display and it may be that some of these were obtained by Watts during this period and were copied by Couzens for this portrait. MB

1 Christopher Kent, 'Cosmopolitan Club,' *Oxford Dictionary of National Biography* (http://www.oxforddnb.com/view/article/... accessed 25 Feb. 2008).
2 *The Times*, 7 June 1847, p.10; *The Times*, 26 June 1857, p.12.
3 Watts Catalogue, I, p.131.
4 Watts 1912, I, p.106.
5 Watts 1912, I, p.44.
6 Blunt 1975, p.50.
7 Watts 1912, I, p.74.

Cat. 12.1 Charles Couzens, *G.F. Watts, c.*1849, pencil on paper, 22.5 × 18.5 cm (8⅞ × 7¼ in), COMWG 2006.9

13. *Satan*, 1847–8

Oil on canvas, 198.1 × 132.1 cm (78 × 52 in)
COMWG117

PROVENANCE: collection of the artist (Little Holland House Gallery); part of the original Memorial Collection, 1905

EXHIBITIONS: Watts Grosvenor 1881, no.70; probably Watts Leighton House 1903, p.10, no.7; Watts Gallery 1904, no.10; Compton 2004, no.55

LITERATURE: Spielmann 1886, pp.2, 32; Arthur Symons, *Studies in the Seven Arts*, London, 1906 (essay dating from 1900), p.89; Macmillan 1903, p.150; Watts Gallery Catalogue 1904, no.10; Barrington 1905, pp.24, 32, 92; Watts Catalogue, I, p.131; Watts 1912, I, pp.96–7, 101; Alston 1929, no.95; Blunt 1975, pp.56–7

Cat. 13.1 *Satan Calling up his Legions*, c.1849–50, pencil on paper, 18 × 11.5 cm (7 × 4½ in), formerly Watts Gallery, art market, London, 2000

This extraordinary painting depicts Satan turning emphatically as he confronts an explosion of light. Its large scale indicates Watts's ambitions on his return from Italy in 1847; he had been painting big pictures and had every intention of carrying on. Fortunately, he had the use of sizeable rooms as a studio in Dorchester House, a palatial residence on Park Lane then nearly completed for his friend, the wealthy collector Robert Holford.

Here Watts planned and, in some cases, began a group of works that featured Satan: *Michael the Archangel Contending with Satan for the Body of Moses*; *Satan, Sin and Death*; *Satan Calling up his Legions*; and the *Temptation of Eve*, showing the figure of Satan with his wings spread out hovering over Adam and Eve. All these works derived thematically from John Milton's epic *Paradise Lost*, a book that had intrigued Watts from his childhood when in 1830, aged thirteen, he had copied Richard Westall's design *Archangel Uriel and Satan* from an edition of 1794–7.

Paradise Lost attracted artists from the time of its publication in 1667. Watts knew and probably responded in particular to paintings of Milton's Satan by British artists of the Romantic era. Many of Henry Fuseli's published engravings from his Milton Gallery of the 1790s portray a forceful and physically beautiful Satan. The designs of William Blake (1757–1827) for Milton's works were known in artistic circles. Indeed, the title page to Blake's poem *Milton* shows a nude figure seen from the back raising his arm amid swirling forms, a close comparison to Watts's *Satan*. In 1827 John Martin published *Paradise Lost* with mezzotint engravings filled with sublime imagery. Thomas Lawrence painted a vast *Satan Summoning his Legions*, which was seen at the Royal Academy in 1797 and sold in 1831, entering the collection of the Academy shortly after. The first of the Houses of Parliament competitions included Milton's poetry among the stipulated subjects. Watts chose a scene from classical history, but other artists opted for Satan. Watts's own drawing of *Satan Calling up his Legions* (cat.13.1) suggests a planned sublime composition in the manner of Fuseli.

The charismatic Miltonic Satan continued to fascinate Watts, although the biblical Satan also featured in his thinking. When the present painting was first exhibited in 1881 at the Grosvenor

Gallery retrospective as *Satan*, Watts included a quotation from the opening verses of the book of Job (1: 7) in the Old Testament: 'And the Lord said unto Satan, Whence comest thou? Then Satan answered the Lord and said, From going to and fro in the earth and from walking up and down in it.' Other titles that attached to the work in later catalogues include 'Whither goest thou Satan' and 'Satan goeth to and fro [on the Earth] seeking whom he may devour'.[1] The encounter between God and Satan provokes the trials of Job, as Satan challenges God to test Job's faith.

When Blake's *Illustrations of the Book of Job* was privately printed in 1825, Watts was only eight years old. But Blake's *Job* had a cult following in artistic and literary circles from the 1820s onwards and copies of the book were circulated among the cognoscenti.[2] An early scene in the poem, plate 2, shows an athletic, dynamic nude Satan gesturing to the enthroned God. Later, in plate 4, after Satan's failure to discredit Job, he exits, a moment not described in the Bible. But Blake includes in the delicate design the engraved quotation 'Going to & fro in the Earth & walking up & down in it' in the upper margin of the plate. Seen from behind, Satan, with his great faceted wings rising on each side, strolls over the curved earth. Significantly, we do not see his face. Watts uses that very quotation for his subtitle and also offers a partial view of side and back of the faceless figure.

The return from Italy prompted a re-evaluation for the artist and his style underwent changes. The techniques of fresco, painting on wet ground, required a broader treatment, as did working on a large scale, found in the social realist paintings (cats 14–16). *Satan* is a fascinating example of Watts's fresco-like style, with extremely simplified handling resulting in a direct and easily readable image. Just as the composition is reduced to its essence, so is the colour. The outline of Satan's figure and head sits against the flat gold of the background. Watts's studies of antiquity are apparent in the visualisation of Satan's head, with his hair arranged much like that of an antique sculpture of an Apollo type. The confrontation between Satan and God results in an elemental collision between the powerful torso of Satan rising from a mass of swirling waves with a defiant gesture and the blinding sunlight emblematic of the power of God. This Satan, presented on a monumental scale with his powerful torso and emphatic gesture, is a force for evil. Indeed, his averted face conveys an even more intensified power and mystery.

Watts did not send the painting to an exhibition at the time he painted it. Such paintings were not in tune with contemporary tastes, yet *Satan* had its admirers. An undated letter from around 1850 indicates that John Ruskin had seen it: 'I don't understand the new picture, but it is glorious, and Satan has his cheek-bone all right.'[3] Ruskin considered Watts 'to my mind the only real painter of History or thought we have in England'.[4] It seems that the writer even bought Watts's *Michael the Archangel Contending with Satan for the Body of Moses*.[5] To have Ruskin consider him as a 'painter of thought' must have encouraged some of Watts's more ambitious ideas, but he never accepted the role of protégé.

Watts kept *Satan* in his studio throughout the Charles Street and Little Holland House years. In 1880 he took it up to prepare it for the retrospective at the Grosvenor Gallery where it was seen for the first time at a public exhibition.[6] He then included it in his newly built gallery at New Little Holland House. By reincorporating *Satan* into his own canon of works, Watts acknowledged that, although it seemed out of step with contemporary art in the late 1840s, by the early 1880s, with his own symbolical works finally praised, its time had arrived. This painting, replete with mystery and power and suggestive of the forces of evil, suited an era when Symbolist tastes were in the ascendancy. Indeed, no writer seemed to comprehend its meaning until Arthur Symons, *fin de siècle* author of *The Symbolist Movement in Literature* (1899), identified 'the malevolent pride of the intellect, in the poise and gesture of a body only partly alive and but slightly formed with beauty' in Watts's *Satan*. BB

1   Barrington 1905, p.32. This is in fact a partial quote from 1 Peter 5: 8 from the New Testament.
2   See the list of buyers of Blake's *Job* in Barbara Bryant, 'A Documentary History of Blake's *Job*', in *The Illustrations of the Book of Job*, facsimile edition with introductory essays, ed. David Bindman (William Blake Trust, London, 1987), pp. 103–47; Mark Evans refers to Alexander Constantine Ionides's knowledge of Blake via his follower, Edward Calvert, in 'Blake, Calvert – and Palmer? The Album of Alexander Constantine Ionides', *Burlington Magazine*, CXLIV (2002), pp.540ff.
3   Barrington 1905, p.24; Cook and Wedderburn 1903–12, XXXVI, p.112.
4   Cook and Wedderburn 1903–12, XI, p.30.
5   Mrs Watts noted that this work was returned to the Watts Gallery in *c*.1910 by Joan Severn, who was Ruskin's caretaker at Brantwood in the Lake District. Ruskin died in 1900, and although it seems odd, he must have had this painting by Watts until then. Now, however, it seems to be lost, perhaps destroyed. Mrs Watts described it as 'never completed' and 'fresco like', 'a suggestion of two figures standing in a great light', a description that suggests a connection with cat.13. In 1851 Ruskin returned a large work to Watts and this was probably *Time and Oblivion* (Eastnor Castle).
6   Barrington 1905, p.92, described it as among the pictures finished at that time and never retouched.

14. *Found Drowned, c.*1848–50

Oil on canvas, 119.4 × 213.4 cm (47 × 84¼ in)
Label on reverse inscribed 'Found Drowned, G F Watts, Little Holland House, Kensington, London Liverpool'
COMWG161

PROVENANCE: collection of the artist (displayed at 30 Charles Street, Old and New Little Holland House); Watts Gallery

EXHIBITIONS: Liverpool Academy 1862, no.377;[1] St Jude's, Whitechapel, 1881, under the revised title of 'One More Unfortunate';[2] Watts Grosvenor 1881, no.90; Watts New York 1884, no.118; Whitechapel Art Gallery 1903; Watts Gallery 1904, no.63; Whitechapel 1974, no.12; *Hard Times*, Manchester City Art Gallery, 1987, no.14; *The Times of Our Lives*, Whitworth Art Gallery, Manchester, 2000, unnumbered; Watts Gallery 2004, no.7

LITERATURE: Spielmann 1886, p.30; Macmillan 1903, p.217 (referred to as 'Found Dead'); Barrington 1905, p.135; Watts 1912, I, p.126; Watts Catalogue, I, p.58; Blunt 1975, p.55, pp.211–12; Linda Nochlin, 'Lost and Found: Once More the Fallen Woman', *The Art Bulletin*, 60, no.1 (March 1978), pp.143, 144

In *Found Drowned* the body of a young woman, arms outstretched in a cruciform position, is framed by a dry arch of Waterloo Bridge and partially immersed in the Thames water in which she has drowned. In her left hand, limp in death, are a chain and heart-shaped locket, and in the distance loom the vague outlines of the Hungerford Suspension Bridge and London's heavily industrial south bank, over which gleams a single star.[3]

The reason for such a specific London topography stems from Waterloo Bridge's reputation as the bridge used by suicides. Its notoriety in this respect found its way into guidebooks, and one, *London*, edited by Charles Knight, notes:

We remember with pain how many unfortunates have stood shivering in those very recesses, taking *their* last farewell of the world in which they have experienced so much misery. We have no idea, nor do we wish to have, of the entire extent of this dreadful evil, which has of late years given a new and most unhappy kind of celebrity to Waterloo Bridge.[4]

The location also provided Watts with the opportunity to express his revulsion at the industrialisation that had caused such social distress, and with deliberate irony he chose the bridge's familiar picturesque arch to frame London's river and cityscape.[5] Another image of a Waterloo suicide, which dates from 1848 and was widely circulated at the time, comprises one of eight plates in George Cruikshank's Hogarthian moral tale, *The Drunkard's Children*, a sequel to the famous *Bottle* series of a year earlier. In this work, as the title describes, 'The drunkard's daughter, having a maniac of a father and dead brother, in desperation and under the influence of alcohol, takes her own life by jumping from a bridge.' Such crude morality and melodrama are removed from Watts's depiction, yet the currency of the theme must have been pervasive.

The reputation of Waterloo Bridge was made even more famous by Thomas Hood's poem, *The Bridge of Sighs*, in which a young woman commits suicide from the bridge.[6] Indeed, another smaller version by Watts of the current painting, bought by the collector Charles

H. Rickards,[7] was entitled *The Bridge of Sighs – 'Take her up tenderly, lift her with care'*, which is quoted directly from Hood's poem, and Watts's image clearly echoes further lines from it:

Look at her garments
Clinging like cerements
Whilst the wave constantly
Drips from her clothing;
Take her up instantly,
Loving, not loathing.[8]

Sympathy for the suicide is evident in both Hood's poem and Watts's painting, and Mrs Barrington in her Metropolitan Museum catalogue writes: 'The subject is identical with that of Hood's poem, but was not taken from it, but suggested by an incident seen by the artist.'[9] Whether Watts did see such a scene is debatable, but it is more likely that the numerous articles in the daily papers reporting *Found Drowned* would have provided a source for his painting. The legal term used in the title of the painting is deliberately open and non-conclusive: it might be an accident, allowing a Christian burial, or suicide, which does not. The point is dramatically emphasised by the outrage that followed when the Reverend Bryan King in 1847 'declined reading the service over the body of a woman who had been "found drowned", according to the verdict pronounced at a coroner's inquest'.[10]

In *Found Drowned* Watts hints at the tragic reasons for the suicide through the heart-shaped locket suggesting a lover's betrayal or an unwanted pregnancy. In Watts, as in Hood, there is drama and sympathy, a criticism of those who judge and whose strict and unforgiving morality leads to premature death – attitudes like those of the Reverend King. For all the 'dark arch' and 'black-flowing river' of Thomas Hood, a single star shines, a symbolic and redemptive sign that echoes Hood's last lines, 'leaving, with meekness, Her sins to her Saviour'. Both hope and despair are present, themes that were to be more famously explored by Watts in a single unbroken string (see *Hope*, cat.59). Here the glowing tones of a single star amid stillness and calmness evoke another world. Mary Watts later described the painting as portraying 'the wreck of a girl's life, with the dark

arch of the bridge she had crossed from the seen to the unseen, the cold dark river, and the deep-blue heaven with its one star watching all'.[11]

Found Drowned belongs to a very small group of four paintings that date to a short period between around 1849 and 1850 and graphically depict the suffering poor: *Found Drowned*, *The Seamstress* (*c.*1849–50; Watts Gallery), *Under a Dry Arch* (cat.15) and *The Irish Famine* (cat.16). Although they were painted in the late 1840s, none of these socially concerned paintings was exhibited until much later in Watts's studio home at Little Holland House. The first to be publicly exhibited and most widely exhibited was *Found Drowned* in the Liverpool Academy of 1862. In 1875 Rickards's version was exhibited at the Dudley Gallery, where the *Athenaeum* noted its lyrical quality: '*Found Drowned* (211), a corpse, lying on a river's brink, at night, with flying gleams of the lost day. The pathetic effect supports the motive of the subject; pictorially this is a dark and strong study of tone.'[12] On its exhibition at the Grosvenor Gallery in 1882 more than thirty years after being painted, critics noted the radical nature of the works, painted at a time when Europe was in turmoil. The *New York Times* called it 'a sad and pitiful representation of the crime and misery that the world is full of and that we pass by unheeding'[13] and the *Spectator* warned: 'Bad policy, Mr. Watts, to confront these "curled darlings" with so vital a question. You come too close to home *Sir* to our consciences to be agreeable.'[14] MB

1 It is difficult to be certain which of the two versions of *Found Drowned* were exhibited at which exhibitions. The label on the reverse suggests that the present version was exhibited at the Liverpool Academy in 1862. Rickards's appears to have been exhibited at the Dudley Gallery (no.211) in 1875 and at the Royal Manchester Institution in 1880.

2 Gould 2004, p.153.

3 From its position in the sky it is likely that the star is in fact the planet Venus. Symbolically, the star is redemptive in meaning, although the association of Venus as the goddess of love reflects the heart-shaped locket in the suicide's hand.

4 Charles Knight (ed.), *London*, 6 vols, 1841–4, III, p.169.

5 Such topography can be seen in many paintings, most famously Canaletto's views through the arches of Westminster Bridge.

6 As the poet noted in a letter of 1844, 'I have all but done a poem on "the Bridge of Sighs" – ie Waterloo, and its Suicides.' Thomas Hood to Frederick Oldfield Ward, 10 April 1844, in Peter F. Morgan (ed.), *The Letters of Thomas Hood*, Edinburgh 1973.

7 A smaller version of *Found Drowned* is in the Walker Art Gallery, Liverpool (inv. no. WAG2104). It is uncertain whether this is a study or smaller copy. In Watts Gallery correspondence dating from 1903 G.F. Watts, who had got the work back from Rickards, agreed to sell it for 50 guineas to James Smith, who later gave it to the Walker Art Gallery, Liverpool.

8 Thomas Hood, *The Poetical Works of Thomas Hood*, London, 1906, p.526, lines 9–14.

9 Barrington 1905, p.135.

10 *The Times*, 2 January 1847, p.4.

11 Watts 1912, I, p.126.

12 *Athenaeum*, 30 October 1875, p.581.

13 *New York Times*, 21 May 1882, a clipping in the Watts Gallery Archive.

14 *The Spectator*, 7 January 1882, p.15.

15. *Under a Dry Arch, c.*1848–50

Oil on canvas, 137 × 102 cm (54 × 40 in)
COMWG171

PROVENANCE: collection of the artist (displayed at 30 Charles Street, Old and New Little Holland House Gallery); Watts Gallery

EXHIBITIONS: Watts Grosvenor 1881, no.100; Toynbee Hall 1891; Watts Gallery 1904, no.67; Watts Whitechapel 1974, no.13; Watts Manchester, Minneapolis, Brooklyn 1978, no.8

LITERATURE: Spielmann 1886, p.32; Cartwright 1896, p.16; Barrington 1905, pp.32, 92; Watts Catalogue, I, p.15; Watts 1912, I, p.126; Blunt, 1975, pp.55, 82, 211–12; Staley 1978, pp.63–4; Gould 2004, pp.28, 160

The most brutal depiction of all the four social paintings of the late 1840s is *Under a Dry Arch*, Watts's most direct response to the poverty that was evident in London at this time. A *Times* article of 1852 exclaimed: 'Does it not appear at first sight a strange result of the terrible statistics of society, that upon an average 1 person out of 20 of this luxurious metropolis is everyday destitute of food and employment, and every night without a place for shelter or repose?'[1] Here is the face of the poor, not the sentimentalised genre depictions that graced the walls of the Royal Academy. The imagery of Watts's painting is closer to the graphic journalism that developed in the 1840s, a severe Hogarthianism that he was later to reject but understood its value. Such a picture, he wrote, 'like my old woman under the archway … has no beauty but it has purpose. It, I hope, arouses pity for human refuse.'[2]

Mary Watts later described the woman as 'dying … with all the anguish of a long life scored upon her face;'[3] F.G. Stephens in his *Portfolio* piece on Watts saw her as 'the wreck of an "unfortunate woman" crouching with her tarnished finery against the wall of Waterloo Bridge'.[4] Is her finery decayed? Her bonnet is certainly reduced to a rag, but was it ever really fine? There is in this painting something more generic: it could be so many personal stories, figures that tugged on Watts's conscience. He wrote in a letter:

> Objects of distress that have come upon my observation in the last two or three days have induced me to reflect seriously that I have no right to throw away any means of being useful … I think every poor shivering wretch I meet has a right to revile me for wanting charity … Today I saw a poor woman whose appearance evinced better days, applying for relief at the workhouse (which was refused). £20 would have gone far to set up the poor trembling brokenhearted creature, which £20 I might easily have had in my power to give her; but beast that I am, I hadn't sixpence.[5]

The painting is dramatic and horrific; the only part of the woman's body that is exposed is her face, which is illuminated by the moon, staring

out of a dark recess. It is a symbolic image of the troubled consciousness of the period, a face, hidden by shadow, barely human but recognisable, Watts's 'human refuse'.

The irony and the protest are aimed in part at the failure of religion and the hypocrisy of the church. The figure is huddled under the dry arch of Blackfriars Bridge, the common location of such dramatic views with St Paul's in the background. St Paul's Cathedral, that great symbol of London with its dome that looks down over the metropolis, may be London's unofficial emblem but it is also an icon that represents the merging of church and state. *Under a Dry Arch* does not, however, present the cathedral's bold resplendent outline but a shadowy apparition framed by the arch of Blackfriars Bridge – not the positive affirmative image but an inherent criticism that both church and state have failed the poor and the dispossessed. In *Bleak House* Charles Dickens describes Jo, the crossing sweeper, at Blackfriars Bridge munching on scraps given by a hypocritical clergyman Mr Chadband:

And there he sits, munching and gnawing and looking up at the great Cross on the summit of St Paul's Cathedral, glittering above a red and violet-tinted cloud of smoke. From the boy's face one might suppose that sacred emblem to be, in his eyes, the crowning confusion of the great confused city; so golden, so high up, so far out of his reach.[6]

We also are reminded of Hood's words in his *Bridge of Sighs* (see cat.14):

Alas! for the rarity
Of Christian charity
Under the sun!
Oh! it was pitiful!
Near a whole city full,
Home she had none![7]

Under a Dry Arch was not publicly exhibited until 1881, some thirty years after it was painted. It remained on view at Watts's studio, where it made an impression on many of those who saw it including Miss Isabel Povey, who sent Watts a poem about the painting.[8] MB

1   *The Times*, 23 March 1852, p.5. The article continues: 'During the year 1850–51 … relieved with soup and bread, 54,208 poor persons at the Kitchen.'
2   G.F. Watts, *What a Painting Should Say?*, undated pamphlet in Watts Gallery Archive, p.4.
3   Watts 1912, I, p.126.
4   F.G. Stephens, 'George Frederic Watts', *Portfolio*, 1887, p.18.
5   Undated letter to Miss Georgiana Duff Gordon, quoted in Blunt 1975, p.54.
6   Charles Dickens, *Bleak House*, 1852–3, ch.19, last paragraph.
7   Thomas Hood, *The Poetical Works of Thomas Hood*, London, 1906, p.527, lines 43–8.
8   Letters to and from Miss Povey, Watts Gallery Archive, GFW/2/64 a, c, December 1891.

16. *The Irish Famine, c.*1848–50

Oil on canvas, 180.3 × 198.1 cm (71 × 78 in)
COMWG132

PROVENANCE: collection of the artist (displayed at 30 Charles Street, Old and New Little Holland House); Watts Gallery

EXHIBITIONS: Watts Grosvenor 1881, no.15; *Romantic Art in Britain: Paintings and Drawings 1760–1860*, Detroit Institute of Art and Philadelphia Museum of Art 1968, no.204. *Hard Times*, Manchester City Art Gallery 1987, no.13

LITERATURE: Spielmann 1886, p.30 (dated 1850); Barrington 1905, pp.32, 92; Watts Catalogue, I, p.78; Watts 1912, I, p.126; Macmillan 1903, p.218; Blunt, 1975, pp.47, 55–6, 211, 220; Allen Staley, '"Art is upon the town!", the Grosvenor Gallery Winter Exhibitions', in Susan Casteras and Colleen Denney (eds), *The Grosvenor Gallery: A Palace of Art in Victorian England*, New Haven and London, 1996, pp.72–3; Gould 2004, pp.29, 160 (fig.26)

Watts's radical volte-face from history painter to painter of contemporary social subjects is nowhere better illustrated than in this commission from the wealthy Ionides to paint the subject of Panthea. Instead of illustrating the story from Xenophon, Watts used the canvas to paint an entirely different subject: the horror of the Irish Famine in 1845–9 when the failure of the potato crop several years in succession caused thousands of deaths.[1] Unlike his depictions of London's poverty, Watts's awareness of the Irish Famine did not come directly from experience, as he did not visit Ireland before he completed the painting. His sources were news reports, periodical illustrations and his association with Aubrey de Vere, whose writings on the state of Ireland in this period were hugely influential. Mary Watts writes:

Amongst the congenial friendships begun at this time was one with Mr. Aubrey de Vere, a life-long friendship, for until his visits to London had to be given up, Mr. de Vere came yearly to spend some hours with his friend … Mr. de Vere, in his hours of uncertainty before he decided to join the Church of Rome, had often paced the studio in Charles Street [1849–50] pondering this question. Perhaps with intuition thus quickened he knew that his friend was also passing through a time of crisis.[2]

Aubrey de Vere's important *English Misrule and Irish Misdeeds: Four Letters from Ireland*, published in 1848, and his poem of the following year, 'The Year of Sorrow. – Ireland – 1849', could not have failed to have made an impact on Watts, and a few lines from the poem are echoed in the painting:

In horror of a new despair
His bloodshot eyes the peasant strains,
With hands clenched fast, and lifted hair,
Along the daily darkening plains.[3]

If such texts influenced Watts's choice of subject matter and perspective in his painting of *The Irish Famine*, it was the black and white imagery of magazines that informed the reality of his depiction. During this period magazine illustrations of the Irish consisted largely of two

kinds: humorous in the pages of *Punch* and other satirical magazines; and journalistic in the *Illustrated London News* (cat.16.1) and, more radically so, in the *Pictorial Times*. Watts's paintings railed against the comic stereotype of the former, which de Vere pointedly mentions in his *English Misrule*: 'The genius of many an artist who has amused the public with Irish sketches yet never breathed Irish air, has evidently been guided by such sight aids as a visit to the Zoological Gardens, or a child's book of demonology.'[4] Clearly, these were not the only images of the Irish that proliferated, but equally Watts ignores the influence of the more bucolic and sentimental depictions of the 'sister isle' in favour of the journalism of the illustrated newspaper, imagery that directly showed the impact of the famine on the Irish. The *Pictorial Times* made clear its aims for such illustrations:

All that is loathsome and offensive is softened by the power of distance … Hence our motive was derived for doing what we have accomplished in former numbers of our journal – a motive that still operates in continuing the task. We wished, so far as is possible, to annihilate distance, to bring our readers into contact with the peasantry of the sister isle, and to contribute our part to the urging of appropriate means for the amelioration of their wretched condition.[5]

Such an aim is clearly echoed in *The Irish Famine* and such sources must have informed Watts, for he only visited Aubrey de Vere in Ireland later, in 1850, after the painting was completed. 'Mr. de Vere', Mary writes, 'remembered that when he first visited the studio in Charles Street.'[6] Indeed, when inviting Watts to visit his home,

THE DAY AFTER THE EJECTMENT.

Cat. 16.1 Anonymous, 'The Day After the Ejectment,' wood engraving, *The Illustrated London News*, 16 December 1848, reproduced with the permission of the Guildhall Library, City of London

de Vere wrote: 'You would find much to interest you deeply in Ireland, besides its scenery, including not a little of which you must have had a second-sight vision before you painted your "Irish Eviction" (afterwards called "The Irish Famine").'[7]

As de Vere points out, the painting appears to have changed its title, but it is clear, with the small bundle of possessions noticeable in the foreground, that it is depicting an eviction. The large scale of the work is notable: a grand Panthea scene becomes a brooding Irish landscape with a family of figures huddled together at its centre. The main figure is the father looking defiantly outwards with clenched fists, angry at the powerlessness of his cause. The use of the family group heightens and reveals the full horror of the famine; Allen Staley has compared the family with that in depictions of the Flight into Egypt, a savage irony that reinforces the painting's argument.[8]

If the painting drew on contemporary illustration, its own approach was of course radically different. Here popular illustration has been transformed into High Art, and little wonder that Hogarth has been cited as a possible model.[9] In contrast to journalism, we do not need to know the name of the baby who is grasping towards its exhausted mother for the milk that is not there, nor the family name, for it could be one of many. Nor, too, do we need to know the particular district of Ireland. This is, rather, a poignant symbol of suffering that gives us a more universal dimension. In *The Irish Famine* Watts was struggling to find an appropriate language for expressing his horror and sense of injustice at events in Ireland. As such, it is exceptional to Watts, but also to British art.[10] MB

1   Pentimento is clearly evident in the painting. See Watts 1912, I, p.126; Blunt 1975, p.47.
2   Watts 1912, I, p.108.
3   Aubrey de Vere, 'The Year of Sorrow. – Ireland – 1849', in *The Poetical Works of Aubrey de Vere*, V, London 1897.
4   Aubrey de Vere, *English Misrule and Irish Misdeeds: Four Letters from Ireland Addressed to an English Member of Parliament*, London 1848, p.195.
5   *Pictorial Times*, 1849, p.92.
6   Watts 1912, I, p.113.
7   Watts 1912, I, pp.108–9.
8   Allen Staley in F. Cummings and A. Staley, *Romantic Art in Britain: Paintings and Drawings 1760–1860*, exh. cat., Philadelphia Museum of Art, 1968, p.288.
9   See David Stewart, 'G F Watts: The Social and Religious Themes', PhD Thesis, Boston University, 1988, p.102.
10 The politics of the painting are derived from de Vere, and Watts's sympathy for the Irish remained throughout his life, although expressed in his writing rather than in paint, such as a letter of 1896 to Gladstone in which he spoke of the 'many generations so frightfully unjust to Ireland' (Watts Papers, Watts to Gladstone, 7 May 1896).

The 1850s: Little Holland House, Travel, Murals

For his new friends, Sara (née Pattle) and Thoby Prinsep, Watts interceded with Lady Holland to grant them a twenty-one-year lease on Little Holland House, the dower house on the Holland Estate from December 1850. He also moved into Little Holland House himself as resident artistic luminary, becoming the central attraction of Sara's bohemian salon. The Anglo-Indian Pattle sisterhood, dubbed 'Pattledom', had an impact on his art and life. He fell in love with Virginia, who, however, married into the aristocracy in October 1850. Other sisters, including Julia Margaret Cameron and Sophia Dalrymple and their children, served as models for Watts. Sophia, his special friend, called him 'Signor', a name that alluded to his years in Italy. In 1853 he made a long-awaited, if brief, return visit to Italy, visiting Venice for the first time.

Watts's former studio on Charles Street became the meeting place for the Cosmopolitan Club, a group of writers, politicians and artists. Watts's friend Tom Taylor invited him, as a noted advocate of 'high art', to contribute to a biography of Haydon published in 1853, in which Watts promoted the values of mural painting. He also painted some murals in private homes, including Little Holland House, and had major projects under way at the Houses of Parliament (fig.43) and Lincoln's Inn.

Travel allowed Watts to advance his art in new ways. At the behest of the Hollands, he spent the winter of 1855–6 in Paris painting portraits in a sophisticated continental style. In 1856 classicist and archaeologist Charles Newton invited Watts to join an expedition to Asia Minor to excavate the site of ancient Halicarnassus. Back at Little Holland House from 1857 onwards, Watts enjoyed a cosseted lifestyle with the Prinseps, whose salon now included Ruskin, Tennyson and the young Pre-Raphaelites. He continued to build his reputation outside the Royal Academy, channelling his ambitions into murals and portraits, which he now pursued as more 'elaborate performances'.   BB

*Self-Portrait ('The Venetian Senator'), c.*1853, oil on canvas, 154.9 × 74.9 cm (61 × 29 ½ in), private collection

17. *Sophia Dalrymple, c.*1851

Oil on canvas, 198 × 78.7 cm (78 × 31 in)
Inscribed lower left 'G F Watts'
COMWG200

PROVENANCE: collection of the artist (Little Holland House Gallery); given by Watts to Sophia's daughter, Virginia Champneys, in the 1890s; by descent to Sophia's grandson, Sir Weldon Darymple-Champneys; his gift to the Watts Gallery, 1981

EXHIBITIONS: *Japan British Exhibition*, London, 1910, no.72; *Artists at Home: The Holland Park Circle, 1850–1900*, Leighton House Museum, London, 1999, no.13; Watts Portraits 2004, no.22

LITERATURE: Watts Catalogue, II, p.44; Blunt 1975, pp.81–2; Bryant 2004, pp.82–3

Cat. 17.1   Frederick Hollyer, photograph of *Sophia Dalrymple and Sara Prinsep, c.*1850–1, Hollyer Album, Watts Gallery Archive, original painting (damaged), oil on canvas, 231.1 × 144.8 cm (91 × 57 in), COMWG137

In its stark simplicity and restrained beauty this portrait is one of Watts's most remarkable images and it has justly become famous in his *oeuvre*. Though a feature of the artist's private collection in his various residences, it only came to wider notice in recent decades once it arrived at the Watts Gallery.

Sophia Dalrymple (1829–1911), one of the beautiful Pattle sisters (see also cats 23, 26), is shown here in her early twenties. While her husband, John Warrender Dalrymple (1824–88),[1] was in India in the Bengal civil service, she lived mainly in London with her sister Sara Prinsep, first in Mayfair and then at Little Holland House. For Watts she became a special friend, the one with whom he was most in sympathy, and it seems fitting that she dubbed him 'Signor' and he in turn called her 'Sorella'. She modelled regularly for him, posing for a series of silver-point drawings that allowed the artist to study drapery folds based on his ideal of Greek antique sculpture.

This portrait of Sophia is also an essay in a classicising style. It belongs to a group of works executed in the years around 1850 when Watts was consciously treating both portraits and subject paintings (cats 13–16) in a newly monumentalised manner based on the frescoes he had seen in Italy. Broad masses and flat colouring, along with thin paint applied rapidly, derived directly from the techniques of fresco painting. This was a radical departure for portraits, and when he sent the first such work in this style, showing Sophia's sister Virginia Pattle, to the Royal Academy in 1850 (Eastnor Castle Collection), it confounded critics and observers.[2] Yet for Watts that particular work proved to be a labour of love, a painting in the grand manner that had no commission, carried out because he

found Virginia to be a living example of the classical style. Grandly tall, she wore robe-like dresses and confined her hair in a net leaving her head in a simple outline. To a later observer she was like 'the Elgin Marbles with dark eyes'.[3]

Watts's attraction to Virginia in 1849 prompted his introduction to the extended Anglo-Indian families of the Pattles and Prinseps. The sisters, raised in France and India, had a unique style. With their robe-like dresses, hair in nets and exotic Indian jewellery, they did not look at all like their English counterparts. With Virginia's marriage in October 1850, Sophia and Sara took centre stage in his life, and in 1851 they moved into the dower house on Holland House estate in Kensington. Unlike the bossy Sara, chatelaine of Little Holland House, Sophia cut a different figure, 'a lovely vision',[4] who brought laughter to the frequent gatherings staged at her sister's salon.

Following the portrait of Virginia, Watts executed two other full-lengths showing sisters Sophia and Sara: cat.17.1, also at the Watts Gallery, and cat.17. The two paintings are related. It was always clear that Sophia's portrait had been something of an unfinished experiment with a section cut and replaced by two narrow pieces of canvas along the right side. But recent conservation has revealed a label explaining that cat.17 was originally a double portrait with Sara. It was exactly like cat.17.1 but with changes in clothing and background.[5] The figure of Sara must have been cut out and removed.

The double portrait (cat.17.1) hung at Little Holland House by June 1853,[6] and probably by this time the other work was also complete. The question of precedence arises but it seems likely that the extant double portrait of the sisters came first. The distinctive quatrefoil balustrade of the balcony of Holland House forms the backdrop.[7] The heavy robes draping the two sisters create a strongly sculptural effect reminiscent of Roman sculpture. Sophia, in a green dress, is partially swathed in a lengthy, golden paisley shawl whose bulky folds are held in front of her figure.[8] Sara wears a red dress, over a white under-gown, with a blue cape. Richly coloured figures sit against the paler, more fresco-like background, but while a powerful image, it is not completely resolved.[9]

One can see that Watts may well have
decided to attempt the double portrait afresh,
keeping the arrangement of the figures. Sophia
is dressed very differently but her pose is similar,
exactly so on the right, especially the positioning
of the hand. The background has changed to a
simple balustrade allowing the figure to lean
back. Essentially, the new idea for Watts this
time was to impose a more classicising approach
to the colouring. The stark whiteness of Sophia's
dress is more in harmony with the fresco-like
handling of the paint. The folds take on the
character of drapery in Greek sculpture. The
horizon line is raised with a landscape of rolling
hills of parkland giving way to a range of bluish
hills. Its positioning directs attention to Sophia's
face and enhances the mood of the portrait, representing a development of the idea as a whole.
We do not know why he cut down the painting
removing Sara, but it may well be because
Sophia proved to be the more compelling personality, as well as the more successfully realised
figure within the painting.[10]

Certainly, in presenting Sophia, Watts suc-
cumbed to her individual allure. Although not
as 'classically' beautiful as Virginia, Sophia had
distinctive looks, with thickly curly reddish-
brown hair and down-turned eyes, the so-called
'Pattle eyes'.[11] Sophia's gaze is steady and haunting. Her Anglo-Indian background is signalled
by unusual jewellery and the Hindu *rakhi*,[12]
symbolic of the love between siblings, tied
around her right wrist. The subcontinent
formed part of her mystique. Other artists, such
as Dante Gabriel Rossetti and Edward Burne-
Jones, also fell for her charms late in the 1850s,
when they entered the circle at Little Holland
House. Widely seen by an array of society figures as well as artists, the portrait of Sophia as a
depiction of a full-length woman in white garb
was an important precedent for Whistler's *White
Girl* (National Gallery of Art, Washington) of
1860 and forecast Aesthetic trends.

Sophia remained close to Watts. Photographs
show them relaxing together at Little Holland
House and she featured in other paintings by
him. But her role as a friend is illuminated most
powerfully as one of the few witnesses to his marriage to Ellen Terry in 1864. He kept cat.17 as a
personal memento until the 1890s, when he presented it to her daughter (cat.42). BB

1   He inherited the Dalrymple baronetcy in 1887, so she did not become Lady Dalrymple until then.

2   Bryant 2004, no.21.

3   Letter of 3–4 April 1859 from Ruskin to Margaret Bell, quoted in Van Akin Burd, ed., *The Winnington Letters*, London, 1967, p.150.

4   Watts 1912, I, pp.156–7, records the comments of a member of the family recalling Sophia.

5   A lone figure in blue can be glimpsed between the balustrades, a suggestion of the larger composition.

6   Twisleton 1928, p.97. In her diary Ellen Twisleton refers to visits to Little Holland House, where she saw 'a portrait of her [Sara] and her beautiful sister Mrs. Dalrymple', which was 'a living and breathing likeness of her … it was the whole figure'.

7   See Bryant 2004, p.83, regarding the location and also a contemporary photograph of Watts and Sophia.

8   It may also be that the bulky folds in of Sophia's dress disguise a pregnancy. Watts might have begun the portrait while working on *Virginia Pattle*, completed for the Royal Academy of 1850. Sophia was pregnant during the first half of 1850 before the birth of a daughter in June. Her second known pregnancy, during late 1853, before the birth of her son Walter in January 1854, post-dates the painting.

9   Sketchley 1904, p.48, notes that it is unfinished; Watts Catalogue, II, p.127.

10 There is a record of yet another, now unlocated, full length of Sara, this one in profile, in the Watts Catalogue, II, p.126 (without illustration).

11 Sir Weldon Dalrymple-Champneys, *The Chevalier de L'Etang and his Descendants*, privately printed, 1972, p.8.

12 The *rakhi* is a bond of protection, or holy thread, tied around the wrist by siblings. William Dalrymple, Sophia's descendant, refers to her wearing the *rakhi*, in *White Mughals: Love and Betrayal in Eighteenth Century India*, London, 2002, p.xlv.

18. Study for *The Triumph of the Red Cross Knight*, c.1851–2

Oil on canvas, 58.5 × 41 cm (23 × 16¼ in)
COMWG20A

PROVENANCE: collection of the artist; given by Watts to Sophia Dalrymple; then given by Sophia to her daughter Virginia Dalrymple Champneys; Sir Francis Champneys in 1910; by descent to Sir Weldon Dalrymple-Champneys; his gift to the Watts Gallery, 1981

LITERATURE (on the fresco): Spielmann 1886, p.32; Cartwright 1896, p.6; Watts Catalogue, I, p.138; Watts 1912, I, pp.133–4, 143; Loshak 1954, pp.47–8

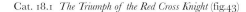

Cat. 18.1 *The Triumph of the Red Cross Knight* (fig.43)

This oil study relates to Watts's fresco executed for the Royal Fine Arts Commission in the Upper Waiting Hall of the House of Lords at the new Palace of Westminster (cat.18.1). By 1852 he was at work on *The Triumph of the Red Cross Knight*, also known as *St George Overcoming the Dragon*, a scene from Edmund Spenser's *Faerie Queene* (1590, 1596). The decorative scheme of the hall contained eight upright panels by various artists showing scenes from the work of native poets. Given the subject matter, this area was called 'the Poets' Hall'. Painted in the medium of fresco, which was totally unsuited to the English climate, these works suffered almost from the outset and were boarded up for much of the twentieth century. A complete conservation programme in the 1980s means that they are now all on view as intended.[1]

Committed after his return from Italy to the idea of mural paintings in public places, Watts welcomed this commission to illustrate Spenser's great poem. John Ruskin, who had become a friend of Watts around this time, considered Spenser the 'poet of beauty'.[2] The Red Cross Knight, later revealed to be St George, had an allegorical role as the Anglican Church. He protects the beautiful virgin Una, herself emblematic of truth and the one true religion. Book I recounts his trials, culminating in a ferocious three-day fight with the dragon. Towards the end of canto XI the knight slays the dragon by running his sword right through his mouth. Then, as Spenser writes,

> So down he fell, and forth his life did
>   breathe,
> That vanished into smoke and clouds swift;
> So down he fell, that the earth him
>   underneath
> Did groan, as feeble so great load to lift …
> So down he fell, and like an heaped
>   mountain lay.

The initial idea for the composition showed the knight with his horse at the centre and contained more figures.[3] He wrote at the time: 'I fear it may be thought too crowded; but I would venture to defend this as being characteristic of the poem.'[4] In preparation for the fresco, which was intended for a narrow compartment, Watts reduced and simplified the design to show the main figures of the Red Cross Knight and Una with fewer subsidiary people: a youth and a mother holding a baby and restraining a toddler. In the distance are the lesser characters of the tale. The heroic figure of the knight stands triumphant, gazing heavenwards, his foot placed on the dead dragon with its gaping mouth. Later Watts drew on the *Faerie Queene* for another painting with the same characters, the opening scene of book I, 'Una and the Red Cross Knight'.

This oil study from the Watts Gallery shows a distinctive handling of paint. The artist parted with it fairly early on, and so it remains without later additions as a good example of his style in the early 1850s. The thin, liquidy medium, applied over a white ground, gives the effect of fresco painting with its blanched colours. There is a notable classicising impulse at work here in the figures of the knight and youth and in the handling of Una's draperies. Rather than choose an episode depicting the bloody battle of the knight and his foe, Watts paints this scene of tranquillity, which relies on the classically stable form of a pyramidal composition.

A visitor to Little Holland House in June 1853 noticed among other works in the artist's studio 'a picture of St. George and the Princess'. Since by this time the fresco was *in situ*, she must be referring to one of the works related to it, possibly this one. She goes on to say, regarding Sara Prinsep's care of Watts, that 'as a reward, [he] paints nothing but idealised figures and faces of herself, and her sisters, and their children'.[5] As we look closer at the model for Una, and recall that the artist gave it to Sophia, it also seems likely that one of the attractive members of the extended Prinsep clan might have modelled, adding a personal dimension to this modest painting. BB

1   Malcolm A.C. Hay, 'The Westminster Frescoes: the restoration of the Victorian murals,' *Apollo*, CXXV (1992), pp.307–10.
2   Noted by Macmillan 1904, p.175.
3   It is known by a drawing in an outline style; another work in the Watts Gallery (COMWG20) gives some idea of it, although much of the handling is later.
4   Watts 1912, I, p.134.
5   Twisleton 1928, p.106.

19. *Geraldine Mildmay*, 1855–6

Oil on canvas, 55.9 × 45.7 cm (22 × 18 in)
COMWG65

PROVENANCE: collection of the artist (Little
Holland House Gallery); part of the original
Memorial Collection, 1905

EXHIBITIONS: on loan to the Tate Gallery from
1921 to *c*.1924

LITERATURE: Watts Catalogue, II, p.107; Watts
Gallery Catalogue 1920, no.37; Short 1924, p.145;
Alston 1929, no.97

This little-known portrait always had a place at
the Little Holland House Gallery during Watts's
lifetime and it formed part of the original
bequest to the Watts Gallery,[1] but it has never
been discussed in the literature. Interestingly, the
trustees did lend it to the Tate Gallery in 1921,
along with other works by the artist. Always
identified as resulting from the artist's trip to
Paris, it documents an experimental phase in his
portraiture in the 1850s, at a time when he was
re-evaluating this genre.[2] But first one must look
at the milieu in Paris where Watts painted it.

During the winter of 1855–6 Watts travelled
to Paris with an invitation to visit the Hollands
who resided there for part of each year.[3] He
executed several notable portraits of their
friends, including Prince Jérôme Bonaparte and
Princess Lieven (both private collection),[4] his
most sustained exercises in French formal
portraiture in the neoclassical tradition. The
foremost practitioner of this mode was J.-A.-D.
Ingres (1780–1867), who had just had a career
retrospective as part of the recent Exposition
Universelle, an event that Watts certainly knew
about even if he did not attend it himself. In
adopting the three-quarter-length format associated with Ingres, which allowed a grander treatment of the figure and setting, Watts extended
his portraiture to new levels of accomplish-
ment.This close-up study of a head, in its
restrained simplicity, lacks the grandeur of
Watts's French portraits but gains in intimacy.
One can see in the thinly applied oil paint and
close observation that this work is allied to the
portraits painted for the Hollands. One can even
imagine that such a work proved to be a relax-
ation for the artist after painting the elderly
luminaries of the French political scene. While
in Paris, Watts might also have considered other
major portraitists, such as Ary Scheffer
(1795–1858), with whose work his own shares a
linear purity.

The sitter has always been referred to as
'Miss Mildmay'. Geraldine Mary St John-
Mildmay (1832/3–1912) is here aged about
twenty-three, yet she appears to be younger. She
and her mother, through family connections
with the Barings, belonged to the literary and
intellectual 'Ashburton set'.[5] With her aristocratic and military links (her father, George
St John-Mildmay, a captain in the Royal Navy,

had died in 1851), Geraldine enjoyed the lifestyle
of an upper-class woman,[6] attending country-
house parties at the splendid seat of the
Ashburtons, the Grange in Hampshire, where at
the salon of the literary hostess, Harriet
Ashburton, she came into contact with the writers Thomas and Jane Carlyle, Henry Taylor and
Tennyson. A particular friend of the Carlyles,
Geraldine visited them in London.

Why Geraldine Mildmay was in Paris, we do
not know; perhaps to attend the Exposition
Universelle, an event that attracted Queen
Victoria and her entourage. She might have had
an introduction to Watts through their mutual
friend Henry Taylor. Although her background
explains how she and Watts crossed paths, it
does not tell about the motives he had for painting the portrait. Almost certainly not a commission, as he retained it in its unfinished state, this
is clearly one of the first of his studies of youthful female beauty.

Painted thinly on a fine-weave canvas, the
blue-green background sets off the profile of the
sitter. Her maroon frock is incomplete, but the
head is finished with extreme delicacy, especially
in the tiny strokes of the brush that suggest the
upturned roll of hair. The simplicity of the
image conveys a mood of quiet contemplation.
Watts later elaborated on the idea of mood in
portraiture in a series of studies of young
women, but this rare example shows his thinking
at an early stage. He valued it and retained it,
perhaps as much for its stylistic purity as for the
sitter herself. This portrait (in a plain frame
with a gold slip) can be seen in one of the
interior views of the Little Holland House
Gallery, propped up in the foreground of the
photograph.[7]   BB

1   It begins to appear in the catalogues of the
    gallery in 1920.
2   Bryant 2004, pp.17–18.
3   Ilchester 1937, pp.412–13.
4   Bryant 2004, nos 26, 27.
5   Twisleton 1928, p.271, in a diary entry of 1855.
6   Geraldine Mildmay married Alfred Buckley in
    1858, two years after this portrait was painted.
7   Illustrated in von Schleinitz 1904, p.15.

20. *In Asia Minor*, 1856–7

Oil on canvas, 20.3 × 58.4 cm (8 × 23 in)
COMWG174

PROVENANCE: collection of the artist (Little Holland House Gallery); Mary Watts; on view at the Watts Gallery by 1920; Lilian Mackintosh (Mrs Michael Chapman), legal descendant of the artist; given by her to the Watts Gallery in 1946

EXHIBITIONS: Memorial Exhibitions, London 1905, no.139, Manchester 1905, no.5, Newcastle 1905, no.66, 'Asia Minor', Edinburgh 1905, no.98; Jubilee Exhibition, The Alpine Club, 1907; on loan to the Tate Gallery from 1921 to *c*.1924; Watts London and Compton 2006, no.8

LITERATURE: Sketchley 1903, p.121; Watts Catalogue, I, p.10; Watts Gallery Catalogue 1920, no.16; Short 1924, p.145; Alston 1929, no.105; Blunt 1975, p.94; Staley and Underwood 2006, p.33

Watts had always planned to travel to Greece to make direct contact with the world of Pheidias. He had learned much about antique art from his classicist friend Charles Newton (1816–94), a former assistant in the British Museum's Department of Antiquities and sometime consular official. In 1856 Newton assumed the leadership of a government-sponsored expedition on behalf of the British Museum, with a grant of £2000 to excavate antique remains at Bodrum, on the Aegean coast of Turkey, famed as the site of the ancient city of Halicarnassus. Newton invited Watts to join, not in any official capacity but as an interested individual,[1] although in fact the artist did provide some valuable testimonials to what he had observed on site.[2]

Watts travelled out on the warship HMS *Gorgon*, along with the crew of royal engineers and sappers, arriving in early November 1856. Although Bodrum was the base of operations, for much of the time the artists were boat-bound; on board, entertainment included the usually serious Watts singing sea ditties. Newton charged him with travelling to Constantinople in order to obtain a 'firman', the necessary document to allow the removal of the sculptures to Britain. On this side trip Watts met Admiral Lord Lyons, commander-in-chief of British forces in the Mediterranean, on whose ship he

then sailed around the Greek islands, taking the opportunity to paint his portrait (National Portrait Gallery; see also cat.21). Watts returned to Bodrum with the firman. Newton had uncovered the remains of Halicarnassus, including antique sculptures that still bore their original colour. Watts himself watched these works coming out of the ground and saw the colour fade on contact with air, an episode that made a vivid impression and fuelled his imagination long after he departed in June 1857 (see cat.48).

This remarkable sojourn in Asia Minor over the winter of 1856–7 provided so many new visual sensations that Watts turned to landscape in oil and watercolour to create both aide-memoires and independent works of art.[3] Travel often prompted him to turn to landscape; one visitor to his studio observed that he 'filled his portfolios with precious memories of foreign lands'.[4] Macmillan noted that Watts joined the expedition 'to become better acquainted with ancient Greek art and modern Greek landscape'.[5] The scenery he observed while on various boat trips impressed him.[6] One of two similar works (cat.20.1), the long horizontal format of *In Asia Minor* imparts a sense of the expanse of the coast continuing beyond the edges of the canvas. The sunset view of a harbour framed by mountains is saturated with

Cat. 20.1   *In Asia Minor*, 1857, oil on canvas, 30.5 × 61 cm (12 × 24 in), COMWG85

colour, ranging from a milky yellow-orange to red, the warm light softening the distant rocky forms. Rising blue-grey clouds echo the shapes of the mountain range. No doubt executed on the spot, this oil study captures the fleeting effects of light, not least in the reflection of the colour in the glassy sea. Though not a major statement, this Mediterranean view is a subtle treatment of the elemental convergence of sky, land and sea. For Watts such landscape studies provided the raw materials for his imagination.

BB

1 Also included in the invitation, probably to give Watts some further companionship, were two young artist friends, Valentine Prinsep (1838–1904), son of Sara and Thoby Prinsep (cat.41) and John Roddam Spencer Stanhope (1829–1908), whom Watts had informally taught some years before.

2 Charles Newton, *Travels and Discoveries in the Levant,* London, 1865, II, p.272.

3 One watercolour, formerly in an album, bears the inscription 'on board the Gorgon'.

4 Cartwright 1896, p.17.

5 Macmillan 1903, pp.28–30.

6 Although Mary Watts records that this view was painted from the site of Halicarnassus, it was clearly done while on a boat looking back towards the coast; see Watts 1912, I, pp.163–7 for an account of the trip.

21. *Admiral Lord Lyons*, 1856

Oil on canvas, 121.9 × 99.1 cm (48 × 39 in)
COMWG170

PROVENANCE: collection of the artist (Little Holland House Gallery by 1896); Lilian Mackintosh (Mrs Michael Chapman), legal descendant of the artist; given by her to the Watts Gallery in 1946 (no.25)

LITERATURE: Spielmann 1886, p.31 (National Portrait Gallery version); Macmillan 1903, p.39; Barrington 1905, pp.27–8; Watts Catalogue, II, p.100; Watts 1912, I, p.164; Bryant 2004, p.23; Gould 2004, p.47

Watts painted two portraits of Admiral Edmund Lyons in 1856, shortly after the end of the Crimean War in which Lyons had emerged a hero. The completed head-and-shoulders portrait entered the National Portrait Gallery in 1883. The other, this three-quarter-length painting and the more ambitious of the two, remains unfinished.

First Baron Lyons (1790–1858) was one of the leading naval heroes of his age and one whom Watts desired to paint. His opportunity came during his trip to Bodrum to visit the ancient site of Halicarnassus with the archaeologist Charles Newton (1816–94). Mrs Barrington recalled that Watts 'and Sir Charles Newton travelled to Greece together. They went *via* Constantinople.'[1] While there, Watts and Newton dined with Lyons at the British Embassy in the winter of 1856 and became guests of Lyons's flagship, *The Royal Albert*, where Watts painted this portrait. Mary expressed disappointment that it was never completed:

> Most regrettably this three quarter length portrait painted on the Flagship Royal Albert remains unfinished at Limnerslease. It lay for years forgotten, a covering of brown paper having been stretched over the face of it. Lord Lyons sent Mr. Watts for a cruise among the Greek islands, saying playfully 'I put you in command.' To this cruise we owe his two conceptions of 'the genius of Greek Poetry' and other works of imaginative beauty.[2]

Watts never forgot his time on the flagship and he delighted in the 'wonderful blueness of the waters seen through the port-holes at night, and often spoke of one night as more splendid than all others when he was dining on board *The Royal Albert*'.[3]

In the three-quarter-length version Watts was able to give posture to the figure and also began to add details of the flags and ensigns on the left. The backdrop of *The Royal Albert*, the formal character of Lyons's stance, and his stern and determined expression strongly express the role of a military hero like Lord Nelson. The admiral's biographer observed that 'Lyons, with his white hair and slight physique, always fancied that he resembled Nelson, and consciously attempted to model his conduct accordingly'.[4]

Although incomplete, the painting is an accomplished portrait in which the character, strength and aggression of Lyons are acutely apparent. Due to its being unfinished, the painting was never publicly exhibited during Watts's lifetime. However, 'a fine pen and ink drawing made for this portrait, is in the Watts collection at Compton' and was exhibited as part of the 1905–6 Memorial Exhibitions.[5] The Watts Gallery now holds only a small pencil drawing of the painting, drawn on the back of a seascape watercolour and part of the Brinsley Ford collection (COMWG2007.624a).   MB

1   Barrington 1905, pp.27–8.
2   Watts Catalogue, II, p.100.
3   Watts 1912, I, p.164.
4   Andrew Lambert, 'Lyons, Edmund, first Baron Lyons (1790–1858)', *New Dictionary of National Biography* (http://www.oxforddnb.com/view/article/17288, accessed 25 Feb. 2008).
5   Watts Catalogue, II, p.100. Exhibited as no.112 at the Memorial Exhibition, London in 1905, catalogued as a pen and ink drawing, 7 × 6¼ in, and dated 1850.

22. *Georgina Treherne, c.1857*

Oil on canvas, 50.8 × 69.9 × cm (20 × 27½ in)
COMWGNC19

PROVENANCE: collection of the artist; Mary Watts; Lilian Mackintosh (Mrs Michael Chapman), legal descendant of the artist; by descent; Sotheby's, London, 1 July 2004, no.297; acquired for the Watts Gallery with the support of the Art Fund

EXHIBITIONS: Watts London 1954, no.19; Watts Aldeburgh 1961, no.25

LITERATURE: Watts Catalogue, II, p.161; Blunt 1975, pp.84–5; *Quarterly: The Magazine of the National Art Collections Fund*, winter 2004, p.24

In the 1850s the handsome women in the Pattle and Prinsep household who surrounded Watts became a feature of his art, not usually as pure portraits but more often as studies of youthful beauty. This unusual image, a double view of the sitter, reflects the artist's fascination with this theme.

Georgina Treherne (1837–1914) had a remarkable life, the subject of several books,[1] but here her activities in the mid-1850s are of interest. After an upbringing in Florence and elsewhere on the continent, her family returned to London in 1856. Her father Morgan Thomas was a barrister and member of the Welsh landed gentry, who changed his name to Treherne in the year of their return, seemingly in an effort at social aggrandisement and with a view to his daughter's presentation at Queen Victoria's court. Georgina, fluent in French and Italian, had an excellent soprano voice, which gained her entry to society musical soirées such as those staged at Little Holland House. Her introduction there probably took place in 1857.[2] Her vivacity attracted many admirers, Watts included. She immediately became familiar with him; he called her his 'Bambina mia', writing: 'The Bambina's vivacity was pleasant to the dull Signor, who was affected by the exhilarating contagion … I miss the effervescing stimulant that was sparkling and overflowing all about the house … Yet I was always in a fidget about the wild little girl.' [3]

Georgina's appeal resided in a strong personality and physical presence. Not a conventional beauty, she was plump and of medium height; she had a curving lower lip, full neckline and slightly dimpled chin. Watts also painted a more formal portrait of her, wearing a dramatically fashionable, black broad-brimmed hat, turning her head coquettishly.[4] Her taste for unusual earrings is noticeable in both portraits. It is also proposed that Georgina is the subject of cat.25.

This double-head study reflects Georgina's nature, as on one side she sings softly and on the other she lies asleep,[5] and she is seen on two different occasions. In the first, while singing, she wears a low-cut evening dress with elaborate hair ornament, looking as she did when performing at Little Holland House. The other view shows a daytime frock and seems to reflect Georgina after one of her bouts of excitability, having fallen asleep. This study with its loose handling and lack of high finish conveys the exuberant personality it depicts.

Georgina's tangled love life caused consternation to all around her. She had attracted a well-born young man, Merthyr Guest, son of Lady Charlotte Schreiber, another habitué of the Little Holland House circle, who had introduced Georgina at court. But while in Brighton in early 1858, she fell for a handsome soldier, Harry Weldon. Torn between two different men, she sought advice. Watts wrote:

> I want you to be very wise in the choice of a husband … if you are fortunate in this respect, you will be as you ought to be, an ornament and a delight to society; if the contrary, I dread more than I can say for the poor little bambina. I do not think you could be happy as the wife of a poor man.[6]

By mid-1858 Georgina was expelled from the inner circle at Little Holland House.[7] She had carelessly used Watts's studio when it was vacant to meet with another suitor, Lord Ward. Her understanding, if not engagement, with Merthyr Guest came to an end, and in April 1860 she married Harry Weldon. At this time, Georgina purchased the portrait of herself in the black hat at a reduced rate; however, Watts kept this oil study for himself. It does not seem to have featured at his gallery and was a more personal memento of the young Bambina. As an early example of a 'musical portrait', it forecast later aspects of Watts's more innovative portraits (see cat.31).   BB

1   Her running of an orphanage, affair with the composer Gounod, near commitment to a lunatic asylum, and litigiousness are described in Grierson 1959, and Thompson 2000. Further biographical information is in John Martin, 'Weldon, Georgina (1837–1914)', *Oxford Dictionary of National Biography* (http://www.oxforddnb.com/view/article/53148, accessed 13 Feb. 2008), which is especially useful on her later life, but does not refer to any of Watts's portraits of her.
2   Grierson 1959, p.18, notes that in July she had met Lady Holland.
3   Grierson 1959, p.19.
4   Watts London 1954, no.23; Grierson 1959, frontispiece (copy of the original portrait, said to date from 1857); Thompson 2000, front cover.
5   A label on the back of the painting suggests that she is singing a lullaby to herself, but it is not clear who wrote the label, which is certainly not in Watts's handwriting.
6   Quoted in Grierson 1959, p.19.
7   When writing to Watts after her marriage, she criticised Sara Prinsep; see Blunt 1975, p.85.

23. *Study of Maria Jackson*, early to mid-1850s

Pencil on white paper, 13 × 7.9 cm (5¼ × 7 in)
Inscribed (in another hand) 'Mrs Jackson'
COMWG2007.690

PROVENANCE: collection of the artist; Mary Watts; Lilian Mackintosh (Mrs Michael Chapman), legal descendant of the artist; by descent until formally included within the Watts Gallery collection

Reputedly born at sea on a passage to or from her family's home in Calcutta, Maria ('Mia') Pattle (1818–92) married a physician, John Jackson (1804–87), in the employ of the East India Company who was dedicated to his work in the subcontinent. Due to poor health Maria lived much of the time in England with their three young daughters, Adeline (1837–81), Mary (1841–1916) and Julia (1846–95). One of the celebrated Pattle sisterhood, Maria belonged to the extended family at Little Holland House. Among the seven female siblings, Julia Margaret Cameron and Sara Prinsep were her elders, while Louisa, Virginia and Sophia (cat.17) were younger. Although their father was a minor nabob in the Bengal civil service, they had grown up in France, informally educated while living with their grandmother near Versailles. The sisters were distinctive in their unconventional dress sense, unusual interests and ability to speak Hindustani. Maria is perhaps less well known than the others (and is now more famous as the grandmother of Virginia Woolf), but she too was a noted beauty.

Living at Little Holland House, the sisters and their children all served as part of Watts's adopted family and he drew them regularly throughout the 1850s.[1] A formal portrait drawing of Maria appeared at the Royal Academy in 1850, the same year as his full-length oil of her younger sister Virginia,[2] so he knew her right from the beginning. She and Watts, both in their early thirties, were exact contemporaries. More frequently she and the other sisters appear in informal sketches executed in the course of their everyday activities. Watts carried his sketchbook to be ready and when 'his eye fell on a particularly beautiful arrangement in posture or line',[3] he called for them to wait for a moment. They were more than just his models, being family friends, and his affection towards them is often evident. In this drawing Maria sits with pen in hand, writing or sketching. Quickly yet carefully sketched in pencil, with minimal means, the three-quarter-length seated figure creates a satisfying composition on the sheet. As in his noted portrait drawing of Virginia (Watts Gallery),[4] Watts studied the sequence of folds in the dress, as well as the sitter herself. Her perfectly even features bear out his later recollection that 'the structure of her face was so fine that the beauty of line only increased with age'.[5] Family tradition held that Maria was ascetic, tender-hearted and spiritual,[6] qualities one can almost identify in her calm and restrained downward gaze. BB

1   A similar drawing of Sara Prinsep is illustrated in Watts 1912, III, following p. 78; see also Watts Whitechapel 1974, no.58.
2   Bryant 2004, no.21.
3   Watts 1912, I, p.157.
4   For an illustration and discussion, see Bryant 2004, no.19.
5   Watts 1912, I, pp.129–30.
6   Elizabeth French Boyd, *Bloomsbury Heritage*, London, 1976, pp.27–8.

24. *A Knight and a Lady*
Study for *Edward III and Philippa*,
mid- to late 1850s

Pencil, pen and ink on white paper, 35.2 × 21.3 cm
(14 × 9 in)
Inscribed upper left 'Alice is a naughty girl' and
lower right (in another hand) 'Study for Edward
III and Philippa / Knight study never painted / 6'
COMWG2007.699

PROVENANCE: collection of the artist; Mary Watts;
Lilian Mackintosh (Mrs Michael Chapman), legal
descendant of the artist; by descent until formally
included within the Watts Gallery's collections

Part of an album of drawings by Watts made in
his lifetime,[1] this sheet is now separate. The
identification of the subject, based on the
inscription on the drawing itself and from the
original album, seems reliable, although it is
certainly unusual in the artist's *oeuvre* both in its
subject matter and style. The inscription in the
album notes that this was a study for an etching.
A related oil on panel, probably dating from
c.1860, follows the composition with slight differences.[2] The chivalric theme focusing on the
fourteenth-century King Edward III (1312–77)
and his wife Philippa of Hainault (d.1369)
reflects the medieval subject matter favoured by
Watts's younger, up-and-coming contemporaries, the Pre-Raphaelites, who frequently visited Little Holland House, and this connection
suggests a date in the mid- to late 1850s.[3]

This drawing shows real historical individuals in an imagined episode. Edward III, victor of

Crécy, prepares to leave for battle as his queen,
Philippa, reaches up to embrace him; in the
more slightly sketched area, they clasp hands.
His reserved demeanour suggests regal stoicism
during this private moment. Watts's scene of
farewell between lovers inevitably recalls
Millais's *A Huguenot on St Bartholomew's Day*
(Makins Collection), an immense success at the
Royal Academy in 1852; also relevant is Ford
Madox Brown's *Chaucer at the Court of Edward III*
(RA 1851; version, Tate Britain).[4] But Watts's
drawing is in a minor key and more intimate in
scale and mood. Better known for chalk portraits
drawings in the 1850s, he rarely used pen in such
a highly worked fashion. This drawing imitates
an etching with its closely hatched, sharp
pen-and-ink lines, and, if the album inscription
is correct, it was intended to be executed as an
engraving, perhaps in emulation of the Pre-
Raphaelites. The style suggests that of Dante
Gabriel Rossetti and the other Pre-Raphaelites,
particularly the drawings they produced for the
engravings in the famous illustrated edition of
Tennyson's poems published by Moxon in 1857.
That same year Watts met the poet at Little
Holland House and soon after painted *Sir
Galahad* (RA 1862; Fogg Art Museum). The
image of the thoughtful knight in armour is one
he adopted in his own self-portraits (see fig.34),[5]
but whether this drawing shows a self-portrait is
open to question.   BB

1   The volume contains a list of removed items in
    which the title *Edward III and Philippa* appears.
2   This oil on panel, formerly at the Watts Gallery
    but not included in the Watts Catalogue, is illus-
    trated in Loshak 1963, p.488, ill.18. He calls it
    simply *Knight and Maiden* and seems unaware of
    the related drawing. One should probably treat
    with caution his suggestion that the image is a
    self-portrait of Watts with Ellen Terry.
3   The casually noted inscription in the upper left,
    'Alice is a naughty girl', might well refer to Sara
    Prinsep's daughter Alice (1844–1919), who
    frequented the artist's studio in Little Holland
    House and might, given the tone of the inscrip-
    tion, be an older child aged between eight (in
    1852) and twelve (in 1856).
4   In the 1780s–90s Benjamin West painted a series
    in the Audience Chamber at Windsor Castle fea-
    turing Edward III and Philippa but these heroic
    representations are counter to Watts's more
    intimate view of the characters.
5   Another example is the later *Eve of Peace* (begun
    1863; Dunedin Public Art Gallery), p.32, fig.18.

25. *Georgina Treherne, c.*1857

Chalk on wove paper, 61 × 50.8 cm (24 × 22¾ in)
COMWG310

PROVENANCE: collection of the artist; Mary Watts;
Lilian Mackintosh (Mrs Michael Chapman), legal
descendant of the artist; by descent until formally
included within the Watts Gallery's collections

LITERATURE: Ann Thwaite, *Emily Tennyson: The
Poet's Wife*, London, 1996, p.614 and pl.11

This beautiful work is an example of Watts's portrait drawings of the 1850s at its very best. He specialised in large-scale chalk studies of heads from *c.*1850 to about 1857.[1] This particular drawing has gained a certain amount of fame as an unusually flattering portrait of Emily Tennyson (1813–96) aged in her mid-forties,[2] but that identification seems improbable.[3] Watts met the Tennysons in 1857 and comparisons with images of Emily at that time show that it could not be her. The drawings that are known (and inscribed) from around this date, at the Fogg Art Museum, for example, show an older woman, with a bonier nose, sunken cheeks and an expression of worn resignation. Here we see a plump young woman no older than her twenties. So the question becomes who is she?

Fortunately, it is now possible to propose a more likely identification of the sitter as Georgina Treherne (1837–1914), the young woman who burst on the scene at Little Holland House in 1857 and who is also the subject of the double oil portrait (cat.22) now in the Watts Gallery. She has the same blue eyes (pale in the drawing),[4] fullness of face, slightly rounded protruding chin, small mouth and taste for exotic earrings. Not only did the drawing lose its identity over the years, but also the full size of the large sheet was masked by a smaller mount. Nevertheless, it is an important record of a type of drawing that Watts had a great reputation for in the 1850s.

Georgina was a notorious coquette, and this image may well be the first of the three portraits Watts carried out of the woman he called his 'Carissima Bambina'. He seems not yet to have grasped her personality and indeed shows her gazing upward in rapt contemplation and calmness, quite unlike her usual frenetic temperament. In fact, it seems to be this drawing that Watts's friend John Ruskin commented on when he wrote in 1873:

> You yourself were paralysed for years by
> your love of the Greek style – you never
> made an entirely honest, complete, unaf-
> fected study of anything. You drew […] for
> instance, trying to make an angel of her –
> She was not an angel, by any means. The
> soft chalk translation of her did you deadly
> mischief at every touch – in the deliberate
> falsification.[5]

Ruskin disapproved of such drawings in chalks but most of Watts's contemporaries considered them very highly. In the early 1850s he exhibited several such portraits, which one reviewer described as 'masterpieces of drawing – they have the mingled softness and strength of drawings by the old masters'.[6] The impressive scale of this portrait of Georgina and the melting softness of the chalk show mastery of the medium, in which the subtly executed shading conveys a wide range of tonal values. The artist famously refused to add shoulders to many of his head studies, which rendered them ineligible for the Academy's annual exhibition, but which allowed complete focus on the head and face, always for Watts the essence of any portrait. This one, which he kept as a private work of art for his own collection, can now at last have its identity restored.   BB

1   See Bryant 2004, no.23, for a discussion of simi-
    lar portrait drawings of Austen Henry Layard
    (National Portrait Gallery).
2   John Carey, review of *Emily Tennyson: The
    Poet's Wife*, in the *Sunday Times Book Review*,
    22 September 1996, p.6 (fig. in reverse)
3   Ann Thwaite, *Emily Tennyson: The Poet's Wife*,
    London, 1996, p.614. In this excellent biography
    the author credits Richard Jefferies of the Watts
    Gallery as 'identifying beyond all reasonable
    doubt a previously unknown portrait'. But this
    identification seems highly unlikely. There are
    some inscriptions, such as 'Lady Emily
    Tennyson', on the lower edge and back of the
    drawing, but these are recent and a new exami-
    nation of the research means that it is now
    possible to identify this portrait. I should also like
    to correct my reference, following Thwaite, to
    this drawing as a portrait of Emily in Bryant
    2004, p.127.
4   Grierson 1959, p.12.
5   Ruskin to Watts, 13 February 1873, partly quoted
    in Blunt 1975, p.63, without naming Georgina as
    the subject; a typescript copy of the letter is in
    the Bodleian Library (Eng. Lett.c.50, ff.195–6).
6   *The Times*, 7 May 1851, p.8.

The 1860s

The 1860s proved to be a decade of change for Watts: he came into the public eye, received universally good critical notices and set an example for the rising younger generation of artists in the circle of Dante Gabriel Rossetti. Patronage improved with an introduction through Tom Taylor to Charles Hilditch Rickards, a philanthropist from Manchester. The artist's finances were now on a better footing and he could paint to sell without commissions. He also devoted more time to sculpture both as an aid to composing and in its own right.

Watts cultivated a distinctive line in portraits and decorative studies of women in a new poetic spirit. His friend, dramatist and critic Tom Taylor, introduced two young actresses to Little Holland House, Kate Terry (1844–1924) and her younger sister Ellen (1847–1928). Enamoured of Ellen's looks and considering her potential as a stimulus to his art, Watts planned initially to adopt her, but then decided to marry her, even though he was considerably older. Still very young and impressionable, Ellen noted in her memoirs that 'the stage seemed a poor place when compared with the wonderful studio'. They married on 20 February 1864 around the time of both of their birthdays, with Watts turning forty-seven and Ellen believing she was about to turn sixteen, but in fact nearly seventeen. A series of remarkable paintings displayed her inherent dramatic abilities. The ill-fated marriage broke down in less than a year, and after a legal separation instigated by Watts, Ellen was sent back to her parents. Her impact on his art lasted longer, as he returned to unfinished paintings of her for years after (cat.30).

At this point, aged in his mid-forties and with imperfect health, Watts decided not to pursue mural projects (which had occupied him continuously in the 1850s) and instead directed his attention to what he came to call 'symbolical' works, in essence 'poems painted on canvas'. His distinctive persona is conveyed in Julia Margaret Cameron's photograph, *The Whisper of the Muse* (fig.45). Still outside the bounds of the Royal Academy, he was elected an Associate when its rules changed in 1867, and later that year a full Academician, a uniquely rapid elevation. BB

The Whisper of the Muse (detail, fig.45)

26. *Countess Somers*, 1860–89

Oil on panel, 121.9 × 89 cm (51 × 35 in)
COMWG71

PROVENANCE: collection of the artist (Little Holland House Gallery); given to Watts Gallery by Mary Seton Watts in 1908 in exchange for another painting from the original core collection of 109 works from 1905

EXHIBITIONS: *Jahresausstellung*, Munich, 1893, no.1650; Watts New Gallery 1896, no.103; Stockholm 1897; *Internationale Kunstausstellung*, Dresden, 1901, no.742; Society of Portrait Painters 1902; Watts Leighton House 1903, no.2 (as 'Portrait of the Countess Somers early manner on panel'); Memorial Exhibitions, London 1905, no.183, Edinburgh 1905, no.71, Manchester 1905, no.126, Newcastle 1905, no.39, Dublin 1906, no.20

LITERATURE: Spielmann 1886, p.32 (1850 version); Watts Catalogue, II, p.145; Watts 1912, I, pp.122–3, 126, 158, 174, 235; Alston 1929, no.31

Watts first saw Virginia Pattle (1826–1910) in 1849 near his Charles Street studio. She was living around the corner in Chesterfield Street with her sister Sara and Sara's husband Henry Thoby Prinsep (1792–1878). An introduction was made and Watts joined a family and circle of acquaintances with whom he was to remain intimately connected for some time. Virginia was renowned for her beauty and charisma, described by a friend as 'one of those happy beings in whose presence is a pleasure, whose simplicity, grace, and beauty capture all beholders'.[1] Watts fell in love with her and painted several portraits around this time.[2] When she married on 2 October 1850, Sir Charles Newton recalled that Watts was 'deeply grieved by the thought that Lady Somers had married; we thought she ought not to marry any *one*'.[3] Ironically, it was reputedly Watts's 1849–50 portrait of her that led her future husband to marry her.[4]

There are a number of portraits of Virginia Pattle and, as she subsequently became, Countess Somers. She recalled later: 'I was never dazzled by another painter's brush … all other brushes were like boot-brushes to me.'[5] Her obituary in 1910 noted: 'Watts's pictures have preserved the charm of her presence, and great beauty such as hers is a gift to the world. Whatever may be said, beauty does not pass away.'[6] This painting was begun around 1860 but not completed until around 1889.[7] Depicting Virginia with a peacock feather in her left hand seated against a tapestry background, it displays the beauty of the Pattles, 'the deep lids drooping over the beautiful eyes'.[8] A photograph exists of the painting before 1889 (cat.26.1) and it is evident that the right-hand sleeve has been radically altered from Renaissance style to more conventional dress.[9] It was only 'sketched in monochrome, and so left', giving a very different impression of the work.[10]

Watts uses thin layers of paint on the panel for the background, the running of the paint clearly visible. Thicker layers of complimentary paint and lighter colouring build up the detail giving it a rich luminosity. Alston refers to it as 'the most important example in this Gallery [Watts Gallery] of the painter's method when using transparent colour and copal varnish … it is remarkable for its fine glowing colour'.[11] The painting was admired by Roger Fry, who thought it one of the great examples of British portraiture. Fry even lectured at the gallery in 1909, and the impressionist swirls of the floral tapestry backdrop and the heavy eyelids and languid pose cannot escape parallels with later Bloomsbury painting.[12] In comparison with his earlier portraits of Countess Somers, she has retained her beauty but lost the innocent look with which Watts initially imbued her. Painted shortly after the death from diphtheria of her youngest daughter Virginia in 1859 at the age of three, it shows a more careworn expression. MB

Cat. 26.1 Frederick Hollyer, photograph of *Countess Somers* (taken at an early stage of completion before 1889), Hollyer Album, Watts Gallery Archive

1   *The Times*, 4 October 1910.
2   See Bryant 2004, pp.76–81.
3   Sir Charles Newton quoted in Watts 1912, I, p.126.
4   See Bryant 2004, p.80.
5   Watts 1912, I, p.122.
6   Obituary of Countess Somers, *The Times*, 3 October 1910, p.13.
7   'Lady Somers sat for this portrait painted on panel about the year 1860, but the sleeve on the right arm, the lower section of the picture, or rather some part of the shirt, and parts of the background remained for many years unfinished. These parts in 1889 were completed by the artist, but he never touched either head or hands save only one small injury to the lower lip, where the colour had blistered from the ground. The statement that the picture was then repainted, is untrue.' Watts Catalogue, II, p.145.
8   Watts 1912, I, p.123.
9   When it was exhibited at the Society of Portrait Painters in 1902, *The Times* wrote: 'the best things – Mr. Watts's pictures, for example – date from a quite distant period. The portrait of "Countess Somers", a picture celebrated long ago, represents the sitter in the costume of the sixties' (13 November 1902, p.15).
10 Watts 1912, I, p.123.
11 Alston 1929, no.31.
12 Fry believed that Watts's portraits of Joachim, Garibaldi and the Countess Somers 'take rank with the finest achievements of English art for all times'. According to Charles H. Thompson, Curator's Report, 1915, the occasion was a 'party of scholars of the Adult Schools connected with the Society of Friends, whose Summer Tour chose Guildford for its centre in 1909, when Mr Fry gave a short address on the work of G.F. Watts'.

27. *Dr Demetrius-Alexander Zambaco,* 1861

Oil on panel, 50.8 × 40.6 cm (20 × 16 in)
Inscribed 'G F Watts London 1861'
COMWGNC20

PROVENANCE: probably commissioned by Euphrosyne Ionides Cassavetti; the sitter; his son Demetrius Francois Zambaco; by descent; … Christie's, South Kensington, 26 April 1988, no.15; bought by the Watts Gallery

LITERATURE: Watts Catalogue, II, p.175; Eileen Cassavetti, 'The Fatal Meeting, The Fruitful Passion', *The Antique Collector*, LX (1989), pp.34–5

Unknown until relatively recently, this portrait records the likeness of a man mainly famous for the fact that his wife Maria left him, later becoming the mistress of the artist Edward Burne-Jones. Demetrius Zambaco (1832–1913) married Maria Terpsithea (Theresa) Cassavetti (1843–1914), a granddaughter of Constantine Ionides and niece of Alexander Constantine Ionides (see cat.4). Her mother Euphrosyne, known as 'the Duchess', married a wealthy merchant Demetrius John Cassavetti. With Watts's status as painter to the Anglo-Greek community, he painted both the parents and Maria as a child in an appealing study of her aged four in Turkish dress standing on a grand sofa, as well as another portrait of her aged eighteen about the time of her marriage (now unlocated; see cat.27.1).[1] But the death of her father in 1858 when Maria was fifteen, made her heiress to a huge fortune of some £80,000 and a desirable catch for a suitor. Strong-willed and independent,

Cat. 27.1 Frederick Hollyer, photograph of *Maria Zambaco*, Hollyer Album, Watts Gallery Archive

she married out of her own circles in London to Zambaco, a Constantinople-born member of the Greek community in Paris and therefore an unknown quantity to her family. Rumours flew around, including one that she 'attached by mere obstinacy to a Greek of low birth in Paris'.[2] But Zambaco was well educated: he had submitted his thesis to the École de Médecine in Paris in 1857 and then specialised in sexually transmitted diseases.[3]

The portraits of Zambaco and Maria, on the same scale and of about the same date, function as a pair.[4] It seems likely that Maria's mother commissioned Watts to depict the young couple in 1861, the year of their marriage, as she knew that her daughter would be moving to Paris. Alternatively, she might have commissioned the portraits as a wedding present. Either way, Watts was fulfilling an unusual request for his friend: to paint her daughter and the man she was about to marry with only the reluctant consent of the family. Watts cannot have known Zambaco well. In the portrait we see a handsome man staring straight ahead, perhaps defensively against the painter's inquisitive gaze, with his arms folded. The sitter's high collar and tight black bow tie also lend a severity to the image and keep his personality under wraps. If this portrait was intended to commemorate Zambaco's union with the extended Ionides and Cassavetti families, it is a curiously sombre image.

In Paris the Zambacos lived comfortably in an apartment off the Champs Élysées.[5] Maria gave birth to a son Demetrius Francois in May 1862, the year her husband published a study of syphilis. She must have travelled back and forth to London since Watts painted her infant son in about 1863/4, a child he claimed was one of the most beautiful he had ever seen.[6] Three years later, in September 1865, a daughter Mary was born, but shortly after this Maria absconded back to London, taking refuge at her mother's residence. Thanks to the terms of the family trust and marriage settlement, she retained her dowry. Zambaco refused to grant her a divorce. In addition to the humiliation of her departure, he must also have been angered that she removed the children to London.

Maria returned to London aged twenty-three, a transformed woman, now dramatically gorgeous, with 'glorious red hair and almost phosphorescent white skin'.[7] She befriended the bohemian artists whom her cousins Alecco and Luke knew, such as Burne-Jones, Rossetti and James McNeill Whistler (1834–1903). As one of the 'three Graces', Greek beauties, who included her cousins Marie and Christina Spartali, she was sought out by artists as a model and many portrayals of her survive, especially in the work of Burne-Jones. She studied art herself, later achieving success as a sculptor and medallist. Maria's affair with Burne-Jones and her attempted suicide scandalised the London art world, but that is another story.[8]

Demetrius Zambaco is an interesting example of Watts's panel portraits of the late 1850s and early 1860s. This support allowed greater detail and precision in handling, with colour built up by the use of glazes, as can be seen in the deep blood-red background of this painting. The hot colouring contrasts with the black of the clothing and pale skin tones, almost suggesting simmering passions kept at bay by the cool-headed doctor. This painting has an added fascination in showing the man Maria Zambaco abandoned. One might ask why she did so: was it his interest in the more unusual avenues of medicine?[9] But of course the portrait itself cannot tell us. BB

1 Watts Catalogue, II, p.32. One unsubstantiated claim is that Maria's family destroyed her portrait when she had her very public affair with Burne-Jones, but this is unlikely. Her own mother introduced her to Burne-Jones and may even have encouraged the liaison, according to Cassavetti 1989, p.35.
2 A comment by George du Maurier quoted in Philip Attwood, 'Maria Zambaco: Femme Fatale of the Pre-Raphaelites', *Apollo*, CXIV, 1986, p.31.
3 Cassavetti 1989, p.35, notes that he was the protégé of France's leading specialist in venereal diseases.
4 It would be interesting to know if the now unlocated portrait of Maria was similarly signed and dated, and on panel.
5 Cassavetti 1989, p.35.
6 He refused to sell the study of Demetrius; it served as the source for *Ganymede* (a copy of which he painted for Maria Zambaco; Watts Catalogue, I, p.62) and *The Childhood of Jupiter* (Watts Catalogue, I, p.27).
7 According to Alexander C. Ionides, junior, *Ion: A Grandfather's Tale* (*Notes and Index*), privately printed, Dublin, 1927, p.28.
8 Discussed in Penelope Fitzgerald, *Edward Burne-Jones: A Biography*, London, 1975, pp.112–15.
9 He continued such work with published studies on disorders of a psycho-sexual nature including his infamous, 'Onanisme avec troubles nerveux' (1882). Eminent in French medical circles, he later worked in Constantinople where he founded a hospital for lepers and worked for the Sultan who dubbed him Zambaco-Pacha.

28. *Mary Bartley, Known as 'Long Mary'*, mid-1860s

Oil on panel, 53.3 × 66 cm (21 × 26 in)
COMWG180

PROVENANCE: collection of the artist (Little
Holland House Gallery); Mary Watts; Lilian
Mackintosh (Mrs Michael Chapman), legal
descendant of the artist; given by her to the Watts
Gallery in 1946

LITERATURE (on the sitter): Watts Catalogue, I,
p.53; Watts 1912, II, pp.44–5; Watts London 1954,
p.52 (nos 140–1)

This double-head study is an informal portrait
of Watts's favourite model Mary Bartley, affec-
tionately known as 'Long Mary', due to her statuesque proportions. Depicted from two different
angles on the same panel, Mary's features come
to life as Watts portrays her in both a frontal
view and a three-quarter study. The artist kept
this work in his own studio collection and, as far
as is known, it has never been exhibited other
than at the Watts Gallery.

The present work is a detailed study of the
sitter's face with scant attention to dress or background detail. This double-portrait format can
also be seen in the study of *Georgina Treherne*
(cat.22), a society beauty associated with Little
Holland House circle, and a double portrait of
Watts's second wife Mary (cat.64), painted
during their honeymoon in 1887 on one canvas.
Watts kept these informal, uncommissioned portraits as working studies and did not intend them
for exhibition.

Mary Bartley, the daughter of a gardener,
worked at Little Holland House as a housemaid
to the Prinseps.[1] Watts obtained Sara Prinsep's
permission to ask Mary to model, as he was
struck by her beautiful proportions, and eventually he persuaded her to pose in the nude. Mary
Watts wrote about Long Mary in her husband's
biography in the context of Watts's nude painting practices:

> It has been said that Signor never made use
> of the model, but this was not the case. To
> the end of his life he occasionally made use
> of one. In earlier years a large number of
> studies were made from a model whom he
> always called 'Long Mary', who sat to him,
> and to him only, from the early 'sixties and
> onwards for several years. He told me he
> never made use of her, or any other model,
> when painting a picture. He said, 'I don't
> want individual fact in my pictures where I
> represent an abstract idea. I want the general
> truth of nature' … When painting, Signor
> referred to these studies made in charcoal on
> brown paper from this most splendid model
> – noble in form and in the simplicity and
> innocence of her nature – a model of whom
> he often said that, in the flexibility of move-
> ment as well as in the magnificence of line,
> in his experience she had no equal.[2]

Many nude studies on brown paper show Mary.[3] She sat for oil paintings as well, including *A Fair Saxon* (cat.28.1), *Rhodopis* (*c*.1865; Watts Gallery) and *Daphne* (RA 1870; unlocated). Studies of her influenced *The Judgement of Paris* (1874; Faringdon Collection, Buscot Park), the Eve trilogy (1868–1903; Tate), *Dawn* (1875–80; private collection) and *Olympus on Ida* (1885; private collection),[4] as well as *Psyche* (1880; Tate). Watts is known to have worked from other models for pictures such as *Arcadia* (cat.58)[5] and *Thetis* (cat.47),[6] but Long Mary certainly provided the artist with the greatest inspiration. Her statuesque proportions and facial features appeared in a series of Watts's subject pictures and sculptures from the 1860s until the end of his life, with the original nude drawings produced at the Little Holland House studio showing her 'flexibility of movement' being used as reference for future works.

In the 1860s, at the same time as using Long Mary as a model, Watts began to treat the nude in painting and sculpture. She may also have posed for *Clytie* (cat.32), along with other models such as the professional Italian, Angelo Colorossi, and a little baby.[7] Long Mary probably served as reference for the Clytie's ample bosom and provided the classical features for her face. It is possible that this study of Long Mary, showing the model's face from two distinct angles, might have been painted to record the oval of her head, as a visual aid for future sculptural works. This approach would have been familiar to Watts through Anthony Van Dyck's portrait *Charles I, King of England from Three Angles* (1636; Windsor Castle), produced as reference for a sculptural bust. But it was essentially Long Mary's impressive stature and powerful physique that lent strength and power to such full-length nude sculptures as the first version of *Dawn* (also known as *Aurora*).[8]

As a non-professional model, Long Mary was by no means in a minority in the Victorian art world. Amateur models often rose to professional status, once approved by the artists for whom they sat. Some models used by the Pre-Raphaelites were 'discoveries' including Fanny Cornforth, a former domestic cook, who sat for Rossetti.[9] As Watts's 'discovery', Mary Bartley had an impact on the course of his work in the 1860s and after. JD

1   Watts Catalogue, I, p.53, the entry for the *Fair Saxon*, for which Mary modelled. She also notes that Mary Bartley 'married from Little Holland House, but died not long after'.
2   Watts 1912, II, p.44.
3   Watts London 1954, no.141; others are in the Watts Gallery and elsewhere.
4   Watts 1912, II, p.45.
5   Watts Catalogue, I, p.5, says that he had a professional model pose.
6   Watts Catalogue, I, p.144, in which Mary records re *Thetis*: 'A study of the nude made in charcoal, in form different from more heroic lines of Long Mary, has the name, probably of the model, as "Miss Smith".'
7   Watts 1912, II, p.45; Angelo Colorossi also sat for Frederic Leighton, Julia Margaret Cameron, John Singer Sargent and Jean-Léon Gérôme.
8   Watts 1912, II, p.45.
9   Smith 1996, p.30.

Cat. 28.1 *A Fair Saxon*, 1868–70, oil on canvas, 66 × 53.3 cm (26 x 21 in), COMWG91

29. *The Building of the Ark*, 1862–3

Oil on canvas, 94 × 74 cm (37 × 29 in)
COMWG111

PROVENANCE: collection of the artist (Little Holland House Gallery); Watts Gallery

EXHIBITIONS: Whitechapel Art Gallery 1901, no.311; Watts Gallery 1904, no.48

LITERATURE: Cartwright 1896, pp.13, 15; Macmillan 1903, p.151; Watts Catalogue, I, p.18; Gould 2004, pp.62, 340

Versed in the Bible from a very young age, Watts 'remembered every detail of the Old Testament stories'[1] and drew on them for many of his paintings. In particular, the book of Genesis with its accounts of the creation and great flood appealed to his imagination and contributed to the content of his great scheme, a cycle of paintings that later became known as 'The House of Life' (see cats 33, 45). The Hebrew prophets, too, served as important subjects for Watts, who found parallels in them with his own ambition as an artist, an aspiration that 'art may speak … with the solemn and majestic ring in which the Hebrew prophet spoke to the Jews of old, demanding noble aspirations, condemning … prevalent vices'.[2]

When in 1862 he was asked by the Dalziel brothers to produce designs for an illustrated Bible, his response was mixed, as letters between him and the publishers testify.[3] I do not want to submit 'mere costume painting',[4] he wrote, but 'consider myself at liberty to depart from mere correctness if necessary for my purpose'.[5] In the discussions of details he further emphasised that it would in no way be a tame illustration: 'My object is not to represent the phrenological characteristics of a mechanical genius, but the might and style of the inspired Patriarch.'[6] In 1863 Watts finally submitted three works: *The Meeting of Jacob and Esau*, *The Sacrifice of Noah* and *The Building of the Ark* (all Watts Gallery).

The illustrations for the Bible were sought from the leading artists of the day including Millais, Leighton, Poynter and Holman Hunt. The project was never completed but over sixty Old Testament illustrations were finally published

Cat. 29.1 *The Building of the Ark* from *Dalziel's Bible Gallery*, 1880, wood engraving after G.F. Watts

Cat. 29.2 G.F. Watts in his Limerslease studio showing *The Building of the Ark* on display, Watts Gallery Archive

in 1881 as *Dalziel's Bible Gallery*. In its review of the book *The Times* considered Watts's work as the most successful:

> Mr. Watts's designs strike us more than any with the sense of beauty and impressiveness of an ideal style, in which symmetrical, pictorial composition brings the subject before us without loss of probability and with sufficient expression in face and attitude, the solemnity and intensity of the whole being well sustained. The 'Noah Building the Ark' and 'Noah's Sacrifice' are remarkable for the fine conception of the principle figure, the expression of the heads, and the general grouping of the subordinate figures.[7]

The Watts Gallery collection has three compositional drawings of the subject (COMWG2007.626, cat.29.3 and COMWG2007.258b), which show that, although there are differences with the surrounding figures, the vision of Noah remains consistent. Noah stands in the centre of the painting holding huge planks of wood for the construction of the ark, which diagonally divides the composition. On the right-hand side Noah's family prepare for the deluge, while on the left only the windswept Noah stands firm, acting as protector, patriarch and visionary against the 'darkening ... clouds, all prophetic of the doom that is hanging over the world'.[8] The wind-blown locks of the beard are reminiscent of Michelangelo, where Noah is perceived as more akin to Moses, whom Watts originally wished to illustrate.

Mary recalled Watts retelling Old Testament stories and how 'just by an accent here and there he would throw new and original comment upon them, quite his own'.[9] Similarly, in his painting he emphasises Noah as a prophet, a point appreciated by a reviewer who wrote:

> In these designs beauty is not sacrificed to characteristic features either in the persons or the motive of the picture, as it is too often in modern works. It is in these great subjects of religious art that we feel especially that the more the painter is impelled by an abstract ideal of his own, the nearer he comes to that which is presented to the mind of those who are not artists, but simply the recipients of thoughts and feelings called up by the revered traditions of ages.[10]

Although very seldom exhibited, *The Building of the Ark* had its first public airing at the opening exhibition of the Whitechapel Art Gallery in 1901 and was met with general praise, including from Roger Fry who wrote: 'outside all fashions and periods ... It is one of his best works.'[11] MB

1   Watts 1912, I, p.17.
2   G.F. Watts quoted by Stead in *Review of Reviews*, June 1902 (Watts Gallery Archive).
3   The Dalziel brothers were the wood engravers, George Dalziel, head of the firm (1815–1902), Edward Dalziel (1817–1905) and Thomas Bolton Gilchrist Septimus Dalziel (1823–1906).
4   British Library, MS 39168, f.52.
5   G.F. Watts quoted in George Dalziel, *The Brothers Dalziel: A Record of Fifty Years' Work*, London 1901, p.246.
6   British Library, MS 39168, f.52.
7   *The Times*, 28 December 1880, p.9.
8   Macmillan 1903, p.151.
9   Watts 1912, I, p.17.
10   *The Times*, 28 December 1880, p.9.
11   Roger Fry quoted in Gould 2004, p.340.

Cat. 29.3 Sketch for *The Building of the Ark*, *c.*1862, ink and pencil on envelope, 18.5 × 13 cm (7½ × 5¼ in), COMWG2007.264

30. *Ophelia*, 1863–4, *c.*1877–80

Oil on canvas, 76.2 × 63.5 cm (30 × 25 in)
COMWG89

PROVENANCE: collection of the artist (Little
Holland House Gallery); part of the original
Memorial Collection, 1905

EXHIBITIONS: Annual Exhibition, Grosvenor
Gallery, 1878, no.59; Royal Institution, Manchester,
1878; Watts London 1881, no.102; St Jude's,
Whitechapel, London, 1884, no.153; Watts
Birmingham 1885, no.131; Watts Nottingham 1885,
no.41; Art Museum, Rugby School, Rugby, 1888;
Guildhall, London, 1892, no.14; Jahresausstellung,
Munich, 1893, no.1641; Society of Artists,
Sheffield, 1894; Watts New Gallery 1896, no.20;
Autumn Exhibition, Liverpool, 1902, no.1011;
Southport 1902; Watts Gallery 1904, no.19;
Memorial Exhibitions, London 1905, no.140,
Manchester 1905, no.182, Newcastle, 1905, no.10,
Edinburgh 1905, no.108, Dublin, 1906, no.3;
*Whisper of the Muse: The World of Julia Margaret
Cameron*, P. & D. Colnaghi & Co., London, 1990,
no.80; *Shakespeare in Western Art*, Isetan Museum of
Art, Tokyo (and other venues), organised by
Takamatsu City Museum of Art, the Shikoku
Shimbun, 1992–3, no.73; Watts Compton 2004,
no.47

LITERATURE: Spielmann 1886, p.31; Watts Gallery
Catalogue 1904, no.19; Barrington 1905, pp.33,
35–6; Watts Catalogue, I, p.110; Sketchley 1912,
pp.150–1; Watts 1912, I, p.328; Alston 1929, no.108;
Loshak 1963, p.485

Watts's painting shows Ellen Terry in the character of Ophelia from Shakespeare's *Hamlet*. She
approaches her watery grave, a moment detailed
in the quotation from Act IV, scene vii:

> There is a willow grows aslant a brook
> That shows his hoar leaves in the glassy
>   stream.
> Therewith fantastic garlands did she make . . .[1]

The artist began this work in the few years
around the time of his short-lived marriage in
1864 to the young actress, Alice Ellen Terry,
and then abandoned it at the time of their
separation.

Almost certainly part of Watts's intention in
marrying Ellen, apart from natural affection and
a desire to protect her, was so that he could
acquire a striking and exclusive model who
would do his bidding.[2] And indeed, as a stage
actress, she moved and presented herself in a
genuinely energetic fashion, a quality apparent
from the photographs taken of Ellen by Julia
Margaret Cameron in 1864. As her friend, the
artist Graham Robertson, later wrote, 'she was
par excellence the Painter's Actress and appealed to
the eye before the ear; her gesture and pose were
eloquence itself'.[3] Her input into Watts's portrayals cannot be ignored. But in 1864 she had
not yet played the role of Ophelia, although it is
telling that her sister Kate did so in a noted
production by Charles Fechter at the Lyceum in
May 1864. This was just a few months after the
marriage of Ellen and Watts, and it is certain
that he knew of and could easily have seen this
play starring his sister-in-law. The event may
well have sparked Watts's interest in the subject,
although he 'recasts' Ellen in the role.

Shakespeare's Ophelia had provided British
artists with rich subject matter since the
eighteenth century, mainly as an opportunity to
depict the effects of mental distraction and mad-
ness in an attractive female sitter. Many of these
depictions are straightforward scenes from the
play itself; others dwell on Ophelia herself in
isolation as she dies, a referred to, but not

enacted, moment in the play. Just over ten years
before, during the early days of the Pre-
Raphaelite Brotherhood, John Everett Millais
painted *Ophelia* (RA 1852, Tate Britain), a work
that has attained iconic status. For Watts the
Shakespearean source provided the framework
for what became a study of the interior mind of
Ophelia in a far more disturbing scene than
Millais's decorous drowning.

Watts's Ophelia lies on an outcrop of rock
gazing downwards to the river below. The entire
scene is claustrophobically enclosed by dark
undergrowth and the long tendrils of the willow
referred to in Act IV. Handled loosely and
broadly, the work has the feel of a study. At one
stage it was left unfinished; even with the additional painting, it has an immediacy and power
that would not be found with more meticulous
execution. Murky in colour, predominantly
brown, only the golden hair of Ophelia and her
pale mauve-coloured cape relieve the scheme.
The elongation of her arm and hand echo the
extended willow branches, which themselves
threaten to pull her downwards. Ellen brought
an expressive inevitability to the pose, as
Ophelia gazes open-mouthed at the beckoning
water, seemingly in a trance. The shadow on her
face portends the death to come.

The painting remained unfinished until the
late 1870s. With the break-up of the marriage,
Watts apparently destroyed many paintings that
Ellen had modelled for and hid others away,
including this one, in his studio. It was only to
emerge some fifteen years later. According to
Mrs Barrington,

> one evening, when the large studio was
> lighted with but one candle, which Watts
> held and shaded by his hand as he threw the
> light on to the 'Ophelia' which he had taken
> out from a heap of old canvasses to show me,
> I saw this picture for the first time. … I sup-
> posed Watts thought there might be some-
> thing in it, or he would not have cared to
> show it.[4]

At this point, the artist reworked the painting, with Barrington lamenting he ever retouched it.

Watts sent the work to the second Grosvenor Gallery exhibition in 1878, where it attracted the notice of Tom Taylor in *The Times*: 'His ideal head of Ophelia, in little more than monochrome, is pathetically beautiful.' It went on to Manchester and then to the major retrospective of Watts's work at the Grosvenor several years later, when Cosmo Monkhouse wrote in the *Magazine of Art* that Ophelia, 'craning over the dark stream, mind and body burnt out with the fierce pale flame that still flickers in her wan cheeks and wild eyes, is very finely conceived'.[5] Its poetic qualities came to the fore; in an era of literal Shakespearean productions and paintings this deeply emotive view of Ophelia provided a counterbalance. Indeed, it was only at the very end of 1878 that Ellen, by now officially returned to the stage, first performed the role of Ophelia in her inaugural appearance with Henry Irving at the Lyceum Theatre.

Barrington, who was a good friend of Ellen's, noted that 'it was not Shakespeare, but his sitter's creation of the part that lent the picture its exquisitely tender pathos'. The actress's golden hair is distinctive as are certain facial features, especially the strong line of the chin. Other writers, such as Graham Robertson and Ellen Terry's biographer in the *Dictionary of National Biography* (1930), also describe *Ophelia* as one of the works she sat for. Yet it is not a portrait as such and is essentially Ellen reimagined.

Watts and Ellen were formally divorced in 1877 and it may well be relevant that, once their relationship was finally resolved, he felt freer to take up a work she had inspired. This is one of his most important portrayals of his young muse and a rare survival, since reputedly he destroyed many of his paintings of her and only a handful remain. Retained by Watts[6] and much exhibited during his lifetime and immediately after, it is the only major depiction of Ellen at the Watts Gallery and has always stood out as one of the jewels of the collection. BB

1   The painting was only exhibited with this quotation in the Memorial Exhibition of 1905.
2   See Bryant 2004, nos 43–6, for other depictions of Ellen Terry by Watts.
3   Graham Robertson, *Time Was: The Reminiscenses of W. Graham Robertson*, London, 1931, p.54.
4   Barrington 1905, p.36.
5   *The Times*, 2 May 1878, p.7; *Magazine of Art*, 1882, p.180.
6   He refused all offers to sell it (Watts Papers, letters to James Smith in 1893 and 1894), saying it and several others 'must be kept to lend'.

MISS ELLEN TERRY AS "JULIET"

WINDOW & GROVE   63ª BAKER STREET, W.
Photographers to   the Royal Family.

Cat. 30.1 Window & Grove, *Ellen Terry as Juliet*, 1882, photograph, 16.5 × 11 cm (6½ × 4¼ in), Watts Gallery Archive, The Rob Dickins Collection

31. *A Lamplight Study: Herr Joachim,* 1867

Oil on canvas, 91.4 × 66.6 cm (36 × 26¼ in)
COMWG34

PROVENANCE: collection of the artist; Little Holland House Gallery; part of the original Memorial Collection, 1905

EXHIBITIONS: Royal Academy 1867, no.619; International Exhibition, London, 1871, no.394; Exposition Universelle, Beaux Arts, Ecole Anglaise, Paris, 1878, no.271; Watts Grosvenor 1881, no.10; Watts New York 1884, no.88; Watts Birmingham 1885, no.124; Watts Nottingham 1886, no.52; *Internationale Kunst-Ausstellung,* Berlin, 1891; Watts Wolverhampton 1894; Watts New Gallery 1896, no.14; *Exhibition of Dramatic and Musical Art,* Grafton Gallery, 1897; Society of Portrait Painters, London, 1902, no.24; Watts Leighton House 1903, no.13; St Louis 1904; Watts Gallery 1904, no.51; Memorial Exhibitions, London 1905, no.27, Manchester 1905, no.65, Newcastle 1905, no.108, Edinburgh 1905, no.72, Dublin 1906, no.19; *Exposition Rétrospective de Peinture Anglaise,* Musée Moderne, Brussels, 1929, no.193; *Exhibition of British Art,* Royal Academy of Arts, London, 1934, no.498; *The First Hundred Years of the Royal Academy 1769–1868,* Royal Academy of Arts, London, 1951–2, no.351; Watts Aldeburgh 1961, no.9; Watts Compton 2004, no.43

LITERATURE: Spielmann 1886, pp.20, 30; Cartwright 1896, p.24; Sketchley 1903, pp.62–4; Macmillan 1903, pp.86–8; Watts Gallery Catalogue 1904, no.51; Barrington 1905, pp.36, 92, 202; Spielmann 1905, p.39; Watts Catalogue, II, p.82; Watts 1912, I, pp.201–2; *Letters from and to Joseph Joachim,* selected and translated by Nora Bickley, London, 1914, pp.256–7; Alston 1929, no.39; Bryant 2004, pp.32, 33 (fig.19)

From the time of its first showing in 1867 this portrait became one of Watts's most highly regarded works. Sent to exhibitions far and wide during his lifetime, including Paris in 1878, he refused to sell it, as it was essential to his personal collection. The portrait depicts the great musician, Joseph Joachim (1831–1907), standing before a piano as he plays his violin. As a youthful prodigy, dubbed the 'Hungarian boy' because of his birthplace, Joachim had a stellar career.[1] He had a position in Hanover until the late 1860s, but his international reputation as a performer took him to all the great European cities, and by the 1860s he regularly spent several months of the season in London with his 'Popular' concerts.[2] His growing celebrity gained him access to the circle of Sara Prinsep at Little Holland House. Still relatively young, in his mid-thirties, at the time he is portrayed, Joachim looks somewhat older in the painting with his soft jowly face and lugubrious expression. The thick wavy hair can be seen in contemporary photographs (cat.31.1), including several (1868) by Julia Margaret Cameron, for whom he modelled swathed in velvet shortly after Watts's portrait.

Watts's own love of music dated from his childhood growing up with a father who made pianofortes (and who seems to have named him after Handel). The artist himself often said he 'ought to have been a musician instead of a painter'.[3] He adored singing and at one point

Cat. 31.1 Elliott and Fry, *Joseph Joachim,* photograph, 16.5 × 11 cm (6½ × 4¼ in), Watts Gallery Archive, The Rob Dickins Collection

took up the violin. Indeed, in Cameron's well-known photograph, *The Whisper of the Muse* (fig.45), Watts holds a violin in a not dissimilar pose to that of Joachim in the portrait. Both Watts and Cameron enjoyed listening to Joachim play at Little Holland House where he gave informal performances, as he did at other private residences in high society. Charles Halle, the subject of another 'musical' portrait (*c.*1870; National Portrait Gallery) by Watts, often accompanied Joachim on the piano. From about this time the violinist also became a feature of Frederic Leighton's musical soirées.[4] Joachim's reputation grew rapidly as one of the prime interpreters of Beethoven's music and as a promoter of his contemporary and close friend Johannes Brahms, whose *Hungarian Concerto* (1857) he specially arranged.

Joachim's extraordinary technical accomplishment was already legendary, so it is not surprising that Watts sought him out for this 'musical' portrait. He intended it as an addition to his 'gallery of worthies' (see p.32), not done on commission but painted for his own collection. On Joachim's first visit to one of Sara Prinsep's Sunday evening soirées, Watts asked him to play Beethoven's 'Adelaide'.[5] Such performances in the dim and glowing surroundings at Little Holland House inspired the portrait. It proceeded in the spring of 1867. The seemingly simple effects were hard won, as Joachim sat on at least five occasions for the artist. The violin itself is somewhat truncated in size in order to achieve the positioning of the hands.

Watts's portrait of Joachim is far from straightforward in its intention or meaning. Accuracy of portrayal was secondary; some contemporaries did not even consider it a particularly good likeness.[6] Since the 1850s the artist had already developed the notion of portraits that expressed 'the poetry of feeling' as well as those that exist as studies of the beautiful. Here he explores the idea of a visual equivalent for the sound of the music and the deep emotion conveyed by a gifted performer. Subtlety of lighting creates a sense of ambiguity. Watts's title for the painting on its first exhibition cites the 'lamplight' before it even refers to the sitter, a peculiarity that calls out for explanation. Joachim plays his instrument within an artificially lit setting. Looming out of the dim background space, the figure is read through the intensely concentrating face and the powerfully active hands, with the right hand drawing the bow over the strings of the violin. Watts's technique of thin glazing creates a sense of impenetrable space, which adds to the mood.[7] The painting presents an embodiment of the performer engaged in the creative act of making music.

Watts's *Joachim* is a major contribution to a particularly fertile period in English art. At the same exhibition of the Academy he also showed a portrait of a woman singing. These two paintings at just this time reveal the artist at the forefront of new theories in art. Relations between music and art were at the heart of the early Aesthetic movement of the 1860s. Critics familiar with such issues, such as F.G. Stephens, commented that in the portrait of Joachim 'the treatment seems to proclaim the essential concord between colour and sound'.[8] Another review of 1867 cited Watts's works in connection with this 'cherished theory',[9] later expressed by Walter Pater's dictum, 'All art constantly aspires towards the condition of music'.

Lamplight Study: Herr Joachim is one of Watts's most inventive portraits, praised by critics and fellow painters.[10] The artist refused to sell it, partly because 'it belongs to my gallery',[11] but he did paint a replica (1868; Art Institute of Chicago) for his patron Charles Rickards. Watts and Joachim continued their strong friendship, with the artist attending the musician's Diamond Jubilee celebration in 1904 shortly before his death.[12] BB

1   Andreas Moser, *Joseph Joachim: A Biography*, trans. L. Durham, London, 1901, p.55.
2   Clive Brown, 'Joachim, Joseph (1831–1907)', *Oxford Dictionary of National Biography* (http://www.oxforddnb.com/view/article/53548, accessed 25 Feb 2008).
3   Barrington 1905, p.94.
4   On the friendship of Leighton and Joachim, see Leonée and Richard Ormond, *Lord Leighton*, New Haven and London, 1975, pp.64–5.
5   Harry Prinsep, the brother of May, recalled the first time Joachim played there.
6   Barrington 1905, p.36.
7   Barrington 1905, p.202. He abandoned this technique shortly after, due to cracks appearing in the surface of the paint in the background, attributing this to an 'unsafe ground'.
8   *Athenaeum*, 18 May 1867, p.666.
9   *Blackwood's Magazine*, July 1867, p.91.
10 Spielmann 1905, p.39, noted that Ford Madox Brown considered it, along with Watts's *Cardinal Manning* (1882; NPG), as 'supreme in style and dignity'.
11 Watts Papers, Watts to Rickards, 30 May 1867.
12 Watts 1912, II, p.321; Blunt 1975, p.217. There is also correspondence between Leighton and Watts when the former endeavoured to find a suitable gift for Joachim in advance of his fiftieth birthday.

32. *Clytie*, late 1860s

Oil on panel, 61 × 51 cm (24 × 20 in)
Inscribed on labels on the reverse 'Clytie 73',
'W. Graham Esq. 264', 'Lent by Major-General
The Honorable Sir Reginald Talbot, K.C.B., State
Govt. House, Melbourne'
COMWG73

PROVENANCE: collection of the artist (Little
Holland House Gallery); … W. Graham Esq.; …
The Honorable Sir Reginald Talbot (?); … Cecil
French, Cecil French Bequest to the Watts Gallery,
1955

LITERATURE: W.M. Rossetti, *Rossetti Papers 1862 to
1870*, London 1903, p.403 (Sunday 18 July 1869);
Watts Catalogue, I, p.140 (listed as *Sunflower* and
unillustrated); Gould 2004, p.75

Watts's painted version of the myth of Clytie
appears never to have been exhibited or
reviewed in Britain, unlike its sculpted counterpart, which caused a sensation at its first exhibition at the Royal Academy, London, in 1868 (see
cat.85). His engagement with the subject is first
recorded in 1867 in a letter from John Denison
to the artist following the former's visit to his
studio and observation of the unfinished bust:

> I have been thinking a good deal of Clytie …
> I have been reading the story in Ovid this
> morning. Clytie, in relations with Apollo, is
> furious at being neglected for Leocothoe. She
> informs Leocothoe's Father of the intrigue
> with his daughter. The Father buries her
> alive. Apollo the Sun breaks down the earth
> by the force of his rays, so that the face may
> show itself above the soil. But no more. She
> is turned into a fragrant shrub. So both these
> Ladies have something [of] the same Fate.
> For Clytie, still neglected, lies on the ground,
> and will not move, and neither eats nor
> drinks, but she watches the course of the
> Sun. It is said her limbs adhered to the soil,
> but she continues to follow with her eyes and
> countenance the course of the Sun. She is
> changed into a flower like a violet 'violaque
> simillimus ora Flos teget.' I did not remem-
> ber the exact story when I was with you.[1]

Whether Watts expressed the subject first in
paint or sculpture is difficult to assess. The first
record of the painting appears in William
Michael Rossetti's diary entry for Sunday 18 July
1869: 'G[abriel] & I went to the Prinseps' – first
time I have been there an unconscionable while.
Watts's *Endymion*, *Daphne*, *Millais*, *Clytie* (same
composition in painting as the bust, perhaps
his most vigorous piece of flesh-painting), new
picture from the Greek head at Oxford, v. lovely
– etc.'[2]

Both the bust and the painting are of a
life-size scale, evoking the physical presence of
Clytie. Watts's treatment of flesh tones was
explored in the series of life-size half-length
nudes that he produced in the 1860s such as
A Study with the Peacock's Feathers (fig.47), *Rhodopis*
(c.1865; Watts Gallery) and *Wife of Plutus* (c.1865–
85; Walker Art Gallery, Liverpool). Of the last,
Mary noted that 'the design for this picture was

probably made about 1865 when the artist was studying from his model "Long Mary" and others, for the sculptured Clytie'.[3]

The composition of Watts's painted *Clytie* is virtually identical to that of the frontal view of the sculptural bust: the head is turned to the far left in a 'lost profile', and the proper right arm is held closely to the chest while the proper left arm is bent sharply backwards, conveying the impression of movement in a moment of uncomfortable transformation. The musculature was taken from the Italian model Angelo Colorossi, who was the basis for the original sculptural treatment of the subject, reminiscent of Michelangelo's work.[4] The focal point of both compositions is the elongated and turned neck, a recurrent motif in Watts's work.

The main difference between the sculpture and the painting can be seen at the base of the bust where sunflower leaves provide a decorative foundation for the sculpture. The painted *Clytie*, in contrast, is depicted against a background of large sunflowers that trap the nymph within the plane of the picture, recalling Rossetti's floral backgrounds. The bottom left corner, showing three sharp sunflower petals, indicates the metamorphosis from human figure into flower. Watts's virtuosity in depicting flesh is achieved by a subtle variation of skin colour and particularly by the balance between pale and warm skin tones, which was carefully planned out on the chalk study for the composition, also in the Watts Gallery collection (cat.32.1).

The metamorphic subject appealed to Watts, and, according to one scholar, *Clytie* can be described 'in Ovidian terms' as 'a reduction from ardent humanity to the flower whose nature (rather than volition) is to turn its head perpetually towards the sun … Clytie's love for Apollo brings the loss of humanity.'[5] JD

1   Letter from John Denison, Speaker of the House of Commons, to Watts, 10 December 1867, Watts Papers.
2   W.M. Rossetti, *Rossetti Papers 1862 to 1870*, London 1903, p.403 (Sunday 18 July 1869). The reference to the painting in Rossetti's diaries was located by Hilary Underwood.
3   Watts Catalogue, I, p.160.
4   Watts 1912, II, p.45.
5   Elizabeth Prettejohn, 'Between Homer and Ovid: metamorphoses of the "grand style" in G.F. Watts', in Trodd and Brown 2004, p.59; Prettejohn's essay considers the idea of metamorphoses in Watts's work and discusses the sculptural *Clytie* (cat.85) and the painted *Wife of Pygmalion* (fig.48) as complementary art works.

Cat. 32.1 Study for *Clytie*, late 1860s, red, white and brown chalks on cream paper, 38.7 × 29.5 cm (15¼ × 11¾ in), COMWG352

33. *Eve Tempted*, begun around 1868

Oil on canvas, 251.5 × 109.2 cm (99 × 43 in)
COMWG142

PROVENANCE: collection of the artist (Little
Holland House Gallery by 1896); Lilian
Mackintosh (Mrs Michael Chapman), legal
descendant of the artist; given by her to the Watts
Gallery in 1946 (no.1)

EXHIBITIONS: Watts New York, 1884, no.123 (a
photograph of the work); Watts New Gallery 1896,
no.152 (possibly, loaned from Little Holland
House); Watts Leighton House 1902, no.16 (lent by
Watts about 1880); Watts Gallery 1904, no.38 (no.9,
small study formerly in Watts Gallery collection);
Memorial Exhibitions, Edinburgh 1905, no.140,
Manchester 1905, no.64, Newcastle 1905, no.62,
Dublin 1906, no.43

LITERATURE: Spielmann 1886, p.30; Cartwright
1896, pp.11, 13; Barrington 1905, pp.33–4, 92, 118,
109, 136–7; Watts Catalogue, I, p.47; Watts 1912, I,
p.262, II, pp.45, 138–41, p.183; Macmillan 1903,
pp.146–8; Bryant 1997, pp.265–6; Gould 2004,
pp.104, 112, 163, 171, 233, 236, 256, 261

A reviewer wrote of the artist's 1905 retrospective at the Royal Academy: 'Mr Watts occupied himself much with the Bible story of Paradise, as well he might; nothing could give fuller scope to his genius both as painter and as the poet of humanity.'[1] Through his paintings of such subjects Watts explored his fascination with the creation and evolution of the spirit of mankind, which formed part of the cycle that in the 1890s became known as 'The House of Life'. Although the scheme to bring the paintings together in one great work never materialised, several individual paintings and groups emerged from this grand vision.

The story of Adam and Eve is depicted in a number of works painted at different points in his career and developed over a long period. Watts had originally conceived of six paintings in the cycle. He wrote to Rickards in 1873, telling him that they

> can hardly be separated, any more than one would think of separating the parts of an epic poem, my intention was to make them part of an epic & they belong to a series of six pictures illustrating the story in Genesis ... 'The Creation of Eve,' 'After the Transgression' & 'Cain' – 3 single figures, & 3 full compositions. Those I always destined to be public property ... I think you will understand that I would keep these designs together and leave them after my death to form part of one whole.[2]

As Watts indicated, the paintings divide very clearly into two groups of related compositions.[3] The most celebrated of these became known as 'the great trilogy of Eve', as Julia Cartwright described them in 1896, which consists of *She Shall Be Called Woman* (c.1875–92; Tate, see cat.33.1),[4] *Eve Tempted* and *Eve Repentant* (cat.34).

In *She Shall Be Called Woman* Watts depicts Eve on her creation as a single ethereal upright figure, a bridge between heaven and earth, 'resembling a rainbow only brighter and purer'.[5] In *Eve Tempted* and *Eve Repentant* Eve is more obviously in the material world and that of the physical senses. The sculptural solidity of Eve's depiction is emphasised in both paintings, expressing in turn sensuousness and grief. The biblical source for *Eve Tempted* is Genesis 3: 6: 'And when the woman saw that the tree was good for food, and that it was pleasant to the eyes, and a tree to be desired to make one wise, she took of the fruit thereof, and did eat.' If Genesis is the original source, the painting has more than an echo of Milton's interpretation of the subject in *Paradise Lost*, a work greatly admired by Watts.[6] Milton writes of the temptation, 'Fixed on the fruit she gazed, which to behold / Might tempt alone',[7] yet it is the sensuous imagery that follows that is more clearly reflective of the lush nature that Watts paints:

> Thick overhead with verdant roof embowered,
> ... flowers were her couch,
> Pansies, and violets, and asphodel,
> And hyacinth – earth's freshest, softest lap.[8]

Mary, writing of *Eve Tempted* in the Manchester catalogue, notes that, with 'her spiritual nature, lulled to sleep by the opulent beauty around her, the colour and scents of fruit and flower, and the fawning animal life, Eve yields to the tempter'.[9] Watts evokes not only the intoxication of physical beauty and sensual pleasure (the spirit dulled) that leads to the Fall but also the moment when mankind understands its own weakness and the stage 'through which human life has to pass'.[10] The panther on its back symbolises lust and physical pleasure: Eve is adorned and lost in nature. Watts paints the seduction and corruption of the material world, where materialism is viewed as the opposite of the spiritual and a danger to it. It is, as Mary describes it, a 'lower ecstasy',[11] rather than the 'higher' spiritual ecstasy of *She Shall Be Called Woman*. More explicitly, according to the catalogue notes of 1905, Watts is 'The moralist "warning in deep tones against lapses from morals and duties" using "the parable to urge his lesson".'[12]

Mrs Barrington points out how Eve is portrayed as 'she bends forward toward the fruit which is tempting her, not plucking it, but allowing herself to be allured by its seductive fragrance'.[13] The depiction of her leaning was conceived by Watts to be highly symbolic, her stance on the point of fall highlighting her weakness and vulnerability. Furthermore, Mary describes the 'elemental lines' that make up the stance of each of the Eves in the trilogy, 'the first representing perfect strength, the second entire weakness, the third a return to the first but requiring support'.[14]

Cat. 33.1 Emery Walker after G.F. Watts, *She Shall Be Called Woman*, coloured mezzotint, 70 × 31 cm (27½ × 12¼ in), COMWG2008.89

The manuscript catalogue of Watts's works lists seven versions of this painting, indicating its importance to the artist. Four versions, 'destined to be public property', are in public collections, the Tate having the most finished one, almost identical in size to this version.[15] The two other, smaller versions are in the collection of the Walker Art Gallery, Liverpool, and Aberdeen Art Gallery.[16] Of the three other versions, none appear to have been exhibited. The Watts Gallery has several sketches for the composition (COMWG2007.290, 635, 639), and the present painting shows clear evidence that it was extended vertically with an additional piece of canvas, which may indicate that Watts was still working out the composition, thus making it the earliest of the two large versions, if not the most finished. MB

1   *The Times*, 31 December 1904, p.10.
2   Watts Papers, Watts to C.H. Rickards, 6 January 1873.
3   Four are included in this catalogue and exhibition: cats 33 and 34 from the Eve trilogy and cats 35 and 36, pendant paintings depicting the creation and denunciation of Adam and Eve.
4   *She Shall Be Called Woman* is sometimes titled *The Creation of Eve* but is not to be confused with the painting of the same title in this catalogue and exhibition (cat.36).
5   Plato, quoted in Watts 1912, II, p.138.
6   'One day when Andrew Hichens sat beside him while he rested in his niche, they talked of *Paradise Lost*' (Watts 1912, II, p.275); Mary also notes that *She Shall Be Called Woman* was, in part, inspired by Milton's lines, 'dark with excessive light' (Watts 1912, II, p.139).
7   Milton, *Paradise Lost*, book 9, lines 735–6.
8   Milton, *Paradise Lost*, book 9, lines 1038–41.
9   Watts Manchester 1905, cat. no.64.
10   Watts 1912, II, p.141.
11   'The paradise of sense has developed a lower ecstasy' (Watts 1912, II, p.141).
12   Watts Newcastle 1905, no.62.
13   Barrington in the catalogue for the Watts Metropolitan Museum, New York, 1885, no.123 (only a photograph appeared in the exhibition, as the original remained in Britain: 'The first and third were not sufficiently finished to send').
14   Watts 1912, II, p.141.
15   The Tate version was exhibited at Birmingham in 1883 and the New Gallery in 1896–7.
16   The Aberdeen version (inv. no.3398) was exhibited at the Grosvenor Gallery in 1881–2, as no.129 (lent by Macdonald); the Walker Art Gallery version (inv. no.2101) was shown at Birmingham in 1883 and Nottingham in 1885–6.

34. *Eve Repentant*, begun in 1868 (1868–1903)

Oil on canvas, 251.5 × 114.3 cm (99 × 45 in)
COMWG141

PROVENANCE: collection of the artist (Little Holland House Gallery); Watts Gallery

EXHIBITIONS: Watts Grosvenor 1881, no.58 (as 'Eve Penitent'); Watts New York 1884, no.123 (a photograph of the work); Watts New Gallery 1896, no.154 (possibly this version, loaned from Little Holland House); Watts Gallery 1904, no.8; Memorial Exhibitions, Edinburgh 1905, no.119; Watts Manchester 1905, no.72, Watts Newcastle 1905, no.68; Watts Compton 2004, no.49

LITERATURE: Spielmann 1886, p.30; Cartwright 1896, p.11, p.13; Barrington 1905, pp.33–4, 92, 109, 118, 137; Watts Catalogue, p.49; Watts 1912, I, p.262, II, pp.45, 138–41, p.183; Macmillan 1903, pp.148–9; Chesterton 1904, pp.29, 126, 136, 139; Alston 1929, no.123; Gould 2004, pp.112, 163, 170–1, 233, 270–2, 284, 349

Cat. 34.1 *Eve Repentant*, 1860s, oil on canvas, 61 × 28 cm (24 × 11 in), COMWG26

The final painting in the Eve trilogy (see cat.33) is *Eve Repentant*, the dramatic moment of realisation and remorse. The primary source is biblical, but the imagery in this, like the others in the series, draws on the poetic detail of Milton's *Paradise Lost*, where nature is overwhelming:

> ... Cover me, ye pines,
> Ye cedars, with innumerable boughs
> Hide me, where I may never see them more.[1]

In *Eve Tempted* Eve engulfs herself in nature; in *Eve Repentant* nature is the hiding place and it shows a different aspect. 'Note how all this beauty and luxuriance disappear in the picture "Eve Repentant"; nature there has taken on a hue of sadness,' wrote Mary in 1905.[2] In this painting the physicality of the forms is even more evident than in *Eve Tempted*, the figure heavier and the leaves and branches more clearly defined, suggesting the weighty burden of sin. Mrs Barrington described the scene for the Metropolitan exhibition: 'in the third she has thrown herself against the stem of a tree, her hands clasped above her head, her figure shrouded by hair ... The colour in ... the "Eve Repentant," shaded blue and saddened into twilight.'[3] The white lilies, symbols of innocence and death, in this case the death of innocence, are figuratively trampled underfoot.[4]

The positioning of the figure of Eve in the trilogy was conceived by Watts as fundamental to its meaning: 'the first representing perfect strength, the second entire weakness, the third a return to the first but requiring support'.[5] Figuratively, she is a buttress to the straight column that she wishes to emulate; she is accepting her sin but aspiring towards the original ideal, or, as Macmillan expressed it, 'her repentance and grief have highest hope. It is not all misery.'[6] Watts described the painting himself as 'Eve restored to beauty and humility by remorse'.[7] Repentance is the cathartic and redemptive act. As many commentators pointed out, the Eve trilogy is symbolic of the stages of all mankind, and Eve, 'a type which may suggest the mother of all the human race'.[8]

The expression of grief and remorse is characteristically Watts, rather than the physiognomy of the face: the contortions and physicality of the body act as the expression. Like *For He Had*

Great Possessions (cat.75), the face is almost totally absent and its obscurity, the powerful tool for expression. With *Eve Repentant* she is hiding herself away in shame and it is her back we see, rather than her front in *Eve Tempted*. Chesterton wrote:

> *Eve Repentant* (that fine picture), in which the agony of a gigantic womanhood is conveyed as it could not be conveyed by any power of visage, in the powerful contortion of the muscular and yet beautiful back, is the first that occurs to the mind.[9]

For Chesterton the back had a very particular meaning:

> [W]hat is beyond all question the most interesting and most supremely personal of all the elements in the painter's designs and draughtsmanship … is, of course, his magnificent discovery of the artistic effect of the human back … It is the part of man that he knows nothing of; like an outlying province forgotten by an emperor. It is a common saying that anything may happen behind our backs: transcendentally considered the thing has an eerie truth about it. Eden may be behind our backs, or Fairyland. But this mystery of the human back has again its other side in the strange impression produced on those behind: to walk behind anyone along a lane is a thing that, properly speaking, touches the oldest nerve of awe.[10]

Macmillan also found

> [t]he third of the trilogy … the finest … We think of the bitter repentance and unutterable sorrow of Eve, not of the power of the mind that conceived, and the hand that brought out her story so vividly before us. As an interpretation of a great human tragedy it has a haunting power. Watts is possessed himself so wholly with his subject, that he has expressed it with that inevitableness of spontaneousness which makes a really noble picture.[11]

The manuscript catalogue lists four versions of this painting, all of which are in public collections. The Tate has the most finished version, almost identical in size to the present one.[12] The two other, smaller versions are in the collection of the Walker Art Gallery, Liverpool, and the Watts Gallery (cat.34.1).[13]   MB

1   Milton, *Paradise Lost*, book 9, lines 1088–90.
2   Watts Manchester 1905, no.64.
3   Mrs Barrington in Watts New York 1884, no.123 (only a photograph of the work in the exhibition).
4   Macmillan 1903, p.148.
5   Watts 1912, II, p.141.
6   Macmillan 1903, p.148.
7   Watts Papers, Watts to C.H. Rickards, 6 January 1873.
8   Mrs Barrington in Watts New York 1884, no.123 (only a photograph of the work in the exhibition).
9   Chesterton 1904, p.139.
10   Chesterton 1904, p.136.
11   Macmillan 1903, p.148.
12   The Tate version was exhibited at the New Gallery in 1896–7.
13   The Walker Gallery version (inv. no.2100) was exhibited at the Grosvenor Gallery in 1881–2, Birmingham in 1883, Nottingham in 1885–6 and Liverpool in 1922.

35. *The Denunciation of Adam and Eve / After the Transgression*, c.1865–8

Oil on panel, 61 × 25.4 cm (24 × 10 in)
COMWG59

PROVENANCE: collection of the artist (Little Holland House Gallery); Watts Gallery

EXHIBITIONS: Watts New York 1884 (a photograph of the work); Memorial Exhibitions, London 1905, no.196, Edinburgh 1905, no.96 (misprinted 95 in the catalogue), Manchester 1905, no.91, Newcastle 1905, no.86, Watts Dublin 1906, no.23, Watts Tate Gallery 1954–5, no.49; Watts Aldeburgh 1961, no.13

LITERATURE: Spielmann 1886, p.39; Barrington 1905, p.133; Watts Catalogue I, p.37; Watts 1912, I, pp.235, 262; Gould 2004, p.112

The pendant to *The Creation of Eve* (cat.36), this painting is also known as *After the Transgression*:

> And the LORD God said, Behold, the man is become as one of us, to know good and evil: and now, lest he put forth his hand, and take also of the tree of life, and eat, and live for ever: Therefore the LORD God sent him forth from the garden of Eden, to till the ground from whence he was taken. So he drove out the man; and he placed at the east of the garden of Eden Cherubims, and a flaming sword which turned every way, to keep the way of the tree of life.[1]

In contrast to the joyous scene of *The Creation of Eve*, *The Denunciation of Adam and Eve* depicts the first man and woman at the foot of a tree, lamenting their fate. At the pinnacle of the column of grieving angels is 'God the Father, with outstretched arms in the act of denunciation'.[2] This figure, powerfully set at the top of the canvas and painted within an aurora of yellow light, judges the cowering figures at its base.

Mrs Barrington notes in comparing the two pendant paintings that 'the descending angels [in this picture] contrast with the ascending angels [in *The Creation of Eve*]'.[3] Perhaps, even more significantly, there is a complete dislocation in this work representing the break with heaven, whereas in *The Creation of Eve* the figures are presented in a continuous link. Watts considered both works to be masterpieces: 'This picture partaking of the nature of a sketch, was rapidly painted and has been ranked as a masterpiece by the artist. He never wanted to carry it further and would not be induced to part with it.'[4] A review of the 1905 retrospective exhibition shared the artist's view: 'This is "The Denunciation of Adam and Eve" (196), a brilliant and rapid study for one of an interesting and little-known pair, illustrating two stages of the story of Eden, which are lent by Mr. Edmund Davis (167, 171).'[5]

Of all six pictures that depict various stages of the transgression, several versions were exhibited in Europe, including at the Galerie Georges Petit in Paris in 1883. In the sensational novel, *À Rebours* (Against Nature), by Joris-Karl Huysmans, published in 1884, Des Esseintes reflects on the nature of London through the

English art that he had experienced; in painting this meant Millais and Watts, and he recalls

> weirdly coloured pictures by Watts speckled with gamboges and indigo, and looking as if they had been sketched by an ailing Gustave Moreau, painted in by an ailing Michel Angelo, and retouched by a romantic Raphael. Among other canvases he remembered a *Curse of Cain*, an *Ida*, and more than one *Eve*, in which the strange and mysterious amalgam of these three masters was informed by the personality, at once coarse and refined, of a dreamy, scholarly Englishman afflicted with a predilection for hideous hues.[6]

The manuscript catalogue lists only two versions of this painting, this one and the completed painting in the Fogg Art Museum, originally sold to Edmund Davis in 1899 with a finished *Creation of Eve*.[7] A third unfinished monochromatic version is in the Watts Gallery collection, 'Mr. Watts', Mary notes, 'often worked simultaneously upon the design in monochrome on a large scale and upon the study for a colour scheme on a small scale.'[8] MB

1 Genesis 3: 22–4.
2 Watts Manchester 1905, no.91.
3 Barrington 1905, p.133.
4 Watts Catalogue, I, p.37.
5 *The Times*, 31 December 1904, p.10.
6 Joris-Karl Huysmans, *À Rebours* (Against Nature), 1884, trans. Robert Baldick, London 1982, p.136. See Staley 1978, pp.82–3.
7 Watts Catalogue, II, p.36; exhibited at the Royal Academy in 1905, no.171; Davis's collection was sold at Christie's on 7 July 1939, *The Creation of Eve* and *The Denunciation of Adam and Eve* fetching £438. A version of the latter painting was exhibited at Watts New Gallery 1896, no.76, but it is uncertain which it was.
8 Watts Catalogue, I, p.37.

36. *The Creation of Eve*, c.1865–8, completed c.1870s

Oil on canvas, 117 × 44 cm (46 × 17½ in)
COMWG11

PROVENANCE: collection of the artist (Little Holland House Gallery); Watts Gallery

EXHIBITIONS: Watts Grosvenor Gallery 1881–2, no.92; Watts New York 1884, no.109; Watts Birmingham 1885, no.168; Watts Nottingham 1886, no.27; Stockholm International 1897; Watts Gallery 1904, no.24; Memorial Exhibitions, Edinburgh 1905, no.35, Manchester 1905, no.159, Newcastle 1905, no.171, Dublin 1906, no.14; Watts London 1954, no.51 (no.52 is another version in the Watts Gallery collection); Watts Compton 2004, no.15

LITERATURE: Spielmann 1886, p.30; Cartwright 1896, pp.10, 13; Barrington 1905, pp.132–3; Watts Catalogue, I, p.45; Watts 1912, I, p.262, II, pp.45, 138–41, 183; Macmillan 1903, p.143; Alston 1929, no.27; Gould 2004, pp.170–1, 233–4, 256, 306

Cat. 36.1 Study for *The Creation of Eve*, 1881–2, oil on canvas, 117 × 43.2 cm (46 × 17 in), COMWG13

The Creation of Eve forms part of Watts's envisioned scheme of six paintings (see cat.33) depicting the story of Adam and Eve and their fall from Paradise, works that 'can hardly be separated, any more than one would think of separating the parts of an epic poem'.[1] Three single figure compositions made up the 'Eve trilogy', and the other three were full compositions, *The Creation of Eve, After the Transgression* (cat.35) and *The Denunciation of Cain* (RA 1872; Watts Gallery), of which this painting is the first of the narrative. Each of the three paintings follows the same format of perpendicular composition, individually responding to the key moment where heaven touches earth, with the angels in turn rejoicing and lamenting. Watts found the structure and colour in these works analogous to music, writing about *The Denunciation of Cain*: 'If I were a poet and musician like Wagner, I could make a fine cantata or oratorio of the subject.'[2] The source for this work is the second chapter of Genesis:

> And the LORD God caused a deep sleep to fall upon Adam, and he slept: and he took one of his ribs, and closed up the flesh instead thereof; And the rib, which the LORD God had taken from man, made he a woman, and brought her unto the man. And Adam said, This is now bone of my bones, and flesh of my flesh: she shall be called Woman, because she was taken out of Man.[3]

The composition shows a host of angels who ascend in a spiral with Adam in the foreground and Eve behind him. 'Their work done,' Mrs Barrington wrote, 'the angels are rising into light, singing a chorus of praise. One is touching Adam with a finger to arouse him from his torpor.'[4] The ascending and interconnected stream of angels link Adam and Eve with heaven, symbolically creating a bridge between the two. The joyous and musical nature of the work was emphasised through the verse from Job that accompanied its exhibition: 'The morning stars sang together and all the sons of God shouted for joy.'[5] If the musicality of *The Denunciation of Cain* is reflected in *The Creation of Eve*, it is in the latter's true pendant, *The Denunciation of Adam and Eve* (cat.35), where the comparisons serve to highlight the meaning of the paintings figuratively

in different keys as in *Eve Tempted* (cat.33) and *Eve Repentant* (cat.34). 'How absolutely different in conception and design', commented *The Times* in 1904, 'is this "Creation of Eve" now before us, a full, rich composition, the figures smaller than life, an exact pendant to that "Denunciation [of Adam and Eve]" which forms the final scene of the tragedy.'[6]

Mrs Barrington notes in comparing the two works that 'the descending angels contrast with the ascending angels in this picture'.[7] Perhaps even more significantly, there is a complete dislocation in *The Denunciation of Adam and Eve* representing the break with heaven, whereas in this the figures are presented in a continuous link. Watts considered both works to be masterpieces, 'the painting takes its place as a masterpiece amongst the work of Mr. Watts. The crisp brilliancy of the touch recalls a quality in the natural landscape, which Mr. Watts was often heard to admire.'[8] A version of this painting that moves towards abstraction was considered at its exhibition in 1896 to be as 'great a mistake' as the late pictures of Turner, where

the artist has tried to make his brush attempt something beyond the power of painting. It is language, they say, and not form and colour, which must express abstract ideas; form and colour can tell nothing beyond themselves, except by appealing illegitimately to the associations of language as embodied in literature.[9]

The manuscript catalogue lists only two versions of this painting, the present one and the completed painting in the Fogg Art Museum, which was originally sold to Edmund Davis the year of its completion in 1899 with a finished *Denunciation of Adam and Eve*.[10] A third unfinished version is in the Watts Gallery collection (cat.36.1), less complete than this and closer to the Fogg version.[11] MB

1 Watts Papers, Watts to C.H. Rickards, 6 January, 1873.
2 G.F. Watts quoted in Watts 1912, I, p.258.
3 Genesis 2: 21–3.
4 Mrs Barrington in Watts New York 1884, no.109.
5 Job 38: 7. According to Watts's own words quoted in the 1905 memorial exhibition

catalogues: '"The morning stars sang together and all the sons of God shouted for joy." The final act concluded, the powers of Creation, symbolised by these spirits of air, rise heavenwards in a triumphant swirl from the scene of their completed work. At the Divine touch, Adam moves, but the stupor of deep sleep is still upon him.'
6 Review of the 1905 Royal Academy Watts exhibition, *The Times*, 31 December 1904, p.10.
7 Barrington 1905, p.133, and Watts New York 1884, no.109.
8 Watts Catalogue, I, p.45.
9 'The Watts Exhibition at the New Gallery', *The Times*, 29 December 1896, p.8. Watts NewGallery 1896, no.87 (as 'The Birth of Eve').
10 Watts Catalogue, I, p.45; exhibited at the Memorial Exhibition, London, 1905, no.167, lent by Mr Edmund Davis esq. (completed in 1899). Davis's collection was sold at Christie's on 7 July, 1939, *The Creation of Eve* and *The Denunciation of Adam and Eve* fetching £438.
11 Exhibited at Watts London 1954, no.52.

37. *May Prinsep, c.1867–9*

Oil on canvas, 66 × 53.3 cm (26 × 21 in)
COMWG88

PROVENANCE: bought from the artist by Charles H. Rickards, 1869; his sale, Christie's, London, 2 April 1887, no.43, 'Portrait of a Lady', for 130 guineas; acquired by May and Andrew Hichens; presented to the Watts Gallery by Mrs Andrew Hichens, 1907

EXHIBITIONS: Royal Academy 1869, no.327; ?*Works of Modern Artists*, Royal Manchester Institution, 1872, no.596, 'A Portrait', lent by C.H. Rickards; ?*Exhibition of Art Treasures*, Royal Manchester Institution, 1878, no.29, 'May' lent by C.H. Rickards; Watts Manchester 1880, no.2 or 34, *A Portrait*, or no.54, 'A Portrait Study', or no.5, 'May'; Watts Grosvenor 1881, no.199 or 203, 'A Portrait', or no.136, 'A Portrait Study'; St Jude's, Whitechapel, 1892, no.69, 'A Young Lady', lent by A.K. Hichens; Watts New Gallery 1896, no.21 as 1867; Memorial Exhibition, London 1905, no.197; Watts Aldeburgh 1961, no.6; *Victorian Paintings 1837–1890*, Mappin Art Gallery, Sheffield, 1968, no.137d

LITERATURE: Spielmann 1886, pp.13, 31, various portraits in Rickards's collection; Watts Catalogue, II, p.128; Watts Gallery Catalogue 1920, no.75; Alston 1929, no.130

One of Watts's most haunting portrayals of youthful beauty, this painting belongs to a particular group of idealised portraits of women in the 1860s.[1] Watts portrayed May, a member of the extended Prinsep family at Little Holland House, on many occasions and her remarkable looks seem to have inspired him in no less than four oil paintings, each of which he sent to the Royal Academy.

Mary Emily (May) Prinsep (1853–1931) was the adopted daughter of Sara and Thoby Prinsep (see cat.41), her uncle. Her father Charles Robert Prinsep (1789–1864) had a career at the bar and as an economist, and, like many of his brothers, he worked for the government in India, attaining the post of Advocate-General of Bengal by the early 1850s.[2] Already an old man when May was born, Prinsep lost his wife Louisa, who died around 1853, the year of May's birth. Along with her older brother Henry (Harry) (1844–1922), May went to live with her relations in Kensington; here she had cousins including Valentine and Alice. Her father's death in 1864, when she was eleven years old, led to adoption by Sara and Thoby.

May's good looks were apparent to all and Watts used her regularly as a model; she posed for the young woman in *The Court of Death* (see cat.67). One habitué of Little Holland House recalled 'the vision of beauty, dear May Prinsep'.[3] Reputedly, her aunt Sara only allowed her to pose for Watts and her cousin Val, presumably excluding someone like Rossetti who was often on the lookout for 'stunners'. But of course May is also widely known through the photographs of Julia Margaret Cameron, sister of Sara Prinsep. In 1866 Cameron first used May, then still only thirteen, as a model for a group of photographic studies taken on the Isle of Wight. One shows her full faced with her hair down, a completely natural effect, others show her costumed to suggest exotic types, such as *La Contadina*, or to evoke characters in poetry, such as Zoe in Byron's *Don Juan*. She appears in a picturesque wide-brimmed hat in Cameron's group *Summer Days* (cat.37.1).

Watts's studies of youthful beauties from the late 1850s onwards reached a culmination with his portrayals of Ellen Terry, but he and Ellen had separated by 1865. She had played a major role in the realisation of his poetical studies of

women, so at this point the artist sought other models. Watts's earliest portrayal of May Prinsep, a painting showing her kneeling and reading, came to be entitled *Prayer* (Manchester City Galleries),[4] although he sent it to the Royal Academy with the title *May* in 1867. It sold immediately to his new client, Charles Rickards of Manchester. He followed it with this head study of May, probably worked on from 1867 until sent to the Academy in 1869. The same client, by now a regular visitor to Watts's studio, showed interest. On 13 March 1869 Watts wrote to him:

> I will send the head to the Exhibition if you wish it certainly & will not call it May. I think your name is a very good one and shall regard it as so christened but I do not know

about so styling it in the Exhibition catalogue as I rather dislike fanciful names for such occasions and would prefer calling it a study but will do what you wish.

Rickards had a partiality for descriptive titles, but it is revealing that Watts considered this work as a study. In the end he just called it *A Portrait* when he sent it to the Royal Academy. Less a reading of character, it is more a poetic study. With May turned away, gazing into the distance, there is a distinct mood of wistfulness. She is dressed simply with her pale gown trimmed with black velvet ribbon and an untied bow at the neck. Focus is on the expanse of her fair skin and profile. One senses the quiet containment of her personality. In essence, the painting was an exercise in capturing beauty

Cat. 37.1 Julia Margaret Cameron, *Summer Days*, c.1866, photograph showing May Prinsep on the left, 10 × 7 cm (4 × 2¾ in), Watts Gallery Archive, The Rob Dickins Collection

within a strictly reduced palette of greys and whites against a darker background, an almost Whistlerian exercise in tonal values.

Watts had one of his first professional assignments as a new Royal Academician at the exhibition of 1869 when he served as one of the three hangers, along with Leighton. In *The Times* Tom Taylor, known as an astute critic, singled out *A Portrait* as 'a dignified kit-cat of a fair young girl in simple grey'.[5] The *Art Journal*, however, was less favourable noting that 'the handling is less that of the old Italians than of modern French'.[6] Yet this did not put off Rickards who had already decided to buy it. Letters reveal references to portrayals of May with various titles, reaching a point when Watts jauntily refers to this picture as 'May the second'.[7] Late in 1869, he sent it to Rickards in Manchester, offering, as he often did, to allow the patron to exchange it if he no longer liked it. The price of one of these smaller paintings was £300, a substantial amount to realise. This collector's fondness for images of May led him to acquire a third work, a full-length portrait that he called *The Ulster* (RA 1879; Manchester City Galleries).

Watts's portrayals of May – there are four in total – indicate something of the close friendship they had. He had known her virtually from birth and she grew up as he watched. When somewhat older than she is in this picture, they had a standard routine of taking a morning ride in the park. On her marriage in 1875 to Andrew Kinsman Hichens, the couple carried on as close friends of Watts.[8] Indeed, it was on a visit to the Hichenses' second home at Monkshatch in Surrey, near Compton, that Andrew urged Watts to consider building a house, so that he could escape London winters for fresher air and countryside. That house became Limnerslease and one could say that it was due to May and her husband that Watts, and therefore the Watts Gallery, ended up in that corner of Surrey. BB

1   Bryant 2004, pp.29–31.
2   He is included in the entry by A.J. Arbuthnot, 'Prinsep, Henry Thoby (1792–1878)', rev. R.J. Bingle, *Oxford Dictionary of National Biography* (http://www.oxforddnb.com/view/article/22811, accessed 26 Feb 2008).
3   According to Lady Constance Leslie, quoted in Watts 1912, I, p.160.
4   Watts Catalogue, I, p.119.
5   *The Times*, 10 May 1869, p.12 ('kit-cat' refers to the standard English canvas size of 36 × 28 in/91 × 71 cm, though in fact the painting is smaller).
6   *Art Journal*, 1869, p.198.
7   Watts Papers, Watts to Rickards, 26 May 1869.
8   See Blunt 1975, pp.186–7, on their friendship.

38. Study for *Lady Constance Lothian and her Sisters*, c.1862

Pencil on paper, 10.5 × 7.5 cm (4 × 3 in)
COMWG2006.52

PROVENANCE: collection of the artist; Mary Watts; Lilian Mackintosh (Mrs Michael Chapman); sold to Brinsley Ford, 1939; bequeathed by Ford through The Art Fund to the Watts Gallery, 1999

EXHIBITIONS: probably Exeter 1946, no.181;[1] Watts London 1954, no.130c; Watts Aldeburgh 1961, no.51

LITERATURE: Ford 1998, pp.105, 255, no.RBF495; Bryant 2004, no.42, pp.128–31

This pencil study is one of several[2] that Watts executed in preparation for a portrait (1862; formerly Watts Gallery, now private collection) of Lady Constance Lothian (1836–1901) and her two younger sisters, Lady Gertrude Talbot (1840–1906) and Lady Adelaide Talbot (1844–1917).[3] The finished portrait, one of Watts's most beautiful works of this period, reflects the artist's close friendship with the main sitter and her family. He was a particular friend of her husband William, whose early death in 1870 inspired his painting *Love and Death* (fig.52, see cats 52–5).

Watts instigated the portrait for his own pleasure without a commission while on a visit to the Lothians' home at Blickling in Norfolk in September 1862. The drawings, including this one, indicate his planning of a three-figure composition, itself something of a technical challenge. Within an arched format Constance, the oldest sister, sits in the foreground and Gertrude draws aside a curtain to reveal a landscape background. By suggesting a narrative Watts treated it not as a formal portrait but as a subject painting, with the action adding a note of drama to the scene.

On the back of this drawing there is a fragment of a watercolour study for the same portrait. Eventually, Watts abandoned the idea of the curtain being drawn aside and instead set the sitters out of doors, with the youngest Adelaide passing flowers to Constance. This loosely sketched drawing records Watts's earliest notion for one of his most poetically inspired portraits. BB

1 Brinsley Ford had several studies (now Watts Gallery, including COMWG2006.51) for this portrait.
2 In the Watts Gallery is COMWB2006.51 with studies on both recto and verso.
3 Watts Catalogue, II, p.156. For the portrait and additional literature on it, see Bryant 2004, no.42.

39. Studies for *The Magdalen* and *Sir Perceval*, 1860s

Red chalk on a paper, irregular, 11.5 × 16.5 cm (4½ × 6½ in)
Inscribed (in ink) 'Miss Ellis Post Office. Praed St. Paddington'
COMWG2006.33

PROVENANCE: collection of the artist; Mary Watts; Lilian Mackintosh (Mrs Michael Chapman); sold to Brinsley Ford, 1939; bequeathed by Ford through The Art Fund to the Watts Gallery, 1999

LITERATURE: Ford 1998, p.258, no.RBF516

Two studies for paintings begun in the 1860s appear on this piece of writing paper: *The Magdalen at the Foot of the Cross* (c.1863–84; version, National Museums Liverpool)[1] and *Sir Perceval* (c.1863–70; bought by Rickards, now Astley Cheetham Art Gallery, Tameside).[2] The loose study for *Sir Perceval* shows the Arthurian knight in motion, a counterpart to the contemplative *Sir Galahad* (RA 1862; Fogg Art Museum).[3]

Though on a small scale, the figure of a woman makes an immediate and powerful impression. The Magdalen, seen in a pose of despair, kneels in a landscape, and the pattern of a cross-like form appears in the sky. Yet this is a modern-day Magdalen, not in a Middle Eastern setting or authentic garb, but a model in contemporary dress. Watts's own social realist subjects, known only to a small circle, did not have the popularity of Pre-Raphaelite modern-life subject matter, Rossetti's *Found*, for example, in the 1850s. Yet for Watts the Magdalen was an archetype of suffering, adhering to his belief in a universalising visual language. The artist worked through the idea in a number of drawings,[4] oil studies (cat.39.1) and a wax model. The arched top of the composition, seen also in other works of the early 1860s (cat.38), did not carry through to the final painting.

The inscription gives a fascinating insight into Watts's working practice in the 1860s. Miss Ellis is almost certainly the name of the model who posed for the female figure. Long Mary (cat.28) served for him while she worked at Little Holland House, but he had recourse to other models on occasion. Miss Ellis, with her only contact via the Post Office, lived on the busy street with Paddington Station, a bustling neighbourhood with a peripatetic population where an artist's model might live cheaply. The conjunction on the same sheet of a modern-life subject and an Arthurian one shows Watts responding to the type of subject matter identified with the Pre-Raphaelites. BB

1   See Morris 1996, pp.469–70. Watts Catalogue, I, p.97, lists another full-scale version, now unlocated.
2   Watts Catalogue, I, p.133. See *William Morris and the Middle Ages*, Whitworth Art Gallery, Manchester, 1984, no.117
3   Bryant 2003, no.194, pp.431–4.
4   Chapman 1945, opp. p.97, ill.22.

Cat. 39.1 *The Magdalen*, 1860s, oil on canvas, 36.2 × 30.5 cm (14¼ × 12 in), COMWG191

40. Study from the 'Oxford Bust', c.1862–7

Pencil on tissue paper, mounted onto thicker sage paper, 28 × 22.2 cm (11 × 8¾ in)
COMWG 2007.608

PROVENANCE: probably removed from one of the albums of Watts's mounted drawings; Mary Watts; Lilian Mackintosh (Mrs Michael Chapman); sold (with others in album) to Brinsley Ford, 1943; given to the Watts Gallery through The Art Fund, 1994

Cat. 40.1 The 'Oxford Bust', plaster cast, 83 × 57 × 33 cm (33½ × 22½ × 13 in), Leighton House Museum, Royal Borough of Kensington and Chelsea

Watts made this sketch from either the antique sculpture dubbed the 'Oxford Bust' or else a plaster cast of it that he had in his studio (cat.40.1). He used the sculpture as a model for *The Wife of Pygmalion: A Translation from the Greek* (fig.48),[1] a key work of nascent Aestheticism in contemporary English art.

Watts had a personal connection with this piece of reconstructed sculpture, which belonged to the famous Arundel and Pomfret Marbles at the Ashmolean Museum at Oxford.[2] His friendship with the classicist Charles Newton (1816–94), then an assistant at the British Museum, dated back some years before 1856 when Watts joined him on his excavation in Asia Minor (see cat.20). Around 1850 the two men trawled through the antique fragments at the Taylor and Randolph Library at Oxford, where they came across some pieces of sculpture that they believed belonged together. These formed the bust of a beautiful woman of the Pheidian era perhaps sculpted by Praxiteles. Once it was reconstructed,[3] the bust's unusual portrait-like qualities prompted its identification as 'Aspasia', the Greek courtesan who became the wife of Pericles in fifth-century-BC Athens. Watts acquired a cast of the whole bust and also had one of the face (still at the Watts Gallery and now properly identified for the first time).[4] When Gladstone admired *The Wife of Pygmalion* at the Royal Academy in 1868, Watts urged him to visit the studio so he could show him the plaster bust of the sculpture that inspired the painting, 'wherein you will see all that you admire in the picture, with infinite beauties altogether missed'.[5]

The 'discovery' of the Oxford Bust by Watts and Newton was not widely publicised until 1867.[6] It is likely that this announcement came about because Watts was then working on a painting in which the bust was brought to life as the wife of Pygmalion, the ancient Greek sculptor. This drawing was integral to this process of 'translating' the antique sculpture to an oil painting. Here Watts responded directly to the sculpture, sketching it accurately, yet hinting that it is not a piece of cold marble. The turn of the woman's head and loose sketchy lines suggest that the model is made of flesh and blood, and the accurate detailing of the ancient garb and head ornament shows his interest in reimagining the antique character as a subject for modern art. This drawing reveals the transition between sculpture and painting in Watts's thinking and as such is a fascinating reflection of how he reinterpreted the antique. BB

1 On the painting, see Staley 1978, pp.73–4.
2 D.E.L. Haynes, *Ashmolean Museum*, Oxford, 1975, p.21. This 'Aphrodite' type is now considered a seventeenth-century pastiche formed from two Roman statues copied from Greek originals.
3 The head and torso, hitherto separate, were attached under the instructions of Newton in consultation with Watts; she was missing a section of hair above the left eye, much of her nose and other parts.
4 It has long laboured under misidentification as the head of 'Long Mary' (see cat.28), but a comparison with the Oxford Bust shows that it is taken from this sculpture.
5 Watts 1912, I, p.237.
6 *Athenaeum*, 20 July 1867, pp.91–2. The firm of Brucciani made and marketed the casts.

The 1870s

During the 1870s Watts consolidated his position in the art world; he exhibited regularly, attracted new patronage and had the continuing support of Charles Rickards who bought many works from the artist. He submitted his diploma piece to the Academy, a large multi-figure composition, *The Denunciation of Cain* (RA 1872), marking him as a painter of serious subjects.

Watts foresaw a departure from Little Holland House as the widowed Lady Holland began to sell sections of the estate. In late 1871 he bought property on the Isle of Wight, where his friends Julia Margaret Cameron and Tennyson already had homes. In 1873 Watts had The Briary built at Freshwater for the Prinseps and spent much time there himself. As the younger Prinseps, such as May (cat.37) to whom he was close, married and went their own way, he adopted another young relation, Blanche Clogstoun. To create a home for himself in London, he bought land on the new Melbury Road, backing onto Leighton's property in Holland Park Road, in an area of Kensington that had become an artists' district. Watts commissioned the architect C.R. Cockerell to build a new home and studio, ready by February 1876. New Little Holland House remained his London residence until his death. A neighbour and amateur artist, Mrs Barrington, made herself indispensable to Watts. In the late 1870s he discovered that Ellen Terry, now back in the theatre world, had some years before set up home with the architect William Godwin and had two children by him. Watts petitioned for divorce (perhaps at Ellen's instigation) and a decree nisi was awarded in March 1877.

In May 1877 the inaugural exhibition of the Grosvenor Gallery on New Bond Street opened as the venue par excellence of the Aesthetic era, where one could see Watts's paintings in conjunction with the works of Burne-Jones, Whistler and Albert Moore. The triumphant appearance of the prime large-scale version of *Love and Death* (fig.52) revealed for the first time Watts's 'symbolical' paintings to the elite of the art world. He sent works to exhibitions in Paris in 1878 and 1880. In 1879, along with Leighton and Millais, Watts painted a *Self-Portrait* (RA 1880) at the request of the Uffizi Gallery in Florence, signalling his international stature. BB

Self-Portrait, 1879 (detail, cat.51)

41. *Thoby Prinsep*, 1871

Oil on canvas, 51 × 41 cm (20 × 16 in)
Signed lower left in red paint 'G F Watts'
COMWG153

PROVENANCE: Painted for Charles H. Rickards
Esq.; Andrew K. Hichens; Mrs A.K. Hichens
(widow); gift to the Watts Gallery 1908

EXHIBITIONS: Watts Grosvenor 1881, no.4; Watts
New Gallery 1896, no.100; Memorial Exhibition,
London 1905, no.49

LITERATURE: Spielmann 1886, p.31; Watts
Catalogue, II, p.125; Watts 1912, I, p.124; Alston
1929, no.131; Blunt, 1975, pl.13b; Gould 2004, p.330

Henry Thoby Prinsep (1792–1878), civil servant
in the East India Company, went to India at the
age of sixteen and excelled there, finally retiring
from service in 1843 when he returned to
London. In 1835 he married Sara Monckton
Pattle (1816–87), daughter of James Pattle of the
Bengal civil service, whose other famous daughters included Virginia, Countess Somers (cat.26),
and Julia Margaret Cameron. In 1850 Prinsep
set up home at Little Holland House,
Kensington, which was advertised as 'a capital
detached family house, making up about 17
beds, well suited for an invalid, or a family with
children, having beautiful lawn with extensive
pleasure grounds'.[1] Watts joined them and
stayed resident for over twenty years, during
which time it became the centre of one of the
most fashionable artistic and literary groups,
where figures such as Tennyson mixed with John
Ruskin and the Pre-Raphaelites. Watts recalled
that Prinsep was 'like a child in the perfect
unconsciousness of his wonderful knowledge
and absence of display – as simple as a child,
and with its charm'.[2]

His fine portrait is full of warmth and character, reaching 'the painter's own standard of

true portraiture, that of finding the man behind
the surface'.[3] Exhibited at the Grosvenor, New
Gallery and Royal Academy Watts retrospec-
tives, it was considered by many to be one of his
greatest portraits, including Rowland Alston
who found it 'finely constructed and full of character'.[4] When the poet W.S. Blunt saw it hanging at the Hichenses' home at Monkshatch,
Compton, he declared it one of the finest portraits in England.[5] The sitter's thoughtful, stu-
dious and generous nature is so apparent that
'Mr Thoby Prinsep will live on in this portrait'.[6]

Watts painted several versions of head
portraits of Thoby Prinsep. This is the second,
which the artist considered the best and was
painted for his collector Charles H. Rickards.
The first was given by Watts to his niece Mrs
Herbert Duckworth. This version was 'laid in by
another hand' and finished by Watts from his
original painting and another sitting.[7] He wrote
to Rickards in February confirming this method:
'As to the head of Mr Prinsep, I think I can get it
copied for you for 50 and if you like to have it
done I will afterwards go over it so in a way
makes the work my own.'[8] Later that year, after
the copy was made, Watts wrote again to
Rickards: 'I think on looking over I can improve
by working upon from nature so I shall get him
to give me a sitting before it goes.'[9] There are
also other versions painted by Watts and not
listed by Mary in her catalogue; 'other heads of
Mr and Mrs Prinsep', she notes, were 'made for
the son Henry Thoby in India.'[10] A Frederick
Hollyer photograph at Watts Gallery (cat.41.1)
illustrates a version where Prinsep is shown
reading.[11] MB

Cat. 41.1 Frederick Hollyer, photograph of
Thoby Prinsep (version with a book), Hollyer
Album, Watts Gallery Archive

1   Advertisement in *The Times*, 21 June 1850, p.10.
2   G.F. Watts quoted in Watts 1912, I, p.124.
3   Ibid.
4   Alston 1929, no.131.
5   Gould 2004, p.330.
6   G.F. Watts quoted in Watts 1912, I, p.124.
7   Watts Catalogue, II, p.125.
8   Watts Papers, Watts to Rickards, 26 February
     1871.
9   Watts Papers, Watts to Rickards, 2 July 1871. In
     August Watts confirmed Rickards's liking of the
     commission: 'I am glad you were pleased with
     the head of Mr Prinsep & hope it will not cease
     to please you upon acquaintance' (Watts Papers,
     Watts to Rickards, 20 August 1871).
11   Illustrated in Gould 2004, p.30, and listed as in a
     private collection.

42. *Miss Virginia Dalrymple*, 1871–2, with later additions *c*.1874

Oil on canvas, 132 × 84 cm (52 × 33 in)
COMWG200A

PROVENANCE: collection of the artist (Little Holland House Gallery); given by Watts to Sophia Dalrymple's daughter, Virginia (Lady Champneys) by the 1890s; by family descent until 1981 when promised by Sir Weldon Dalrymple-Champneys, Virginia's son, as a gift to the Watts Gallery; confirmed by Norma, Lady Dalrymple-Champneys, 1986, and received by the gallery on her death, 1998

EXHIBITIONS: Royal Academy 1872, no.215; Watts Grosvenor 1881, no.71, as 'Mrs. F. Champneys' (or 175: *Portrait Study of a Lady in a Green Gown – Landscape Background*); *Japan British Exhibition*, London, 1919, no.87, as *Mrs. Champneys*

LITERATURE: Spielmann 1886, p.30 (following the Grosvenor catalogue, lists the *Mrs. F. Champneys* owned by the artist and the painting shown at the RA in 1872 as two different works);[1] Watts Catalogue, II, p.35; Edwina Ehrman, 'Velvet two-piece dress worn by Virginia Julian Dalrymple', unpublished (Watts Gallery), 2006

As this portrait entered the Watts Gallery from a private collection relatively recently, its unusual qualities can only now be assessed. It is an extraordinary image showing Watts going beyond the accepted conventions of the portrait into a more imaginative and innovative realm. As a portrayal of a beautiful young woman, the painting expands on earlier work by the artist in this area (see cat.37) with a new focus on colour, fashion and setting. Using the larger three-quarter-length format, Watts opted for an atypical pose, showing his subject out of doors, sitting on the fallen branch of a tree. The intense green of the dress is arresting. Obviously experimental, the portrait was not a commission.

Virginia Julian Dalrymple (1850–1922), Sophia Dalrymple's daughter, posed for the portrait. Just as the mother had often sat to the artist (see cat.17), so had her children at Little Holland House.[2] Watts had known Virginia for her entire life; when she was a child, he drew her portrait several times (one dating from 1853 is at the Watts Gallery) and in 1865 also painted her in a deep blue dress (version, Fogg Art Museum). She belonged to the extended bohemian circles surrounding her aunt Sara and mother Sophia, herself a muse to artists such as Burne-Jones and Rossetti. Photographs show Virginia to be an attractive young woman with a somewhat more rounded face than that seen in the portrait. Her blond colouring favoured her father John rather than Sophia, whose dark hair and eyes disclosed her Anglo-Indian background. Virginia was in her early twenties and unmarried[3] when Watts began the work, using the gardens of old Little Holland House as the setting.[4]

The portrait was under way by late 1871 as Watts notified his patron Charles Rickards: 'The Lady in Green portrait is one of the family (Virginia Dalrymple) a cousin of May's.'[5] Watts painted May for the Royal Academy in 1869 (cat.37), a work acquired by Rickards, who perhaps had shown interest in this one as well. A full-scale oil study (formerly Chapman collection) showing the figure in the same dress and pose also indicates that the landscape background was not part of the initial idea. By early 1872 Watts announced that the portrait would go to the Royal Academy where it appeared for the opening in May that year.

The most striking feature of the portrait is the intense green of Virginia's dress. In a note to his sitter he postponed her visit to the studio, 'as good light is indispensable' for what he had to do.[6] It seems as if Watts was challenging himself to produce a portrait with such a dominant colour. A similar artistic test on display here is how to depict a complicated pose. Virginia sits on a branch close to the ground with the thick folds of the dress sweeping around her figure.

This portrait seems to be as much about the intricacies of modern fashionable garb as it is about the sitter. Virginia wears a green velvet, day or walking dress.[7] Watts requested that she give him the dress, as he would certainly have needed time to paint it on a lay figure when his model was not there, such were the complications of its construction. It comprises two sections:[8] a gored skirt and a bodice with its neckline decorated with orange silk braid with bow-knot ties. From ruched velvet epaulettes on the shoulders a similar trim of tiny bows flows down the sleeve. Black silk bows on the front of the bodice relate to the black silk tie around the waist. Contrasting with the green of the dress is the coral jewellery worn by Virginia. Probably dating from *c*.1870, as Edwina Ehrman notes, the dress accords with the fashionable silhouette of *c*.1868–9, so it was a relatively recent fashion statement, without being absolutely up to the minute. The colour was certainly unusual and, along with the style of the dress, serves to characterise Virginia's Aesthetic taste.

This eye-catching portrait, on an impressive scale and with its powerful colouring, attracted comment when it appeared at the Academy's exhibition. Watts's great supporter, Tom Taylor in *The Times*, noted that 'the lovely golden haired maiden, Miss Virginia Dalrymple, in the brightest Venetian green satin, who only needs, we venture to think a different background to give even more value to her vivid robe and sweet young face'.[9] Colour also preoccupied F.G. Stephens in the *Athenaeum*, where he referred to the 'green, which, at present, seems a little crude, but not opaque; the face could not be improved'.[10] The colour prompted Taylor to compare Watts's portrait with Venetian art but it struck a modern note as well.

Interestingly, at the same exhibition Frederic Leighton showed *After Vespers* (RA 1872; The Art Museum, Princeton University) of a young girl in three-quarter-length view also wearing a strongly coloured green dress. At exactly the same time Rossetti painted *Veronica Veronese* (1870–2; Delaware Art Museum), noteworthy for the saturated green velvet dress of the music-making woman.[11] Might these artist friends have set themselves a common artistic challenge (or heard about each other's new paintings)?

Virginia Dalrymple brilliantly demonstrates how Watts expanded on the conventional notion of the portrait by moving it into the realm of subject painting. With its implied narrative, the portrait takes on new meaning. Essentially, it shows a beautiful young woman who, having walked into the woods, stops to rest on a fallen branch, a lily in her hand. The portrait is brought out into nature, not a pristine garden setting, but a wilder, more disquieting place. The massive tree trunk rising behind the figure creates a dark area that casts a sinister note over the scene. The landscape background with its autumnal hues suggests the passing of time. Within this setting Virginia in her green gown seems to be part of the landscape. Her fairness and youth contrast with the aged tree, her deep viridian garb signifying the forces of life and growth that will also age and die. In its unexpected departure from the norms of portraiture Watts's painting is a resolutely modern, wholly new approach to the genre. BB

1   It might be that the work referred to as *Mrs. F. Champneys* was the early portrait of Virginia as a child.
2   Sophia's two other children (Virginia's brothers) were Hew (1848–68) and Walter (1854–1920).
3   In 1876 she married Francis Champneys, an obstetrician and brother of the architect Basil Champneys. Francis, highly eminent in his field, became a baronet in 1910; see J.S. Fairbairn, 'Champneys, Sir Francis Henry, first baronet (1848–1930)', rev. June Hannam, *Oxford Dictionary of National Biography* (http://www.oxforddnb.com/view/article/32358, accessed 19 Feb 2008).
4   According to a later label on the back of the painting written by a member of the Dalrymple-Champneys family.
5   Watts Papers, Watts to Rickards, 4 October 1871.
6   Watts Papers, Watts to Rickards, undated letter, c.1871.

7   The dress survives in remarkably good condition, explained by the fact that Watts kept it for more than thirty years. It was only returned to Virginia after 1904. Later her descendants donated it to the Watts Gallery.
8   I am indebted to Edwina Ehrman's excellent analysis of the dress for an understanding of its construction and dating.
9   *The Times*, 4 May 1872, p.5.
10 *Athenaeum*, 11 May 1872, p.596. Despite these comments, it seems that Watts did repaint the face during 1874, as he mentioned in a letter to Rickards (Watts Papers, 29 November 1874).
11 Rossetti's later *Day Dream* (1880; Ionides Bequest, Victoria and Albert Museum), with Jane Morris dressed in a green gown and sitting in a tree surrounded by branches, seems indebted to Watts's portrait of *Virginia Dalrymple*.

43. *The Prodigal*, 1872–3

Oil on canvas, 61 × 51 cm (24 × 20 in)
COMWG44

PROVENANCE: collection of the artist (Little Holland House Gallery); Watts Gallery

EXHIBITIONS: possibly Watts Leighton House 1903, no.23 (as 'A Prodigal' about 1864); Memorial Exhibitions, Manchester 1905 (two Watts Gallery versions: probably no.17, as 'The Prodigal', is this version and no.88, 'The Prodigal' 1873, the other), Newcastle 1905 (two Watts Gallery versions: probably no.35, as 'The Prodigal', is this version and no.75, 'The Prodigal' 1873, the other), Dublin 1906, no.39

LITERATURE: Spielmann 1886, p.31 (RA version); Barrington 1905, p.92; Watts Catalogue, I, p.120; Macmillan 1903, pp.165–6 (other Watts Gallery version); Gould 2004, p.89

Cat. 43.1 *Samson*, 1871, oil on panel, 55.9 × 25.4 cm (22 × 10 in), COMWG75

Watts painted versions of two of Christ's most well-known parables, the Good Samaritan and the Prodigal Son, both of which deal with the triumph of love and mercy over established traditions and prejudices. His *Good Samaritan* (fig.41) was dedicated to the prison visitor and reformer, Thomas Wright (1789–1875), in support of his work. *The Prodigal* is based on Christ's parable from the Gospel of St Luke (15: 11–32) about two sons, one of whom, claiming his inheritance early, 'wasted his substance with riotous living'. After facing starvation and the humiliation of feeding from the scraps of a swineherd, he returns to his father to ask for forgiveness, which is granted.

If the parable is about the forgiveness of the father, it is also about the realisation by the individual of his errors or, as Macmillan expressed it, 'as an example of the larger liberty which sin offers to the deluded soul, and which ends in destitution and in the company of swine'.[1] Another version in the Watts Gallery collection portrays a full-length Prodigal Son sent to the fields to feed swine.[2] In this portrait the son, in profile, looks to the left of the picture and is dressed in a sheepskin and rags.

The manuscript catalogue notes that the present version is 'a study made from a well known Italian model, who also sat for the above [full-length *The Prodigal*] and for "A Venetian Nobleman"'.[3] It is probable that the sitter for the painting was Angelo Colorossi (1839–1916), a model favoured by leading artists including Leighton, Burne-Jones, Alma-Tadema and Simeon Solomon. Mary notes that 'the muscles for the "Clytie" were carefully studied from a well-known Italian male model, of the name of Colorossi',[4] and although he is not mentioned by name with regard to this painting, the likeness is strong.

As well as being the portrait of a well-known Italian model, the painting also gives a psychological portrayal of the character from the parable. The son's ragged clothing indicates the miserable position that he has reached, and the contemplative stare, his own realisation of the fact. The strength and determination evident in his aspect denotes the wilfulness that has led to this situation and the forming resolution to return to his father, in many respects a more difficult choice. The colours are subdued and warm, the handsome features of the model brooding. Unlike the passive desperation of Watt's full-length version, there is a restlessness in this painting shown in the straining neck suggesting an epiphany.   MB

1   Macmillan 1903, pp.165–6.
2   *The Prodigal Son* (seated), 1872–3: Royal Academy, 1873, no.281; Watts Grosvenor 1881, no.184 (as 'The Prodigal Son, 1873' with 'And he sent him into the fields to feed swine', Luke 15: 15); Camberwell 1902, as 'Prodigal (full length)'; Memorial Exhibition, London 1905, no.10, Edinburgh, Newcastle, Dublin, 1905. A note from Blunt in Watts Catalogue, I, p.120, says a head study of this model was with Adams, 92 New Bond Street, W1. 'Mr Watts's "Prodigal" (231), at the side of Eve, is an effective, low-stone study of a picturesque model' (*The Times*, 3 May 1873, p.12).
3   *Venetian Nobleman*, 1872–4, exhibited at Manchester 1905. Watts also used the same model and almost identical portrait in his study for *Samson* (cat.43.1)
4   Watts 1912, II, p.45.

44. *Farm Buildings, Freshwater, Isle of Wight, c.*1874–5

Oil on canvas, 53.3 × 66 cm (21 × 26 in)
COMWG166

PROVENANCE: collection of the artist (Little Holland House Gallery); part of the original Memorial Collection, 1905

EXHIBITIONS: Watts London 1881, no.111; Hanley, Staffordshire, 1890; Guildhall, London, 1892, no.19; Memorial Exhibitions, Manchester 1905, no.153, Newcastle, 1905, no.49, Edinburgh 1905, no.116; Watts Whitechapel 1974, no.30; *Whisper of the Muse: The World of Julia Margaret Cameron*, Colnaghi, London, 1990, no.62; Watts London and Compton 2006, no.14

LITERATURE: Watts Catalogue, I, p.59; Bayes 1907, p.xi; Staley and Underwood 2006, p.40

There are three known views of Freshwater by Watts: *Farm Buildings, Freshwater, Isle of Wight* (cat.44); *Freshwater, near Farringford* (cat.44.1) and *Freshwater in Spring* (private collection).[1] Painted in the same period in 1874–5, all were selected by the artist for his important solo exhibition at the Grosvenor Gallery in 1881–2.[2]

Watts's connection with Freshwater originated from his friendship with Alfred Tennyson and Julia Margaret Cameron, whom the artist visited on the Isle of Wight. Following his first marriage to Ellen Terry in 1864, Watts holidayed with his young wife in Freshwater, where she was photographed by Cameron and the couple went on walks with Tennyson. Watts's friendship with the Poet Laureate was well known to the Victorian public. In this context *Farm Buildings, Freshwater*, when exhibited at Watts's Memorial Exhibitions in 1905, was catalogued as 'A scene near Tennyson's house in the Isle of Wight. The picture pleasantly suggests the friendly intercourse of the painter and the poet.'[3]

Shortly before the lease on Little Holland House was due to expire in 1874, Watts commissioned the Arts and Crafts architect, Philip Webb, to build a house in Freshwater for himself and the Prinseps. The Briary was completed by 1873 and *Farm Buildings, Freshwater* was painted from Watts's bedroom window in the house. *Freshwater, near Farringford*, produced on a canvas of the same size and featuring a similar palette and composition, can be viewed as its companion piece, as it shows a continuation of the same view stretching to the right, with a repetition of the smaller farm building from a slightly different angle.[4] The two views were most probably started in the winter, as the artist wrote to his important collector Charles Rickards in February 1874: 'I am here out of the cold and fogs of London and I am painting a study from my window.'[5] Watts enjoyed the English countryside and received guests at Freshwater. His friend Mrs Barrington recorded an Easter visit to see Watts in 1873, recalling the frequent walks the artist took 'along the country roads in the soft grey hat he always wore and a loose cape flying in the wind'.[6]

Watts suffered from poor health. His doctors recommended winters away from London, and between 1876 and 1886 he spent that season in his studio at Brighton in Lewes Crescent, and from 1891 at Limnerslease, his winter residence in Compton, Surrey. Health-dictated travels also extended to foreign destinations, including a honeymoon in Egypt with second wife Mary in 1886–7 and an extensive stay in Malta in the winter of 1887. All these locations provided the artist with inspiration for landscape studies.

In *Farm Buildings, Freshwater*, the cold blue and grey sky, the leafless trees in the foreground and the dark subdued palette with a predominance of brown suggest that the season is winter, probably early morning or late evening due to limited light. The artist was known to have worked from very early morning well into the night. The main difference between cat.44 and its counterpart *Freshwater, near Farringford* is the nature of the light, particularly visible in the sky, which is cold and grey in cat.44 and warm with a yellow and orange glow in the other. As *Freshwater, near Farringford* was exhibited at the Grosvenor Gallery under the title *Evening at Freshwater, Isle of Wight*, it is likely that *Farm Buildings, Freshwater* was painted at dawn. As an artist Watts was interested in the differing quality of the lighting conditions seen in two very similar views of the same locality. Despite its apparently ordinary rural landscape subject showing thatched buildings with incidental detail such as a barrel and ladder propped against the roof, *Farm Buildings, Freshwater*, with its dark subdued palette and rich texture, conveys a mood of sadness and nostalgia. JD

1   Illustrated in Blunt 1975, pl.IIa.
2   Watts Grosvenor 1881, nos 111, 116, 83.
3   Memorial Exhibitions, Edinburgh 1905, p.52, and Manchester, p.42.
4   Staley and Underwood 2006, p.40.
5   Watts to Rickards, 13 February 1874, quoted in Watts Catalogue, I, p.59.
6   Barrington 1905, pp.4–5.

Cat. 44.1 *Freshwater, near Farringford*, 1874–5, oil on canvas, 53.3 × 66 cm (21 × 26 in), COMWG163

45. *Chaos*, 1875–82

Oil on canvas, 104 × 317.5 cm (41 × 125 in)
COMWG143

PROVENANCE: collection of the artist (Little
Holland House Gallery); part of the original
Memorial Collection, 1905

EXHIBITIONS: Watts New York 1884, no.108; Watts
Birmingham 1885, no.111; Watts Nottingham 1886,
no.10 (all three called 'a sketch', but unclear if this
means a full-size sketch, i.e. the Watts Gallery
painting, or a smaller one); Rugby School 1888;
People's Palace 1888, no.24 (Watts Gallery or Tate
version); Toynbee Hall, London, 1888; *A Collection
of Mountain Paintings and Photographs*, The Alpine
Club, London, 1894 (Watts Gallery or Tate version); Watts Manchester, Minneapolis, Brooklyn
1978, no.23; *The Nature of Painting*, Arts Council of
Great Britain, Museum and Art Gallery, Sheffield,
etc. 1983–4, no.21; Watts Compton 2004, no.11

LITERATURE (on the subject): Spielmann 1886, p.4,
cat. p.30; Macmillan 1903, pp.193–4; Sketchley
1904, pp.86–7, 122; Barrington 1905, pp.93, 100,
131–2; Watts Catalogue, I, p.25; Watts 1912, I,
pp.101–3, 105, 275–7, 301–2, II, p.105; Watts
Gallery Catalogue 1920, no.69; Alston 1929, no.61;
Blunt 1975, pp.65–7; Staley 1978, no.23; Morris
1996, pp.466–7; Bryant 1997, pp. 164–7; Trodd and
Brown 2004, pp.60–61; Staley and Underwood
2006, pp.20, 22 nn.13, 14

One of only two large-scale versions of this major composition, *Chaos* is a powerful statement of what one writer called 'Watts's cosmology'.[1] The painting is less highly finished than the one that the artist included in his bequest to the Tate Gallery in 1897.[2] The idea for the design dates from around 1850 when Watts conceived an ambitious mural cycle eventually dubbed 'The House of Life'. He intended *Chaos* to be 'the opening chapter of a book'.[3]

Within the sprawling composition the tumultuous chaos of the earth's formation, painted in scorching orangey tones, contrasts with an intermediary stage where a lone figure emerges from the sea. The concluding section, to the right, depicts a period of calm as reposing giants are paired with a row of dancing female figures robed in green drapery and flying through the air. In fact, this final section existed first as a separate oil painting called *The Titans* (cat.45.1), exhibited in 1875 at the annual exhibition in Manchester.[4] These powerful titans typified the mountains formed during the making of the earth, while the graceful chain of flying figures represents the passage of time. Watts expanded the composition during the 1870s and by the mid-1880s versions went to major exhibitions in New York, Birmingham and Nottingham.[5] Cat.45 is the first of the larger versions worked on, but it was left unfinished on the advice of fellow artists Edward Burne-Jones and Frederic Leighton, who were especially impressed with the figures of time sailing through the air. At that point, *c.*1875, Watts instructed his then assistant Matthew Ridley Corbet (1850–1920) to lay in the design on a new canvas, only slightly smaller in length; this version he completed for his bequest (Tate Britain), keeping the unfinished one for himself.[6]

In composing this multi-figure scene, Watts created a series of maquettes of individual poses in wax and clay (later cast in plaster),[7] including an Atlas-like figure forcing his back against a crushing rock, another writhing in anguish and one 'in the swollen tides [who] marks the beginning of the strides of time'.[8] Watts noted that

there were 'fifty figures in it, perhaps more', so the maquettes (on approximately the same scale as the actual figures in the painting) served as vital reference points to convey the physical reality of this invented subject.

In 1884 Watts's first explanation of this 'general history of mankind' appeared in the catalogue for the Metropolitan Museum of Art's exhibition.[9] Here he posited the notion that the upheaval taking place reveals the earliest moments of 'our planet' transforming into a 'vaporous uncertainty of atmosphere, of unborn creatures', until the figure emerging from the 'swollen tides marks the beginning of the strides of time'. The title *Chaos*, established by 1884, harked back to Watts's preoccupation with Miltonic subjects (see cat.13) in the years around 1850. *Paradise Lost* (book X, 282–3) speaks of 'waste wide anarchy of Chaos, damp and dark' on the edge of hell. Relevant, too, for Watts's thinking was the primeval chaos of Greek mythology, the nothingness from which the first elemental beings emerged, as related in Hesiod's *Theogony* and Ovid's *Metamorphoses*.

Watts's view and his language are almost certainly dependent on recent scientific debates concerning the formation of the world. Well

aware of Charles Darwin and the controversies caused by his publications, the artist had sought to paint his portrait.[10] In *Chaos* dynamic figures enact this evolutionary drama within a symbolic landscape of a distinctly post-Darwinian cast, with pre-history visualised in the language of the artist. Upheaval and creation are linked as great chunks of rock force their way up through fiery vapours and clouds of smoke. The 'swollen tide' with one single figure emerging reflects the idea of the first signs of life crawling onto the land from the water. The view in the background opens out to an expansive distant view of white mountains set against a golden light, before giving way to the titans and figures symbolic of time passing.

Later Watts wished he had called it *Cosmos* or *Chaos Passing to Cosmos*, as this title more fittingly described the emphasis on evolution presented in the painting. He made this clear when he commented in his retrospective explanation in 1896 in the catalogue of the exhibition at the New Gallery. The painting shows 'the emergence from convulsion to evolution in material and social condition'.[11]

The subject came in for much comment during Watts's lifetime, such was its unusual flavour in

Cat. 45.1 *The Titans*, 1869–75, oil on panel, 71.1 × 111.8 cm (28 × 44 in), COMWG109

an era of more straightforward subject paintings. Originally, he let it be known that the idea of the giant figures of the reposing continents was 'suggested to him when looking at the cracks and stains on the dirty plaster of a wall',[12] but this seems to be a piece of myth-making on the part of an artist, who had read Leonardo's *Treatise on Painting* and wanted to ally himself with the geniuses of the Renaissance. Truer to the spirit of *Chaos* was the highly individualised philosophy of William Blake, who also invented and depicted his personal mythology.

As one of Watts's most powerful designs, *Chaos* is a remarkable attempt to visualise the kind of subject matter not previously considered material for artists and, as such, it has particular relevance to the modern era. BB

1   Sketchley 1904, p.87.
2   For a discussion see Bryant 1996, no.49.
3   On the landscape element in *Chaos*, see Staley and Underwood 2006, p.20.
4   Although Watts sold this painting soon after the exhibition, Mary Watts bought it back in 1928 and it entered the collections of the Watts Gallery in 1931 (Watts Compton 2004, no.11).
5   The small design called *The Titans*, once a treasured item belonging to Watts, was given to the Fitzwilliam Museum by Mary Watts in 1916; see also Watts Whitechapel 1974, no.33, for another study called *The Titans*; a smaller version finished in the late 1890s went to a collector in Liverpool, James Smith, and is now at the Liverpool Museums.
6   Mary Watts in Watts Catalogue, I, p.25; Staley in Staley and Underwood 2006, p.22 n.14, considers that the Tate version is the first one.
7   Bryant 1997, pp.165–6.
8   The description of this figure appears in Watts New York 1884.
9   Reprinted in Barrington 1905, pp.131–3.
10 Cartwright 1896, p.25; Watts 1912, II, p.142.
11 Prefatory Note, Watts New Gallery 1896, p.5
12 Watts 1912, II, p.105.

46. *Orpheus and Eurydice*, 1872–7

Oil on canvas, 66 × 38 cm (25½ × 15 in)
COMWG79

PROVENANCE: sold by the artist to Charles Rickards, 1877; his sale, Christie's, London, 2 April 1887, no.40, bought by Williams; ... Barbizon House, London; Cecil French, by whom bequeathed to the Watts Gallery, 1955

EXHIBITIONS: Watts Manchester 1880, no.49; Watts Grosvenor 1881, no.36, as 'Orpheus and Eurydice: Design for the Larger Picture'; *Dei ed Eroi: classicità e mito fra '800 e '900*, Palazzo delle esposizioni, Rome, 1995, no.9; Watts Symbolism 1997, no.37; Watts Compton 2004, no.44

LITERATURE: Spielmann 1886, p.31; Barrington 1905, p.203; Watts Catalogue, I, p.112; Bryant 1997, pp.142–3; Bryant 2003, no.195, pp.434–6

The Greek legend of Orpheus and Eurydice is a tale of death and loss. Ovid (*Metamorphoses*, 10) and Virgil tell of Eurydice's death from a snake bite and her subsequent passage to Hades. Her husband, the musician Orpheus, resolves to reclaim her. He descends to the underworld where the playing of his lyre charms Pluto and Proserpine, thus securing Eurydice's release on the condition that Orpheus does not look back. On their climb back up to daylight and safety, Orpheus is unable to resist gazing back at his beloved and with his backward glance Eurydice vanishes. In Watts's painting we see the moment when she collapses and expires. Orpheus has dropped the lyre to reach out for his wife, but the pallor of her skin indicates death is already upon her as she falls into the gloom of Hades forever.

In celebrating the musical hero, the myth of Orpheus had a long-standing appeal to artists, not least Watts, who returned to it again and again from the 1860s onwards. The continual fascination for him centred on the moment of loss, which he painted in various versions in different formats, beginning with a well-known small composition with half-length figures (formerly Forbes Magazine Collection, now private collection) exhibited in 1869. Watts then expanded the figures to full-lengths with a draped Eurydice. After exhibiting one such work in 1872, he decided to portray this female figure as a nude, culminating in a grand full-length (Salar Jung Museum, India) exhibited to much acclaim at the Grosvenor Gallery in 1879 and then in Paris in 1880. This painting had a significant impact in establishing Watts's reputation in French Symbolist circles in the 1880s.

This smaller version of *Orpheus and Eurydice* can be identified as the 'design' for the eventual large painting of 1879.[1] Watts's method of working involved a 'design' for the large picture that was always planned as the eventual outcome.[2] These smaller works, used for experimenting with composition, colour and tonal values,[3] were more than simply studies and often ended up as finished pictures themselves, which Watts

exhibited or sold once he no longer required them. They were particularly suitable as cabinet pictures for connoisseurs, whereas the large versions were destined for public exhibition and public collections. Indeed, Charles Rickards eventually acquired this picture.

In this reduced-scale 'design' Watts experimented with the idea of the nude, reflecting a feature of his work that came to the fore in the late 1860s (see fig.48 and cat.32). Painted during a time when he used 'subdued tints' with little colour, the overall monochrome treatment and unreality of the grey light offer a more visionary approach to the subject, which emphasises the extreme paleness of Eurydice's skin. Much is obscured and hidden: Eurydice's face merges into the shadows, while Orpheus, a dynamic nude, whose face also remains partially concealed, reaches emphatically to claim the already corpse-like body of his wife. Even the lily, traditionally a symbol of innocence, here portends the end of life. The fallen lyre, as in *Hope* (cat.59), has lost all its strings but one, signalling the end of music. In connecting the idea of death with love and with the nude, the work resonates ominously. This visualisation does not offer ideal, beautiful nudes but is rather a disturbing study of bodily death and eternal loss.

The main version of *Orpheus and Eurydice* of 1879 retained the central idea of the design, but exploited the landscape setting – a rocky, bleak space – to convey the dark mood of the subject. Watts eventually sold it,[4] but he continued to work on another large version of the subject (cat.46.1) now in the Watts Gallery. In this final incarnation details are swept away for a powerful image of the two figures locked in a swirl of movement, emblematic of the inevitability of death. BB

1   Bryant 1997, no.37.
2   For this process see Bryant 1987–8, pp.54–7.
3   Barrington 1905, p.203, notes that one of the smaller versions, possibly this one, was an example of 'subdued tints'.
4   Barrington 1905, pp.92 and 126.

Cat. 46.1 *Orpheus and Eurydice*, c.1900–3, oil on canvas, 185.4 × 104.1 cm (73 × 41 in), COMWG134

47. *Thetis, c.*1870–86

Oil on canvas; 193 × 53.3 cm (76 × 21 in)
Inscribed lower left 'G F Watts'
COMWG42

PROVENANCE: collection of the artist (Little
Holland House Gallery); sold 1889/90 to Thomas
Agnew and Sons;[1] bought in May 1890 by Edward
Cecil Guiness, 1st Earl of Iveagh; his collection;
after his death in 1927 on loan from the Iveagh
Trustees to Kenwood, London; presented by
Rupert Edward, 2nd Earl of Iveagh, to the Watts
Gallery in May 1951

EXHIBITIONS: Memorial Exhibitions, London 1905,
no.193; Watts Manchester, Minneapolis, Brooklyn
1978, no.15; *Victorian Dreamers: Masterpieces of the
Neo-Classial and Aesthetic Movements*, organised by the
British Council, Isetan Museum of Art (Tokyo
Shimbun), Tokyo (and other venues), 1989, no.4;
Exposed: The Victorian Nude, Tate Britain, London,
2001, no.29; Watts Compton 2004, no.51

LITERATURE: Spielmann 1886, p.32 (smaller ver-
sion of 1866); Sketchley 1904, pp.93, 101, 103, 150;
Barrington 1905, p.93; Watts Catalogue, I, p.144;
Watts 1912, I, pp.235–6; *Catalogue of the Iveagh
Bequest Ken Wood, c.*1928, no.70; Watts Gallery
Catalogue 1957, p.19, no.7a; Staley 1978, pp.70–1;
Julius Bryant, 'Lord Iveagh as a Collector' and
'Purchases from Agnew's by Sir E.C. Guinness', in
Kenwood: Paintings in the Iveagh Bequest, New Haven
and London, 2003, p.418

In Greek mythology Thetis, a sea nymph and
one of the Neriades, married Peleus and gave
birth to Achilles, whom she dipped in the river
Styx as a baby. Later, the Iliad tells of how she
rose from the sea to console her warrior son.
Watts's aim in selecting this character was not to
dwell on Homeric or Ovidian narratives. Thetis
is characterised as a sea creature by the setting,
but in all other respects this is a study of the full-
length nude and as such an exercise in the tradition of treating the human figure as artists from
the Renaissance onwards had done. It was, however, a modern and consciously up-to-date portrayal of the nude based on direct observation
and yet reinvented for its audience.

During a phase of renewed interest in classical subjects in the mid-1860s Watts planned
several nude figures including small oils of *Thetis*
and *Daphne* (both private collection). *Thetis*,
exhibited at the Royal Academy in 1866, drew
the admiration of advanced artists such as
Rossetti[2] and patrons such as Frederick Leyland,
who, after seeing it, asked to meet Watts.[3] With
such interest, the artist went ahead with his
planned large-scale version of the subject, the
Thetis now at the Watts Gallery. Although Watts
might well have started the work in the late
1860s, most of the painting is characteristic of
the period between 1877 and 1886, as one can
see in the built-up golden highlights of Thetis's
hair. Barrington wrote that it was among those
works begun and finished during the years she
was an intimate of the artist's studio. It was not
considered ready for Watts's retrospective at the
Grosvenor Gallery in 1880, nor did it appear at
any of the many showings of his work in Britain
and abroad during that decade; by 1890 he had
sold it to Agnew's and it only went to public
exhibition in 1905. In his review for the *Art
Journal* R.E.D. Sketchley considered it 'perhaps
the loveliest of Watts's nudes, lovelier, because
more entirely designed for delight in beauty in a
young pure figure'.[4]

In the 1860s Watts treated the nude in a
series of studies. He drew the model Long Mary
rapidly and succinctly in charcoal on large
sheets of brown paper (see fig.49). In some studies she adopts traditional poses, in others she is
in motion. With this direct experience of the
human figure, Watts planned several large oil
paintings: *Thetis* on the seashore;[5] *Daphne* (RA

1870; unlocated), a wood nymph set against the
profuse growth of a laurel tree associated with
her transformation; and *Psyche* (completed 1880;
Tate Britain). Watts had painted nudes as part
of more expansive compositions during and
after his trip to Italy, but not yet as single figures.
Studies showing the nude depicted on a tall,
upright canvas had ample precedents in contemporary European art, as in the work of Ingres,[6]
but were also the logical outgrowth of Watts's
own interests in classical subjects from the 1850s
onwards and in the nude figure, as in the bust-
length *Study with the Peacock's Feathers* (fig.47). After
1866, when Watts's small *Thetis* was first publicly
seen, such concerns became more widespread in
British art in the work of Leighton, Whistler and
Albert Moore. Yet, perhaps one reason why
Watts did not finish the larger *Thetis* promptly is
that he realised that the market for such work
was limited. In 1873 he wrote regarding another
nude figure painting: 'it is a perfectly naked figure and though I hope my endeavours to render
it perfectly unobjectionable on that score have
not been wholly unsuccessful still such subjects
are more fit for a Gallery than a dwelling
house.'[7]

Watts depicted *Thetis* on a tall, narrow canvas
so that the length and long limbs of the figure
are even more elongated. She wrings the sea
water out of her hair. Her face is averted so that
her nudity is displayed in neutral fashion. The
physical presence of this slender Thetis is
restrained, even withdrawn. In line with this
approach is the thin dry quality of the paintwork
and muted colour scheme of pale blues and
greys evoking fresco painting. The canvas grain
shows through and in parts the paint is very
sketchy, with some of the edges all but unfinished as on the lower right side.

Thetis, probably nearly complete by 1880,
remained in the studio, and was then finished
off prior to its sale to Agnew's. Shortly after, in
1890, one of the greatest art buyers of the age,
Edward Cecil Guinness, added it to his still
growing collection, paying the substantial price
of 1200 guineas.[8] Guinness personified the type
of client a dealer such as Agnew's could attract,
but Watts himself would not have known him,
his own sales in this period being mainly to
Liverpool collector James Smith. Guinness, later
1st Earl of Iveagh, retained the work in his

personal collection, lending it to the Memorial Exhibition in 1905; later, after his death in 1927, his executors lent it to Kenwood where it hung upstairs in the China Room, as part of a display intended to evoke the private quarters of Lord Iveagh. Apart from the war years, it remained an incongruous feature of the mainly old master and eighteenth-century holdings at Kenwood until 1951. Probably at the urging of Anthony Blunt (never one with undue affection for the Victorians),[9] who was then official adviser to the Iveagh Bequest, the 2nd Earl, presented *Thetis* to the Watts Gallery. BB

1 Mary Watts in the Watts Catalogue incorrectly gives the date of this sale as 1899. Lord Iveagh bought the painting in 1890.

2 On the connections between Watts's painting and later nudes by Leighton, Whistler and Albert Moore, see Staley 1978, pp.70–1.

3 Watts Papers, Rossetti to Watts, n.d. [spring 1866]. Leyland did not in fact buy this painting, although he later owned Watts's portrait of Rossetti.

4 *Art Journal*, 1905, p.79.

5 Mary Watts claimed Watts made a study for *Thetis* inscribed 'Miss Smith', a well-known model in Pre-Raphaelite circles. There are various small oil studies of nudes some titled *Thetis*, but these are titles given later, not by Watts. These works are not associated with cat.47 in any significant way apart from being nudes.

6 Ingres's *La Source* (1856; Musée d'Orsay) is the most famous example. Watts could have known about this work by its reputation from his trip to Paris in 1855–6 at the time of the retrospective of Ingres's work at the Exposition Universelle or more obviously from the International Exhibition of 1862 in London, but he need not have personally visited Ingres's studio.

7 Watts 1912, I, p.261.

8 See Appendix C, 'Lord Iveagh's Purchases of Pictures from Agnew's', in George Martelli, *Man of his Time: A Life of the First Earl of Iveagh*, London, 1957, p. 353 (9 May 1890, mistakenly listing 'J.F. Watts'). My thanks to Julius Bryant for kindly providing this reference, as well as for further information on Iveagh's collecting of contemporary art and Watts's *Thetis* in the collections at Kenwood.

9 Anthony Blunt's brother Wilfrid became Curator of the Watts Gallery in 1959.

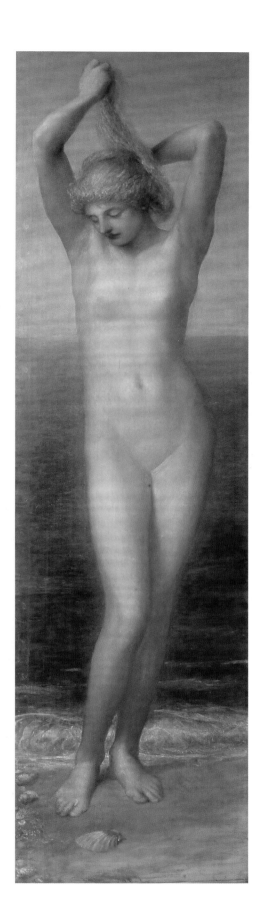

48. *The Genius of Greek Poetry*, c.1857–78

Oil on canvas, 66 × 54 cm (26 × 21 in)
COMWG22

PROVENANCE: collection of the artist (Little
Holland House); Watts Gallery

EXHIBITIONS: Watts Grosvenor 1881, no.176; Watts
New York 1884, no.121; Watts Birmingham 1885,
no.171, Nottingham 1886, no.9; People's Palace
1888, no.13; Rugby School, July 1888; Tottenham,
April 1891; Chicago 1893, no.489; Memorial
Exhibitions, Edinburgh 1905, no.134, Manchester
1905, no.98, Newcastle 1905, no.109, Dublin 1906,
no.30; Watts Aldeburgh 1961, no.65; Watts
Manchester, Minneapolis, Brooklyn, no.25; *The
Wilde Years: Oscar Wilde and the Art of his Time*,
Barbican Art Galleries, London, 2000–1, no.189;
Watts Compton 2004, no.27 or 28

LITERATURE: Spielmann 1886, pp.10, 30 (Davey
version); Cartwright 1896; Barrington 1905, pp.93,
109, 135–6; Watts Catalogue, I, p.63; Watts 1912, I,
p.235, II, p.74; Macmillan 1903, pp.124–5; Alston
1929, no.15; Blunt 1975, pp.94, 202; Staley 1978,
pp.25–6; Gould 2004, pp.154 (pl.XXIV), 155, 210,
275; Bryant 1997, pp.204–6

Ancient Greek art, with which Watts was fascinated, was the major source of inspiration for
this painting. From his youth, as Mary poetically
describes,

> his imaginative mind could roam the windy
> plains of Troy, or climb the heights of
> Olympus. Moving through the dim light of
> the London atmosphere, in his dull little
> room he saw 'the bright-eyed Athene in the
> midst bearing the holy aegis, that knoweth
> neither age nor death,' and dreamed that he
> too might be an aegis-bear of that which
> cannot grow old.[1]

Such enthralment led him in 1856 to tour the
Greek islands and visit the site of ancient
Halicarnassus, where the bright landscape was
imbued with the stories and myths of ancient
Greece. The attraction of Greece was the
history and art that for him was apparent everywhere in the landscape. The brightness and
sharpness of colour that he experienced on his
visit acted upon his imagination, and on his
return he began this painting, which was not
completed until 1878. Mary later wrote of her
visit to Greece with Watts in the 1880s:

> The Bay of Salamis was blue to its depths,
> blue poured into a cup of gold; the sky was
> blue, not that dye of a paint, but as if fold
> over fold of some ethereal web laid over and
> over again to infinity. 'We have got some-
> thing for life,' he said as we turned away. 'If I
> could paint that, I feel it would be worth a
> lifetime, even if I did nothing else.' He never
> did paint that picture, but had he not already
> summed up the whole sentiment of that hour
> in the picture he had called the 'Genius of
> Greek Poetry'?[2]

The painting is neither typically a landscape
nor a figure composition, making its interpretation a problem to commentators.[3] What Watts
clearly expresses is the importance of the landscape on the imagination and more specifically
how the art and religion of ancient Greece were
intimately connected with its landscape. He wrote:

> Greece was the natural home of the arts.
> Those who have visited Asia Minor, or sailed
> among the Islands of the Greek Seas, have
> seen assembled in serene harmony all that is
> most exquisite in nature, a concurrence of
> conditions that may well account for the
> birth and development of the divine facul-
> ties. The graceful mythology of the Greeks,
> which probably scarcely amounted to a
> superstition, was the outcome of constant
> communion with such loveliness.

Watts further emphasised the point by contrasting the northern landscape and how it acted
upon the human imagination:

> The less perceptive, though perhaps more
> imaginative, people of the north, who derive
> their conceptions more from habits imposed
> by an ungenial climate, from mists and dark-
> ness, display an inbred fancy and a grotesque
> arrangement of thought.[4]

Mrs Barrington notes that the painting would be
more easily explained if it was shown next to its
pendant, 'The Genius of Northern Poetry'. This
painting was either never fully conceived or no
longer survives, but Barrington's tantilising
description of it as 'darker, more mysterious, less
human in attributes'[5] emphasises the north–
south dichotomy that Watts explores. Barrington
also writes of an unexpected source for *The
Genius of Greek Poetry*: 'Wordsworth's lines beginning "The world is too much with us" had suggested this picture to Watts.'[6] It seems unlikely
that, if it was a source, it was a central one,
although the sentiment of the sonnet echoes a
dichotomy, less here between north and south,
but between the monotheism of the nineteenth
century and the pantheism of the ancient world:

> Little we see in Nature that is ours;
>   … I'd rather be
> A Pagan suckled in creed outworn;
> So might I, standing on this pleasant lea,
> Have glimpses that would make me less
>   forlorn;
> Have sight of Proteus rising from the sea;
> Or hear old Triton blow his wreathed horn.

On the painting's exhibition at the
Metropolitan Museum in New York in 1885,
Barrington expressed the central ideas of the

work in the catalogue, although the catalogue of the People's Palace exhibition in London in 1888 had the longest and clearest explanation of the painting and its visual expression of ancient Greek pantheism. There is little doubt that this would have involved consultation with the artist and was made clearer for an audience new to art and the ideas it expressed.

We have here a huge naked figure, seated and reclining with his elbow on a rock which juts from the edge of a cliff overlooking the sea. He is contemplating many spirits which are intended to suggest the forces of nature at work as they act together or against one another. They throng the golden clouds of the sky, and are thus driven by the wind over land and ocean; others are moving rapidly in the air, where one of them, like a falling star, describes a fiery arc; some are swimming in the sea, disporting in its wavelets and calmer spaces; some, man-like, race upon the shore, and some traverse the land. The Genius looks at these moving, happy, and powerful spirits with profound interest and, with one hand at his lips, seems to be marvelling at the wonders of the world. The painter intends to illustrate the fact that the ancient Greeks recognised (and imagined that they some-times actually saw) the forces of nature acting in human forms. Accordingly to them every brook had its guardian, the air was full of spirits, a nymph lived and perished with every tree; there were goddesses of the sands, deep sea, mountains, rocks, and waterfalls, while even temporary incidents, such as storms and floods, were under the dominion of their own genii.[7]

The central figure of the Genius is drawn from the reclining figures of Dionysus and Ilissos that Pheidias carved for the east and west pediments of the Parthenon. Pheidias was one of Watts's greatest inspirations, and this figure, held at the British Museum, was used by the artist in several compositions. The sculptural nature of this painting must have influenced the sculptor Sir Edgar Boehm's comment that the work was 'Mr Watts's greatest imaginative work'.[8] A small bronze of this painting (cat.87) highlights further the exploration of sculptural space within the

work and the artist's use of three-dimensional models to inform his painting.

The painting was begun in the late 1850s and not completed until about 1878. It is built up of layers of dry scumbles, which serve to enhance the sculptural quality of the Genius and the rocky promontory against the luminous sea. In it Watts successfully combines a golden light with the brilliant blue that he experienced on his visit to Greece. There are two other versions of the painting,, at the Fogg Art Museum and Preston Art Gallery, but this is the most exhibited. The Preston version, another highly finished one, was exhibited at the Watts exhibitions at the New Gallery in 1896–7 (no.74), the Royal Academy in 1905 (no.85) and the Tate Gallery in 1997 (no.78). MB

1   Watts 1912, I, p.15.
2   Watts 1912, II, p.74.
3   Bryant in Watts Symbolism 1997 (no.78).
4   Watts 1912, III, pp.50–1.
5   Barrington 1905, p.136.
6   Barrington 1905, p.109.
7   *The People's Palace for East London, Catalogue of the Finest Collection of Modern Paintings*, exh. cat., People's Palace, Mile End Road, London 1888, pp.8–9.
8   Watts Catalogue, I, p.63.

49. *Paolo and Francesca, c.1872–84*

Oil on canvas, 152 × 130 cm (60 × 51 in)
COMWG83

PROVENANCE: collection of the artist (Little Holland House Gallery); Watts Gallery

EXHIBITIONS: Grosvenor Gallery 1879, no.73; Watts Grosvenor 1881, no.51; *Exposition Internationale de Peintre*, Galerie Georges Petit, Paris, 1883, no.2; Watts New York 1884, no.89; Watts Birmingham 1885, no.132; Watts Nottingham 1886, no.18; Guildhall 1892, no.18; Chicago 1893, no.488; Watts New Gallery 1896, no.95; *L'Exposition Générale des Arts et de l'Industrie*, Stockholm 1897, no.1436; Watts Gallery 1904, no.26; Memorial Exhibitions, London 1905, no.180, Edinburgh 1905, no.86, Manchester 1905, no.125, Newcastle 1905, no.106, Dublin 1906, no.47; Watts London 1954, no.59; Watts Whitechapel 1974, no.26; Watts Manchester, Minneapolis, Brooklyn, no.28; Munich and Madrid 1993, no.70; *The Victorians: British Painting 1837–1901*, Washington 1997, no.32; Watts Symbolism 1997, no.48; Watts Compton 2004, no.64

LITERATURE: Spielmann 1886, p.31; Cartwright 1896, p.29; Macmillan 1903, pp.167–70; Barrington 1905, pp.92, 125–6; Watts Catalogue, I, p.117; Watts 1912, I, p.64; Alston 1929, no.33; Loshak 1963, pp.484–5; Blunt, 1975, p.149; Staley 1978, pp.86–7; Gaja 1995, pp.32–9; Bryant 1996, pp.121–4; Bryant 1997, pp.162, 164

'One day we read for pastime how in thrall
Lord Lancelot lay to love, who loved the
   Queen;
We were alone – we thought no harm at all.

As we read on, our eyes met now and then,
And to our cheeks the changing colour
   started,
But just one moment overcame us – when

We read of the smile, desired of lips long-
   thwarted,
Such smile, by such a lover kissed away,
He that may never more be parted

Trembling all over, kissed my mouth. I say
The book was Galleot, Galleot the
   complying
Ribald who wrote; we read no more that
   day.'

While the one spirit thus spoke, the other's
   crying
Wailed on me with a sound so lamentable,
I swooned for pity like as I were dying …[1]

So in *The Divine Comedy* Dante describes the adulterous lovers Paolo and Francesca giving their own account to the poet in a circle of hell where the souls are blown by the 'blast of hell that never rests from whirling'. Caught together and killed by Francesca's husband, the lord of Rimini, the black wind that blows them in hell is symbolic of the lust that they gave in to. The subject, like that of Lancelot and Guinevere about whom they were reading, was a popular one for artists. In 1856 the story of Paolo and Francesca was produced as a play performed at the Lyceum Theatre, taking 'so frequent a theme for pictorial art' to the stage.[2] William Blake, John Flaxman, Ary Scheffer, Ingres, Rossetti, Leighton, Charles Halle and Gustave Doré, all found inspiration in the story.

The two scenes that the story offered to the visual artist for depiction was their first kiss and the two souls being blown around the circle of hell. Rossetti takes both scenes, while Scheffer, whose version is closest to Watts's, takes hell and depicts Dante and Virgil looking on. Watts had become fascinated with the subject in the 1840s whilst he was in Italy. 'Many pencil drawings',

the manuscript catalogue notes, 'were made at Careggi for this subject',[3] and several drawings from around 1845 show ideas for a composition based on the illicit kiss.[4] The artist would have been aware of John Flaxman's illustrations to Dante published in 1793, and possibly Scheffer's painting, which was influenced by Flaxman and first exhibited in 1835.[5] Similarly, in Watts's first version of the painting dating from around 1847 Francesca is nude. The painting was exhibited at the British Institution and, according to one critic, was 'distinguished by the vigour of the drawing, and by an adherence to the Florentine principle of using colour only as a subservient to the exhibition of form'. Certainly, it was considered the best of Watts's work there, highlighting 'the pensive countenance of Francesca Rimini'.[6]

Watts himself painted four versions of the subject including this one, which is the last and most complete. The first version painted around 1847 (152.5 × 122 cm, private collection) was exhibited at the 1848 British Institution; the second version, *c.*1865, oil on panel (45 × 35 cm), was previously in the collection of Lord Brownlow and David Loshak; and the third, from around 1870 (66.1 × 52.5 cm), was owned by Rickards and is now in Manchester City Galleries. The strong linear quality that was so admired in the first is consistent throughout all the versions, the composition fluctuating very little, but there are also marked changes, perhaps most noticeably the addition of drapery: Francesca loses her nudity and the draperies begin to emphasise the movement of the hellish black wind. When we reach this final version, Paolo and Francesca are more visibly deathlike, more obviously shades in hell, with sunken eyes, worn out from the wind that allows no rest.

David Loshak writing in 1963 observed that Watts 'apparently tended to identify Francesca with his lady-loves'.[7] Loshak proposes Lady Holland as the model for his early drawings of the kiss, while he considers the 1865 *Paolo and Francesca* to be modelled on Watts's first wife Ellen Terry and the present version, on Countess Somers. As a result, Allen Staley suggests that Paolo is a personification of Watts himself. It is unclear who the model for the 1870 Francesca was, but she is distinct from the other three. Unusually, the figures of Dante and Virgil appear in the lower left of this painting, which,

like the 1865 version, is a small study, owned by the collector Rickards and exhibited at the Dudley Gallery in the winter of 1870. This was essentially an exhibition of cabinet pictures, often studies for larger paintings, and among several works by Watts were small versions of *Love and Death* and *Paolo and Francesca*. Despite its scale, the latter still attracted the praise of critics:

Mr. Watts's other figure design is an exquisite monochrome of Francesca and Paolo, as Dante saw them in the Inferno, whirled round amid the fiery shower in the embrace of love that defies death and torment. The sad sweetness of the pale head that reposes on the bosom of the shrouded lover has never been surpassed in any version of this often-painted subject. Mr. Watts's group in beauty of design quite holds its own with the famous one of Ary Scheffer, and *in chiaroscuro* as well as expression seems to us at once worthier of the subject and truer of the description.[8]

The present final version is a very clear development of the earlier works and was painted mainly between 1872 and 1875, though reworked in the early 1880s: 'The painting is formally finished,' Watts wrote, 'but I have repainted and improved it.'[9] In an engraving of how it was first completed in the *Magazine of Art* of 1878 the figures of devils can be clearly seen tormenting the adulterous shades as they are swept along.[10] The dark claustrophobic fumes evident in its completed state replace the limbs of devils. When it was first exhibited in 1879 at the Grosvenor Gallery, the painting was read as a story illustrating the power of love: 'the pair of lovers as Dante saw them whirled by the wind through the black-air in never-ending embrace … tell of the triumph of love, over death … the intense lovingness of the embrace of Paolo and the restfulness of Francesca's face upon his breast.'[11] Mrs Barrington in her catalogue entry for the Metropolitan Museum exhibition interpreted it similarly, as 'tender love abiding through endless suffering'. Malcolm Warner in the 1997 Washington exhibition, *The Victorians*, has suggested a far bleaker reading of the painting in which infinity together is gradually wearing out their love.

If Loshak is correct in identifying the model for Francesca as Countess Somers, his lost love, who was perhaps still a regretful memory, that awareness may add to our reading of the painting. When it was exhibited at his Grosvenor Gallery retrospective, although it was greatly praised, it was seen as

only second to Ary Scheffer's conception of the same subject. In composition, indeed, we prefer our English painter's work, but it has not the pathos of the German picture, nor is it finished with the same elaboration. How fine it is may, perhaps, be understood by those who compare with it M. Gustave Doré's rendering of the same subject.[12]

The tenderness of earlier versions appears to have diminished, giving way to the sunken eye-sockets and sheer weariness, 'hopeless of any rest' in Dante's words. Love is all that remains, and you wonder if this will give way to bitterness. But this is the very reason that they are in hell and has as much to do with the trials, torments and compulsions of love as it has to do with love triumphant. With endless love the agonies never cease. Explored over nearly four decades, this is one of Watts's most powerful paintings and a pinnacle of the artist's achievements both technically and imaginatively. MB

1   Dante, *The Divine Comedy: Inferno*, canto V, lines 127–41, translated by Dorothy L. Sayers, London, 1951, pp.100–1.
2   'Lyceum Theatre', *The Times*, 15 July 1856, p.12.
3   Watts Catalogue, I, p.116.
4   See Gaja 1995, p.35 (illustrated).
5   See Staley 1978, no.28.
6   'British Institution', *The Times*, 7 February 1848, p.8.
7   Loshak 1963, p.484.
8   'Winter Exhibitions', *The Times*, 5 November 1870, p.4.
9   Watts Catalogue, I, p.117.
10 *Magazine of Art*, I, 1878, p.242.
11 'The Grosvenor Gallery', *The Times*, 2 May 1879, p.3.
12 *The Times*, 26 January 1882, p.8.

Cat. 49.1 Frederick Hollyer, Photograph of *Paolo and Francesca* (early stage of final version; cat.94)

50. *The Return of Godiva*, early 1870s–1900

Oil on canvas, 185.4 × 109.2 cm (73 × 43 in)
COMWG136

PROVENANCE: collection of the artist (Little Holland House Gallery): Watts Gallery

EXHIBITIONS: von Schleinitz records it as first exhibited in 1885, location unspecified; Royal Academy 1900, no.207; Southport 1901, no.45; Watts Gallery 1904, no.83 (as 'The Lady Godiva'); Memorial Exhibitions, Manchester 1905, no.104, Newcastle 1905, no.130, Edinburgh 1905, no.127; Herbert Art Gallery and Museum, Coventry 1982, no.50; Compton 2004, no.69

LITERATURE: *Athenaeum*, 11 January 1879, p.58; Spielmann 1886, p.30; Macmillan 1903, pp.178–80; Sketchley 1904, pp.138–9; von Schleinitz 1904, p.58; Phythian 1906, p.177; West c.1906, pl.21; Erskine 1906, p.189; Watts Catalogue, I, p.64; Gould 2004, pp.144, 335–6

Begun in the early 1870s, Watts did not complete *Lady Godiva* until 1900 when he sent it to the Royal Academy exhibition. Later, when it was shown at the Memorial Exhibition in Manchester in 1905, a quotation from Tennyson's eponymous poem of 1842 appeared together with explanatory text:

> Godiva, wife of a grim earl who ruled in Coventry. When he laid fresh taxes on his people she prayed him passionately to lighten the burden on the starving town.
>
> And from a heart as rough as Esau's hand,
> He answered: 'Ride you naked through the
>   town
> And I repeal it …'
> So left alone, the passions of her mind
> As winds from all the compass shift and blow,
> Made war upon each other for an hour,
> Till pity won. She sent a herald forth,
> And bade him cry with sound of trumpet, all
> The people; therefore as they loved her well,
> From then till noon, no foot should pass the
>   street,
> No eye look down, she passing; but that all
> Should keep within, door shut and window
>   barred …
> And she rode forth clothed with chastity. –
>   Tennyson.
>
> This picture represents the moment when her supreme task of love fulfilled she faints into the arms of her waiting women, who wrap robes around her.

Originally Lady Godgifu ('Gift of God') of Mercia (fl.1040–80), Lady Godiva was primarily revered for her dedication to the Church and exceptional beauty, including extremely long hair. Godiva married her second husband Leofric of Coventry (968–1057) in 1035, and the couple were recorded as benefactors and founders of a number of monasteries. No early chronicle mentions Godiva's tax dispute with her husband or the naked ride, which is generally considered to be legend rather than history.

Watts's treatment of the subject is rare. More common depictions of the story illustrate Godiva's conversation with Leofric, preparations and prayer before the ride, or the ride itself. The last is by far the most popular subject due to its sensual appeal and is best exemplified by John Collier's famous treatment of the subject of 1898 (Herbert Art Gallery, Coventry). Watts probably also knew William Behnes's sculpture of the subject (Coventry City Council House) exhibited at the Academy exhibition of 1844 and inscribed with a quotation from Tennyson.[1]

Watts's painting depicts the dramatic moment of Lady Godiva's return to her castle. Exhausted, she dismounts from the horse, falling into the arms of her dedicated female attendants, who cover her naked body with robes. Interestingly, Godiva's reception at the castle on completing the ride is not mentioned in Tennyson's poem, therefore Watts's interpretation of this episode is imagined. Unusually, Watts employs little narrative or contextual detail in the form of architecture or historical costume. The stone wall, cobbled street and loose robes of the protagonist's attendants are only suggestive of a medieval past. The spires in the far distance become symbolic of Coventry's skyline.

The emphasis on the dramatic impact of the central figure composition is recorded as the artist's original intention in two slight pen-and-ink compositional sketches (cat.50.1), as well as a detailed monochromatic oil study (early 1870s; COMWG151), all displaying the same central focus on Godiva supported by attendants and the indistinct indication of the horse's head in the far left.[2]

The depiction of Godiva's virtually lifeless body largely covered in shroud-like white drapery occupies the central diagonal axis of the composition. Her body is supported by a maternal figure (in the top centre) surrounded by a group of other attentive figures, and is more suggestive of religious imagery of martyrdom in old master painting and sculpture than of popular narrative representations of this medieval legend.[3] Evocative of the Deposition of Christ and covered in the white drapery of the shroud, Godiva is lowered into the arms of a veiled tender figure reminiscent of the Virgin. The three kneeling angelic attendants reinforce the religious imagery deployed by Watts. The picture focuses on Godiva's martyr-like suffering and sacrifice undertaken to redeem the people of Coventry.

Exhibited at the Royal Academy exhibition of 1900, the picture attracted the attention of the critic of *The Athenaeum*:

Mr. Watts, in *The Return of Godiva* (207), has hit upon an entirely unused incident in an ancient legend, and he had poetic truth on his side when he decided to represent the heroic lady as no longer young. It no doubt occurred to him that when she was past her prime Godiva's trial would be immeasurably greater, and her sacrifice more heroic.[4]

According to Mary, Watts's Godiva was 'painted as a protest against the many studies of merely the nude model exhibited under this title'.[5] Started in the 1870s and well advanced by 1876, as recorded by Barrington, *Lady Godiva* was part of Watts's most important group of works, which the artist called his 'Anthems'.[6] As demonstrated by an early Hollyer photograph of the first version of this picture, the original composition revealed more of Godiva's bosom, subsequently made more indistinct by the artist. In 1906 J.E. Phythian drew a parallel between *Lady Godiva* and two other images of womanhood:

Three ... pictures by Watts may be linked into a short chain: The Daughter of Herodias [*c.*1885; private collection], in the splendour of sensuality and pride; The Magdalen [cat.39.1], in the sad hues of spiritual abasement; and Lady Godiva, a picture of a woman's chivalry; she faints away into the arms of her attendants, after the fearful strain of her devoted heroism; but the colour is bright, because the moment, after all, is a joyous one.[7] JD

1   A number of painters depicted various episodes from Tennyson's poem such as Lady Godiva's conversation with Leofric by Edmund Blair Leighton (1892; Leeds Museums and Galleries) or preparations and prayer before the ride in *Lady Godiva's Prayer* by Sir Edwin Landseer (*c.*1865; Herbert Art Gallery, Coventry).
2   Notably, Godiva's bosom featuring in the monochromatic oil study disappears behind her long hair in the finished picture, while the towers of Coventry prominent in the study become less distinct in the finished painting.
3   Such as Peter Paul Rubens, *The Descent from the Cross* (central part of the triptych), 1611–14 (Cathedral, Antwerp, Belgium).
4   *The Athenaeum*, 12 May 1900, Watts Gallery Archive.
5   Watts Catalogue, I, p.64.
6   Barrington 1905, pp.92–3.
7   J.E. Phythian, *G.F. Watts*, London, 1906, p.177.

Cat. 50.1 Study for *Lady Godiva*, *c.* 1870, pen and ink on paper, 18 × 12 cm (7 × 4¾ in), COMWG2006.15

51. *Self-Portrait*, 1879

Oil on canvas, 66 × 53.3 cm (26 × 21 in)
Inscribed lower left 'G F Watts 1879'
COMWG9

PROVENANCE: sold by the artist to Charles
Rickards, 1879; his sale, Christie's, 2 April 1887,
no.45, bought by Agnew for 147 guineas; Edward
Atkinson, Fowey, Cornwall; his sale, Christie's,
9 March 1912, no.160, bought by the Fine Art
Society; acquired by Mary Watts; her collection
until December 1913 when given to the Watts
Gallery

EXHIBITIONS: Watts Manchester 1880, no.6

LITERATURE: Macmillan 1903, p.83; Watts Gallery
Catalogue 1920, no.23; Watts Catalogue, II, p.168;
Alston 1929, no.49; Bryant 2004, pp.164–5

In 1879 a request came from the Uffizi Gallery in Florence through the new President of the Royal Academy, Frederic Leighton, for Watts and Millais to join him in painting their own self-portraits for the famed gallery of artists' self-portraits in that collection. To Watts this recognition came in the aftermath of his successes at the first two exhibitions of the Grosvenor Gallery and at the International Exhibition in Paris in 1878. In 1880 he completed the portrait showing him posed before his painting *Time, Death and Judgement* (cat.68), and it was sent to Italy.[1] His reputation now had an international reach.[2]

For this important commission Watts worked on several new ideas for self-portraits, his first since the mid-1860s. It is possible to see the close connections between the three portraits begun in 1879. An unfinished study (p.214) related to the Uffizi portrait shows Watts facing to the right against a plain background,[3] which in the final work becomes the more specific backdrop of *Time, Death and Judgement*. In cat.51 he also wears a painter's smock with a white collar just visible but instead tries out a different pose, facing the opposite direction in strict profile against a red-curtained background. The boldness of the lavish red contrasts with the more reticent touches of the brushwork in the painting of the beard.

Unusually among his fellow British artists, Watts had always paid particular attention to the virtues of self-portrayal. On a practical level, he commented in 1869: 'I paint myself constantly, that is to say whenever I want to make an experiment in method or colour and am not in the humour to make a design.' But he also had known the Uffizi's collection of artists' self-portraits from his years in Florence, once calling it the 'most interesting gallery I know'.[4] In November 1879 he discussed his plans for the Uffizi's commission with his patron Charles Rickards in Manchester who already possessed one of Watts's self-portraits (*c.*1863; private collection), a work related to his famous portrait of 1864 (Tate Britain).[5] He even sent a self-portrait, apparently the one that he intended to send to the Uffizi, for Rickards to see. There is a possibility that it may be the same as cat.51.[6] So fascinated with the idea of his artist friend being commissioned by the Uffizi, Rickards pressed him for a current self-portrait to add to his large

collection, but Watts resisted, saying 'you have one already and I cannot think you want another'.[7] But eventually he relented: 'I must tell you that before leaving town I began a head of myself very much against my own feelings somehow, but you have seemed to make such a point of it that I could hardly help doing it.'[8] Characteristically, Watts sought a high price, citing another recent painting of himself that could have made £1,000, but he allowed Rickards privileged client status, reeling him in with a lower price of 200 guineas rather than the 500 guineas he would charge to an ordinary client.

Aged sixty-two, Watts presents himself as a modern old master painter, wearing the characteristic skullcap he adopted in the manner of Titian, the sixteenth-century Italian artist. One contemporary described this as 'ruby-coloured', which may have suggested the depth of the red background also evocative of Venetian art. Fully signed and dated, this portrait is a vivid statement of Watts's seriousness of purpose at this stage in his career. It only entered the Watts Gallery because Mary Watts bought it after an auction in 1912; when she presented it in 1913, the curator Charles Thompson recorded that this was a valuable acquisition as 'a likeness of Mr. Watts at a time when little other really exact record of his appearance exists'.[9] BB

1   Bryant 2004, no.59.
2   On Watts's growing international reputation see
     Bryant 1996, pp.109ff. and Bryant 1997, pp.65ff.
3   Illustrated in Bryant 2004, p.37.
4   Watts Papers, Watts to Rickards, 10 February
     1869; quoted in Watts 1912, I, pp.244–5.
5   Bryant 2004, no.48.
6   If this were the case, then the Watts Gallery
     self-portrait is the original Watts intended for the
     Uffizi, but unfortunately the correspondence
     between Watts and Rickards for the crucial time
     period concerned is not complete, so it is not
     clear if Rickards returned the portrait he was
     sent and Watts painted another or he kept the
     one Watts originally intended to send to Florence,
     prompting the artist to paint another one.
7   Watts Papers, Watts to Rickards, 19 November
     1879.
8   Quoted in Watts Catalogue, II, p.168, but not
     among the Watts/Rickards letters.
9   Curator's Report, 15 November 1913. The Uffizi
     portrait had gone to Italy in 1880, so would not
     have been well known in England, and the study
     for it (p.214) was an unfinished work.

52. Study for Death in *Love and Death*, 1870s

Pencil on paper, 11.7 × 9.1 cm (4½ × 3½ in)
Inscribed (possibly in another hand) 'Love & Death'
COMWG 2007.317

53. Study for Death in *Love and Death*, c.1870

Pencil on paper, 14 × 8.5 cm (5½ × 3¼ in)
COMWG 2007.321

54. Study for Death in *Love and Death*, c.1870

Pencil on paper, 15.5 × 9 cm (6 × 3½ in)
COMWG 2007.324

55. Compositional study for *Love and Death*, c.1870

Pen and sepia ink on paper, 8.2 × 4.5 cm
(3¼ × 1¾ in)
COMWG 2007.325

PROVENANCE (for 52–5): collection of the artist;
Mary Watts; Lilian Mackintosh (Mrs Michael
Chapman), legal descendant of the artist; by
descent until formally included within the Watts
Gallery's collections

These drawings, a selection from a group of studies on the same subject, provide a unique insight into the evolution of Watts's major composition, *Love and Death*.[1] He regarded this design as one of the two 'most important things I can do and shall ever do'.[2] The number of exhibited versions is evidence of the value that he placed upon *Love and Death*; indeed, many of his contemporaries considered it his masterpiece. The first finished version (unlocated) appeared at exhibition in late 1870; the prime large-scale version (fig.52; cat.55.1) was exhibited to great acclaim at the Grosvenor Gallery in 1877.

In *Love and Death*, as in all of Watts's best symbolical compositions, he aimed at a universal audience, yet there was a specific impetus, as he witnessed the long decline into death of his friend William Schomberg Kerr (1832–70), 8th Marquess of Lothian and husband of Constance (see cat.38). In 1874 he stated: 'I wished to suggest the passionate though unavailing struggle to avert the inevitable.'[3] In the painting the winged figure of Love, a nude youth, endeavours to hold back the draped female figure of Death whose faceless persona and relentless forward motion towards a shadowy doorway lend a disturbing and palpable sense of tragedy.

The drawings show the first idea of the subject, with Death crossing a threshold not as the traditional ghastly skeleton who appears in older art, but as a draped female. Watts first portrayed Death with the conventional emblem, a scythe (cat.53). Moving on from that notion, the small but vigorous pen-and-ink drawing (cat.55) reveals the now established composition, with Death advancing to the doorway, here blocked by Love. Death still has a massive scythe over one shoulder but now enforces its dominance over Love with an outstretched arm. This drawing effectively sets out the composition in terms of light and dark, with diminutive Love falling backwards into the murky dark spaces. The other two drawings (cats 52, 54), though small-scale works in themselves, concentrate specifically on the arrangement of Death's drapery. In the earlier cat.54 the sheer monumentality of the figure is conveyed by the thick folds, whereas in the other drawing, relating to a later version, Death is more elongated and the drapery flows into longer lines. Watts's study of

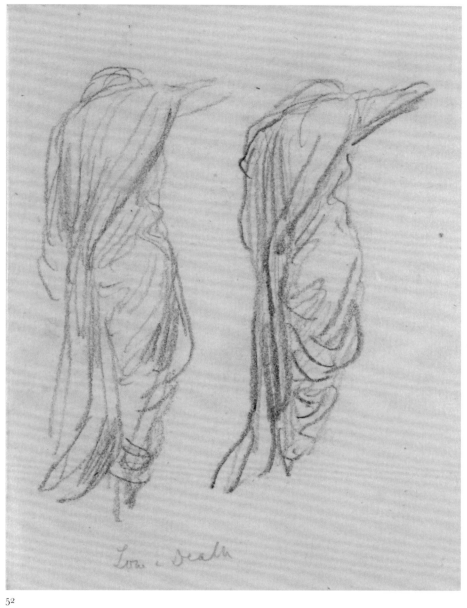

52

53

54

55

drapery in ancient sculpture here enters the realm of his imaginative subject paintings. These drawings show how the artist's ideas evolved at the key moment when the composition of *Love and Death* took shape. BB

1   For a discussion of the prime finished version at the Whitworth Art Gallery see Bryant 1997, pp.166–8; see also Bryant 1996, pp.116–17.
2   Quoted in Watts Catalogue, I, p.89.
3   Watts to Rickards, December 1874, quoted in Watts 1912, I, pp.283–4.

Cat. 55.1 Frederick Hollyer, photograph of *Love and Death*, Hollyer Album, Watts Gallery Archive

56. Study for *The Spirit of Christianity*, early 1870s

Black and red chalk on paper, 52 × 31.5 cm (20½ × 12¼ in)
COMWG 2006.8

PROVENANCE: collection of the artist; Mary Watts; Lilian Mackintosh (Mrs Michael Chapman), legal descendant of the artist; by descent until formally included within the Watts Gallery's collections

This drawing is a study for the painting under way in the early 1870s (versions: cat.56.1 and Tate Britain). Watts mentioned the oil, then entitled *The Sacred Heart*, in letters to his patron Rickards, promising him a reduced copy (1874; art market, 2003). When he exhibited a large version at the Royal Academy in 1875, it bore the less overtly religious title, *Dedicated to All the Churches*. Unusual in referring to religion specifically, Watts did not in fact consider it 'a religious picture, certainly not a doctrinally religious picture'. Essentially, it was 'the symbol of compassionate tenderness'.[1] To Watts religion had a purpose as 'the effort of mankind to reach out to an idea of the Infinite'.[2]

An impressive study on a quite substantial scale, this work shows the overall composition of the painting, with the 'genius of religion' floating in the clouds and below her a cluster of fat putti endeavouring to shelter beneath her capacious robes. Like the artist's most successful designs, the simplicity of the oval shape that contains the figures creates a memorable image. The overall softness of the handling in chalks recalls Watts's portrait drawings of the 1850s (cat.25). Here the treatment accords with the idea of the spirit who inhabits a realm removed from the everyday. Indeed, the medium and handling help to convey the visionary nature of the subject. BB

1   Watts to Rickards, quoted in Watts 1912, I, p.279.
2   Watts 1912, III, p.326, an undated comment by Watts.

Cat. 56.1 *The Spirit of Christianity*, 1872–5, oil on canvas, 91.4 × 53.3 cm (36 × 21 in), COMWG122

The 1880s

In the 1880s Watts had the benefits of a reputation that was secure, and he was able to explore grand themes in his allegorical paintings or, as he described them, 'poems painted on canvas'. His artistic career was celebrated at the highest level, first with a retrospective exhibition at the Grosvenor Gallery in 1881–2 and then a solo exhibition at the Metropolitan Museum of Art, New York, in 1884–5. His honours were equalled at home with a Doctor of Laws (LLD) from Cambridge and a Doctor of Civil Law (DCL) from Oxford, the robes of which he familiarly wore in later life.

He built a gallery extension onto his studio home at Little Holland House and opened it to the public from two to six pm every weekend. His belief that art should be accessible to all was reflected in this project and in his support of schemes that took art into the poor areas of London through exhibition and the creation of new galleries. In the 1880s Watts painted some of his most memorable and iconic images, including *Hope* (cat.59), which inspired artists and thinkers internationally, and *Mammon* (cat.62), his great protest against the destructive motivating force of greed that was prevalent in society.

On 20 November 1886 he married Mary Seton Fraser-Tytler (1849–1938) in Epsom, Surrey. Their extended honeymoon between 1886 and 1887 took them to Egypt, Constantinople, Athens and Messina, and many of his great landscapes, including *A Sea Ghost* (cat.65), were inspired by the visit.   MB

Self-Portrait, *c*.1879, oil on canvas, 63.5 × 50.8 cm (25 × 20 in), National Portrait Gallery, London (NPG/406)

57. *The Dean's Daughter (Lillie Langtry)*, 1879–80

Oil on canvas, 66 × 53.3 cm (26 × 21 in)
COMWG43

PROVENANCE: collection of the artist (Little Holland House Gallery); part of the original Memorial Collection

EXHIBITIONS: Royal Academy 1880, no.4; Watts Grosvenor 1881, no.193; Watts Birmingham 1885, no.148; Watts Nottingham 1886, no.2; *Second Exhibition of the Society of Portrait Painters*, Royal Institute, Piccadilly, London, 1892, no.194; *Fair Women*, Grafton Gallery, London, 1894, no.139; *Exhibition of Dramatic and Musical Art*, Grafton Gallery, 1897, no.182; Watts Gallery 1904, no.37; Memorial Exhibitions, London 1905, no.61, Manchester 1905, no.109, Newcastle 1905, no.89, Edinburgh 1905, no.79, Dublin 1906, no.52; Watts Aldeburgh 1961, no.2; *The Masque of Beauty*, National Portrait Gallery, London, 1972, no.44; *All the World's A Stage: Australian-British Theatre Exhibition*, organised by the British Council at the Sydney Opera House, Sydney, 1973; *The Wilde Years: Oscar Wilde and the Art of his Time*, Barbican Art Galleries, London, 2000–1, no.191; *Look at Me, Look at You: An Exhibition of Portraits*, organised by the South London Art Gallery, Carnegie Library, 2002, no.4; Watts Portraits 2004, no.58

LITERATURE: Spielmann 1886, p.31; Macmillan 1903, p.87; Watts Gallery Catalogue 1904, no.37; Barrington 1905, p.86; Spielmann 1905, pp.47–8; Watts Catalogue, I, p.35, II, p.88; Langtry 1925, pp.57–9; Alston 1929, no.42; Blunt 1975, pp.147, 215–16; Bryant 2004, p.162

One of Watts's best-known portraits, this work portrays Lillie Langtry, a great celebrity of the day and the first 'professional beauty'. Born Emilie Le Breton (1853–1929), she grew up on the island of Jersey, acquiring the name 'Lillie' due to her white skin, with an additional reference to the native flower of her Channel-island home. The daughter of the Dean of Jersey, hence the title of Watts's painting, she married Edward Langtry in 1874.[1] In 1876 they moved to London where Lillie made an impact with her striking looks. Graham Robertson, a young artist, compared her to 'the lost Venus of Praxiteles', adding it was 'the first and only time in my life I beheld perfect beauty'.[2]

After an invitation to a soirée, Lillie made her entrance into society, where artists were very much part of the bohemian fringes of the aristocracy. She understood that her beauty, as her main asset, had to be translated into a commodity. Millais, Frank Miles and Whistler became her first promoters, as did the young Oscar Wilde with his poem 'The New Helen', published in July 1879, a panegyric to her as the reincarnation of the classical temptress. Indeed, one reason for her immediate elevation to public figure was her affair with the Prince of Wales (1841–1910). Soon she was modelling for Burne-Jones's *Golden Stairs* (1872–80; Tate).[3]

Watts invited Lillie to sit to him at new Little Holland House in the autumn of 1879 when she was at the height of her fame. The artist painted it for his own collection, not as a commission. Lillie personified the cult of beauty associated with the Aesthetic movement. She had already posed for portraits by Watts's friends, Millais, Edward Poynter and Val Prinsep, in addition to being the subject of photographic postcards featuring 'professional beauties' of the day (cat.57.1). Lillie possessed an individual sense of style evident in Watts's portrait. Her chignon in the shape of a figure eight set low on the neck became known as the 'Langtry knot'. Early on, she wore only black as she was in mourning for her brother; later it became her own fashion statement. Dressed characteristically, she arrived wearing outdoor clothing, not high fashion. Completing her outfit was a small flat bonnet of an everyday sort, tied with bow and festooned with an ostrich feather. Watts's sympathy for bird life was such that he promptly removed the

Cat. 57.1 *Lillie Langtry*, photograph, 14.6 × 10.48 cm (5¾ × 4⅛ in), Watts Gallery Archive, The Rob Dickins Collection

feather.[4] Apart from this change, he painted her as she appeared, with no jewellery, flowers or elaboration of any kind to augment her natural beauty. Her famed profile is set against a background of green, with which Watts intended to enhance the flesh tones.[5] The painting of her face, with the subtlest bloom of pink glowing from her cheeks, is one of the most delicate passages in any of his portraits.

Watts greatly enjoyed the company of Lillie, who became a frequent visitor to his studio. They chatted for hours, with her visits not always solely about posing for this portrait or the other that he had under way using her as a model.[6] Her beauty itself inspired him. He sent the portrait to the Royal Academy in 1880 under the title *The Dean's Daughter*, which harked back to her more innocent days. The public display of the portrait further enhanced the cult status of this 'professional beauty'. Watts probably never intended to sell this portrait. Shown at his gallery and in a range of exhibitions, it established his familiarity with current public figures, lending an aura of glamour to his collection of portraits. BB

1   For biographical information, see Theo Aronson, 'Langtry, Lillie (1853–1929)', *Oxford Dictionary of National Bibliography* (http://www.oxforddnb.com/view/article/37652, accessed 19 Feb 2008).
2   Quoted in Laura Beatty, *Lillie Langtry: Manners, Masks and Morals*, London, 1999, p.36.
3   Langtry 1925, p.59.
4   Watts himself seems to have promoted this anecdote, as when in 1884, prior to the exhibition of his works at the Metropolitan, he recounted the story to the reporter 'Walsingham' from a New York newspaper (cutting of 13 September 1884, Watts Gallery Archive).
5   Discussed in Bryant 2004, p.162.
6   Langtry 1925, p.58; she also posed for a girl holding a basket of flowers at forty or more sittings, but much later Watts replaced the face (Watts Catalogue, II, p.88).

58. *Arcadia*, 1878–80

Oil on canvas, 193 × 61 cm (76 × 24 in)
COMWG39

PROVENANCE: collection of the artist (Little Holland House Gallery), part of the original Memorial Collection, 1905

EXHIBITIONS: Grosvenor Gallery, London, 1881, no.57; Watts Grosvenor 1881, no.26; Watts Birmingham 1885, no.184; Watts Nottingham 1886, no.37; *Jahresausstellung*, Munich, 1893, no.1653; Hampstead 1894; Watts Gallery 1904, no.69; Memorial Exhibitions, Manchester 1905, no.19, Newcastle, 1905, no.43

LITERATURE: Spielmann 1886, p.29; Cartwright 1896, p.14; von Schleinitz 1904, pp.88, 93; Watts Gallery Catalogue 1904, no.69; Watts Catalogue, I, p.5; Alston 1929, no.44; Gould 2004, pp.154–5

Arcadia is a sparsely populated, mountainous region of the Peloponnese in Greece named after Zeus's son Arcas. In classical mythology and literature Pan, the god of flocks and herds, ruled this pastoral paradise, inhabited by shepherds and shepherdesses, along with nymphs and satyrs. An unspoiled wilderness where romantic love flourished, Arcadia appeared in Virgil's *Eclogues*.

Watts's painting *Arcadia* is a life-size study of a female nude, partially draped, standing in a classical setting in front of a stone fountain with an indication of lavish vegetation of orange trees and a deep blue Mediterranean sky. Described in the catalogue of the Memorial Exhibitions of 1905 as 'A daughter of the happy land of the Greek poet, a nursling of the sun', it is essentially decorative.[1] Throughout his career Watts admired the classical tradition and turned to mythological narrative stories and figures for subject matter. In an article on Watts in 1896 Julia Cartwright discussed *Arcadia* in the context of its mythological subject:

> In his 'Arcadia' … graceful form is combined with delicate colour, and the violet tones of the maiden's draperies blend with the purple of the iris blossoms growing by the marble fountain. Many of these subjects [suggested by classical myths] … were painted out of pure delight in lovely form and colour, in the glowing hues of sun and sky.[2]

Watts first employed the narrow vertical canvas for *Thetis* (cat.47) a decade earlier, later painting others in the same format, including *Daphne* (RA 1870; unlocated), *Psyche* (1880; Tate) and *Dawn* (1875–80; private collection), which won him artistic recognition among fellow artists and the interest of collectors. Ingres, the nineteenth-century French classicist, used this format in *Venus Anadyomene* (1848; Musée Condé, Chantilly) and *La Source* (c.1856; Musée d'Orsay, Paris); the latter was well known and had been exhibited in London in 1862.[3] Watts was in the forefront of the classical revival of the 1860s, and his painting of the nude in a vertical format became widely used by Leighton, Albert Moore and other artists.[4]

According to Mary Watts, the artist used a professional model and specifically sought 'to give the warmer tones of the flesh, produced by the sun in more southern climates than our own'.[5] This was a bold artistic choice, since only white was considered appropriate because of its 'connotations of purity, refinement and impassivity'.[6] The figure in *Arcadia* has a dark complexion characteristic of Italian models (who were very popular with other contemporary artists, including Leighton) and a curvaceous body. Her features are distinctive and individualised and she has a fashionable Victorian hairstyle. This depiction of an individual rather than a general type risked offending propriety and may have prompted the artist to employ an opaque classical drapery to cover most of the model's body, and direct her gaze away from the viewer, avoiding too direct a visual encounter. Watts's choice of a mythological title for his work might have also been a strategic decision aimed at giving propriety to this sensual nude.

In *Arcadia* the mythological setting without narrative results in an exotic scene affecting all the senses: rich Mediterranean colours stimulating the sight, fountain spring splashing against the smooth surface of the reservoir evoking the sound of water, and cut irises in the basket and orange trees suggestive of the rich natural fragrance of this idyllic setting. The skilful juxtaposition of the geometric white stone surface of the fountain with the beauty of the female figure enhances the sensual appeal of the picture. JD

1   Memorial Exhibitions, Manchester and Newcastle 1905, pp.5 and 18 respectively.
2   Cartwright 1896, p.14.
3   Alison Smith, ed., *Exposed: The Victorian Nude*, exh. cat., Tate Britain, London, 2001, no.27.
4   The format is discussed in Smith 1996, pp.107, 111.
5   Watts Catalogue, I, p.5.
6   Smith 1996, pp.121–32.

59. *Hope* c.1885–6

Oil on canvas, 150 × 109 cm (59 × 43 in)

Lent from a private collection

PROVENANCE: presumably sold by or on behalf of Watts by Agnew's, who on 23 June 1887 sold it to Joseph Ruston of Monk's Manor, Lincoln, for £2,300; Ruston Trustees sale, Christie's, London, 4 July 1913, no.113, bought by Gooden & Fox for £1,575; for their client Sir Jeremiah Colman Bart. of Gatton Park, Surrey; his sale, Christie's, London, 18 September 1942, no.113; bought by Mitchell for £94.10; ... Ben Welch; sold to Ronald Staples and remaining with his family until *c.*1960 when sold back to Ben Welch ...; private collection; Sotheby's, London, 26 November 1986, no.55; bought by the present owner

EXHIBITIONS: Grosvenor Gallery, 1886, no.61; Memorial Exhibitions, London 1905, no.201, Newcastle 1905, no.160; *Exposition Rétrospective de Peinture Anglaise (XVIII et XIX Siècle)*, Musée Moderne, Brussels, 1929, no.191; *The Victorians: British Painting 1837–1901*, National Gallery of Art, Washington, DC, 1996, no.33; Watts Symbolism 1997, no.76; Watts Compton 2004, no.81

LITERATURE: Spielmann 1886, p.30 (as unfinished); Claude Phillips, 'The Ruston Collection, The Modern Pictures–I', *Magazine of Art*, XVII (1893), pp.40–2; Cartwright 1896, p.11; Sketchley 1904, pp.98–100; Macmillan 1903, pp.200–4; Chesterton 1904, pp.94–108, 135; Barrington 1905, pp.37, 93, 162; Watts Catalogue, I, p.71; Watts 1912, II, pp.57, 106, 150, 163; Mullen 1974, foreword and no.66; Blunt 1975, pp.xviii, 62, 155, 212, 220; Rosemary Treble, *Great Victorian Pictures*, Arts Council of Great Britain, exh. cat., Royal Academy of Arts, 1978, p.88; Staley 1978, p.90; Bryant 1987, pp.62–5; Morris 1996, p.487; Warner 1996, pp.135–6; Bryant 1997, pp.67ff and 201–2; Paul Barlow, 'George Frederic Watts's *Hope*: Where There's Life, There's ...', *Tate Etc.*, issue 2 (autumn 2004), pp.108–11

A blindfolded young woman sits on a sphere, floating among the clouds in an undefined region marked only by one shining star; the figure, clad in thin white drapery, bends awkwardly and strains to listen to the sound she creates from the one string left on her archaic lyre. As Watts's most famous and enduring icon, *Hope* is unique in his *oeuvre*. It has a traditional association with one of the three theological virtues, but relies on a programme invented anew by the artist. The simple composition can be read as an unencumbered visual statement, but its meaning is multi-layered. *Hope* has entered into popular iconography and proved to be a topic of much discussion ever since its first public exhibition in 1886.[1]

Hope exists in two main oil versions: this one, the first and prime version,[2] and the second, which was painted with the help of an assistant and was presented to the Tate Gallery by the artist in 1897. The composition began as a series of small sketches (Watts Gallery) of a bent figure swathed in drapery and pressing her ear to a lyre.[3] By the time he painted the half-scale oil sketch (1885; National Museums Liverpool),[4] later given to his friend and neighbour, Frederic Leighton, Hope appeared on a globe within a setting of blue sky and indeterminate mists. Such was its popularity that Watts produced other lesser versions, all purchased during his lifetime. The only complete version of *Hope* at the Watts Gallery is a large drawing in red chalk (cat.59.1), almost certainly executed after the oil.[5]

On completing the first version in early 1886, Watts commented on its potential popularity. One buyer offered £1,500 before the exhibition, but as he planned to include it in his potential bequest to the nation, he decided to paint another one. Apparently, Watts believed the second one to be an improvement,[6] so he sold the first one and via Agnew's it entered the noted private collection of Joseph Ruston who lived in Lincoln. The second version was much exhibited in the following years, including at the Exposition Universelle in Paris in 1889. Slight differences exist between the two versions. The figure in this first version wears greyish-white drapery and is seen against a brushier background of bluish-green. One writer considered the first version far superior as it was 'subtler in colour ... and more crisply touched in the white diaphanous draperies'.[7] Details are more precise

and a smile seems to play over the lips of Hope. The star set in the sky injects a note of optimism edited out of the more sombre second version.

Watts's personal feelings in 1885 pervaded the thinking behind the subject. The details of the star and lyre with all strings broken but one, as well as the overall blue tonality, suggest a mood of sadness at variance with the title. As Chesterton famously commented, it might easily be called 'Despair'. While painting *Hope* in December 1885, Watts was more than usually melancholy, as he wrote to Madeline Wyndham: 'There seems to be neither peace nor prosperity or happiness, what is best worth having is I think only to be found in ourselves ... for myself, I am not always sorry that the end of my time is not so very far off.' In the same letter he explained that his adopted daughter Blanche, now married, had lost her one-year old baby Isabel after an illness.[8] Two sentences later he described his new composition: 'Hope sitting on a globe, with bandaged eyes playing on a lyre which has all the strings broken but one out of which poor little tinkle she is trying to get all the music possible, listing with all her might to the little sound.'[9]

Watts exhibited the new painting at the Grosvenor Gallery, the venue par excellence of the Aesthetic Movement, and indeed there are intriguing parallels with works by Rossetti, Burne-Jones and Albert Moore.[10] Music-making also identified *Hope* with one of the central preoccupations of Aestheticism summed up by Walter Pater's dictum, 'All art constantly aspires towards the condition of music'.[11] Watts had incorporated the idea of music as a way to reinvigorate portraiture in such works as *A Lamplight Study: Herr Joachim* (cat.31) of 1868 and *Blanche, Lady Lindsay* (private collection) of 1877. But Hope's lyre plays what one writer called 'vague uncertain music'. Inextricably linked, music and colour act together; one writer recalled that the effect that Watts 'wished his pictures to have upon the eye, resembles that which the performance of some melodious piece of music would have upon the ear'.[12] The analogies between music and colour confirmed an Aestheticist impetus. Watts's sense of colour allowed for the creation of 'delicate refined colour-harmonies'. This revitalised interest in colour and atmosphere was new to his work in the 1880s.[13] When F.G. Stephens announced *Hope* in late

April 1886, he called it a 'piece of tone harmony' with 'poetical' colour:

> Hope's dress is of a dark aerial hue, and her figure is revealed to us by a wan light from the front and paler light of the stars in the sky beyond. This exquisite illumination fuses, so to say, the colours, substance, and even the forms and contours of the whole and suggests a vague dream-like magic.[14]

In addition to colour, light creates a mood of dreamy suggestiveness, avoiding clearly defined forms in favour of a dissolving atmosphere. Watts's venture into pastel drawing in the 1880s came about thanks to this new interest in shimmering effects of light and colour. Critic Cosmo Monkhouse discerned its 'tender opalescence',[15] and another writer was drawn to comment on its otherworldy 'blue and phosphorescent green'.[16] Such effects added a mystery and enigma to *Hope*, thus placing it in the forefront of Symbolist currents in European art, especially once the second version was seen in Paris in 1889.

Later commentators delved into the meaning of the painting with the kind of fervour reserved for a devotional image, expending pages of interpretation and speculation. One of the most eloquent analysts was G.K. Chesterton, who imagined how, when an unwary observer came on this 'queer twilight picture, a dim and powerful sense of meaning began to grow upon him'.[17] Without conventional avenues into the painting, the observer had to read it for himself. This was not the hackneyed image of Hope with her anchor or otherwise fettered in a cell but a new idea of the subject. Sketchley observes that 'Watts liberates her, sets her above the world … Hope has attained the summit of earthly possession, but has gained the world at a loss, almost, of her own soul.'[18] Cartwright considered that 'all the trouble and disquiet of modern times is in that picture, all the doubt and questioning of these latter days'.[19] Macmillan related its meaning back to Watts's own outlook, when he wrote:

> [Watts] has the sadness born of the doubt and deep unrest characteristic of these days – the experience of the vanity and unsatisfactoriness of all earthly things. No man is more sensitive to the physical and moral confusion that lies on the very surface of man's life. But

no man feels more than he the consolations and hopes that abound amid the darkness and despondency. His is a gospel of hope and not despair.[20]

In creating an image without a traditional reading, Watts opened it up to a range of potential meanings, available to anyone who cared to investigate its manifold mysteries, then and now. BB

1 To give but two examples: Watts Whitechapel 1974, no.66, refers to reproductions of *Hope* being given to Egyptian troops after their defeat in the war of 1967; Bryant 1987, p.64, cites cartoonist Nicholas Garland's adaptation of the image in 1982 for *The Spectator* featuring the embattled Labour leader Michael Foot.
2 See Bryant 1987 regarding this version, which, unseen since the 1940s, emerged at auction in 1986 when it made a then record price for a Victorian painting (£869,000).
3 COMWG2007.508a–512a and 509b; several are illustrated in Blunt 1975, pl.12.
4 Illustrated in colour in Bryant 1986, p.65; see also Morris 1996, p.487.
5 Watts London 1974, no.66.
6 Watts 1912, II, p.106.
7 *Magazine of Art*, XVII (1893), p.40.

8 See Bryant 1997, p.202. Although contradicted by Gould 2004, p.406 n.1, in fact the infant, Isabel Joan, was born on 21 October 1884 and died on 4 November 1885, a month before the letter quoted. Her sister Adeline Verena Ishbel was born later, in 1886.
9 Watts Papers, Watts to Madeline Wyndham, 8 December 1885.
10 Discussed more fully in Bryant 1997, p.202.
11 As Pater wrote in 'The School of Giorgione' from *The Renaissance: Studies in Art and Poetry* (1877; the third edition of *Studies in the History of the Renaissance*, first published in 1873).
12 Macmillan 1903, p.203.
13 Bryant 1997, pp.71ff.
14 *Athenaeum*, 24 April 1886, p.56.
15 *The Academy*, 15 May 1886, p.350.
16 Sketchley 1904, p.100.
17 Chesterton 1904, p.98.
18 Sketchley 1904, p.100.
19 Cartwright 1896, p.11.
20 Macmillan 1903, p.204.

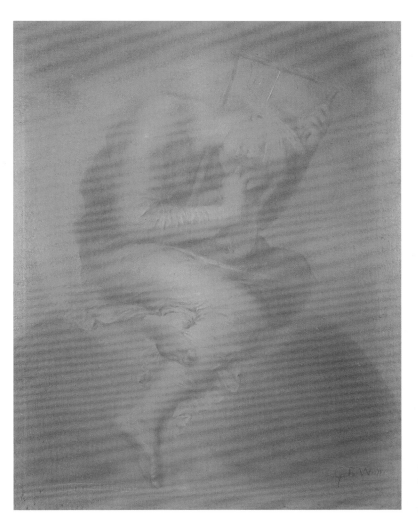

Cat. 59.1 *Hope*, *c*.1885–6, sanguine, 139 × 107 cm (54¾ × 42 in), COMWG304

60. *Love and Life*, c.1882–4

Oil on canvas, 66 × 44 cm (26 × 17 ½ in)
COMWG175

PROVENANCE: collection of the artist (Little
Holland House Gallery); Watts Gallery

EXHIBITIONS: Watts Gallery 1904, no.28; Memorial
Exhibitions, Edinburgh 1905, no.80, Manchester
1905, no.147, Newcastle 1905, no.82, Dublin 1906,
no.74; Watts Manchester, Minneapolis, Brooklyn,
no.30a

LITERATURE: Spielmann 1886, p.21; Cartwright
1896, p.10; Barrington 1905, pp.68, 129–30, 204;
Watts Catalogue, I, p.94; Watts 1912, II pp.48–9,
150, 215, 234–5, III, pp.227–8; Macmillan 1903,
pp.34, 36, 248–52, 264; Sketchley 1904, pp.124–6;
Shrewsbury 1918, pp.70–8; Blunt, 1975, pp.154–7;
Staley 1978, pp.169–70; Gould 2004, pp.149, 168,
171, 173, 175, 187, 190, 193, 199, 203–4, 209, 216,
233–4, 238, 251, 263, 272, 275, 278, 283–7, 294, 314,
319

Cat. 60.1 Outline study for *Love and Life*, c.1882–4,
pencil on paper, 11 × 9 cm (4 ¼ × 3 ½ in),
COMWG2007.515

This painting was one of the most famous of all
Watts's images during his lifetime and one that
he considered 'my best composition'. He wrote
at length on the painting, whose image led to
numerous paintings (Mary's catalogue lists
seven), finished drawings and sculpture. Mrs
Barrington notes that its 'design was made in
1883' and that its prime version was painted
between February and June in 1884.[1] Of its
conception, the artist wrote:

> I have for years been endeavouring to under-
> stand and illustrate a great moral conception
> of life, its difficulties, duties, pains and penal-
> ties, and I find that justice should be the
> mainspring of all our actions, and tender-
> ness, pity, love should give the direction; I
> think my best composition is upon this sub-
> ject; Love and Life, naked, bare life sustained
> and helped up the steeps of human condi-
> tions, the path from the baser existence to the
> nobler region of thought and character. This
> religion of Love has been acknowledged
> from the earliest times – then with an uncer-
> tain utterance – but is now beginning to be
> acknowledged as the foundation of all. This
> is forgotten in the heat of personal impulses,
> and from forgetfulness has sprung almost all
> the injustice and misery in the world. This is
> what my painted parable would recall. I
> would suggest frail and feeble human exis-
> tence aided to ascend from the lower to the
> higher plane, by Love with his wide wings of
> sympathy, charity, tenderness and human
> affection. Love is not intended to be either
> personal or carnal. It is the great love St.
> Paul speaks of which can be dwelt on and
> amplified to any extent.
>
> Nature is grievously insulted; it is true she
> accommodates herself wonderfully to the
> conditions imposed upon her by her rebel-
> lious or unfortunate children. But she does
> not forget her dignity, and will ever take
> vengeance for disregard of her will; she may
> permit the account to run a long time, but
> she always sends in the bill and sternly exacts
> payment.[2]

The 'painted parable', as Watts describes it,
presents two allegorical figures, unclothed 'for
they are only symbols', together on Life's rocky

path.[3] Love in the work of Watts, as in life, has many aspects. In this painting a mischievous Eros is rejected in favour of a depiction of love closest to the love preached in Christianity, which 'St Paul speaks of'. He has a caring and paternal face, winged, propping and guiding Life, a guardian angel. Life, in contrast, is depicted as a frail young woman, lost without the steadying hand of Love. In reaction to criticisms of the frailty of Life, Watts responded by asking 'What is life in the midst of immensities?'[4] Macmillan also takes up this point of supposed weakness in the painting by suggesting that her slightness and meekness have another meaning: that life is little if nothing without love.[5]

Love and Life appears in many exhibitions, due in part to the number of versions available and to Watts's fascination with the subject. In many of the catalogue entries, beginning with Mrs Barrington at its exhibition in New York, it was listed as a companion painting to *Love and Death* (*c.*1885–7; Tate). Yet the depiction of Love in these two pictures is remarkably inconsistent as Staley observes,[6] almost contradicting one another. G.K. Chesterton in a little-known article on the artist went further in suggesting that, where optimism was concerned, Watts was less convincing: 'It is remarkable that when the artist tried to paint optimistic companion pictures to his pessimistic pictures they did not wholly succeed. Surely none can maintain that "Love and Life" is as fine as "Love and Death".'[7] Love triumphant over death and adversity may have been close to what Watts wished to express in *Love and Life*, considering it 'perhaps his most direct message to the present generation',[8] but Chesterton's comment is as poignant as it was in 1904.

Love and Life is one of Watts's paintings that found fame internationally, in America's case infamy. In 1893 the director of the Luxemburg Museum in Paris, Léonce Bénédite, visited London to collect examples of British art for his gallery. He bought a version of *Love and Life*, which is now in the Louvre. Watts later wrote to Bénédite: 'It belongs to a class in which I have endeavoured to identify art with thought, and for which I have never intended to take money, I beg to say that the honour of its acceptance is only too great a recompense.'[9] A French critic, Robert de la Sizeranne (1866–1932), writing in the *Review des Deux Mondes*, saw the largest version of the painting (222.2 × 121.9 cm; Tate Britain) in 1886 in South Kensington, which made an enormous impact upon him:

> I had then the conviction that mythology was a genre false, feeble, and superannuated … I was still of the opinion when I set foot on the staircase. When I reached the last, I no longer believed that myth was dead; nor that to expand the form of a fact to the impersonal, the sexless, the universal, was to take from it the ardour of sentiment, the dramatic element of life.[10]

At the Watts retrospective exhibition in the Metropolitan Museum of Art another version of *Love and Life* was exhibited. It later travelled to the World's Columbian Exhibition in Chicago in 1893 and was given by Watts to the people of America, where it was accepted by Act of Congress in 1894. It was sent for hanging, on the wishes of the president Grover Cleveland, to the White House. An outcry from the W.C.T.U. (Women's Christian Temperance Union), headed by the Superintendent of Purity in Literature and Art, Mrs Emily D. Martin, effected its removal from the presidential home to the Corcoran Gallery, Washington, where it remained until 1902. The objection to the painting was its immodesty, and when President

Cat. 60.2 Maquette for *Love and Life*, *c.* 1882–4, plaster on metal armature, 65 × 55 × 41 cm (25½ × 21¾ × 16¼ in), COMWG2008.124

Roosevelt moved the painting back to the White House in 1902, a further outcry followed: 'It will be very disillusioning for the women', wrote Mrs Martin once more, 'who have admired him [Roosevelt] to learn that he has given a place on the walls of the White House to this vulgar nude painting by Watts.'[11] This time the president stood firm and letters of support followed. Sibyl Wilbur O'Brien, writing to the *New York Times* in 1902, protested against its removal from the Corcoran, saying that it was a loss to the public who could no longer see the vision of 'love inspiring the fainting human soul'.[12]

The present version of the painting is 'an early sketch for this subject, but carried somewhat further in the latest years of Mr. Watts's life', the manuscript catalogue records. 'It nevertheless remains unfinished, an experiment in a markedly different colour scheme.'[13] The 1905 memorial exhibition catalogues date it 1882, which contradicts Barrington's contention that it was conceived in 1883. There are seven versions listed by Mary, of which this version appears to be the earliest.[14] A sculpture for the painting and several sketches are in the Watts Gallery collection (cats 60.1–2; COMWG2007.96a, 515, 516, 697). MB

1 Barrington 1905, p.129.
2 G.F. Watts, quoted in Watts 1912, III, pp.227–8.
3 Watts 1912, II, p.235.
4 Watts 1912, II, p.234.
5 Macmillan 1903, pp.248–52.
6 Staley 1978, no.30a.
7 G.K. Chesterton, *The Christian World*, 7 July 1904, p.78.
8 G.F. Watts, quoted in Macmillan 1903, p.248.
9 Watts Catalogue, I, p.93.
10 Robert de la Sizeranne, quoted in Watts Catalogue, I, p.92.
11 Press clipping, 15 December 1902, Watts Gallery Archive.
12 Sibyl Wilbur O'Brien, letter to the editor, *New York Times*, 21 December 1902.
13 Watts Catalogue, I, p.94.
14 This is one of at least seven versions, aside from the finished chalk drawings, including the White House version now in a private collection; the Tate version, exhibited at the Grosvenor Gallery in 1885, South Kensington in 1886 and the New Gallery in 1896–7; the Walker Art Gallery version; the Louvre version; and two others in private hands but formerly belonging to Mrs Ruston (painted in 1883) and Albert Wood, respectively.

61. *The Messenger, c.*1880–5

Oil on canvas, 111.8 × 66 cm (43¾ × 26 in)
COMWG37

PROVENANCE: collection of the artist (Little Holland House Gallery); part of the original Memorial Collection, 1905

EXHIBITIONS: St Jude's, Whitechapel, 1886, no.225; Toynbee Hall, October 1888; Kunstausstellung Dresden, 1901, no.739 (large or small version); Southport 1902 (large or small version); Spring Exhibition, Whitechapel, 1903, no.274 (?small version); Watts Gallery 1904, no.29; Memorial Exhibitions, Manchester, 1905, no.53, Newcastle, 1905, no.136; *Death, Heaven and the Victorians*, Art Gallery and Museum, Brighton, 1970, no.35; Watts Compton 2004, no.90

LITERATURE (on the subject): Spielmann 1886, p.31; Meade 1894, p.15; Cartwright 1896, pp.1, 9; Bateman 1901, p.42; Macmillan 1903, pp.252–4; Sketchley 1904, pp.81, 88, 91, 100; Watts Gallery Catalogue 1904, no.29; Barrington 1905, pp.93; Watts Catalogue, I, p.99; Watts 1912, II, p.257; Alston 1929, no.85; Bryant 1997, pp.74–5; Lanigan 2000, pp.231–3

Little published and even less seen, Watts's *Messenger* is one of his most enigmatic subjects. As a finished oil study for the large-scale *Messenger* (1884 onwards; version at Tate Britain, part of the Watts Gift of 1897[1] – see cat.70.1 – and another formerly in Germany[2]), this work formed part of Watts's ongoing 'cycle of Death';[3] indeed, its alternative title was *The Messenger of Death*. The reality of the subject stimulated Watts again and again. Death was an actual character with whom he had a personal connection. Writing to a friend at the time *The Messenger* was under way, he commented: 'As to Death, my friend Death! you know also what I feel about it, the great power always walks by my side with full consciousness on my part, inevitable but not terrible.'[4]

The Messenger offers a continuing exploration of a theme that the artist first examined in versions of *The Court of Death* (see cat.67), *Love and Death* (fig.52), then *Time, Death and Judgement* (cat.68). Death appears again as a beautiful woman, and, as in *The Court of Death*, she carries an infant so tiny that it must be a newborn, signalling that life continues even though Death is carrying out her task. Her action is slow and stately; she stands with only the slightest movement, the touch of her finger, on the wrist of the man. As writers in Watts's own time noted,[5] here Death is the consoler who comes to relieve the suffering of a man worn out by life's vicissitudes.

It seems that Watts completed this study to a satisfactory degree while the larger painting was still in progress. It is unusual to find Spielmann specifically cataloguing such a 'smaller picture', dating it to 1885, as ordinarily these go unmentioned. But it indicates the status that this smaller work had, not as an unfinished study but complete in its own right. It contains the essence of the subject: Death's approach to the suffering man in the foreground (as shown in the first studies for the work, cats 69–70). What this version does not have is the array of objects on the *vanitas* theme, such as the orrery (astronomical globe), mallet, palette and violin, characterised as the insignia of the arts and worldly pursuits that no longer have any purpose for the man. Nor does it show the suggestion of architectural forms to the right side, such as the pyramid. This study relies on a simple presentation of the scene with a division of the background into tones of grey, associated with Death, on one side and, on the other, a plain blank wall against which the seated, semi-recumbent man is seen. An interesting drawing (cat.61.1), published in Meade's article of 1894,[6] also shows the face of the man averted, so that a reading of his plight depends on his posture and the strained angle of his neck as he rests backwards. More visible in that drawing was the book placed under the arm of the man; the abandoned book of life is closed and ignored.

The first public viewing of the subject (probably this version) came in 1886 at the exhibition at St Jude's, Whitechapel, when it was entitled *The Messenger of Death*. It seemed appropriate that this venue was associated with Canon Barnett's efforts to uplift and educate poor east Londoners to whom Watts's consolatory message might have had real benefit. Their own, often tragic, personal circumstances would end, not as nothingness but with a suggestion of hope seen in the conjunction of Death and new life. Later, in 1896, the 9-foot-high painting destined for the national collection appeared at the New Gallery.[7] Watts referred to it indirectly when discussing the works for this exhibition:

> You cannot adequately label them, because they represent ideas much too far off, taking one outside experience. I want them to take you as music might, and lead you further even than I myself intended. If I write a few words of explanation with them they will have to be very few. One can say perhaps that I mean not Death himself but his Messenger, coming under various aspects.[8]

Preoccupied with death, Watts had become an honorary member of the Society for Psychical Research in the mid-1880s.[9] As he hinted at in the comments above, he hoped for his paintings to take observers outside their own experience. His exploration of realms of the spirit and the spiritual reveals that he was seeking explanations for a range of phenomena that were removed from day-to-day reality. An artist's aim in painting the very moment of death, as the messenger from an other-worldly realm applies her finger to the victim, would be to encapsulate the passage from one world to another. Yet, even down to her unusual headdress, a winged crown of victory, Death and her world prevail. Early on, an unnamed quotation appeared with the title *The Messenger*:[10] 'Rest after toile, / Port after stormy seas, / Death after life, / Doth greatly please.' This can now be identified as an incomplete fragment from Spenser's *Faerie Queene* (I, ix, 40), a poem much favoured by Watts (see cat.18), and its later addition reinforces the message of the work that Death should hold no fear for her victims.

In a view of the Little Holland House Gallery, *c*.1896, the present version of *The Messenger* is positioned near the large *Court of Death*, and by *c*.1903/4 it had been hung next to the smaller version (cat.67). The artist's placement reinforced this pairing on the theme of Death. Such themes had even wider currency on the continent where Symbolism in art and literature enjoyed high regard in artistic and literary circles. Perhaps spurred on by seeing *The Messenger* at the Dresden exhibition, in 1903 the young German Karl Ernst Osthaus (1874/5–1921) commissioned Watts to complete a large version of *The Messenger* for his newly opened Folkwang Museum of Art in Hagen, Westphalia, a public collection of contemporary art. This version is now unlocated,[11] but until 1921 it allowed Watts's work to play a fascinating role in company with the European avant-garde, which included Rodin, Cézanne, Seurat and Matisse among others. BB

Cat. 61.1 Frederick Hollyer, photograph of drawing related to *The Messenger*, Hollyer Album, Watts Gallery Archive

1 This painting has not hung at the Tate in many years. It is illustrated in Bryant 1997, p.74.
2 Illustrated in Gould 2004, p.220, where it is incorrectly cited as being in the Watts Gallery.
3 Macmillan 1903, p.253ff.
4 Watts Papers, Watts to Madeline Wyndham, 4 April 1885.
5 Sketchley 1904, p.88.
6 Meade 1894, p.15; this photograph by Hollyer also appeared as the opening illustration in Cartwright 1896, p.1. For another drawing see Lanigan 2000, no.94.
7 Watts New Gallery 1896, no.134.
8 Watts 1912, II, p.257.
9 See my essay, 'G.F. Watts and the Symbolist Vision', in Watts Symbolism (Exhibitions) 1997, pp.65–81, for a discussion of Watts's interest in other-worldly phenomenon.
10 When a related drawing was exhibited at Agnew's, this quote appeared; also in Bateman 1901, p.42. The same quote accompanied the title in the first catalogue of the Watts Gallery in 1904.
11 The Folkwang Museum did not survive the death of its founder in 1921 and the collections were sold; after World War II it was reconstituted as the Karl Ernst Osthaus-Museum in Essen.

62 *Mammon, Dedicated to his Worshippers, c.1885*

Oil on canvas, 54 × 31 cm (21 × 12½ in)
COMWG49

PROVENANCE: … Watts Gallery purchased from Mr Arthur Spencer in 1948

EXHIBITIONS: Watts London 1954, no.69; Watts Whitechapel 1974, no.37; Watts Compton 2004, no.70

LITERATURE: Spielmann 1886, pp.15, 21–2, 31; Macmillan 1903, pp.194–6; Chesterton 1904, pp.108–113, 115; Barrington 1905, p.93; Watts Catalogue, I, p.98; Watts 1912, I, p.263, II, p.149; Shrewsbury 1918, pp.113–18; Blunt, 1975, pp.211, 214; Bryant 1997, pp.169–70; Gould 2004, pp.184, 191, 212, 227, 235, 312–14

The figure of Mammon derives from the New Testament. Originally the Aramaic word for wealth and riches, it was transcribed by the Greeks as μαμωνας (mamonas), becoming personified, like Πλουτος (Ploutos), into the god of wealth. The gospels of Matthew (6: 24) and Luke (16: 13) both contain the lines 'Ye cannot serve God and Mammon', whose meaning is echoed in many of Watts's works. 'Mammon', he wrote, 'sits supreme', whereas 'great art, as a child of the nation, cannot find a place; the seat is not wide enough for both'.[1]

Mammon as an allegorical figure is to be found in two works of epic poetry, Spenser's *Faerie Queene* and Milton's *Paradise Lost*, which acted as important sources for Watts. In Milton the idea of Mammon is close to Watts's belief that spiritual health is the direct opposite of materialism. The rich man in *Progress* (cat.79) has his eyes cast down – Watts describes him as 'money grubbing' – like the Mammon of *Paradise Lost*:

Mammon, the least erected Spirit that fell
From Heaven; for even in Heaven his looks
 and thoughts
Were always downward bent, admiring more
The riches of heaven's pavement, trodden
 gold, than aught divine or holy else enjoyed
In vision beatific.[2]

Spenser's rich symbolic imagery inspired a number of paintings by Watts. In *The Faerie Queene* Sir Guyon encounters Mammon in his cave, or 'house of Richesse', surrounded by walls of gold, money, and the skulls and bones of those who worshipped him. The gross figure of avarice speaks to the knight and tempts him with words that had the same relevance in the nineteenth century:

Then *Mammon* turning to that warriour, said;
Loe here the worldes blis, loe here the end,
To which all men do ayme, rich to be made:
Such grace now to be happy, is before thee
 laid.[3]

Watts increasingly believed that society was being made rotten by the worship of wealth and riches, and his portrait of Mammon is a harsh one. In this viewpoint the artist was not alone, as

Carlyle wrote in *Past and Present*: 'Mammon *is* not a god at all; but a devil, and even a very despicable devil'.[4] Taking the image further, the historian described him as a 'serious, most earnest Mammonism grown Midas-eared',[5] an aspect depicted in Watts's painting. In 1897 Canon Barnett wrote after walking through London: 'What is possible when houses are so close, the air so thick, and when people love to have it so! It seemed as if Watts were right and Mammon were God.'[6] For Watts Mammon was 'the deity of the age, more cruel than Moloch, cold and unlovely, without dignity or magnificence, the meanest of the powers to whom incense has been offered'.[7] Mary also recalled that Watts 'would often preach against Mammon worship, and the hypocritical veiling of the daily sacrifice made to this deity' and even suggested that 'he was going to propose to one of our sculptors to make a statue of Mammon, that it might be set up in Hyde Park where he hoped his worshippers would be at least honest enough to bow the knee publicly to him'.[8] Such irony was appreciated by many figures striving for social change.

At its first exhibition in 1885 in Birmingham the catalogue described the work:

'Mammon. Dedicated to his Worshippers' is the righteously scornful title of a singularly powerful work. Here is the god of wealth, robed in gold and scarlet: brutal, course, bull-necked, loathsome. See how he crushes down, with his clumsy foot and unsparing hand, whatever is weak and gentle and timid and lovely. Note that this being is not wantonly cruel. It is more brutal indifference; utter heedlessness of the things on which he treads or which his vile hand bruises.[9]

Watts presents an insidious god, whose worshippers inadvertently cause misery and rot the foundations of art and society. *Mammon* became one of his most famous images, despite the fact that there are only two known versions of the painting: this one, a sketch, and the prime version in the Tate, neither of which were widely exhibited.[10] Its reproduction in photography and print made it a very recognisable image in the late nineteenth century, as Macmillan suggested in 1903:

Mr Hollyer has done his work admirably, and brought this most instructive painting within reach of the poorest person … Mammon, should yet be placed beyond reach of the multitude, and valued at a price which none but a rich man could pay. It must be made accessible to the general public by some cheap medium; and Mr Hollyer, by his photographic reproduction of it, has furnished this cheap medium.[11]

It became such a well-known image that the *Daily Express* printed two large line drawings side by side: one of the head of Watts's *Mammon* and the other of Mr J.D. Rockeller, whom it described as 'the greatest money tyrant the world has ever known'.[12] The visual comparisons were made more than obvious, but Watts's great conception was that of a type: as Chesterton observed, the image 'in essence I have seen before, something which in spirit and in essence I have seen everywhere. That bloated, unconscious face, so heavy, so violent, so wicked, so innocent, have I not seen it at street corners, in billiard-rooms, in saloon bars, laying down the law about Chartered shares.'[13] The artist's image of Mammon was seen by many to be expressing outrage against the evils of society – Shrewsbury even suggested that it was a diatribe against slavery in the Congo and the white slave trade – but others saw some hypocrisy in the painting.[14] In this smaller sketch Mammon is perhaps even more brutal in conception than in the larger version: his gouty foot, symbolic of high living, and the harshness of the colour and form convey the idea in its raw form. MB

1   Watts 1912, III, p.268.
2   Milton, *Paradise Lost*, book I, lines 679–83.
3   Edmund Spenser, *The Faerie Queen*, book II, canto VII, verse 32.
4   Thomas Carlyle, *Past and Present*, London, 1872, p.58.
5   Ibid., p.146.
6   Watts Whitechapel 1974, no.37.
7   Watts 1912, III, p.268.
8   Watts 1912, II. p.149.
9   Watts Birmingham 1885, no.161.
10   Neither version appears in the 1905–6 Memorial Exhibitions.
11   Macmillan 1903, pp.195–6.
12   'Imaginary and Real, Mr. G.F. Watts' Idea of the Money Tyrant as Compared with Mr. J.D. Rockeller', *Daily Express*, 10 September 1904, clipping in Watts Gallery Archive.
13   Chesterton 1904, p.109.
14   *The Outlook*, 9 May 1901, for example, accused Watts of hypocrisy in his view of the South Africa war: 'We can fancy that some decades hence men will stand before Watts's picture of Mammon, and will say, "Strange; in the life-time of the painter a great war was brought about by Mammon solely in his own sordid interests … And the painter looked on and approved".'

63. *After the Deluge (The Forty-First Day)*, c.1885–91

Oil on canvas, 104 × 178 cm (41 × 70 in)
COMWG145

PROVENANCE: collection of the artist (Little Holland House Gallery); Watts Gallery

EXHIBITIONS: ?St Jude's, Whitechapel, 1886, no.9 (as 'The Sun'); New Gallery 1891, no.238; Watts New Gallery 1896, no.155 (as 'After the Deluge'); Cork 1902; Watts Gallery 1904, no.44; Watts Gallery Memorial Exhibitions, Edinburgh 1905, no.122 (as 'After the Deluge (41st Day)'), Manchester 1905, no.70, Dublin 1906, no.22; Watts Symbolism 1997, no.60; Watts Compton 2004, no.113; Watts London and Compton 2006, no.17; *The Seventh Splendour*, Verona 2007

LITERATURE: Spielmann 1886, p.30 (as 'Cessation of the Deluge'); Macmillan 1903, pp.150, 153, 263; Bayes 1907, pp.vii, xi, xviii; Watts Catalogue, I, p.1; Watts 1912, II, pp.57, 192; Bryant 1997, pp.179–80; Gould 2004, pp.250, 252

And the flood was forty days upon the earth; and the waters increased, and bare up the ark, and it was lift up above the earth … And the waters prevailed upon the earth an hundred and fifty days. (Genesis 7: 17, 24)

This remarkable painting is a vast empty seascape dominated by an extraordinary sunburst, whose rays reach outwards beyond the edges of the canvas. The simplicity of its composition is as extraordinary as the use of paint it adopts to represent the phenomena of the sun bursting through the clouds that have hung over the earth for forty days. It takes as its subject the forty-first day when the raining stops to reveal the earth covered by water and slowly begins to recede. The quotation that accompanied its exhibition at the New Gallery in 1891 and 1897, most probably the artist's own description of the work, describes the wonderful scene: 'A transcendent power of light and heat bursts forth to re-create; darkness is chased away; the waters, obedient to the higher law, already disperse into vapoury mists and pass from the face of the earth.'

The title of the work, *After the Deluge*, refers to its biblical subject, although the quotation cited shows the imaginative breadth that Watts used in dealing with this subject. The reference to Genesis was undoubtedly important to Watts, and the explicit linking of awesome natural phenomena to God is fundamental to Watts's conception. Mary recalled:

A visitor looking at 'After the Deluge' remarked that into such a scheme of colour he felt it would not have been impossible to introduce the figure of the Creator. 'Ah no,' Mr. Watts replied. 'But that is exactly what I could wish to make those who look at the picture conceive for themselves. The hand of the Creator moving by light and by heat to re-create. I have not tried to paint a portrait of the sun – such a thing is unpaintable – but I wanted to impress you with the idea of its enormous power.'[1]

In *The Genius of Greek Poetry* (cat.48) Watts expressed a pantheistic vision of a landscape; in *After the Deluge* Apollo has been superseded by a monotheistic god revealed through nature. It is not like Ruskinian landscape, the fidelity to the specific details of nature that show the divine, but rather the great and dramatic sweep painted in general terms, the painting of an idea. As Walter Bayes observes, this is 'a landscape from which all that is coarse and material has been eliminated, and which offers a residuum that is a kind of sublimation of all the most poetic elements in nature'.[2]

After the Deluge is not solely concerned with divine manifestation through natural phenomena but is also about divine retribution and salvation in re-creation; according to Genesis, 'And God saw that the wickedness of man *was* great in the earth, and *that* every imagination of the thoughts of his heart *was* only evil continually', but because of the deluge 'all flesh died that moved upon the earth, both of fowl, and of cattle, and of beast, and of every creeping thing that creepeth upon the earth, and every man'.[3] Noah and his family alone survived the flood, a prophet standing against a sinful world, a subject expressed by Watts in his paintings of Noah and Jonah. Creation, or more specifically re-creation, is a means of redemption; Macmillan describes this image of salvation:

The waters are abating, though the mighty Deluge still asserts its destructive force. But there is hope and promise … The whole sky is taken possession of by the Bow in the clouds, formed by the power of light and heat, dissipating the darkness and dissolving the multitude of waters into vapour, and consisting of a succession of circular rainbows, one beyond the other, with rays of light passing through and uniting them, lighting up all the dark remains of the storm.[4]

The painting was first exhibited at Whitechapel in 1886 under the deceptively simple title, as he was apt to do at this venue, of 'The Sun'. Watts continued to work on the painting and in a letter to Mrs Henry Holiday asked her to see the work as it developed: 'If perchance you should be going to The Grange I should be pleased if you would look in. I want you to see the Sun picture … the cessation of the deluge! I have done a great deal to it since you saw it.'[5] To paint a portrait of the sun was a bold move by any artist, particularly in late nineteenth-century London. It is both a work of the imagination and a study of the effects of light, showing 'the solar glow breaking through turbid mist'.[6] In this sense it anticipates the glorious sunburst of Edvard Munch and his contemporary Vincent Van Gogh.[7] It is also a great vortex in form, radiating and drawing into itself; as Mary put it, 'It is the painter's intention that it should be thus. "The heavens declare Thy glory Oh God!".'[8] MB

1   Watts Catalogue, I, p.1.
2   Bayes 1907, p.xi.
3   Genesis 6: 5 and 7: 21.
4   Macmillan 1903, p.153.
5   Watts Papers, Watts to Mrs Henry Holiday, 30 October, 1886.
6   Bayes 1907, p.xviii.
7   See Bryant in Watts Symbolism 1997, no.60.
8   Watts Gallery 1904, p.14. It is also used in Watts Manchester 1905, no.70.

64. *Mary Watts*, 1887

Oil on canvas, 50.8 × 25.4 cm (20 × 10 in)
COMWG 1

PROVENANCE: collection of the artist; Mary Watts; by descent to Lilian Mackintosh (Mrs Michael Chapman), legal descendant of the artist; given by her to the Watts Gallery 1946

LITERATURE: von Schleinitz 1904, pp.117, 120; Watts Catalogue, II, p.170; Watts 1912, II, p.77; Watts Gallery Catalogue 1957, no.8; Gould 2004, pp.215–16

Cat. 64.1 *Mary Watts*, 1887, oil on canvas, 48.3 × 35.6 cm (19 × 14 in), COMWG7

This informal study of Watts's second wife Mary is a companion piece to a more conventional three-quarter-profile portrait (cat.64.1). Painted during the couple's honeymoon in 1887 while they were staying in a hotel in Pera in Constantinople, both were produced on one canvas and Mary catalogued them together in the manuscript catalogue: 'He began because his hand was wearied by idleness a sketch in oil colour of me. Painted straight off in four colours on a single-prime canvas.'[1] Such a double-portrait format was not unusual for the artist (see cats 22, 28), although in this case it may just have been a convenient use of the canvas obtained in a foreign city. Shortly after completion, he separated it into two autonomous works.[2] Mary's sister Geraldine (Mrs Edward) Liddell acquired (or was given) the signed and dated portrait (cat.64.1), clearly the prime version, which went to a range of exhibitions, including the annual exhibition of the New Gallery in 1897 and the memorial exhibitions of 1905–6; Mrs Liddell bequeathed it to the Watts Gallery in 1931. The two pictures were only reunited in 1946 when Watts's adopted daughter Mrs Michael Chapman presented the back-view study to the Watts Gallery.

On 20 November 1886 the sixty-nine-year-old G.F. Watts married thirty-seven-year-old Mary Seton Fraser Tytler (1849–1938),[3] whom he had known since about 1870. She was a Scottish-born artist who had trained at the Slade School of Art and South Kensington School, and later became an active member of the Home Arts and Industries Association. Watts had previously been briefly married to the actress Ellen Terry, who served as his muse for many works of art, including *The Sisters* (1863; Watts Gallery), *Choosing* (1864; National Portrait Gallery) and *Ophelia* (cat.30) among others. However, there only seem to be three known portrait studies of Mary, the two companion studies under discussion here and a 'lost profile' oil study of Mary in a straw hat (1887; Watts Gallery),[4] also painted during the artist's honeymoon. She is not known to have served as a model for any of Watts's subject pictures.

To his old friend Lady Holland Watts wrote shortly before his departure on the honeymoon trip that his new wife was 'a first rate intellect & beautiful character – she is still young enough to make the office of nurse (for it won't be much

else) a sacrifice, but she believes that sympathy with my work & objects will compensate for much'.[5] Watts seems to have regarded Mary as a carer and an intellectual companion rather than as a muse and visual inspiration. Indeed, the honeymoon destination was largely dictated by medical reasons since Watts was unwell at the time, and, according to an anecdote, the artist's domineering confidante Mrs Barrington reportedly warned Mary that Watts would die on the voyage.[6] Watts suffered from poor health in Malta from where he wrote to Barrington that 'the Signora has had a pretty bad time with me' and praised his wife for 'a gentle and wise companionship which makes things easier'.[7]

If the love between them was not particularly romantic, the artist did nonetheless care deeply for Mary and expressed it in a letter shortly before their marriage:

I shall be disappointed if you do not bloom out like a flower that is transplanted into favourable soil. I want you to feel, if I do not profess the passionate feeling which would not be becoming to my age, I can love you very much with the love that joins itself closely round goodness and had its roots deep down in perfect trust.[8]

Throughout eighteen years of dedicated marriage, Mary devoted her life to looking after Watts and supporting him in all artistic undertakings. She co-founded the Watts Gallery in 1904 and, following the artist's death, wrote a three-volume biography of Watts and recorded the artist's prolific output in a three-volume manuscript catalogue. Watts, in turn, supported his wife's artistic projects including the design of the Compton Mortuary Chapel.

In this intimate oil study the devotion between the artist and his new wife found expression in his focus on the delicacy and vulnerability of the female neck, accentuated by the stylised collar with a stiff white frill and tightly pulled back hair. JD

Cat. 64.2 Frederick Hollyer, photograph of *Mrs G. F. Watts by a Window*, 1880s, Watts Gallery Archive, The Rob Dickins Collection

1   Watts Catalogue, II, p.170.
2   The critic in the *Athenaeum*, 22 October 1887, p.543, mentions a new portrait of Mary Watts, suggesting that the two images had been separated by then. The artist often improved the composition of his works by extending or cutting the canvases down; see cat.17.
3   She was the daughter of Charles Edward Fraser-Tytler and Etheldred St Barbe of Aldourie Castle, Inverness-shire; on Mary and the marriage, see Blunt 1975, pp.169–77.
4   As identified by Hilary Underwood.
5   Gould 2004, p. 203: Watts to Lady Holland, 19 November 1886 (British Library MS 52163, f.132).
6   Chapman 1945, p.127.
7   Barrington 1905, p.168.
8   Watts to Mary, Chapman 1945, pp.119–20.

65. *A Sea Ghost*, 1887

Oil on canvas, 45.7 × 71.1 cm (18 × 28 in)
COMWG100

PROVENANCE: collection of the artist, (Little
Holland House Gallery), Watts Gallery; part of the
original Memorial Collection

EXHIBITIONS: New Gallery 1889, no. 52; Sheffield
1894; Watts New Gallery 1896, no.52; Memorial
Exhibitions, Manchester 1905, no.40, Newcastle,
1905, no.120, Edinburgh 1905, no.52; Watts
London and Compton 2006, no.20

LITERATURE: Bayes 1907, p.xi; Watts Catalogue, I,
p.132; Watts 1912, II, p.83; Staley and Underwood
2006, pp.12, 47

A Sea Ghost was inspired by the weather conditions during G.F. Watts's honeymoon voyage with his second wife Mary in 1887. In 1912 Mary wrote extensively about the honeymoon travels around Egypt and related the circumstances behind Watts's artistic conception of the picture in detail:

> At Messina our boat was told off to tow a disabled sister ship of the same line (the Messageries), and all passengers were given the option of staying on board, to travel more slowly, or of removing to another Messageries boat ready to start at once. We, who preferred slowly coasting round Italy, were in the minority, and therefore had all the advantage of the less crowded ship; and the cruise was full of pleasure. A summer sea fog drifted about us one day, through which Corsica was suddenly revealed like opal and pearl, and then lost again. The disabled ship loomed strangely through the fog, and the two pictures 'Off Corsica' and 'The Sea Ghost' were painted later from the impressions of that day.[1]

The artist must have completed the work by 1889 when it was exhibited at the New Gallery. A Sea Ghost was shown together with Fog off Corsica (private collection), alongside a selection of various subject pictures spanning the artist's entire career.[2] Notably, one critic dismissed the two seascapes as 'dreams, pretty fancies, impressions, if you like, of the painter's latest days till now … at all events, a contrast sufficiently marked, to the noble still life or incident-picture, "The Wounded Heron [cat.3]"', a picture painted about fifty years earlier and surprisingly also exhibited at the New Gallery that year. A Sea Ghost was an indistinct painterly impression of a view from memory. Indeed, another review of the same exhibition describes the work as 'a phantom ship, sailing out of a fog bow that reminds one of Whistler'.[3] Whistler's monochromatic landscapes like Nocturne: Blue and Silver– Cremorne Lights (1872; Tate) were deliberately suggestive rather than naturalistic.

At its first exhibition A Sea Ghost was described as 'a ship seen in a mist'.[4] Other contemporary descriptions of the subject of the work mention fog and its halo effect. Watts was interested in different atmospheric phenomena, but primarily for their aesthetic effect, as is evident in later works such as Rain Passing Away also called The Rainbow (1884; private collection), Sunset on the Alps (1888–94; Watts Gallery) and Study of Clouds (1890–1900; Tate). Painted mostly from memory as recollections of the first impressions of a view, these late landscapes from the last two decades of Watts's life were sometimes recorded in sketches on location, but always completed in the studio and not from life. As Allen Staley points out: 'Although inspired by an actual experience, the painting [Sea Ghost] is more a dreamlike vision than an objective rendering of atmospheric effects in the manner of the French Impressionists.'[5] As a mature artist, Watts believed that 'to render nature truly – that is, to give her inward beauty – one must make careful studies first … looking much and well at nature, and then coming away and trying to paint the impression left on the mind'.[6] This approach was adopted for many late landscapes.

Mary listed A Sea Ghost as 'painted from notes made on board a … boat … The fog in the Mediterranean gave him this subject.'[7] A later commentator pointed out that 'Watts's landscapes … are typical – rather, perhaps, elemental. Light and colour, sky, earth and sea, tree and flower, the great generic facts of nature, not the multitudinous detail of individual forms, are what he sets before us.'[8] The above assessment of the nature of Watts's landscapes reflects their generic quality abstracted from reality through the artist's memory.

The intriguing title, A Sea Ghost, might have been the artist's attempt to disregard the specifics of the locality where the picture was originally conceived and to identify the ephemeral quality of the view, which clearly haunted the painter's memory like a vision (or 'impression left on the mind'), as the intended essence of the work. The motif of a ghost ship, an apparition vessel on the sea, had a presence in English literature of the Romantic period through The Rime of the Ancient Mariner (1797–8) by Samuel Taylor Coleridge and Rokeby (1813) by Sir Walter Scott. Richard Wagner's opera about the most famous ghost ship, The Flying Dutchman (1843), also popularized the subject.

Watts's ambition to keep some of his works for the benefit of the general public invites comparisons with Turner. In A Sea Ghost the static symmetry of the semi-circular composition with the central silhouette of the ship moving smoothly forward evokes calmness and grandeur. This effect is reminiscent of Turner's The Fighting Temeraire (1838; National Gallery, London)[9] and the more expressionistic Light and Colour (Goethe's Theory) – The Morning after the Deluge –Moses Writing the Book of Genesis (1843; Tate), in which Turner employed a similar, strikingly circular composition with a central vertical axis of symmetry.

Watts painted landscapes throughout his career, originally as private studies and recreations and eventually as important publicly exhibited works. Correspondence between Watts and the collector James Smith suggests that A Sea Ghost, which the artist was offering for sale in 1892 for 300 guineas,[10] gradually increased in personal value to Watts. Eventually he decided to keep it in his studio with other important works, explaining that 'those must be kept to lend'.[11] JD

1   Watts 1912, II, p.83.
2   Other New Gallery works by Watts included A Wounded Heron (cat.3), Good Luck to Your Fishing (1889), The Wife of Plutus (1885) and Fata Morgana (1846–89).
3   Unidentified review of the 1889 New Gallery exhibition, clipping in Watts Gallery Archive.
4   New Gallery Catalogue, 1889, no.52, p.26.
5   Staley and Underwood 2006, p.47.
6   Watts 1912, II, p.114.
7   Ibid, p.132.
8   From entry no.30 for An Afterglow, Scotland (1899) in the Edinburgh Memorial Exhibition catalogue (1905).
9   See Staley and Underwood 2006, p.47.
10   Watts Papers, Watts to James Smith, 29 April 1892: '"Fog off Corsica" and "Sea Ghost" same occasion and locality almost, three hundred guineas each.'
11   Watts Papers, Watts to James Smith, 5 August 1894: '"Ophelia" is not to be sold, nor is "Ganymede" nor "The Sea Ghost", those must be kept to lend.'

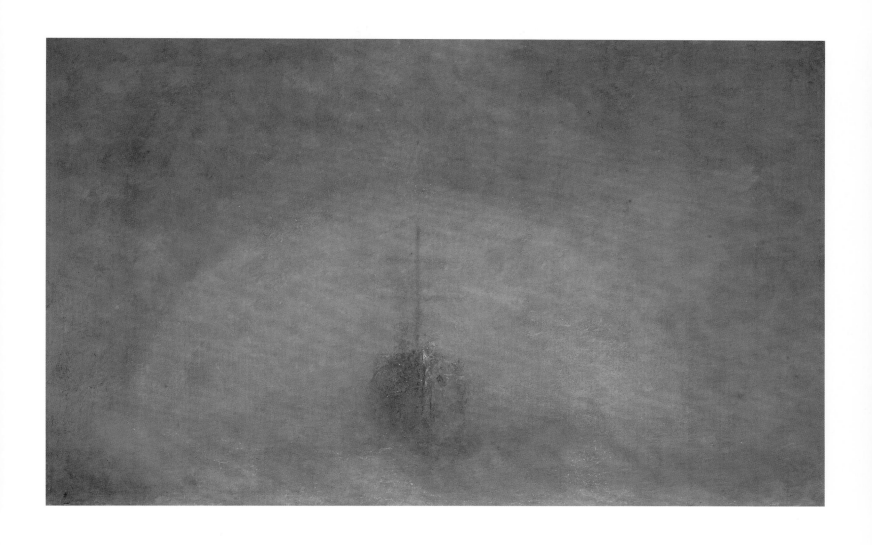

66. *Sunset on the Alps: A Reminiscence* 1888–94

Oil on gilded canvas, 142.2 × 109.2 cm (56 × 43 in)
COMWG113

PROVENANCE: collection of the artist (Little Holland House Gallery); part of the original Memorial Collection, 1905

EXHIBITIONS: *A Collection of Mountain Paintings and Photographs*, The Alpine Club, London, 1894, no.114 ('An Alpine Peak'); Watts New Gallery 1896–7, no.149; People's Palace Exhibition, 1897; Watts Gallery 1904, no.39; Memorial Exhibitions, 1905, Manchester, no.67, Newcastle, no.172; *Landscape in Britain 1850–1950*, Arts Council of Great Britain, London, 1983, no.12; Watts Symbolism 1997, no.62; Watts Compton 2004, no.53; Watts London and Compton 2006, no.23

LITERATURE: Watts Gallery Catalogue 1904, no.39; Bayes 1907, p.xix, pl. XVIII; Watts Catalogue, I, p.139; Watts 1912, II, pp.126–7; Alston 1929, no.120; Blunt 1975, p.182; Bryant 1997, p.182; Staley and Underwood 2006, p.50

While travelling in Europe with Mary Watts during the spring of 1888, Watts had a burst of activity sketching and painting landscapes. He had taken the cure for gout at Aix-les-Bains in southern France, but with further ill health his doctor recommended rest in more bracing air, so they journeyed to Monnetier in Haute-Savoie, Switzerland, by rail. At 2,000 feet above sea level the landscape offered some totally new sights. Watts saw the view in this painting from a train window at the village of La-Roche-sur-Foron, called 'the gateway to the high Alps', far above the river valley of the Arve. He observed the landscape 'steeped in the crimson of the setting sun, suddenly a line of snowy peaks blazed out on the background of giant cumulus clouds', likening it to 'a celestial city'.[1] His new-found attraction to the high Alps had much to do with the conjunction of mountain peaks and sky. Then aged just over seventy, the artist could still be moved by dramatic views in nature and continued to take advantage of such experiences as inspiration for his art.

Although based on direct observation (there is a small watercolour and gouache study[2]), Watts did not paint the oil until he returned to London, when he dramatised the view considerably. From the same journey he conceived several other Alpine landscapes, such as *The Alps near Monnetier* (cat.66.1) and *Sant'Agnese, Mentone* (1888; J.H.J. Lewis),[3] but as horizontal compositions, these lack the grandiose power of *Sunset on the Alps*. Here on a massively enlarged scale and in a suitably vertical format, the cloudscape dominates, filling more than half the composition. Indeed, the clouds take on the character of mountain forms themselves, overpowering the earth-bound peak with their untamed rising movement. This gloriously ascending crescendo results in an image of optimism, even joy. One travels metaphorically from the darker foreground area up the smooth curve of the white tinged mountain to the brilliantly rich orange of the clouds. The experimental choice of a gilded canvas lends a hot glow to the tones and the crumbly textures of dry pigment give a palpitating intensity to the colours.

Watts exhibited this painting in 1894 with the title 'An Alpine Peak', providing a description: 'a reminiscence of a vision of one of the peaks of the Mont Blanc chain'. By 1896 he preferred the title *Sunset on the Alps: A Reminiscence*, allowing the quality of memory to enter into the meaning of the work. Reworking personal experience in unexpected and intensely personal ways corresponded to the Symbolist trends in the 1880s and 1890s. This 'reminiscence' resulted in Watts's most visionary landscape. BB

1   Watts 1912, II, p.126.
2   Discussed in Bryant 1997, p.182; this study, once in the collection of Brinsley Ford (see Ford 1998, no.RBF541), is now at the Watts Gallery.
3   See Watts London and Compton, 2006, nos 22, 24.

Cat. 66.1 *The Alps near Monnetier*, 1888–95, oil on canvas, 48 × 107 cm (19 × 42 in), COMWG80

67. Study for the *The Court of Death*, late 1880s

Oil on canvas, 94 × 61 cm (37 × 24 in)
COMWG81

PROVENANCE: collection of the artist (Little Holland House Gallery); part of the original Memorial Collection, 1905

EXHIBITIONS: St Jude's, Whitechapel, 1891, no.90; ?St Jude's, Whitechapel, 1894, no.154; Clifton Gallery, 1902; Southport 1902; Watts Leighton House 1903, p.8, no.1 as 1886; Watts Gallery 1904, no.20; Memorial Exhibitions, London 1905, no.150, Manchester 1905, no.23, Newcastle 1905, no.45 as 1881; *Death, Heaven and the Victorians*, Art Gallery and Museum, Brighton, 1970, no.34; Watts Compton 2004, no.102

LITERATURE (on the subject): Spielmann 1886, pp.7 (illus. of related version), 21, 30; Robert de la Sizeranne, *La peinture anglaise contemporaine*, Paris, 1895 (trans., London, 1898, pp.110–12); Cartwright 1896, pp.9 (no.34), 12, 30; Sketchley 1903, pp.77, 91; Macmillan 1903, pp.233–6; Watts Gallery Catalogue 1904, no.20; Barrington 1905, pp.33–4, 92, 164–5, 203; Watts Catalogue, I, p.31 (no.34); Watts 1912, I, pp.219, 228, 235, 284, 307–8, 319, II, pp.58, 135, 265, 289; Alston 1929, no.124 as 1880–1900; Blunt 1975, pp.186, 204–5; Morris 1996, pp.480–3; Bryant 1997, p.74

Watts considered *The Court of Death* his greatest and most complete design. This oil study featured in his gallery at Little Holland House; it is the only version of this major subject at the Watts Gallery. In 1902 Watts put the finishing touches to the final version (1870s onwards; Tate Britain), but the composition had evolved over the previous half century. In the early 1850s the artist designed 'The Angel of Death',[1] originally intending that it should adorn a mortuary chapel for paupers,[2] presumably in the manner of a secular altarpiece. It seems that the earliest idea for the composition occurred at about the same time that Watts painted the social realist pictures (cats 14–16), which had been prompted by his observation of and empathy for London's poor. The mortuary chapel for the poor never materialised, but the altruistic beginnings of this design took another form as Watts planned for *The Court of Death* to be part of his public

Cat. 67.1 The studio at Limnerslease showing among other works the final version of *The Court of Death*, *The Illustrated London News*, 29 July 1893, Watts Gallery Archive

Cat. 67.2 Frederick Hollyer, photograph of *The Court of Death* (unfinished state), Hollyer Album, Watts Gallery Archive

bequest to the nation. It also belonged to the amorphous, never-realised House of Life scheme (see cat.45).

Watts invented the symbolic programme for the subject, uniting the idea of regeneration with death: his own explanation first appeared in the catalogue of the Grosvenor Gallery retrospective in 1881.[3] The design went through various changes from the 1850s onwards with the fundamental idea remaining constant: a female angel, symbolising Death, sits on her throne 'composed of architectural ruins denoting the perishability of all things human'.[4] Gathered below, paying homage or obeisance to her, are figures representing different conditions and ages of man: a nobleman relinquishing his crown, a soldier surrendering his sword, a poor cripple, a young woman sometimes called 'Sickness' (modelled by May Prinsep, see cat.37), a beggar woman, a child, a lion and, in two versions, a black slave. In the foreground the 'book of Life' lies open. Death cradles a newly born or even, as Watts wrote, 'an unborn child' to imply 'even the germ of life is in the lap of Death', which he considered 'the most poetic idea in the picture, the keynote of the whole'.[5] By 1886, when Spielmann published his catalogue of Watts's works, the title had changed to *The Court of Death* and the powerful figures of Mystery and Silence flanked the Portal of the Unknown in the background.[6]

Given the complexity of the composition and the variations introduced, Watts produced many versions. A large cartoon was in hand in 1863 (Manchester City Galleries), but he also worked on smaller versions, such as the one borrowed in 1864 by Ruskin who called it 'the new Trionfo della Morte Madonna', adding the exhortation: 'You know – you must learn to paint like Titian!'[7] A finished design (private collection) appeared at the Dudley Gallery in 1871 (and was sold in 1874); another one was completed for Rickards (early 1870s–81; Walker Art Gallery, National Museums Liverpool) and much exhibited in the 1880s.[8]

At this stage in his career Watts did not execute finished drawings for major compositions; rather, his practice was to sketch the design on the canvas itself.[9] For changes and alternative colour schemes he painted smaller oil sketches. The studies for *The Court of Death* are good

examples of this practice.[10] The Watts Gallery oil sketch shows the composition in its latest phase from the 1880s, by which time the artist had decided on the final composition.[11] Certain details, such as the beardless nobleman in ermine-trimmed robes, relate most closely to the final version of the painting. Experimentation with different colour schemes, as in this version, meant that finer detail would not be needed and the handling is freer and looser. Indeed, Barrington commented that one of the small canvases of *The Court of Death* (possibly cat.67) was 'the finest example of this unity of colour, tone, and atmosphere' seen in an exhibition of 1903.[12] This oil study represents an essential stage in the evolution of this major composition, but it also has its own virtues as a display of Watts's richer textures and more sonorous coloration in the 1880s.

The Court of Death is thematically related to Watts's *Love and Death* (fig.52), which he also worked on from the 1860s. Both rely on a personification of Death, not as a terrifying force but as an inevitability. That this powerful, winged figure commanded the tributes and homage of all was (and still is) a pessimistic notion, but the gloriously rich colours, especially the powerful hot-orange burst behind Death, allow a semblance of hope. BB

1. Twisleton 1928, p.106, where in her diary of 1853 she records seeing a design for it in Watts's studio.
2. Watts 1912, I, p.228.
3. A further explanation with some variations appeared in the catalogue of the New Gallery exhibition of 1896, p.6, no.135.
4. Spielmann 1886, p.30.
5. Watts 1912, I, p.308.
6. 'Notes on a visit to Mr. Watts at Limnerslease, Guildford', Watts Papers, 27 September 1898.
7. Watts 1912, I, p.219.
8. For a full discussion of this version, including Watts's refusal to accede to Rickards's request to add a cross and omit the baby, see Morris 1996, pp.481–2.
9. As noted by Cartwright 1896, p.8; on p.12 the illustration seems to be the Watts Gallery version.
10. Several are listed in Watts Catalogue (the discussions confuse various versions); two were sold as part of the Chapman dispersals.
11. Spielmann 1886, p.24.
12. Barrington 1905, p.203.

68. *Time, Death and Judgement,* late 1870s–1896

Oil on canvas, 243.8 × 168.9 cm (96 × 66½ in)
COMWGNC27

On view at St Paul's Cathedral for the duration of the exhibition in London

PROVENANCE: given by the artist in 1897 to the Dean and Chapter St Paul's Cathedral at the request of Canon Henry Scott Holland; hanging in the nave of the cathedral until 1977; on long loan from the Dean and Chapter to the Watts Gallery

EXHIBITIONS:[1] ?Grosvenor Gallery, 1878, no.62; ?Walker Art Gallery, Liverpool, 1878, no.77; ?St Jude's, Whitechapel, 1884, no.9; ?Watts Birmingham 1885, no.174; ?Watts New York 1884, no.103; ?St Jude's, Whitechapel, 1886, no.64; *Jahresausstellung von Kunstwerken aller Nationen*, Glaspalaste, Munich, 1893, no.1638; Watts New Gallery 1896, no.144; Walker Art Gallery, Liverpool, 1896; West Ham, 1898; Memorial Exhibitions, Manchester 1905, no.68, Newcastle 1905, no.47, Edinburgh 1905, no.73, Dublin 1906, no.57; Watts Compton 2004, no.85

LITERATURE (on the subject): Spielmann 1886, pp.23, 24, 32; Cartwright 1896, pp.9, 10; Bateman 1901, p.57; Sketchley 1904, pp.147, 157; Macmillan 1903, pp.236–8; Chesterton 1904, p.30; Barrington 1905, pp.92, 94, 112, 116, 118, 127–8; Watts Catalogue, I, p.146; Watts 1912, I, pp.228, 235, 307, 319, 327–8, II, pp.86, 215; *Henry Scott Holland: Memoir and Letters*, ed. Stephen Paget, London, 1921, pp.146–7; Short 1924, p.122; Blunt 1975, pp.144–5 (on the unveiling of the mosaic), 229; Staley 1978, nos 29a–b, pp.87–8; Bryant 1997, no.123, pp.263–4; Pantazzi 2006, pp.53–5, 58, 62–3

As one of Watts's best-known and most important subjects, *Time, Death and Judgement* summarises his belief in art as a force to communicate powerful ideas in an artistic language 'universal in its appeal'.[2] He asserted that it was the only subject to 'come before his inner sight as a picture'; indeed, to another writer he described it as a 'vision',[3] underlining its role as a key example of the poetic impulse in the artist's work. G.K. Chesterton considered it one of Watts's 'great stoical pictures'.

Thematically linked most closely with *Love and Death* (fig.52), this painting also features colossal figures representing types intended 'to appeal purely to human sympathies, without reference to creed or dogma of any kind'.[4] First entitled *Time and Death*, before the addition of the third figure, the composition had a lengthy gestation from the mid-1860s onwards. Watts's

usual practice was to paint several large-scale versions, sending them to exhibitions, reworking them and only finishing them finally when they left his studio altogether. Three major versions of this subject exist: one given by the artist to Canada to commemorate Queen Victoria's forthcoming jubilee in 1887 (now in the National Gallery of Canada); this one, given in 1897 by Watts to St Paul's Cathedral in London; and a third given to the Tate by the artist in 1900.[5] The first two were under way in the mid-1870s with one sent to public exhibition at the Grosvenor Gallery in 1878;[6] reworked,[7] but still unfinished, one of these probably went to Birmingham and New York in 1885.[8] Both were in Watts's collection in 1886 when Spielmann refers to the great picture and the replica; shortly after, in 1886, Watts presented one to Canada.[9] The handling of this work reveals the

rich yet restrained colouring of the 1880s. The St Paul's picture, on a much rougher canvas, shows greater intensity of colour and more loosely applied paint with pronounced highlights scumbled over the surface.

The youthful figures of Time and Death, beautiful but passive presences, are 'wading hand in hand together through the waves of the stream of life',[10] according to the text in the catalogue for the 1884–5 exhibition in New York, which continues: 'He [Time] is represented as advancing in strides, marking the recurrence of conditions – the hours, days, months and years. Death, his inevitable mate, glides silently by his side, doing her work at unexpected, uncalculated moments.' The massive orb behind the figures is the sun against which Time, with his warm flesh tones, is seen, whereas Death, with her ghostly pallor, is associated with a pale, crescent moon (not easily visible) to the right side. Although Time bears the conventional symbol of the scythe, unlike traditional representations, he is a vigorous youth not a wizened old man. Death, with obvious kinship to the figure in *Love and Death*, is swathed in shroud-like draperies, with eyes barely open, gazing at the wilting flowers she bears. Judgement, wearing robes of flaming red, flies overhead in the wind. With face averted, this figure seems a terrifying force as it gestures both forwards and backwards into space holding its 'deciding scales' and the fiery 'avenging sword'.

As the main versions of *Time, Death and Judgement* are on a colossal scale, with figures conceived in a sculpture-like mode, they seemed suitable as architectural decoration. Indeed, in the catalogue of 1884 the commentary approved by Watts noted that the painting's influence 'would probably be best felt were it seen in a niche by itself, in a cloister or a church, not in an art gallery or museum'.[11] In that year he authorised the reproduction of the subject as a mosaic to decorate the exterior of the church of St Jude's in Whitechapel in the East End of London, where Watts's friend Canon Barnett staged art exhibitions for his impoverished congregation.

Appropriately, *Time, Death and Judgement* had yet more exposure in an ecclesiastical setting when the Canon of St Paul's, Henry Scott Holland (1847–1918), asked Watts to donate a work of art to the great cathedral church.[12] The erudite theologian Scott Holland had already met the artist at Oxford in July 1882, when Watts received his Doctor of Letters. They shared similar views on social reform. In 1884 he took up the position of canon at St Paul's, but while serving at this high level, he also worked to alleviate social problems in the East End and founded the Christian Social Union. His interests extended to contemporary art, and although he knew Burne-Jones well, it was nonetheless Watts's New Gallery retrospective in 1896–7 that fired his enthusiasm. He wrote to Julia Cartwright Ady, whose article on Watts appeared in the previous year:

Two visits to the Watts collection have made me burn with desire to see two great works of his in St. Paul's. They are to go to the

nation: and would not the nation wish to see them there where they would best tell? They should hang in the two great panels at the entrance of the nave, where they would comfort all the weary tramps who doze and dream. Is it at all conceivable? It would be useless to have any but the largest for such a position. But I think Time, Death, and Judgement, for instance, would be large enough to speak there.[13]

Scott Holland's determination to acquire two works did not abate, as he wrote further of his

sincere belief that this would be he right way to honour his gifts … that in this way they

would best deliver their deepest message. They would reach the poor and needy, who sit and dream all down our nave: they would be a wonderful power in the middle of the throngs.[14]

Artist William Blake Richmond lent his support. He was involved with the ongoing decorative schemes at St Paul's, including the installation of mosaics after designs by Watts and others dating from the early 1860s.[15]

The gift was not immediately forthcoming as the painting was at the New Gallery exhibition, but in mid-1897 *Time, Death and Judgement* arrived at St Paul's. To the 'dear old man', the canon wrote, 'our heartfelt thanks, in the name of all the

Cat. 68.1 Interior of St Paul's Cathedral showing the Great North-East Pier, July 1915, photograph reproduced by permission of English Heritage, NMR

tramps in the nave … [the painting] is perfectly splendid, glowing, beautiful. It quite peoples the church. I have been revelling all day in the glory of it.'[16] Might the impact of the painting, if not its actual meaning, also be reflected in Scott Holland's famous and oft-quoted sermon of 1910:

Death is nothing at all
I have only slipped away into the next room
I am I and you are you
Whatever we were to each other
That we are still.

Watts's more fatalistic impetus is summarised by the two quotations from his favourite book of the Bible, that existentialist's resource, Ecclesiastes. On the top of the handsome black frame the same quote that he attached to *Time and Oblivion* (fig.39) is inscribed, 'Whatsoever thy hand findeth to do, do *it* with thy might; for *there* is no work, nor device, nor knowledge, nor wisdom, in the grave, whither thou goest', while at the lower edge we read: 'He that observeth the wind shall not sow; and he that regardeth the clouds shall not reap.'[17] Such messages may have been intended for Scott Holland's grateful tramps, but they were also indicative of Watts's own essentially pessimistic outlook.

With a prominent position on one of the massive piers at the end of the nave (cat.68.1), just before one enters the dome space, Watts's universal vision of *Time, Death and Judgement* took its place in the great cathedral as a kind of secular altarpiece. That the artist's own memorial service was enacted in that same space seven years later adds to the remarkable resonance of this painting in this particular location, to which it has currently, albeit temporarily, returned. BB

1 There is some question as to which versions were exhibited from the 1870s to the 1890s.
2 As Watts commented to Rickards in 1876, quoted in Watts 1912, I, p.307.
3 Barrington 1905, p.94; Sketchley 1904, p.147.
4 Watts's comment to Rickards in 1876, quoted in Watts 1912, I, p.307.
5 For a discussion of all the versions and the meaning of the subject, see Bryant 1997, pp.263–5.
6 Only an earlier oil design in Rickards's collection was at the retrospective in 1881.
7 For an important drawing of Death, formerly at the Watts Gallery and now at the National Gallery of Canada, see Lanigan 2000, no.93, and Douglas E. Schoenherr, *British Drawings from the National Gallery of Canada*, Ottawa, 2005, no.52.
8 Mary Watts indicates that the St Paul's painting was exhibited at New York, Birmingham and later at the New Gallery exhibition.
9 According to Pantazzi 2006, p.52, who writes about the Canadian version, an additional piece of canvas was added to the top of that picture to allow more space for the figure of Judgement.
10 Watts New York 1884, no.103, quoted in Barrington 1905, p.128.
11 Ibid.
12 John H. Heidt, 'Holland, Henry Scott (1847–1918)', *Oxford Dictionary of National Biography* (http://www.oxforddnb.com/view/article/33939, accessed 3 March 2008).
13 *Henry Scott Holland: Memoir and Letters*, ed. Stephen Paget, London, 1921, p.147. Paget does not note that Mrs Ady is Julia Cartwright, but it is clear that, with Scott Holland's friends in the art world, he knew her well.
14 Ibid., p.148.
15 The recent volume, *St. Paul's: The Cathedral Church of London, 604–2004*, ed. Derek Keene, Arthur Burns and Andrew Saint, New Haven and London, 2004, refers to Watts's mosaics but not to the acquisition of *Time, Death and Judgement* by the Dean and Chapter.
16 His desire for a second painting to form a pairing took longer to realise. He approached Watts again but was less keen for the work on offer, *The Spirit of Christianity*, seemingly preferring a more rousing example, such *as The Rider on the White Horse*. It was not until ten years later, when he broached the subject with the artist's widow Mary Watts, that he received *Peace and Goodwill*, as noted in the Minutes of the Trustees of the Watts Picture Gallery, 20 February 1907 (my thanks to Mark Bills for providing me with a copy of the Minutes).
17 Ecclesiastes 9: 10 and 11: 4.

69. Studies for *The Messenger*, *c*.1880

Pen and ink on blue laid paper, 31.8 × 20.3 cm (12 ½ × 8 in)
Paper watermarked 'E. Towgood 1878
COMWG2007.610

PROVENANCE: collection of the artist; Mary Watts; Lilian Mackintosh (Mrs Michael Chapman), legal descendant of the artist; by descent until formally included within the Watts Gallery's collections

This small sheet of three studies provides an insight into Watts's initial ideas for his enigmatic painting *The Messenger* (cat.70.1; see cats 61, 70). The watermark of 1878 gives a useful indicator of a *terminus post quem*; it is likely that he began planning the subject around 1880 as a continuation of his 'cycle of Death', following on the acclaim received by *Love and Death* (fig.52) at the Grosvenor Gallery in 1877 and *Time, Death and Judgement* (cat.68) in 1878. As with so many of Watts's best designs, the essence of the composition is visually very simple, an encounter between Death and the reclining man.

Here the artist has been thinking on paper, loosely sketching on a piece of everyday stationery. The ink lines defining the drapery flow in freely executed circular motion, as the two main characters form an enclosed shape. A slight study at the top of the sheet shows an elaborate knot of twisted fabric, a reminder that for Watts drapery painting had an important function in a composition. He advised students to 'draw constantly from drapery'[1] and he followed his own advice. As in *Love and Death*, the female is initially faceless; it is the gesture of her touching the man that is important. Even in this initial study she is clearly holding the infant, but all the accessories of the more elaborate symbolical design came later. BB

1   Watts 1912, III, p.16.

70. Study for *The Messenger*, early 1880s

Black chalk, heightened with white, on grey paper laid on canvas, 169 × 92 cm (66½ × 36¼ in)
COMWG303

PROVENANCE: collection of the artist; Mary Watts; Lilian Mackintosh (Mrs Michael Chapman), legal descendant of the artist; by descent until formally included within the Watts Gallery's collections

LITERATURE: von Schleinitz 1904, p.115, fig.99

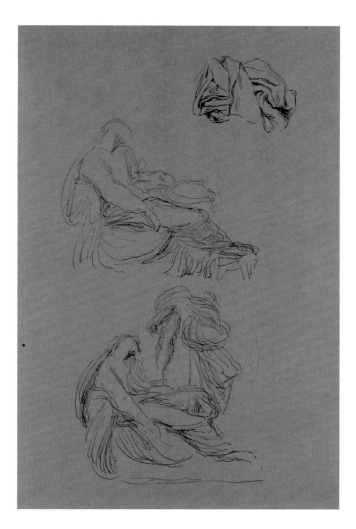

Cat. 70.1 Frederick Hollyer, photograph of *The Messenger*, Hollyer Album, Watts Gallery Archive

In contrast to the loosely executed first idea studies of cat.69, this drawing is a major statement in which the figure of Death is extracted from the composition to create an independent work of art. On unusually large scale, it is an impressive portrayal of the dominant figure in *The Messenger*.

This drawing is on the same scale as the figure in the oil painting (cat.70.1), so it served a role in the creation of a convincing full-size standing figure. The drapery is carefully worked, more elaborate in this drawing than in the painting. The white chalk highlighting, now somewhat less readable than originally, indicates the flow of the drapery over the figure. Certain details are more visible here than in the oil, especially the infant, who seems inert in the arms of Death and may, as in *The Court of Death* (see cat.67), represent the unborn child or the 'germ of life'.[1] Also very evident here is the beautiful face of Death gazing downwards, passionless and passive.

Watts's working procedure for large compositions included detailed studies for single figures, but on occasion these studies took on a life of their own with the artist sometimes even exhibiting and publishing them. For *The Messenger* there was an unfinished design, now known by Hollyer's photograph (cat.61.1) published in an article by Meade in 1894 and Cartwright in 1896.[2] The present work was also published independently by von Schleinitz in 1904. The figure of Death, so clearly the protagonist of the unfolding drama, took a starring role in these drawings. Watts also extracted the same figure from *Love and Death* for separate treatment in an impressive drawing (National Gallery of Canada).[3] The artist's obsession with death, an essentially Symbolist subject, informs these drawings. In such chalk studies the soft focus heightens the mood of silence and mystery, nowhere more evident than in this depiction of Death from *The Messenger*. BB

1   Watts 1912, I, p.308.
2   Meade 1894, p.15, and Cartwright 1896, p.1.
3   Lanigan 2000, no.93.

71. *The Minotaur*, mid-1880s to 1890s

Charcoal with white chalk highlighting on wove brown paper, 73.8 × 56.4 cm (29 × 22¼ in)
COMWG2008.149

PROVENANCE: collection of the artist; Mary Watts; Lilian Mackintosh (Mrs Michael Chapman), legal descendant of the artist; by descent until formally included within the Watts Gallery's collections

EXHIBITED: Watts Compton 2004, no.63

This large-scale drawing is so close to Watts's *Minotaur* (1885; Tate Britain)[1] that it seems not to be a study preparatory to the oil but rather a copy after it. Such large drawings do occur in the artist's *oeuvre* as, for example, the red chalk *Hope* (cat.59.1).[2] He probably executed this version of *The Minotaur* to retain in his own collection since the oil was regularly absent, lent to exhibitions and displays, until it went to the Tate Gallery in 1897 as part of Watts's gift to the nation.

Watts portrays the Minotaur of ancient myth and legend as recounted by Virgil, Ovid and, later, Dante. A hybrid man-animal – the grotesque offspring of an adulterous union between Queen Pasiphae, the wife of King Minos of Crete, and a bull – the Minotaur was confined in the labyrinth on the island of Crete. Every nine years a group of Athenian youths were sacrificed to his blood lust until Theseus slew him. In both Watts's painting and this drawing the Minotaur gazes from a lofty tower atop his prison. His whole world is restricted to the labyrinth, but his momentary release here is to look at the sea and sky. In his vast hand he crushes a small bird, whether from sheer cruelty or because he is so absorbed in his own plight is open to question, but the bird's predicament taps into a characteristic Wattsian theme (see cats 3, 77). The clear design, with a single figure silhouetted against the sky, provides an unencumbered visual statement typical of Watts.

The painting is usually cited as the artist's direct response to the scandal of child prostitution exposed by crusading journalist W.T. Stead, editor of *The Pall Mall Gazette*, in a series of articles, 'The Maiden Tribute of Modern Babylon', published in July 1885.[3] While Watts was undoubtedly aware of this cause célèbre, one needs to take into account his knowledge of the subject in older art, his own previous treatment of mythological paintings as universalised images and his connections with contemporary artists to provide a more accurate and nuanced interpretation. The handling of the paint in the hazy blue seascape of the oil is in itself a tribute to Whistler.

With colour such an important feature of the painting, in which the hot tones of the Minotaur's body contrast with the cool blues of the sea and sky, it must have proved a challenge to convey the same elements in a drawing. Indeed, here the seascape is de-emphasised, allowing the much maligned creature to take centre stage. A rich tonal range is achieved with variations in shading that focus attention on the Minotaur. White chalk picks out the musculature, knotted folds of skin on his back and certain salient details such as the tiny bird. White highlighting also directs focus to the Minotaur's eye, a detail more noticeable in the drawing and essential to Watts's meaning, which is as much about the inner life of the Minotaur as his cruelty. BB

1 Watts Catalogue, I, p.100.
2 Watts Whitechapel 1974, no.66.
3 I have discussed this episode in more detail in 'Interpreting *The Minotaur*: Social Tract or History Painting', presented at the Watts Annual Conference in September 2007; a publication is forthcoming.

72. Study for *'The All-Pervading'*, 1887

Pen, sepia ink and wash on laid writing paper,
12.7 × 20.2 cm (5 × 8 in)
Inscribed (not by Watts) 'Malta'
COMWG 2007.504

PROVENANCE: collection of the artist; Mary Watts; Lilian Mackintosh (Mrs Michael Chapman), legal descendant of the artist; by descent until formally included within the Watts Gallery's collections

This small drawing represents Watts's first idea for the major work, *'The All-Pervading'* (cat.72.1), part of his gift to the Tate Gallery in 1897.[1] The inscription 'Malta' dates it specifically to the tour Watts and Mary took in the winter of 1887–8, a year after their marriage, when they stayed on the island in the seaside town of Sliema around the bay from Valletta. Although attracted to the nearby sea, which inspired his Symbolist seascape *Neptune's Horses* (1888–92; Fenton House, National Trust), Watts found the initial impulse for *'The All-Pervading'* not in the natural environment but in the reflections and refractions of light from a huge glass chandelier in a spacious room he used as a studio, or so Mary Watts recorded.[2]

A draped figure sits enclosed by its huge wings, holding the 'Globe of the Systems', as Watts termed it when describing the large painting in the catalogue to his exhibition at the New Gallery in 1896. He considered the figure as 'spirit that pervades the immeasurable expanse'.[3] The art-historical antecedents for the powerful figure were Michelangelo's Sibyls on the Sistine Ceiling, characters who also had the ability to gaze into the future; indeed, in her pose she appears like a crystal-ball reader. But star-gazing is equally relevant, as the globe of the systems represents the stars and galaxies throughout the universe, so the work shares a thematic link with *The Sower of the Systems* (cat.82). The spirit's face is obscured in darkness, created with washes of sepia ink, lending an uncertainty to this forecast of the future. In striking this disturbing note here and in other works

Cat. 72.1 Frederick Hollyer, photograph of *'The All-Pervading'*, Hollyer Album, Watts Gallery Archive

of the late 1880s, the imagery moves into distinctly Symbolist territory. This drawing, as a
first idea, presents a simple ideogram, the form
contained within an oval shape. That such a
seemingly slight drawing became the basis for a
large-scale oil reveals the potency of Watts's
imagination in producing memorable images.
BB

1   For a full discussion of the painting, see Bryant
     1997, no.125, pp.267–8.
2   Watts 1912, II, pp.104–5. A later oil study is in the
     Watts Gallery, exhibited Watts Compton 2004,
     no.114, and Watts painted a later version for the
     Mortuary Chapel, listed in Watts Catalogue, I,
     p.2.
3   Watts New Gallery 1896, no.129.

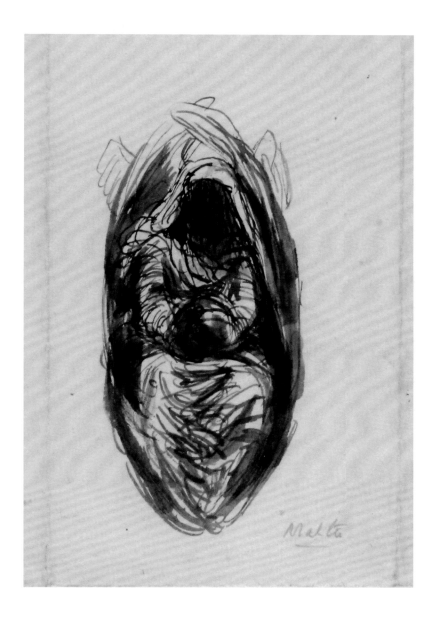

The Grand Old Man at Compton

In 1890 Watts leased land at Compton and had a house built by Ernest George named Limnerslease. Around this time Watts and his wife were introduced to an orphan named Lilian Mackintosh (later Mrs Michael Chapman) whom they adopted and who became heir to part of their personal estate. In 1903 Watts created a purpose-built gallery and moved all his paintings from Little Holland House Gallery to the Compton gallery, which opened to the public on 1 April 1904.

Watts's reputation was consolidated both nationally and internationally with exhibitions in Paris and Munich, and in Britain he was a household name. Images of the grand old man of painting with his Titianesque cap and robes were familiar throughout the country. Furthermore, Watts developed a working relationship with the photographer Frederick Hollyer (1838–1933) in order to record his output and circulate his paintings to a wide audience. He also instigated a memorial garden of 'everyday heroes' in the form of a 50-foot-long open gallery situated in public gardens on the site of the former churchyard of St Botolph, Aldersgate, and called Postman's Park. Along the walls of the gallery Watts placed tablets, each describing acts of bravery that resulted in the loss of the hero or heroine's life. Despite his age and increasingly longer periods away from London, Watts remained remarkably active and a ceaseless experimenter, producing the remarkable and almost abstract painting, *Sower of the Systems* (cat.82), exhibited at the New Gallery in 1903.

Watts died on 1 July 1904 after he had seen the Watts Gallery open in Compton and major bequests to the National Portrait Gallery and National Gallery of British Art (now Tate). International obituaries followed; tributes were published in books; the composer Charles Villiers Stanford (1852–1924) wrote music for his funeral and dedicated his Symphony No.6 to the artist; and a touring Watts Memorial Exhibition travelled to the Royal Academy, London, and to Newcastle, Edinburgh, Manchester and Dublin between 1905 and 1906. The Compton collection of Watts's paintings, which was inherited by Mrs Chapman, was divided on her death in 1972 and works previously in the collection went into private hands.   MB

Portrait of the Painter, 1904 (cat.83)

73. *Sympathy*, 1892

Oil on canvas, 66 × 53 cm (26 × 20⅞ in)
Labels on reverse inscribed 'W.A. Smith'
COMWG95

PROVENANCE: collection of the artist (Little Holland House Gallery), Watts Gallery; part of the original Memorial Collection

EXHIBITIONS: Society of Portrait Painters, 1895, no.29; Watts New Gallery 1896, no.146; South London Gallery 1899; Memorial Exhibitions, Manchester 1905, no.29, Newcastle 1905, no 94, Edinburgh 1905, no 41; Watts Gallery 1904, no.47

LITERATURE: Watts Catalogue, I, p.141; Gould 2004, p.299

Cat. 73.1 *Florence Nightingale (1820–1910)*, unfinished, 1868, oil on canvas, 66 × 53.3 cm (26 × 21 in), COMWG152

Watts's intriguing portrayal of a nurse bears a title more typical of one of his subject paintings. In 1895 he exhibited it at the Society of Portrait Painters as *'Sympathy': A Portrait*. The entry from the New Gallery catalogue describes the painting as a 'Half-length figure, facing, of a lady in the costume of a nurse', without identifying the sitter.[1] The manuscript catalogue refers to the picture as 'This portrait of a nurse, Katharine Webster', about which 'Mr Watts remarked with astonishment on the difficulty of portraying the face in full view'.[2] Despite this identification, Mary placed this work in the volume on 'Subject Pictures'. By not naming the sitter in the title of the present picture, the artist invited readings going beyond the specific. Watts also played with the boundaries between genres elsewhere, often through his choice of titles.

Hinting at a double reading, the entry in the catalogue for the Memorial Exhibition in Edinburgh noted: 'Because sympathy is born of sorrow, Watts has given a subject-title to what otherwise we should have looked at only as a portrait.' The writer implies that the nurse is being used to symbolise the concept of sympathy rather than being a straightforward portrait of an individual. Subject pictures for Watts often meant the visual manifestation of an abstract idea, most famously epitomised in his evocation of *Hope* (cat.59). By entitling the picture *Sympathy*, Watts provides a signpost for interpreting it as an evocation of the emotion. According to Blunt, 'Miss Webster was nurse-companion to Mrs Watts',[3] and the painting could therefore also be read as the artist's private tribute to the work ethos of an individual nurse as well as the profession of nursing as a vocation. Its title may, in contrast, be ironic, depicting the emotionally detached face of professionalism, reinforced by the sternness of the symmetry. The nurse in a frontal pose gazes directly at the viewer with an uncomfortable aura of severity offering an instant engagement with the picture.

As an artist, Watts had a belief in the importance of celebrating the deeds of great individuals, manifested in a series of portraits of eminent Victorians known as the 'Hall of Fame'. In a letter to *The Times* of 1887 Watts formally put forward the idea to give equal prominence to the extraordinary deeds of ordinary people, 'forgotten heroes', through a public monument that came to fruition in the form of the Postman's Park memorial. It seems that *Sympathy* is a manifestation of the same ambition in painting. Watts was a great supporter of women's causes, and the only two portraits of female figures most likely intended for the Hall of Fame were in fact that of Florence Nightingale (cat.73.1), the nursing movement reformer, and one of Josephine Butler (1894; NPG), campaigner for women's rights and moral reform. Just as Watts's moving portraits of these two famous women convey qualities of sadness, purposefulness and a deep social conscience, Watts's representation of the archetypal nurse in *Sympathy* seems to deliberately suggest a conflict between bitterness and severity combined with sadness, determination and commitment to a challenging vocation.

The use of a frontal pose for this picture is uncharacteristic of most of Watts's portraiture and something that he found difficult. As Mary noted, the artist employed a complex technique for the picture:

A monochrome of raw sienna and white over which warm ochre was rubbed and removed almost entirely … Afterwards the surface scraped … and lastly dry flesh tones were applied, again removed in parts leaving a thin film of colour. The drawing in each of these stages was carefully preserved.

This approach resulted in a uniform, yet rich background of a single colour, from which the figure emerges with great effect and with no distraction in the form of background detail. A review in 1895 commented on both the emotion conveyed and the beauty of the painting calling it 'very tender and pathetically expressive … quite a masterpiece of harmony and colour'.[4] JD

1   Watts New Gallery 1896, p.63.
2   Watts Catalogue, I, p.141.
3   Pencil notation by Blunt in Watts Catalogue, I, p.141.
4   *Athenaeum*, 19 October 1895, p.540.

74. *John Stuart Mill*, completed by 1894

Oil on canvas, 66 × 53.3 cm (26 × 21 in)
Inscribed lower left 'G F Watts'
COMWG86

PROVENANCE: collection of the artist (Little Holland House Gallery); Mary Watts; Lilian Mackintosh (Mrs Michael Chapman), legal descendant of the artist; given by her to the Watts Gallery in 1946

EXHIBITIONS: Blackburn, 1894, no.293; Internationale Kunstaustellung, Dresden, 1901, no.741; Watts Leighton House, 1903, p.10, no.18; Watts Gallery 1904, no.68; Memorial Exhibitions, London 1905, no.34, Manchester 1905, no.89, Newcastle 1905, no.128, Edinburgh 1905, no.49, Dublin 1906, no.41

LITERATURE: Cartwright 1896, pp. 22, 26; Macmillan 1903, p.75; Watts Gallery Catalogue 1904, no.68; Watts Catalogue, II, p.108; Watts 1912, I, pp.273–6; Alston 1929, no.64; Richard Ormond, *Early Victorian Portraits*, London, 1973, I, pp. 316–17; Richard Ormond, *G.F. Watts: The Hall of Fame*, National Portrait Gallery, London, 1975, pp. 11, 18

Cat. 74.1 *John Stuart Mill*, photograph, 7.6 × 5 cm (3 × 2 in), Watts Gallery Archive, The Rob Dickins Collection

In 1873 Watts painted the great philosopher and liberal thinker, John Stuart Mill (1806–73),[1] as a commission from the politician Sir Charles Wentworth Dilke (1843–1911).[2] That portrait is now in the collections of the City of Westminster in London, while the replica painted immediately after is at the National Portrait Gallery as part of Watts's gift. Cat.74 is the third portrait of Mill by Watts and technically a replica of a replica. It seems likely that he completed it around 1894[3] for his own collections to replace the painting he gave to the National Portrait Gallery in that year.

Mill's considerable reputation as a political economist and humanitarian was based on publications such as *Principles of Political Economy* (1848) and 'On Liberty' (1859), as well as his support for women's suffrage. At a late stage in his life he had taken under his wing Charles Dilke, a wealthy young Member of Parliament and author who desired a record of his mentor by Watts.[4] Mill was agreeable, writing in March 1873: 'I have hitherto disliked having my portrait taken; but I am unwilling to refuse the high compliment paid me by Mr. Watts and yourself.'[5] The portrait proceeded at Little Holland House before Mill's departure for his home in Avignon in the south of France where he died in early May.

In Watts's portrait Mill, looking downwards, is seen as great thinker with light illuminating his noble brow. The warm flesh tones of the highly worked area of the face create a powerfully textured surface and are evocative of the power of Mill's mind. Macmillan wrote appreciatively in 1903 that 'on the high placid brow of John Stuart Mill … thought sits as on a throne, and glorifies his thin, precise, ascetic features'.[6] Later commentators have also written eloquently on the power of this portrait: as Richard Ormond observes, 'it surveys the geography of old age with searching intensity'.

The original commission came at a time when Watts had already amassed many portraits for his personal collection through his own efforts. Although the artist did not instigate the commission, Mill was very much the kind of person whom he sought for his gallery of 'worthies'; indeed, he considered Mill 'one of our most profound thinkers'.[7] During the sitting the two men discovered a shared concern for social

reform. The introduction provided a way to expand his collection of eminent individuals, so he painted the second version for himself, considering it in some ways better than the original. Dilke, however, preferred the original, as it was from life and Mill had been famously averse to posing for portraits. Watts was happy with the second one, which had wide exposure, even travelling to the exhibition of his works in New York in 1884.

The third version of Mill's portrait differs from the first two; not surprisingly, it is more characteristic of Watts's later style, dating mainly from the early 1890s. As one might expect, the treatment of the face is more generalised, the deep contours are now rendered more softly and an overall grey tonality eradicates any lifelike warmth in the skin. Although some commentators both then[8] and more recently have taken this version to be a falling off, it is, however, rendered in a more Symbolist mode. With no living presence in front of him and the sitter by then a distant recollection, the artist produced a more remote and withdrawn image. Using his own twenty-year-old portrait, Watts recreated an echo of the great man for an audience of the 1890s. BB

1   Jose Harris, 'Mill, John Stuart (1806–1873)', *Oxford Dictionary of National Biography* (http://www.oxforddnb.com/view/article/18711, accessed 2 March 2008).
2   Roy Jenkins, 'Dilke, Sir Charles Wentworth, second baronet (1843–1911)', *Oxford Dictionary of National Biography* (http://www.oxforddnb.com/view/article/32824, accessed 2 March 2008).
3   The photograph reproduced in Cartwright 1896, p. 26, presumably taken within the previous few years, seems to show this work in progress without a finished background.
4   In the same year Dilke commissioned a portrait of himself (National Portrait Gallery) and his young wife, who died in 1874.
5   Quoted in Watts 1912, I, p.273.
6   Macmillan 1903, p.75.
7   Macmillan 1903, pp.275–6.
8   Mary Watts became embroiled in a long-running controversy about the status of this replica by inaccurately describing it as dating from 1874 in the Memorial Exhibitions of 1905–6. Dilke hounded her about the matter (see 'Book of MS Letter Relating to the Dilke Portrait', City of Westminster Archive), and, stung by his criticisms, she wrote in 1912 (p.274), 'Signor made yet another. It was not to be expected that the level could be sustained, and this replica – certainly in Sir Charles Dilke's opinion – lacked some of the inspiration in the other two paintings.'

75. *For He Had Great Possessions*, 1894

Oil on canvas, 94 × 46 cm (37 × 18 in)
Signed and dated lower left in red paint 'G F Watts 1894'
COMWG36

PROVENANCE: Charles S. Goldmann Esq.; Sir Thomas Devitt (?); sold at Christie's, 16 May 1924, for 165 guineas (?); purchased by Watts Gallery from Abbott & Holder for £100 in 1959

EXHIBITIONS: Ancoats Brotherhood near Cross, Manchester 1894; Grosvenor Museum, Chester 1895; Hampstead 1897; Memorial Exhibitions, London 1905, no.62, Newcastle 1905; Watts Aldeburgh 1961, no.221; Watts Compton 2004, no.70a; *The Seventh Splendour*, Verona 2007, no.72

LITERATURE: Cartwright 1896, p.14; Macmillan 1903, pp.165, 263; Watts Catalogue, I, p.57; Watts 1912, II, p.182; Chesterton, 1904, pp.57, 139; Shrewsbury 1918, ch.X, pp.100–6 (Tate version); Blunt, 1975, pp.147, 211; Gould 2004, pp.277, 286, 289, 291 (pl.xxxiv)

A single figure in profile, turbaned and dressed in a rich costume, faces right, his head downcast. Who he is is made clear in the title of the work rather than the elaborate costume, which does not reveal any specific place or time. The source is from the New Testament, the story of the rich young man who appears in all three of the synoptic gospels: Matthew (19: 16–30) Mark (10: 17–30) and Luke (18: 18–30). In Matthew and Mark they both use the identical phrase, 'ην γαρ εχων κτηματα πολλα', translated in the King James Bible as 'For he had great possessions', the title of this painting. The story tells of a rich young man who asks Christ what he must do to gain eternal life. Jesus answers that he must give his wealth to the poor and follow him, something the young man is unable to do. He 'went away grieving, for he had great possessions', and Christ tells his disciples that 'it is easier for a camel to go through the eye of a needle, than for a rich man to enter into the kingdom of God' (Mark 10: 25).

Watts's choice and depiction of the story is characteristically his own. His use of the New Testament, for the most part, focused on the parables and lessons of Christ, such as the Prodigal Son (cat.43) and the Good Samaritan (fig.41), rather than depicting scenes from his life. Watts saw their contemporary relevance, particularly for a society that he felt was riddled with Mammonism (see cat.62). Through this painting he makes clear his belief that spiritual health is the direct opposite of materialism. The stifling effects of such materialism are portrayed as a source of great social injustice as well as of the containment and destruction of the spiritual. It is not simply a social matter but also a religious one, and rarely does he make this point so lyrically and succinctly.

The single figure is alone and isolated. He is smothered by the rich clothes that he wears, to the point where his face is only just visible. A reviewer wrote: 'It is one of the finest of Mr. Watts's imaginative works and one of those that best tells its story. No one but a master could have suggested despondency by the bowed head of the man or "great possessions" by the blazing emeralds on his finger.'[1] Watts conveys the wealth and burden of riches through the weight of the clothes that hang heavily upon him. The rich man's indecision about his choice is suggested,

according to Mary, by his 'irresolute right hand, half closed, and with the jewel on it'.[2] The decision is almost made, he is unable to give up his wealth and his sadness comes from a suspicion that it is the wrong decision. Shrewsbury poetically described it as 'longing to lead some path more holy'.[3]

'It was very usual', Mary wrote of this picture, 'when developing a subject picture for Mr. Watts to dash down three or four lines on a bit of paper, even on his blotting book, in the midst of other occupations. He used no model.'[4] It appears, from this and the numerous sketches of subject pictures that survive, that the central idea and image of the work were often conceived by Watts before they reached the paper. Variations occur, but the central image remains, illustrating Watts's great ability to envisage a complex idea in a visual image. The success of this painting is due to the fact that the striking image invites the viewer to find parallels and comparable personalities in their own life, something that Watts intended. Thus Shrewsbury writes: 'In my own mind this picture is always associated with the wealthiest man I have known intimately … [a] millionaire [who] passed sorrowfully through an embittered old age.'[5] And on the death of Lord Astor a friend wrote, 'there came a tragic cast upon him, which often reminded me of Watts's picture, "For he had great possessions"',[6] showing that the image had brilliantly expressed its subject and struck a deep chord with those who saw it.

There are three versions of this painting listed in the manuscript catalogue: an oil sketch (1893; unlocated), cat.75, and the largest and most finished version in the Tate Gallery. Compared to the Tate painting, the present work is 'a smaller, slightly earlier version, with different background, formerly belonging to Charles S. Goldmann. At one time it was better known … and was frequently reproduced.'[7] MB

1 *The Times*, 5 May 1894, p.16. This is a review of the version now in the Tate Gallery.
2 Watts 1912, II, p.182.
3 Shrewsbury 1918, p.101.
4 Watts Catalogue, I, p.57.
5 Shrewsbury 1918, p.103.
6 *The Times*, 20 October 1919, p.16.
7 Watts London 1954, p.44.

76. *Can these Bones Live?*, 1897–8

Oil on canvas, 152 × 191 cm (60 × 75 in)
Inscribed indistinctly in Anglo-Saxon top left, previously translated as: 'Alfred me planted'; label (now removed): 'Can these Bones Live No.23 G'
COMWG15

PROVENANCE: collection of the artist (Limnerslease); Watts Gallery

EXHIBITIONS: New Gallery 1898, no.167; Camberwell, South London Gallery, 1900 (as 'Dry bones'); Watts Gallery 1904, no.4; Memorial Exhibitions, Edinburgh 1905, no.81, Manchester 1905, no.127, Newcastle 1905, no.51, Dublin 1906, no.76; Watts Compton 2004, no.106

LITERATURE: Watts Catalogue, I, p.22; Macmillan 1903, pp.197–8, 257; Alston 1929, no.2; Gould 2004, pp.315, 319, 321

The title of this painting *Can these Bones Live?*, simplified for the South London Art Gallery audience as 'Dry Bones', is taken from Ezekiel when God speaks to the prophet in the barren valley before reviving the skeletons that lay there: 'And he said unto me, Son of man, can these bones live? And I answered, O Lord GOD, thou knowest.'[1] It refers to the central question of the work, which Watts restated to a visitor to his Limnerslease studio in 1898, 'Is it to be a conflagration or the light of day?', for the bones in the painting refer to the state of the nation.[2] 'The whole thing stands for my opinion of the civilization of the present time when viewed from an artistic standpoint', Watts told Charles Mulford Robinson. 'Yes. Oh! Yes, it is certainly pessimistic. But I have to be, for I can't see how the tendency of our age, how its Mammonism, is to be overcome.'[3] The bones of men can be clearly seen, but the central symbol, according to Watts, is the oak tree, which represents England crushed by the weight of a golden pall, symbolic of how materialism and greed were destroying a great nation.[4] The architect of the Watts Gallery, Christopher Hatton Turnor, noticed that Watts 'persistently wore a black band on his arm. After a time I asked him who he was in mourning for? – no one – "I mourn the stupidity of my country for their inelasticity and lack of vision"!'[5]

On the oak of England Watts placed barely visible words. 'On a tree trunk', a reviewer wrote, 'is an inscription in which we cannot profess to read any word but "Ælfred".'[6] Catalogue entries prepared by G.F. and Mary clarify its meaning: 'On the stem of the tree the words are carved in Anglo-Saxon "Alfred me planted".'[7] For Watts, as for many Victorians, the Anglo-Saxon king Alfred was the father of the nation. 'Alfred', Watts wrote, 'must still be our leader; he laid the foundation of England's power.'[8] The king is the symbol of a healthier and more spiritual nation, whose foundations, symbolised by the tree, are being destroyed. Such symbolism suggests that the dry bones of the painting are those of an ancient British king whose spirit might live again, echoing both Ezekiel and Arthurian legend.

The central images of the tree and pall represent the major theme of the painting, the spiritual decline of the nation, while the richly

symbolic still life surrounding them give the signs and reasons for that decline. To the right of the painting 'implements of labour lie broken and disused', expressing the artist's concern at the erosion of the work ethic and its replacement with fruitless industry.[9] On the left of the painting is the 'golden pall, under which destruction, death and corruption are represented'.[10] These consist of birds' wings used for the millinery trade (see cat.77), an assassin's knife, 'a champagne glass faintly seen in the verdure' representing 'intoxication', and 'two horses hooves … filled with dice' representing gambling.[11] The Symbolist painter Fernand Knopff, reviewing the painting for *The Magazine of Art*, described the scene in the 'lurid shade' of the golden pall as 'a strange spark of colour among them here and there – sick gems, as one might fancy'.[12]

On the year of its first exhibition at the New Gallery in 1898, Watts asked a visitor to Limnerslease 'Did you read it?', for 'he [Watts] told us that often he did not want to make his meaning clear but that his intention was to suggest thoughts to the spectator to make him think and let him find his own solution'.[13] *The Times* found it a 'perplexing picture' and quoted the lines of Wordsworth's *Solitary Reaper*.[14] Ironically, it was the supposed didactic nature of the work that came to divide critical opinion about it. *Can these Bones Live?* raised the question of the relationship between the message of the picture and the art of the picture, or, as Knopff expressed it, 'does not this coercive effect on the mind divert it too much from the consideration of the work itself?'[15] 'From the point of view of the art of painting,' the *Building News* wrote, it 'is perfectly unjustifiable.'[16] Similarly, for more modern critics, such as Rowland Alston, Curator of the Watts Gallery from 1931 to 1958, this work was a sermon 'in which art is servant to religious or morally formulated ideas', unlike most of Watts's other works, whose symbols he saw as 'merely signposts'.[17] In 1952 *The Times* found the symbolism 'strikingly inapplicable' and too literal in its expression.[18]

In Watts's own lifetime, Macmillan noted, '[i]t has been objected that the symbolism of the picture is too forcible, and leaves no room for quietly picking out and dwelling upon the beauties and sublimities of the work'.[19] He explains

that this was the intention of the artist and its coercive strength is its success. Certainly, most critics were agreed that it was a provoking picture with extraordinary colouring. One reviewer wrote that 'the picture means death and transitoriness of human things', recalling the artist's *Sic Transit* (1891–2; Tate) exhibited at the New Gallery in 1892.[20] Fernand Knopff, after raising his question (above) concluded, 'Now these pictures of Mr. Watts's are very "well done"; is it not wise, then, to admire in silence? That, at any rate, is my opinion.'[21] MB

1   Ezekiel 37: 3.
2   Watts Papers, 'Notes on a visit to Mr. Watts at Limnerslease, Guildford', 27 September 1898, p.12.
3   Charles Mulford Robinson, 'A Talk with the Artist at his Home in London', London June 26, *New York Times*, 15 July 1899.
4   Drapery studies for the pall exist in the Watts Gallery collection, nos COMWG584a and 584b.
5   Christopher Hatton Turnor, Manuscript Journal, p.219, private collection.
6   *The Times*, 19 May 1898, p.8.
7   Watts Catalogue, I, p.22.
8   G.F. Watts in Watts 1912, III, p.305.
9   M.S. Watts in Watts Edinburgh 1905, no.81.
10 Watts Catalogue, I, p.22.
11 Charles Mulford Robinson, 'A Talk With the Artist at his Home in London', London June 26, published in the *New York Times*, 15 July 1899.
12 Fernand Knopff, review of 'The New Gallery', *The Magazine of Art*, April 1898, pp.430–1.
13 Watts Papers, 'Notes on a visit to Mr. Watts at Limnerslease, Guildford', 27 September 1898, p.12.
14 'Standing in front of this perplexing picture one feels inclined to adapt and apply to the painter the question of Wordsworth –
        Will no one tell us what he sings?
        Perhaps the plaintive numbers flow
        For old, unhappy, far-off things,
        And battles long ago!'
    The Times, 19 May, 1898, p.8.
15 Fernand Knopff, review of 'The New Gallery', *The Magazine of Art*, April 1898, p.431.
16 *Building News*, April 1898, p.412.
17 Alston 1929, no.2.
18 '"Watts's literature", Yeats said, "is bad literature", and there are still quite enough works left hanging to enable the visitor to verify this point. "Can these bones live?" is perhaps hung in the first gallery [Watts Gallery] as an extreme example; it shows the oak, emblem of England, collapsed under the weight of a pall of gold – it was not Watts's fault that the symbolism should now be so strikingly inapplicable, but it does show

how careful an allegorical painter should be – with below it some skeletons surrounded by indications, such as dice wine cups, for the wicked lives led by the rich.' *The Times*, 5 August 1952, p.8.
19 Macmillan 1903, p.257.
20 *The Times*, 19 May 1898, p.8.
21 Fernand Knopff, review of 'The New Gallery', *The Magazine of Art*, April 1898, p.431.

77. *A Dedication* ('To all those who love the beautiful and mourn over the senseless and cruel destruction of bird life and beauty'), 1898–9

Oil on canvas, 137 × 71 cm (54 × 28 in)
COMWG157

PROVENANCE: collection of the artist (Little Holland House Gallery), Watts Gallery

EXHIBITIONS: New Gallery 1899, no.103; Watts Gallery 1904, no.88; Memorial Exhibitions, Edinburgh 1905, no.26, Manchester 1905, no.61, Newcastle 1905, no.151; Watts Compton 2004, no.62

LITERATURE: Watts Catalogue, I, p.36; Blunt 1975, pp.9, 215; Gould 2004, pp.316, 330

The subject of Watts's painting *A Dedication* was an issue that had been rumbling throughout the latter half of the nineteenth century and came to a head in the 1890s. For decades the destruction of birdlife for fashion was having a devastating effect on wildlife and even threatening the extinction of species such as the great crested grebe in Britain and Ireland. Professor Newton openly denounced the bird-wearing fashion in a letter to the *Times* in 1876, but possibly the most influential was a long letter by the naturalist William Henry Hudson (1841–1922) in 1893. By this time the issues had been expressed in books such as Eliza Brightwen's *Wild Nature Won by Kindness* (1890), and the campaign had crystallised with various groups joining together in 1891 as a national organisation called the Society for the Protection of Birds (the Royal prefix being added in 1904). In his letter Hudson eloquently stated the case, noting early the support of the eminent:

> Many of those who have been trying to save the birds have doubtless ere now experienced the feeling which caused Ruskin to throw down his pen in anger and sickness of heart when engaged in writing 'Love's Meinie'. Small wonder that he could not proceed with such a work when he looked about him to see all women, even his worshippers, decorated with the remains of slaughtered songsters![1]

The figures that Hudson cited were perhaps the most shocking and caused a whole wave of responses that continued throughout the decade:

> It was estimated nine years ago that 20 to 30 millions of birds were annually imported by this country to supply the home demand … In some of the thoroughfares … I saw trays and baskets full of tropical birds exposed – tanagers, orioles, kingfishers, trogons, humming birds, &c. – from 2d. to 4½d. per bird. They were indeed cheap – so cheap that even a ragged girl from the neighbouring slums could decorate her battered hat, like any fine lady, with some bright-winged bird of the tropics.

It is against this background that *A Dedication* takes up the cause through the depiction of an

angel weeping over such wings that Hudson had observed wholesale in the thoroughfares of London. The angel in blue is faceless, her head buried in her hands at the sight of the feathers in front of her. A rich symmetry divides the canvas vertically, evoking an angelic design motif and echoing European Symbolist painting. In the background is the 'solemn aureole' of a setting sun,[2] the angel's wings mirrored on either side of the painting contrasting with those disembodied on what appears to be a pagan altar. The satyr-like figure on the front of the altar represents the vanity that is the root cause of the feathers laid in sacrifice. The majestic colouring, with the red sleeves complementing the golden hair of the angel and the burning glow of twilight, transforms a simple composition into a remarkable painting: a design into a work of art.

Watts's involvement in the campaign, and in many such causes, is well recorded, although the cause against cruelty to birds evoked a greater response in Watts. The death and destruction of birds had come to have a special meaning for him. Mary records that at an early age the artist had tamed a sparrow but had then inadvertently killed it, causing the boy great distress.[3] The death of a bird had a strong symbolic significance for Watts, and in paintings like *A Wounded Heron* (cat.3), but more particularly *The Minotaur* (cat.71), he depicts innocence destroyed, the innocent bird crushed by sinful passions. In *A Dedication* vanity takes entire species to the brink of extinction. According to Blunt, the model for the painting was Watts's adopted daughter, Lilian Chapman.[4]

A Dedication was first exhibited at the New Gallery in 1899, to favourable reviews of the painting but mixed ones of its subject. *The Times* was dismissive:

> We fear that the ladies who wear feathers in their hats do not take their act so seriously as Mr. Watts does, and that some of them will only smile when they find a great artist taking the trouble to paint a majestic angel– weeping over what? Over a shelf-ful of the wings of birds! It is a little startling to read so severe a sermon, and from such a quarter, over an offence which well-meaning commit in all unconsciousness.[5]

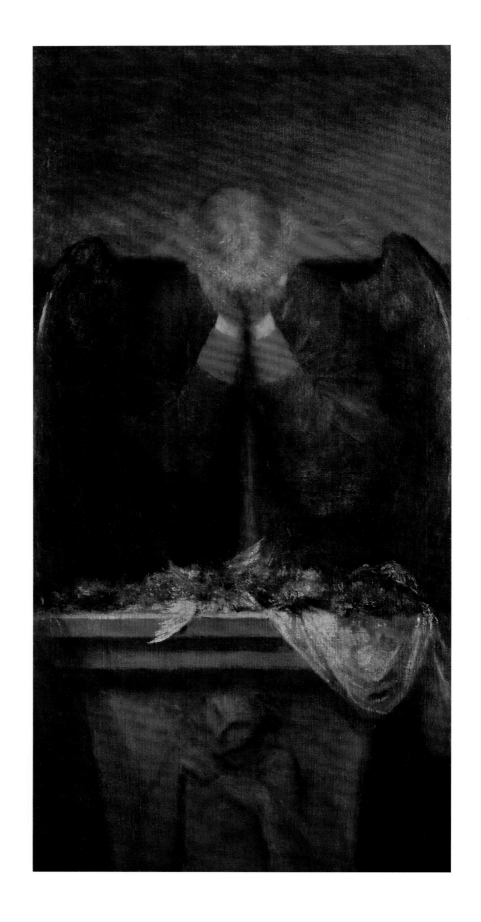

In contrast, the *Art Journal* reproduced the work and was wholly sympathetic to the artist's aims and his means of expressing it.

> With all the righteous indignation at his command, Mr. Watts has sought to translate into the language of paint his denunciation of those who are indirectly responsible for the wholesale slaughter of wild birds for the sake of their plumage. In any other hands the subject would smack of hyperbole.[6]

Despite its praise of the treatment of such a rigid message, it went on to note that it was the painting not the message that would take precedence, for even 'if the lesson be lost after all, here is still another example of Mr. Watts' genius'. The *Athenaeum*, perhaps proving this point, entirely missed its sermon, mistaking the bird feathers for flowers but admiring its 'passionate simplicity as well as nobility of style'.[7]

The painting made a powerful image, and on the year of its exhibition it was used as a symbol of protest on the frontispiece of the anti-imperialist poem *Satan Absolved* by W.S. Blunt (1899) and also in a leaflet produced by the Society for the Protection of Birds.[8] MB

1 W.H. Hudson, 'Feathered Women', letter to *The Times*, 17 October 1893, p.6.
2 *Art Journal*, 1899, p.186.
3 Watts 1912, I, p.13.
4 A pencil note from Wilfrid Blunt in Watts Catalogue, I, p.36, notes: 'Mrs Chapman told me that she posed for this picture.'
5 *The Times*, 22 April 1899, p.4.
6 *Art Journal*, 1899, pp.185–6.
7 *Athenaeum*, p.568.
8 See Gould 2004, pp.316, 330.

78. *The Slumber of the Ages*, 1898–1901

Oil on canvas, 107 × 94 cm (42⅛ × 37 in)
COMWG53

PROVENANCE: collection of the artist (Limnerslease), Watts Gallery; part of the original Memorial Collection

EXHIBITIONS: New Gallery 1901, no.123; Watts Nottingham 1901; Watts Manchester 1901; Liverpool 1901; Dublin 1902; Watts Gallery 1904, no.14; Memorial Exhibitions, Manchester 1905, no.66, Newcastle 1905, no.116, Edinburgh 1905, no.110, Dublin 1906, no.64; Watts London 1954, no.83; Watts Compton 2004, no.104

LITERATURE: Chesterton 1904, p.18; Erskine 1906, p.192; Alston 1929, pl.X; Gould 2004, pp.327, 340

Mary states that:

> for this picture Mr Watts made some use of his early design, painted fifty years before on the walls of Old Little Holland House and then called 'Humanity in the Lap of Earth'. On a canvas upon which the design had been made in watercolour, by Mrs. Charles Wylie, he developed this later conception.[1]

The mother and child composition, *Humanity in the Lap of Earth* (cat.78.1), had originally formed part of a decorative scheme painted in a small dining room at old Little Holland House in the 1850s. In 1878 the painting was given to Mrs Barrington,[2] who considered it 'the most beautiful of these wall paintings' and had it framed separately.[3] *Humanity in the Lap of Earth* was also 'one of the pieces of work which Watts himself admired',[4] particularly the figure of the child which represents Humanity. *The Slumber of the Ages* developed five decades later and uses an almost identical image of the child, while dramatically replacing its attentive mother with a disconcertingly disengaged figure, possibly asleep as suggested by the title, but with her pale complexion and a lifeless posture suggestive of a corpse. Although Watts regularly reworked and refined many designs over the years, his dramatic transformation of an early Holland House wall painting into a morbid allegorical vision prompted his wife to consider *The Slumber of the Ages* as a prime example of 'the growth of the artist's own power of imaginative vision'.[5]

Watts commented on this work:

> All such pictures are symbolic. They do not represent fact, but are forms used to suggest ideas, as notes in music or as gestures of an actor. In this picture the great stretches of time, since the earth ceased to be a formless mass, are represented as a mighty mother, with man, the child upon her lap, growing to conscious knowledge of himself and his place in the scheme of creation.[6]

The female figure symbolises Time as well as suggesting Earth, while the child, almost identical to his first version of this composition, remains as Humanity. Each of these symbolic figures was expressed in a number of different

paintings, notably Earth as a nude in a floral wreath carrying fruits of the earth in *Earth* (1894–5; Watts Gallery) and as a nude mother figure surrounded by infants in *Evolution* (1898–1904; Watts Gallery). The motif of a young child or baby is a particularly idiosyncratic symbol of great prominence in Watts's work, as Mary later noted:

> In Mr Watts's art the little child is used as an expression of his thought in a manner which is entirely his own. His range includes the symbolic infant in the lap of death-Humanity in the 'Slumber of the Ages', the 'Whence-Whither' and many others suggesting serious reflection, whilst in the lighter moods he has given us many such as 'A tormentor', 'A villain I'll be bound' and others too numerous to mention here.[7]

The Slumber of the Ages was painted as part of a series, the planned 'House of Life' scheme that included *Chaos* (cat.45), *Evolution, Whence? Whither?* (1903–4; private collection) and *Destiny* (1904; Watts Gallery), and mostly featured the motif of the little child symbolising humanity: 'the story of mankind as it comes to us through biblical, mythical, poetical, and verifiable history, viewing it from the standpoint of the present time'.[8] However, on its first exhibition in 1901 the *Morning Post* critic considered it primarily in aesthetic terms, though hinting at a more profound meaning:

> For the vagueness of import of 'The Slumber of the Ages' its executive quality atones. Dignified in manner, the picture is invested likewise with individuality as regards chromatic treatment. A woman in grey leans backward, her lips parted as she sleeps. Beyond her, far away, a great red sun is roughly mirrored on a dull blue sea. On her knees sits an infant, motionless, but with alert, wide-opened eye.[9] JD

1   Watts Catalogue, I, p.133.
2   On vacating old Little Holland House in 1878, all the frescoes and wall paintings were removed from the walls. See Barrington 1905, p.99.
3   Barrington 1905, p.101.
4   Ibid.
5   Watts Catalogue, I, p.133..
6   This description appeared in the original Watts Gallery Catalogue of 1904 (pp.5–6) and was subsequently reproduced in the catalogues for the Newcastle Memorial Exhibition of 1905 (p.37) and the Edinburgh Memorial Exhibition of 1905 (p.50), where the entry was preceded by the note 'The following is Mr. Watts's own description'.
7   Watts Catalogue, I, p.133.
8   Edinburgh Watts Memorial Catalogue (1905), p.48 (entry on *Evolution*).
9   *Morning Post* (clippings volume, Watts Gallery Archive), 22 April 1901.

Cat. 78.1 *Humanity in the Lap of Earth*, *c.* 1850s, fresco from Little Holland House, Leighton House Museum, Royal Borough of Kensington and Chelsea

79. *Progress*, c.1902–4

Oil on canvas, 282 × 143 cm (111 × 56¼ in)
COMWG139

PROVENANCE: collection of the artist (Little
Holland House Gallery); Watts Gallery

EXHIBITIONS: Watts Gallery 1904, no.108;
Memorial Exhibitions, London 1905, no.169,
Edinburgh 1905, nos 137, 46 (Misses Colman, York
version), Manchester 1905, nos 118, 92 (Misses
Colman, York version), Newcastle 1905, nos 176, 57
(Misses Colman, York version); Watts Whitechapel
1974, no.43; Watts Compton 2004, no.108

LITERATURE: Macmillan 1903, p.199–200;
Barrington 1905, pp.34, 100–1, 204; Watts
Catalogue, I, p.120; Watts 1912, II, pp.303, 313;
Shrewsbury 1918, ch.VII 'The Triumph of Right',
pp.79–86; Alston 1929, no.22; Gould 2004, pp.24,
229, 236, 345, 352

Watts was fascinated with ideas of creation, evolution and progress. 'The two greatest ideas man
has hitherto had', he wrote, 'are gravitation and
evolution. These best and most truly explain
creation. By these all natural phenomena are
explained … All is progression, revolution,
evolution, and gravitation towards renewal.'[1] In
this painting Watts seeks to embody the idea of
'progress and non-progress' through five
figures.[2] The catalogue entry for its exhibition at
the 1905 Watts exhibition explained the figures:

> The rider on the white horse 'conquering
> and to conquer' has been used as the symbol
> of Progress. From the light there turns away
> – one to search for wisdom by the aid of a
> burnt out candle, another to grub in the
> muck for gold, a third to sleep; while a fourth
> is looking at the light.[3]

The central figure – a bowman on a charging
white horse enveloped in a mighty sunburst –
represents the idea of progress. 'The rider on
the white horse', Watts wrote, 'must represent
the progress of spiritual and intellectual ideals',[4]
and Alston reaffirmed this view, describing the
figure as 'enveloped in a golden glory along his
path to the realization of the Divine ideal'.[5] The
dynamism of the horse and rider, a man har-
nessing power, relates to the artist's conception
of *Physical Energy* (cat.86) and *The Rider on the*

White Horse (*c.*1868–82; Walker Art Gallery). The
choice of the bowman as a symbol for progress
is explained by Watts's admiration for what he
believed was the training given to ancient
Persian youths:

> The Persians taught their youth to ride,
> shoot, and speak the truth. This epitomises
> the whole question; to ride means to have a
> firm seat, supple joints and muscles, to give
> to movement and progress light hands on the
> reins, with iron wrist to curb when necessary.
> Does this not comprise all government? To
> shoot with a bow means, observation, judge-
> ment precision, strength; here are symbolised
> all the active requirements of life.[6]

The figures on the ground represent aspects
of humanity and what Barrington describes as
'non-progress', characterised by the scholar, the
rich man and the 'sluggard'. The scholar
searches for knowledge in an old volume, leaning forward because of the small light emitted
from his tiny candle and oblivious to the great
light that explodes all around him. The rich man
is similarly oblivious to the sunburst and Watts
'mentioned particularly the figure in garlands of
smearched gold, grovelling in the dust "money
grubbing" as he called it that day'.[7] Here, as in
many other works, Watts presents material
values as the direct opposite of spiritual ones,
literally so, with the figures turned down and
away from the spiritual revelation behind him.
The lazy figure is also unconscious of any idea
of progress, lost in his own drowsiness. In
another sense the three figures constitute more
traditional representations of the deadly sins –
vanity, lust, sloth and greed – which are viewed
here as a hindrance to physical and spiritual
progress. The fourth figure in the foreground is
an ordinary man energised by the vision of
progress, which Barrington noted 'suggests
power arising more, I think, from the psychic
than in the physical condition of the worker'.[8]

The golden glow that bathes the painting
illustrates Watts's admiration of late Titian and
his emulation of the master's techniques. The
idea was first conceived on a smaller scale, and
'a note made at Harrogate, July 1888, describes
Mr. Watts's first mention of his thoughts then in
his mind for this picture … This small version

Cat. 79.1 Study for
Progress, pen and ink on
paper, 13.5 × 18.5 cm (5¼
× 7¼ in), COMWG2007.605a

was soon afterwards in progress, but not considered complete till 1904.'[9] This first version, the only other one of this painting, was exhibited in 1890 at the Royal Society of British Artists and at the New Gallery in 1904; it was sold to Misses Colman and is now in York City Art Gallery. Its significance was seized on by commentators in 1904, the *Daily News* seeing progress as 'moving over the world to awaken Primitive Man to Agriculture, to Industry in other kinds, and supremely to Wisdom'.[10]

Watts, having 'much excited interest in the subject',[11] wanted to make a much larger version, so a

large picture was begun in 1902 and replaced 'The Court of Death,' in the studio at Limnerslease, where it had the advantage of being lowered to the basement room when required. It never left the studio until after the painter's death – He did not consider that it was completed. One evening in May 1904, a visitor, expecting that this late hour was given to rest, found him instead standing at the top of his platform steps and at work upon the upper part of this picture.[12]

This version was exhibited with the smaller version in the 1905 exhibitions at Edinburgh, Newcastle and Manchester. MB

1   G.F. Watts in Watts 1912, III, p.296.
2   Barrington 1905, p.101.
3   The 'conquering and to conquer' is a reference to the book of Revelation (6: 2): 'And I saw, and behold a white horse: and he that sat on him had a bow; and a crown was given unto him: and he went forth conquering and to conquer.'
4   Watts Catalogue, I, p.121.
5   Alston 1929, no.22.
6   G.F. Watts in Watts 1912, III, pp.321–2.
7   Watts Catalogue, I, p.121.
8   Barrington 1905, p.204.
9   Watts Catalogue, I, p.121.
10 *Daily News*, 'Watts and Sargent Pictures,' 1904, clipping in Watts Gallery Archive.
11 Barrington 1905, p.204.
12 Watts Catalogue, I, p.120.

80. *End of the Day*, 1902–3

Oil on canvas, 76 × 63 cm (30 × 25 in)
COMWG68A

PROVENANCE: collection of the artist (Limnerslease); Watts Gallery

EXHIBITIONS: New Gallery 1903, no.92; Watts Gallery 1904, no.17; Memorial Exhibitions, Edinburgh 1905, no.131, Manchester 1905, no.146; Watts London and Compton 2006, no.31

LITERATURE: Watts Catalogue, I, p.41; Gould 2004, p.348

Towards the end of his life, while resident at his country home in Compton, the surrounding countryside provided a rich source of inspiration for Watts's painting. This late landscape is characteristically Surrey and confirms Mary's comments that it was 'painted at Limnerslease from impressions gained from surroundings'.[1] Rather than a directly observed view, Watts paints an imagined landscape based on his impressions, which gives him the opportunity to explore more freely the abstract qualities of the painting. Its rich colour and varied textures and surfaces make it a particularly atmospheric vision. The reduction of areas to blocks of colour and defined surfaces echoes the works of the Post-Impressionists that were shortly to make an impact in Britain. Yet the picture owes less to Gauguin than it does to the paintings of the Italian masters: *The Times* reviewer wrote on its first exhibition: '"The End of the Day" (92) is a noble vision such as Titian might have seen.'[2]

Watts sent three of his landscapes to the New Gallery in 1903, *Green Summer* (no.139), *The Two Paths* (no.88) and *End of the Day*. *The Times* reviewer noted of the exhibition:

The landscapes are not very strong, if we are to except the three remarkable contributions of Mr. Watts in this department; and they are rather ideal visions than landscapes in the literal sense in which painters and their public commonly understand the term … One's first thought is not to refer it to some choice vue in nature, but to cast about for some phrase of the great poets that corresponds with it.[3]

The intensity of colour serves to heighten the expression of the evening glow that floods the painting and reflects its title, as well as referring to that point in the artist's own life, which was at its twilight. Warm colours predominate, wholly unlike the Surrey landscape in winter and spring when it was painted, which again highlights its abstract and expressive qualities. Watts wanted to 'suggest warmth and the blood circulating',[4] and its warm glow and subjective vision recall the colours of his late self-portrait (cat.51) with its reflective impression of himself at the end of his life. 'Art', wrote Watts, 'is not a presentation of Nature, it is a representation of sensation.'[5] MB

1 Watts Catalogue, I, p.41. Mary writes 'A companion to "Surrey Woodland"', and a note in pencil by Wilfrid Blunt reads 'Also called Surrey landscape'.
2 *The Times*, 25 April 1903, p.14.
3 Ibid.
4 G.F. Watts, quoted in Gould 2004, p.348.
5 Watts 1912, II, p.44

81. *Endymion, c.*1903–4

Oil on canvas, 104.1 × 121.9 cm (41 × 48 in)
COMWG150

PROVENANCE: collection of the artist (Little Holland House Gallery); Mary Watts, exchanged for another painting from the original Memorial Collection in 1908

EXHIBITIONS: New Gallery, 1904, no.132; Memorial Exhibitions, London 1905, no.174, Manchester, 1905, no.97, Newcastle, 1905, no.150, Edinburgh 1905, no.60, probably Dublin 1906, no.49; Watts Whitechapel 1974, no.49; *Symbolism in Europe*, Museum Boymans-van Beuningen, Rotterdam (and touring to Brussels, Baden-Baden, Paris), 1975–6, no.254; *Androgyna*, Berlin, 1986–7; *Victorian Dreamers: Masterpieces of the Neo-Classial and Aesthetic Movements*, organised by the British Council, Isetan Museum of Art (Tokyo Shimbun), Tokyo (and other venues), 1989, no.6; *Simbolismo en Europe: Nestor en Las Hesperides*, Canary Islands, 1990, p.183; *Heaven on Earth: The Religion of Beauty in Late Victorian Art*, Djanogly Art Gallery, University of Nottingham Arts Centre, Nottingham, 1994, no.72; *Dei ed Eroi: Classicità e mito fra '800 e '900*, Palazzo delle Esposizioni, Rome, 1996, no.49

LITERATURE (on the subject): Spielmann 1886, p.30; Cartwright 1896, pp.14, 17; Macmillan 1903, pp.107–9; Sketchley 1904, pp.103, 109; Watts Gallery Catalogue 1904, no.41, as unfinished; Chesterton 1904, pp.126, 135–6; Watts Catalogue, I, p.42; Watts 1912, II, p.313; Alston 1929, no.16; Watts London 1954, p.37, Stewart 1993, p.302; Trodd and Brown 2004, p.22

As a subject, the classical myth of Diana and Endymion attracted Watts on several occasions over a forty-year period from the late 1860s onwards, much as he also revisited scenes from Greek mythology featuring Orpheus and Eurydice (see cat.46) and Ariadne. All were tales of love in one form or another, often thwarted or doomed. In the case of Diana and Endymion, the well-known legend of the moon goddess who visits her beloved as he slept, the myth had sources in classical literature (Theocritus, for example). But Watts seemed fairly unconcerned with the specifics of the story or, indeed, an exact source. When the first version was exhibited in New York in 1884, the description in the catalogue related: 'The shepherd Endymion lies asleep, while Selene, the crescent moon, according to the old story, descends and bends over him, enamoured of his beauty.' Apart from 'the old story', the subject had antecedents in antique art and had always engaged artists from the Renaissance to the later Romantics in painting and sculpture, with images such as Canova's *Sleeping Endymion* (1819–21; Chatsworth), as well as poets.[1]

Watts began the work, then entitled *Diana and Endymion* (cat.81.1),[2] around 1868,[3] completing it over the next few years. By 1872 the prominent collector and MP William Graham owned it. Unlike the later painting in the Watts Gallery, this one is cabinet-sized, yet, paradoxically, the treatment is monumental with the entire focus on the figures that fill the space. Intending to paint it on larger scale, Watts apparently outlined the design on a canvas almost twice the size, but did not carry on with it at that time, returning to it much later, in 1903.[4] Spielmann catalogued it as a study in 1886 and this is the work that became no.81.

In the first version the inspiration of sculpture is prominent; indeed, the work is conceived like a bas-relief. Endymion is clearly modelled on the antique *Theseus* (now considered to be Dionysus) from the Elgin marbles. To Watts these were the touchstones of artistic excellence at the outset of his career and in fact he possessed a reduced-scale cast of this figure (see fig.67).[5] Colour played a lesser role in this painting, essentially involving a palette in a minor key of whites, greys and browns. The defined forms of the goddess Diana, and the powerful arc of

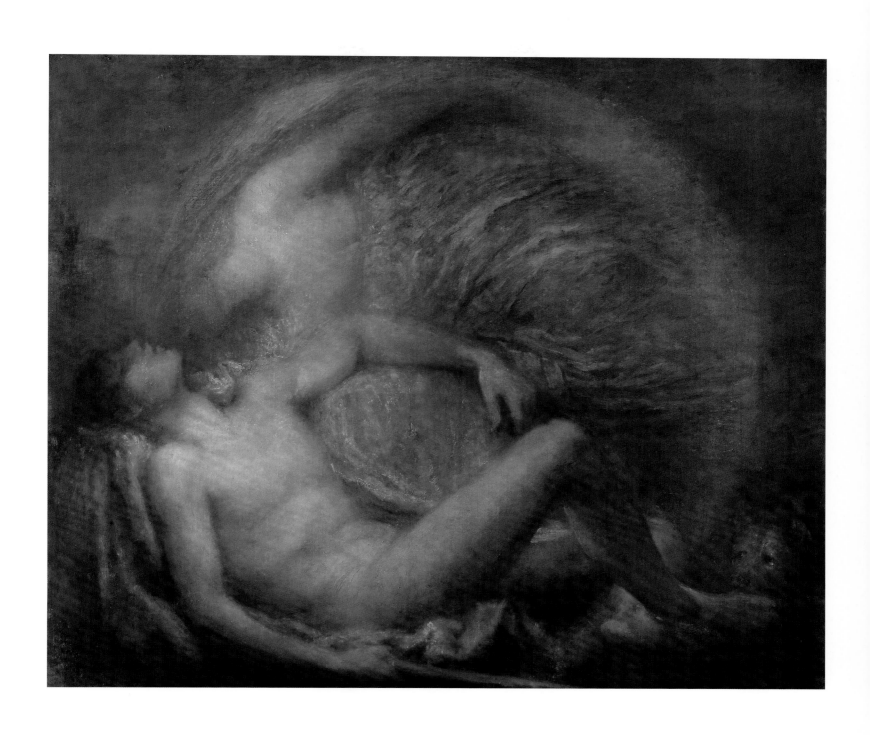

her body as she flies down to kiss Endymion, characterise this memorable image.[6] Chesterton, who considered it 'probably the artist's masterpiece', wrote vividly of 'the splendid rushing whirlpool of curves … It is a rushing and passionate meeting of two superb human figures'.[7]

Much praised and seen widely at exhibitions, this work went to auction in 1886 and attracted a considerable price at the Graham sale. Frank Short, one of Watts's trusted engravers, issued a mezzotint, which was exhibited at the Royal Academy in 1891. With his interest in the subject seemingly revived, in the early 1890s Watts completed a different composition altogether in a tall, upright format and featuring a landscape setting,[8] exhibiting it at the Royal Academy in 1893.[9]

In 1903, according to Mary Watts, early one morning she found 'Signor had taken up the canvas which in the late sixties he had laid in an outline of his *Endymion* … he decided to make this larger picture more visionary and mystic, the moon goddess only luminously visible.'[10] It was 'little more than an outline' but he rapidly completed it. Revisiting the work of his own past was common practice for Watts. Yet might there also have been another impetus? At the Royal Academy in 1902 Edward Poynter (1836–1919) exhibited *The Vision of Endymion*,[11] a composition showing Diana within a circle of light as she descends to a grassy knoll in woodland where her lover sleeps. Seeing the work of Poynter, a fellow Academician, Watts may then have recalled his own incomplete Endymion, now ripe for a stylistic interpretation that had real implications for its meaning.

Essentially, the new version is revised in terms of light and colour, with the figure of Diana dissolved into the form and tints of a rainbow seen against a midnight blue sky.

The more upright composition turns the overall design into a square shape, which allows for the expansion of the Diana figure upwards. Oil paint is handled like pastel, the dry medium of each pure colour unmixed and dragged over the surface to create effects of scattered light, allowing the forms themselves to appear as constructs of light, devoid of material form. The connection between the two protagonists is lessened; there is no touching of lips with the expectant kiss of the first version denied. The goddess's face is now barely discernible, which imparts a strange unreality to the encounter. This dematerialised Diana exists as vision,[12] lending a sense of the unknown to the scene.

In this particular subject, painted first in the late 1860s and revised in the early years of the new century, more profound questions engaged the octogenarian artist. As if to demonstrate his own still-potent artistic powers, Watts turns the story into an elemental drama as the forces of light confront the earth-bound mortal. The new spirit in this work came to critical attention when Watts sent the work to the New Gallery in 1904 (just two months before his death). *The Athenaeum*'s writer found 'a certain Blake-like mystery and intensity'. Comparing it to the earlier version, he wrote: 'it may not charm us quite so much, but it impresses us far more deeply. The spirit of the Moon Goddess, huge, pale, and dimly seen, broods over her recumbent lover with an insistence that is almost terrible.'[13]

BB

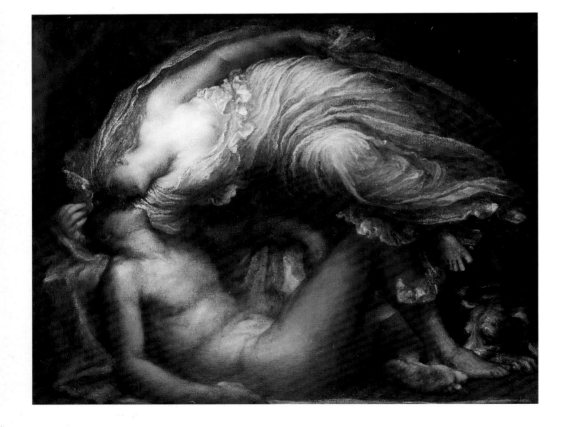

Cat. 81.1 *Endymion*, c.1872, oil on canvas, 52 × 65 cm (20½ × 25½ in), private collection

1   Keats's *Endymion* (1817) would also have been known to Watts, who admired his poetry.

2   The most recent discussion of this version is Angus Trumble, *Love and Death in the Age of Queen Victoria*, exh. cat., Art Gallery of South Australia, Adelaide, 2001, p. 118.

3   Ford Madox Brown, who saw it in progress in 1869, wrote to Watts that it was 'a masterpiece … as full of power in execution as it is poetic in conception', as quoted in ibid, p.8.

4   Watts Catalogue, I, p.42.

5   Ian Jenkins, '"G. F. Watts's Teachers": George Frederic Watts and the Elgin Marbles', *Apollo*, CXX (1984), p.176–9.

6   Intriguing compositional parallels exist with William Blake's illustrations to Blair's *Grave* (1808), *The Death of the Strong Wicked Man* and, according to Watts Whitechapel 1974, no.49, *The Soul Hovers over the Body* in the same volume. Possibly also related in composition are Burne-Jones's design of the late 1860s for Cupid and Psyche from Morris's *Earthly Paradise*, of which watercolours, a painting and an engraving exist. A range of other images may well have fed into Watts's visualisation.

7   Chesterton 1904, p.136.

8   Watts Catalogue, I, pp.42–3, as apparently begun *c*.1877.

9   Two versions exist: one was sold from the Watts Gallery to Cecil French, who included it with his bequest to the Hammersmith and Fulham Libraries (see David Rodgers, *Catalogue of the Cecil French Bequest*, London, 1997, no.52); another is in a private collection.

10   Watts 1912, II, p.313.

11   There are two very similar versions at the Manchester City Galleries: one dated 1901 and called *Diana and Endymion*, and one, presumably RA 1902, dated 1902. On the much later version of 1913 see *Heaven on Earth*, Djanogly Art Gallery, Nottingham, 1994, no.43.

12   When Mary Watts (II, p.313) commented 'what a dream for him [Endymion] to have!', she noted that Watts replied 'with a half-regretful smile, "Yes, but it was only moonshine after all"'. Stewart 1993, p.302, considers the painting a 'Theosophical reworking' of the earlier one.

13   *Athenaeum*, 23 April 1904, p.537.

82. *The Sower of the Systems, c.*1902

Oil on canvas, 66 × 53.3 cm (26 × 21 in)
COMWG101

PROVENANCE: collection of the artist; part of the original Memorial Collection, 1905

EXHIBITIONS: Watts London 1954, no.84; Watts Aldeburgh 1961, no.8; *La Peinture Romantique Anglaise et les Préraphaélites*, Petit Palais, Paris, 1972, no.323; Watts Whitechapel 1974, no.48; Watts Manchester, Minneapolis, Brooklyn 1978, no.34a; *Zwei Jahrhunderte englische Malerei: Britische Kunst und Europa 1680 bis 1880*, Haus der Kunst, Munich, 1979–80, no.382; *The Victorians: British Painting 1837–1901*, National Gallery of Art, Washington, DC, 1996, no.34; Watts Symbolism 1997, no.134; Watts Compton 2004, no.115

LITERATURE: Macmillan 1903, p.288; Watts Catalogue, I, p.134; Watts 1912, II, pp.105, 245, 302; Watts Gallery Catalogue 1920, no.96; Alston 1929, no.111; Staley 1978, pp.92–3; Warner 1996, p.136; Bryant 1997, pp.81, 280–1

This half-size finished oil study was preparatory to the large version of the subject exhibited at the New Gallery in 1903. Both show a figure, cloaked in blue, rushing into deep space, casting golden yellow and orange swirls of light into the darkness. The larger version (Art Gallery of Ontario, Toronto), as befits an exhibition picture, is slightly more defined, especially the treatment of the folds of the garment enveloping the figure and the hair flowing behind. The swirling light is more readable as curving arcs of colour, almost like galaxies of stars. In both the hand of the sower is silhouetted against an explosion of orange light. In cat.82 the handling is freer, looser and with dramatic passages of slashing brushwork and broken colour. The vibrant blue-greens and oranges collide with each other in this energised composition.

Because Watts painted *The Sower of the Systems* in his very last years, it did not have the international exposure that some of his other works did,[1] which is an irony as in many ways it spoke most directly to the new century and has indeed been claimed by modernists for its proto-abstract qualities. Like *Chaos* (cat.45), a seemingly random visual effect, the curiously refracted rays of light thrown by a night-light on the ceiling of the artist's bedroom, seems to have prompted the idea,[2] but one should bear in mind the myth-making surrounding an artist like Watts, who set himself and his art above the conventions of the day.

According to his wife, this work represented Watts's attempt at painting an unpaintable subject. Absorbed with the idea that 'There is only one great mystery – the Creator,' Watts commented: 'We can never return to the early ideas of Him as a kind white-bearded old man. If I were ever to make a symbol of the Deity, it would be as a great vesture into which everything that exists is woven.'[3] Indeed, the 'vesture', a garment of some sort, could just be seen as the swirling cloak in this painting. Along the same lines, Watts invoked the story of a child who, on being asked to draw God, produced 'a great number of circular scribbles, and putting his paper on a soft surface, struck his pencil through the centre, making a great void. This was utterly absurd as picture, but here was a greater idea in it than in Michael Angelo's old man with a long beard.'[4] Michelangelo's God in *The Creation of the Sun and Moon* and *The Creation of the Planets* on the Sistine Ceiling are the most significant art-historical precedents for the Creator,[5] but such traditional images had less validity for Watts in 1902. More related might be the works of the American Symbolist, Elihu Vedder (1836–1923), whose image of *The Pleiades* shows a group of figures casting stars through the darkness in similar swirling forms.[6] Watts commented on his own attempts 'at giving utterance and form to my ideas'. Such ruminations seem to relate in a general way to *The Sower of the Systems*, but there is a more particular context as well. What the painting shows is indeed an act of creation, specifically of the stars, constellations and galaxies of the firmament.

Watts's fascination with star-gazing dates back to his residence at old Little Holland House. Among the Prinseps' circle was the astronomer Sir John Herschel,[7] who actually witnessed the great comet of 1857 in the gardens there. In nearby Campden Hill another eminent astronomer Sir James South had an observatory, where Watts observed Saturn and its rings through a telescope. The artist commented 'it was a sight that dwarfed all others'.[8] His interests may well have led him to the works of the writer on astronomy, Agnes Mary Clerke, whose *Popular History of Astronomy during the Nineteenth Century* (1885) went through many editions. In her later book, *The System of the Stars*, published in 1890, she asserted that 'the entire contents, stellar and nebular, of the entire sphere belong to one mighty aggregation'.[9] This book put the complications of the subject into the language of the layman. At the very least, it may well have influenced the title of Watts's painting. He sought scientists for his portraits (although he did not succeed in attracting as many as he wished). To him, they were 'dwelling … in a kingdom of infinite wonder – larger than that of the poet or artist'.[10] In 1899 he wrote: 'Science has revealed to me laws, or rather the law, by which the physical universe is governed; awestruck by its sublimity and unity, I have learned to wonder, excepting at The Why!'[11] It is this sense of the infinity beyond the known world that lies at the heart of *The Sower of the Systems*. BB

1   Nor did it appear in the initial displays at the Watts Gallery.

2   Watts 1912, II, p.302.

3   Watts 1912, II, p.245.

4   Ibid.

5   Staley 1978, p.93, also cites as relevant the vague form of God in *Dividing Light from Darkness* and the swirling lines of light in *Dividing the Waters from the Earth*.

6   The design was published in *The Rubaiyat of Omar Khayyam* (1884), and an oil painting of the subject appeared in Vedder's one-man show in London in 1899, as noted in Bryant 1997, p.281 (and see p. 202 for further discussion).

7   An unfinished portrait drawing is described in Watts 1912, I, p.203.

8   Watts 1912, I, pp.203–4.

9   Quoted in H.P. Hollis, 'Clerke, Agnes Mary (1842–1907)', rev. M.T. Brück, *Oxford Dictionary of National Biography* (http://www.oxforddnb.com/view/article/32444, accessed 16 March 2008).

10   Watts 1912, I, pp.203–4.

11   Watts Papers, Watts to W.T. Stead, 6 January 1899.

83. *Portrait of the Painter (1904)*, 1904

Oil over monochrome tempera on canvas, 64 ×
46 cm (25½ × 19 in)
Exhibition labels from Manchester 1905 and
Walker Art Gallery, Liverpool, 1995 on reverse
COMWG6

PROVENANCE: collection of the artist
(Limnerslease); Lilian Mackintosh (Mrs Michael
Chapman), legal descendant of the artist; given by
her to the Watts Gallery in 1946 (no.45)

EXHIBITIONS: Memorial Exhibitions, London 1905,
no.192, Edinburgh 1905, no.13, Manchester 1905,
no.143, Newcastle 1905, no.97, Dublin 1906, no.5;
Watts Aldeburgh 1961, no.3; *Face to Face*, Walker
Art Gallery, Liverpool, 1994–5, no.55

LITERATURE: Watts 1912, II, p.319; Watts
Catalogue, II, p.169

Cat. 83.1 George Frederic Watts, photograph,
c.1904, Watts Gallery Archive

By the end of the nineteenth century G.F. Watts
was considered one of the greatest artists of his
age and his face was familiar to a wide public.
His white trimmed beard and skullcap were as
characteristic as his pet name 'Signor'. The
image of the old master is how Watts has
become most popularly known, eyes cast downwards, contemplative and spiritual. In this very
late self-portrait Watts strikes this distinctive
pose. In his touring memorial exhibition, which
opened at the Royal Academy in 1905, Mary
records that 'this portrait was made the centre
of the large gallery', appearing on a specially
constructed screen.[1]

Surprisingly, Watts's source for the painting
was not a looking glass, but 'a fine photograph
instead of the mirror, and to this he owed the
contemplative expression, absent in other
portraits, which all who knew him best held to
be the most characteristic' (cat.83.1).[2] There is a
remarkable fidelity to the likeness in the photograph that he uses, although as a painting it
displays other influences.[3]

According to Mary, it was 'painted but a few
weeks before his last illness',[4] a direct contrast to
the early self-portrait (cat.1), yet both are
supremely conscious of the image they project,
as Chesterton commented: 'His famous skull
cap, which makes him look like a Venetian
senator, is as pictorial and effective as the boyish
mane.'[5] The pose, which Watts adopted for so
many of his photographs, reflects the spirituality
that increasingly absorbed him. 'My first impression of him', wrote Mrs Stirling, 'was that of a
man whom intense spirituality had dominated,
almost annihilated, the material; he seemed
curiously ethereal, with the serenity of a being
accustomed to dwell in the presence of the
Unseen.'[6] The skullcap, a familiar and characteristic accessory, echoed Titian, senator and
cardinal. His fine clothes were the doctoral robes
of the Oxford University honorary DCL
(Doctor of Civil Law), which he received in 1882
and added to the meditative and pensive image
he projected. 'As a likeness,' Mary wrote, it 'is
the most perfect that exists.'[7]

The form and likeness of the painting, as
mentioned, are clearly taken from the photograph, but the painting owes more to Titian.
Watts looked to early painting techniques for the
painting's construction, using tempera as a
ground. 'He had been discussing the use of tempera for ground work in oil-painting with Mr.
Kerr Lawson, and to try this method he made a
study of his own head with a monochrome tempera, and over this painted in oil-colour.'[8] An
earlier state of the painting was photographed
by Hollyer and appears as a frontispiece to
Walter Bayes, *The Landscapes of George Frederic
Watts* (1907).

The painting is almost a mirror image of the
late Titian self-portrait of 1566 (Prado, Madrid),
echoing its profile, beard, skullcap and robes.
Indeed, Watts's fascination for Titian led to the
artist being dubbed the 'Titian of Limnerslease'
by George Meredith, and later the title was
forged onto a medal that was awarded him on
his eightieth birthday and presented by M.H.
Spielmann.[9] Its warm colours and painting
technique are as masterful as the image it presents of the artist, the grand old master of the
Victorian era. MB

1   Watts Catalogue, II, p.169.
2   Ibid.
3   The photograph, like the painting, was given to
     the Watts Gallery by his adopted daughter, Lilian
     Chapman.
4   Watts Catalogue, II, p.169.
5   Chesterton 1904, pp.42–3.
6   A.M.W. Stirling, *Life's Little Day*, London 1924,
     p.220.
7   Watts 1912, II, p.319.
8   Ibid.
9   Watts 1912, II, pp.233, 259. The medal is now in
     the Watts Gallery collection.

84. Studies for 'In the Land of Weiss-nicht-wo', c.1893

Pencil, pen and sepia ink on paper, 10.9 × 14 cm (4¼ × 5½ in)
Inscribed 'Travelling companions' and (in a later hand) 'Weissnictwo'
COMWG 2007.514

PROVENANCE: collection of the artist; Mary Watts; Lilian Mackintosh (Mrs Michael Chapman), legal descendant of the artist; by descent until formally included within the Watts Gallery's collections

This rapidly executed sketch shows Watts's first idea for the painting of two chubby little boys in a flower-strewn landscape that he eventually entitled 'In the Land of Weiss-nicht-wo' (cat.84.1).[1] Mary Watts records that, before he completed this work, they referred to it as the 'Gemini'.[2] Yet, judging by the inscription on the drawing, in the same ink as the drawing itself and presumably Watts's own hand, his working title was *Travelling Companions*.

The drawing shows two little figures, perhaps originally conceived as putti as one can see wings as lighter pencil lines later overlaid by ink, and two slighter studies of nudes. Cupids and putti appeared in Watts's work when he sought to inject a lighter note. But he seems to have decided to render these two as children rather than spirits, hence the inking over of the first pencil sketch. The tiny studies of these rounded little figures show a visual idea already nearly fully formed. One holds his arm outward, the other clasps his tiny fists to his chest. In the painting these sketches translate as one tot with his arm out, palm upward, holding a butterfly, while the other grasps a bunch of grapes from which he feeds himself.

As Cartwright noted when she saw this work in the studio in 1896, even in Watts's child paintings deeper meanings were never absent.[3] Here the artist offered a comment on the duality of human nature, containing both the carnal and the spiritual, with the emblematic butterfly representing the soul. Thus the two 'travelling companions' make their way through life as if on a journey with no idea what fate has in store. The drawing encapsulates the moment that the artist decided on the visual expression of the idea, but the verbal match of its title came at a later stage. Watts aimed for the larger meaning, but still with a twist of humour, when he borrowed a phrase from Thomas Carlyle's *Sartor Resartus* (1838), for a formal title that translates as 'In the land of I-know-not-where'.[4] BB

1   Watts Catalogue, I, p.76, where Mary Watts noted that it was painted rapidly on rough canvas.
2   Watts 1912, II, p.220.
3   Cartwright 1896, p.17.
4   Apart from the title, there is no other apparent connection with Carlyle's book, as noted in Watts London 1954, no.79. Watts had painted Carlyle's portrait in 1868.

Cat. 84.1 'In the Land of Weiss-nicht-wo', 1894, oil on canvas, 91.4 × 71.1 cm (36 × 28 in), COMWG46

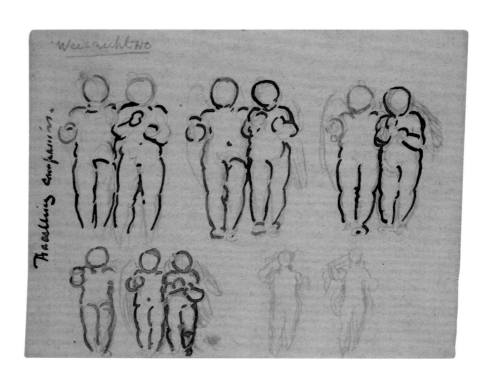

Sculpture

Watts's prolific output as a painter and portraitist tends to overshadow his comparatively small number of major sculptural works. However, Benedict Read's seminal *Victorian Sculpture* (1982) classifies him as a 'painter-sculptor', one of a number whose relatively modest sculptural production was disproportionately influential. This was the case with Watts's *Clytie* (cat.85), the only sculptural subject he exhibited during his lifetime. The marble *Clytie* and the work of another painter-sculptor, the bronze *Athlete Strangling a Python* (1877) by Lord Leighton, galvanised the New Sculpture movement, which dominated the last quarter of the nineteenth century.

Throughout his career Watts, like other painters of the period, made small sketches in wax or clay, often cast in plaster, of figures for his painted compositions. Several survive, including those for *Chaos* (cat.45), *Love Steering the Boat of Humanity* (1899–1901; Watts Gallery) and *The Curse of Cain* (1885–6; Watts Gallery). In addition, several larger, more finished studies were cast in plaster for the figures in *Love and Life* (cat.60), *Love and Death* (a nude study of Death; fig.52) and *The Genius of Greek Poetry* (cat.48), which was later cast in bronze. Watts's earliest sculptural work independent of the paintings was produced during his time in Italy (1843–7), when he first modelled the *Head of Medusa* (cat.89) in clay.

Watts seems to have produced no independent sculptural work during the 1850s but in 1864 exhibited *Time and Oblivion* (fig.39), describing it as 'a design for sculpture', and in 1866 proposed making 'a colossal bronze statue'. Neither materialised but his intentions were signalled. Sculpture interested him, at least in part, as an alternative to fresco, which he had hoped to introduce to public buildings but without success. In 1867 he was elected a Royal Academician, which appears to have been instrumental in his adopting sculpture as a serious pursuit. In the same year he had a new sculpture studio built and started the clay model for *Clytie* and the marble *Monument to Thomas Cholmondeley* (see p.62), the first of a series of memorial works made over the following five years.

A decisive moment for Watts's sculpture came in 1870 when he stopped modelling in clay, because it gave him rheumatism. He took up the coarse plaster medium of *gesso grosso*, which he used to model his first significant commission, received the same year, the *Monument to Hugh Lupus* (fig.75). This equestrian work of heroic scale was cast in bronze in 1884. Sketches Watts made in preparation for this were adapted for another equestrian work, the colossal *Physical Energy* (cat.86). He obsessively reworked, dismantled and re-built this for the next twenty years and, despite being cast in bronze in 1904, he continued to make revisions to the model until shortly before his death the same year. The third of these major works, the colossal *Monument to Lord Tennyson* (figs 62, 77; see cat.88), was started in 1898 and cast in 1903. Although *Hugh Lupus* was realistically detailed to meet the patron's demands, in *Tennyson* and *Physical Energy* Watts exploited the properties of *gesso grosso*, constructing broadly generalised forms complemented by rough and significantly anti-naturalistic surface texture. These properties resulted from close engagement with material and process, very much the concerns of a sculptor. SB

85. *Clytie*, 1868–81

Bronze, 94 × 62 × 47 cm (37 × 24½ × 18½ in)
COMWG2008.152

EXHIBITIONS: Watts Grosvenor Gallery 1881–2, no.205; Watts New Gallery, 1896–7, no.157; Chicago, 1893, no.48; *British Sculpture 1850–1914*, Fine Art Society, London, 1968, no.189

LITERATURE: Rossetti and Swinburne 1868, pp.27–8 and 35–6: Gosse 1894, p.139; Macmillan 1903, pp.34, 273–4; Barrington 1905, pp.40–2; Watts 1912, I, pp.237, 241, 277, II, p.45; Chapman 1945, pp.82, 175; Gutch 1968, pp.693–4, 697; Staley 1978, p.73, no.16 ; Blunt 1975, pp.190–1; Read 1982, pp.278–9, 286; Beattie 1983, p.147; Haight 1992, pp.204–8; Hutchings 2000, pp.33–4; Alison Smith (ed.), *Exposed: The Victorian Nude*, exh. cat. Tate Britain, London, 2001, p.115, no.48; Brown 2004, pp.96–101; Trodd and Brown 2004, pp.57–9; Gould 2004, p.58, no.34; Brown 2007, pp.11, 40–1

Clytie was Watts's first large autonomous sculpture in the round. He started work on the clay model in 1867 and the original marble carving was shown, unfinished, at the Royal Academy in 1868, where it was enthusiastically reviewed by W.M. Rossetti and A.C. Swinburne. In 1894 Edmund Gosse hailed it retrospectively as the precursor of the New Sculpture movement. The significance and popularity of *Clytie* are apparent in the considerable number of replicas made of the work in a range of media.

A bronze cast lent by Lord Mount-Temple was shown at the Grosvenor Gallery in 1881–2 in the important retrospective of 205 works by Watts, who presented another bronze to the Tate Gallery in 1900. The bronze seen here was gifted to the Watts Gallery by Lilian Chapman, Watts's adopted daughter.[1] The original marble carving (fig.74), bought from Watts by Lord Battersea, was presented to the Guildhall Art Gallery by Lady Battersea in 1919. There are also two other marble versions: that in Manchester City Art Gallery, made for Charles Rickards, was carved by Watts's assistant Aristide Fabbrucci (as stated on the plaque); the version in the Harris Museum and Art Gallery, Preston, also carved by Fabbrucci, was purchased from Mrs Fabbrucci in 1906. In both cases Watts probably executed the final chiselling, as was common practice at the time.

A number of plaster casts produced as early as 1869, the year following the RA exhibition, clearly indicate the impact that *Clytie* had made. The first mention of these is in connection with the cast sent by Watts to George Eliot early in 1870. The bust was carried into Eliot's drawing room by Burne-Jones and Rossetti on 9 January 1870, and two days later she wrote to Watts thanking him for 'the finest present I ever had in all my life'.[2] The painter John Lavery owned a plaster cast, as did the sculptor Albert Toft. In 1947 Toft (who had known Watts) presented a plaster cast to Birmingham City Art Gallery, writing to explain that:

> Watts had but three or maybe 4 replicas of this made. The late Duchess of Rutland had one, another is in the possession of an artist [Lavery presumably], the one I offer you has been in my possession over 50 years. Though this great work is in plaster, it is not of the

glaring white colour, but is more like an old marble in colour and quality.[3]

In 1938 a plaster cast was accepted by the Watts Gallery as a gift from Miss Mona Dolman made through the National Art Collections Fund. This copy is painted black. A plaster cast originally owned by Lilian Chapman is now in a private collection, and another was acquired by the Art Institute of Chicago in 2006. In 1912 'the well-known bust of Clytie by G.F. Watts' was reported to be in Panshanger Manor, Hertford, although the medium is not mentioned.[4] In addition, a terracotta *Clytie* in the grounds of the Watts Gallery was one of an unknown number made by the pottery run by Mrs Watts at Compton. SB

1   Listed in the Minutes of the Watts Gallery Trustees meeting on 14 July 1940, where it is described as 'Clytie, bronze head'.
2   Haight 1992, p.206.
3   Birmingham City Art Gallery inventory, no. 1947, p.70.
4   William Page (ed.), *A History of the County of Hertford*, vol. III, Victoria County History, London, 1912, p.470.

86. *Physical Energy*, 1914, reduction by Thomas Wren after Watts (re-cast *c.*1988)

Bronze, 44.5 × 48 × 20.5 cm (17½ × 19 × 8 in)
COMWG2007.931

EXHIBITIONS: *Paintings and Drawings of the Pre-Raphaelites and their Circle*, Fogg Art Museum, Cambridge, Mass., 1946; Watts London 1954, no.158; *British Sculpture 1850–1914*, Fine Art Society, London, 1968, no.188; Watts Whitechapel, 1974, no.72; *Gibson to Gilbert: British Sculpture 1840–1914*, Fine Art Society, London, 1992, no.63; Watts Compton 2004, no.111

LITERATURE: Gutch 1968, p.698, n.20; Cooper 1975, p.77; Hutchings 2000, pp.42–3; Brown 2007, pp.49–53

Watts's colossal *Physical Energy* exists as three full-size bronze casts in London, Cape Town and Harare. The idea developed alongside *Hugh Lupus* (fig.75), commissioned by the Duke of Westminster in 1870. The original design for *Hugh Lupus* was a generalised nude figure on horseback, but the Duke insisted on detailed historical costume and accessories. Once *Hugh Lupus* was complete, Watts reverted to his original design, which, with some modifications, was developed as the colossal *gesso grosso* model for *Physical Energy* now at Compton. Analogous small sculptural sketches and studies by Watts, though often identified as being for *Physical Energy*, were actually made for *Hugh Lupus* and include a plaster model and sketches at Compton and a bronze cast from a wax sketch (Fine Art Society). Watts himself never produced a finished study for *Physical Energy*.

The present statuette, a reduction after *Physical Energy*, originates in a model made by Thomas Wren in 1914. Wren assisted Watts from 1900 until his death, after which he continued to work for Mrs Watts. Either she or the gallery trustees asked him to model a reduction after the full-size *gesso grosso* model of *Physical Energy*. The plan was to make a series for commercial purposes and copies were sold from the Watts Gallery, the Fine Art Society and other outlets. Wren recalls that around fifty were to be cast by Parlanti's but the outbreak of war curtailed production. Only four casts inscribed 'Physical Energy, G.F. Watts' (right side, front) and 'T.H. Wren 1914' (right side, rear) have been located to date (Laing Art Gallery, Newcastle; Harris Museum and Art Gallery, Preston; Walker Art Gallery, Liverpool; Gibberd Art Gallery, Harlow). Subsequently, casts began to appear without Tom Wren's name and the date, including that noted in an inventory of 1928 in the Liverpool University Gallery and another (now lost) acquired by the Fogg Art Museum in 1929.

Correspondence in the Watts Gallery Archive clarifies a number of issues, including the fact that at some point (possibly prior to 1928) Parlanti's foundry had lost or damaged Wren's original plaster model and the moulds. All subsequent casts, therefore, are *surmoulages* – bronzes cast from moulds made from an existing bronze. None include Wren's name and the date, only the title 'Physical Energy' which has

led to them being frequently misattributed to Watts. The first instance is in the catalogue to the Fogg's 1946 exhibition where the cast is described as by Watts. When a similar description appeared in the catalogue for the 1954 Tate exhibition, Wren wrote to correct the misapprehension: 'I not only wish to inform you but to convince you, that this model was made by me in the early days of the 1914 war.'[1]

Subsequent descriptions of these casts vary in their attribution of authorship, although those that appear fairly regularly at auction are routinely attributed to Watts. It is impossible to know exactly how many of these reduced bronzes are in circulation, and their finish and patination varies considerably. The cast exhibited here is from a small edition made in the late 1980s on the instigation of John Lewis, Chairman of the Watts Gallery Trustees. Apart from the Wren version there are two later bronze reductions by other hands, associated with the full-size cast in Harare.[2] The interest in reductions of *Physical Energy* indicates the importance of a sculptural design that, though intended for a colossal scale, retains its essential power when viewed as a comparative miniature.
SB

1   Letter from Tom Wren to the Arts Council, dated 14 January 1955, Watts Gallery Archive.
2   See Brown, 2007, pp. 50–1.

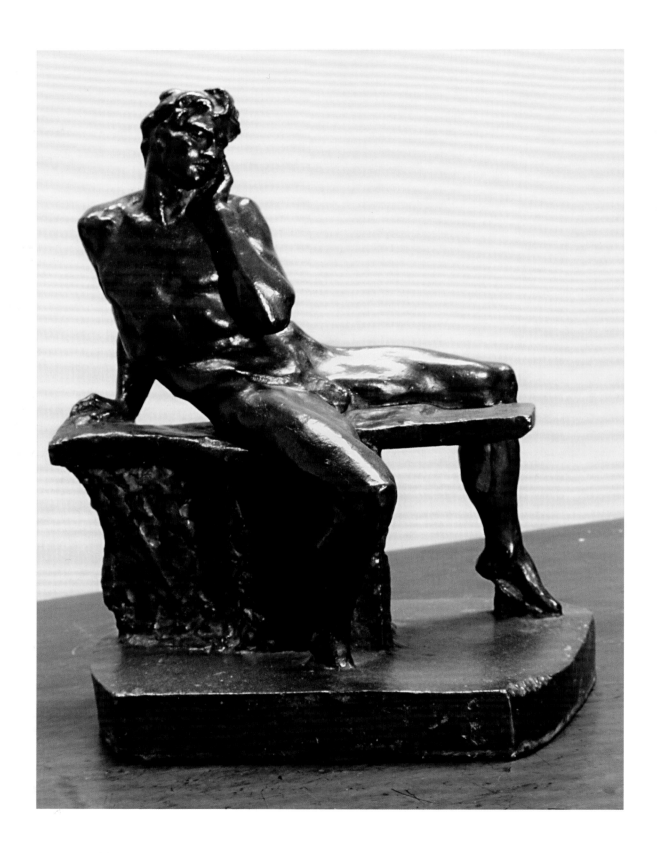

87. *The Genius of Greek Poetry*, cast after 1904

Bronze, 25.5 cm (10 in)
COMWG452

EXHIBITIONS: Watts London 1954, no.156; Watts Aldeburgh 1961, no.65; *British Sculpture 1850–1914*, Fine Art Society, London, 1968, no.185; Watts Compton 2004, no.28

LITERATURE: Barrington 1905, pp.135–6; Watts 1912, I, p.235, II, p.74; Alston 1929, opp. pl.iv; Staley 1978, p.83; Read 1982, p.273

This bronze cast shows the central figure in Watts's painting, *The Genius of Greek Poetry* (cat.48). According to Mrs Watts, the design for this composition originated soon after his trip to Asia Minor in the winter of 1856–7, during which he visited Greece. The first painting evolved over many years, was completed in 1878 and exhibited at the Grosvenor Gallery in 1881. Two other variations are in the Fogg Art Museum, Cambridge, Massachusetts, and the Harris Art Gallery, Preston. The pose of the main figure appears in a number of paintings executed by Watts in the late 1850s and ultimately derives from the 'Elgin marbles', particularly the Ilissos, of which he possessed a reduced plaster cast. The seated figure and its rocky support are surrounded by small, wraith-like sprites and are the only concrete forms in a composition dominated by ethereal effects. As such, it is unsurprising that Watts's treatment of the figure appears notably sculptural in quality. According to Alston, Mrs Watts stated that:

> Sir Edgar Boehm considered it the finest specimen of Mr Watts's art. He also mentioned how much his work appealed to sculptors. This, Mr Watts explained, was partly because he himself thought much about form, and partly because there were few designs of his, which would not be suitable for sculpture.[1]

In preparation for the painting, Watts modelled a study of the main figure, from which this small bronze was cast. Loshak, Staley and Gould all report the study as being in wax, though this cannot now be traced.[2] However, among the works gifted to the Watts Gallery by Lilian Chapman, Watts's adopted daughter, and listed in the trustees minutes on 4 July 1940 is a 'plaster study of the Genius of Greek Poetry'. Watts's wax models tended to be rougher and more generalised than those modelled in clay and then cast in plaster. However, the Chapman plaster cannot be traced either and it is possible it was destroyed in the process of making this bronze cast, some time after 1940. Handley-Read describes this bronze as 'cast posthumously' and this is certainly the case.[3] Gould however, dates the cast to 1856–7 and states: 'Watts made a wax model and cast it in bronze – presumably for

future reference.'[4] There is nothing to support this assertion and there is no reason why a model 'for future reference' should be cast in bronze. It is perhaps more likely that this cast resulted from the plans of the then curator of the Watts Gallery, Rowland Alston, to have Parlanti make bronze casts of small sculptural works in the collection. A letter to Alston from Parlanti sent in 1939 mentions that 'you told me that you had some sketches by the late Mr Watts that you were considering having cast in bronze after approval of the trustees'.[5] *The Genius of Greek Poetry* remains one of only two known examples of small bronzes to have been cast from a model made by Watts himself, rather than one made by another hand (see cats 86 and 88).

The Watts Gallery also conserves two small plaster sketches for the figure of *The Genius of Greek Poetry*, one of which shows the figure on its slab-like support, the other, the torso and thighs only. Also in the collection, and of the same scale, a plaster sketch of a bearded figure seated on a rock appears to be related to *The Genius of Northern Poetry*, apparently planned by Watts as a pendant to the Greek painting. Mrs Barrington alludes to this work but it seems not to have progressed beyond this initial stage. SB

1   Alston 1929, opp. pl.iv.
2   Loshak 1954, p. 54; Staley 1978, p.83; Gould 2004, p.56.
3   Lavinia Handley-Read, *British Sculpture 1850-1914*, London, 1968, p.35.
4   Gould 2004, p.56.
5   Letter from Parlanti dated 19 April 1939, Watts Gallery Archive.

88. *Tennyson*, *c*.1903, reduction by Thomas Wren after Watts

Bronze, 34.3 cm (13½ in)
COMWG478

EXHIBITIONS: *British Sculpture 1850–1914*, Fine Art Society, London, 1968, no.189

LITERATURE: *New York Times*, 18 June 1898; Watts 1912, II, pp.283–4; Gutch 1968, p.698, n.21; Hutchings 2000, p.20

This small bronze is a reduction of Watts's colossal statue of Tennyson and his wolfhound Karenina at Lincoln (figs 62, 77) and was cast from a model by Thomas Wren. It is undated but was among the works offered as a gift to the Watts Gallery by Lilian Chapman (Watts's adopted daughter) and noted in the minutes of the trustees meeting on 4 July 1940, where it is described as '1 bronze copy of Tennyson by T. Wren'.

Since the 1850s Watts had been a close friend of Alfred Lord Tennyson, the Poet Laureate, painting his portrait six times, the first in 1857 and the last in 1890/1. Tennyson, a native of Lincolnshire, died in October 1892, and a memorial committee was formed that proposed to place a stained glass window in Lincoln Cathedral in his honour. By 1898, however, the window had not materialised and it was belatedly agreed that a statue would be a more fitting memorial. Earl Brownlow, Lord Lieutenant of Lincolnshire, approached Watts for advice on commissioning this, but Watts asked to be allowed to make the statue himself, not as a commission but without payment if the county would cover the expense of casting in bronze. Mrs Watts reports: 'This was agreed upon, and he made a small model in wax for approval by Lord Brownlow and the committee.'[1]

There is a very rough wax sketch (55 cm/21½ in high) at the Watts Gallery that includes only a rudimentary indication of Tennyson's dog. Though in a poor state of repair, it is highly unlikely that this is the wax model referred to by Mrs Watts. Rather its characteristics are of a preliminary sketch, broadly establishing the pyramidal form and pose of the figure. There is however, a more detailed, bronzed plaster model (42.5cm/16¾ in) in the Tennyson Research Centre, Lincoln. This belonged to the Tennysons' collection and is almost certainly a cast from the wax model presented to the memorial committee. Like the wax at Compton, the surface of the plaster shows the same distinctive areas of scoring created by a toothed modelling tool. There are also significant differences between this plaster cast and the finished design, indicating that it is indeed a preparatory maquette rather than a reduction made after the work, like that by Wren.

Watts started work on the full-sized *gesso grosso* model of *Tennyson* in 1898, building it up on an armature used for his first version of *Aurora* (1870–5), which he disliked and destroyed. This recycling of an armature made for a smaller work caused problems and Mrs Watts mentions 'the fundamental mistake of a shallow base', which led to the Tennyson figure being broken up and a new beginning made.[2] It has been suggested that the wolfhound was subsequently introduced as a further structural support. However, fragments of the dog are discernible in the wax sketch and it appears in its entirety in the plaster model at Lincoln. The *gesso* model was eventually sent for casting in late 1903, although Watts died before seeing the completed bronze erected in the precinct of Lincoln Cathedral in 1905.

Wren's bronze reduction, with its notably deep base, replicates the appearance of the colossal statue at Lincoln though without the textured surface effects. Hutchings proposes that Wren made the reduction on the instigation of Mrs Watts who feared her husband would die before Singers had finished casting the full-size bronze.[3] This possibility is supported by the lack of evidence that any other bronzes were cast from Wren's model. It seems unlikely, therefore, that the reduction was intended for an edition for commercial purposes, as was the case with Wren's reduced model of *Physical Energy* (cat.86). There are, however, a number of plaster casts after Wren's model of *Tennyson* in private collections.

The Watts Gallery also conserves the full-size *gesso grosso* model from which the colossal bronze at Lincoln was cast and, on the same scale, two plaster studies by Watts, one of Tennyson's entire head and one of half the head. SB

1 Watts 1912, II, p.283.
2 Watts 1912, II, p.284.
3 Elizabeth Hutchings, *Discovering the Sculptures of George Frederick Watts O.M., R.A.*, Newport, 1994, p.20.

89. *Head of Medusa*, 1846–73

Alabaster, 54 × 44 × 37 cm (21¼ × 17¼ × 14½ in)
COMWG455.1

EXHIBITIONS: Watts Compton 2004, no.46

LITERATURE: Watts 1912, I, pp.65–6; Gutch 1968, pp.694, 697; Staley 1978, pp.78–9; Blunt 1975, pp.189–190; Read 1982, p.279; Hutchings 2000, pp.33–4; Brown 2004, pp.87–8

The *Head of Medusa* is Watts's earliest autonomous sculptural design, dating from 1846 during his time in Italy (1843–7) when he stayed at the Villa Careggi, Florence. A fellow guest, Lady Caroline Duff Gordon, mentions, on 19 September 1846, that Watts 'models a good deal … he has just done a very clever Medusa's Head'.[1] Mary Watts states that in Italy he modelled in clay and wax: 'The one remaining example of his work in the round belonging to this date is the head of the dead Medusa, which was twice carried out in alabaster, the last chiselling being done by his own hand.'[2] However, apart from the present example, the only other carving is the marble version now in the Whitworth Art Gallery, Manchester.[3]

The marble carving, commissioned by Watts's Manchester patron Charles Rickards, dates from 1871–3 and was started after Watts completed the alabaster memorial to Bishop Lonsdale (1869–71; Lichfield Cathedral). Writing to Rickards on 2 July 1871, Watts remarks: 'I am so charmed by the colour and texture of alabaster … that I am thinking of doing Clytie in that material.'[4] For Allen Staley 'Clytie' was a slip of the pen for 'Medusa' implying Watts's intention to make a second version in this material.[5] The same letter refers to the 'really beautiful block of marble' used for Rickards's carving. It appears curious, therefore, that Watts stained the marble, seemingly to simulate the effects of alabaster. Watts also told Rickards that his carving was in alabaster, writing to him in October 1874 to correct this. Staley attributes the error to Watts having subsequently carved an alabaster *Medusa*. However, the Wattses' copy of the 1887 auction catalogue for Rickards's collection, following his death, lists among Watts's works: '59. Medusa. Bust executed by the artist in Rome.' In pencil either Watts or his wife crossed out 'Rome' and substituted 'Florence', but this is the only annotation.

There is no provenance for the version in alabaster, a material that both Watts and Mary insistently associate with the design, apparently erroneously. This fails to dispel the possibility that an alabaster carving, made in Italy, later impressed Rickards who then commissioned a copy for himself. The staining of the marble may bear this out. Furthermore, for a novice sculptor, alabaster would be more amenable than marble and facilitate a 'last chiselling'. Staley sees the *Medusa* as 'originating in some form in Italy' and

both carvings as being from the 1870s, and Gould dates the alabaster 1871–3, while Blunt and Brown both support the earlier dating.[6]

The Rickards marble carving, inscribed '1873', has encouraged speculation that the alabaster version and the design itself originated in the 1870s. Gutch argues this on stylistic grounds, identifying it as Watts's 'most Pre-Raphaelite work', which could therefore not predate the group's formation in 1848.[7] Stylistically, however, the *Medusa* has affinities with the head of the supine woman in Watts's painting *Found Drowned* (cat.14). This inverted figure, with the crown of the head foremost, reflects the orientation of the Medusa's head in the Uffizi painting formerly attributed to Leonardo and now identified as a seventeenth-century Flemish work. Here, the Medusa's head lies on a stone slab, a presentation adopted in Watts's high relief carving where the head rises from an octagonal slab.

The subject clearly reflects Watts's response to Florence's celebrated Medusan imagery. Along with the 'Leonardo' painting, the Uffizi also houses Caravaggio's *Medusa* tondo, and Cellini's bronze *Perseus with the Medusa's Head* stands in the Loggia dei Lanzi. That the subject and the city were synonymous is evident in the title of Shelley's poem, 'On the Medusa of Leonardo … in the Florentine Gallery' (1819). By 1867 Pater's *The Renaissance* described this painting in terms anticipating the Medusa's prominence in later Symbolist and decadent imagery. Watts's conception, however, accords more closely with the late Romanticism of his Italian paintings. SB

1   Letter to Lord Holland, Holland House Papers, British Museum, Add. MS 52013.
2   Watts 1912, I, p.65.
3   A plaster cast at the Watts Gallery (Watts Compton 2004, no.4), presumably taken from the original clay model, would have been used for pointing up the carvings.
4   Watts Papers, Watts to C. H. Rickards, 2 July 1871.
5   Staley 1978, p.79.
6   Ibid. See also Gould 2004, p.62; Brown 2004, p.87; Blunt 1975, p.190.
7   R.E. Gutch, 'G.F. Watts's Sculpture', *Burlington Magazine*, vol. 110, November 1968, p.694.

Watts Gallery Archive

The Watts Gallery Archive contains many papers of George Frederic Watts (1817–1904) and Mary Seton Watts (1849–1938), as well as a collection of photographs and records of the creation and development of the Watts Gallery. It also includes material related to Watts's first wife Ellen Terry and letters to and from artists and historic figures. The collection has recently acquired the Rob Dickins Collection of over 4,000 Victorian photographs.   JD

G.F. Watts as Edward the Confessor (detail, cat. 102)

Photographs of G.F. Watts

90. G.F. Watts in the garden at Limnerslease, by George Andrews, 1895, 49.5 × 42 cm (19½ × 16½ in), Rob Dickins Collection at the Watts Gallery – illustrated p.x

91. G.F. Watts in his studio working on *Ariadne* (1888), by Donovan & Son (St James's Street, Brighton), 1888–9, 31 × 35.5 cm (13 × 14 in) – not illustrated

92. G.F. Watts in his studio at Limnerslease, photographer unknown, 26.5 × 23.5 cm (10½ × 9¼ in) – not illustrated

93. G.F. Watts with his wife Mary, photographer unknown, 24.5 × 29 cm (9¾ × 11½ in) – not illustrated

Hollyer photographs

At the height of his career Watts developed a working relationship with the photographer Frederick Hollyer (1838–1933) in order to record his output and circulate his paintings to a wide audience.

94. Photograph of *Paolo and Francesca* (cat.49) by Frederick Hollyer, retouched probably by Watts, 63.6 × 47.9 cm (25 × 18¾ in)

95. Photograph of *Hope* (cat.59) by Frederick Hollyer, c.1880s, 51 × 40 cm (20 × 15¾ in)

94

95

Prints

96. Black and white photogravure after *Hope* (cat.59), by Emery Walker, 33.9 × 26.4 cm (13¼ × 10½ in), inscribed 'Copyright Mrs G.F. Watts, December 10, 1913, Printed at the Watts Picture Gallery, Compton, Surrey, Emery Walker Ph. sc., Published by Franz Hanfstaengl, London', COMWG2008.77.1 – not illustrated. Following the death of Watts in 1904, Sir Emery Walker (1851–1933) set up a studio at the Watts Gallery and worked closely with Mary Seton Watts on the production of commercial photogravure reproduction prints of Watts's well-known works, allegedly using the artist's original paint pigments.

97. *Vanity Fair* cartoon by 'Spy' (Leslie Ward) of G.F. Watts, 'He paints portraits and ideas', 26 December 1891, chromolithograph, 38 × 25 cm (15 × 9¾ in), COMWG2008.159 – illustrated fig.57

Ephemera

The Watts Gallery owns a number of ephemera and memorabilia associated with Watts, including some objects from his studio in Melbury Road, Kensington, later used at Limnerslease, Watts's Compton house. These include Watts's two tables for mixing and storing paints, original easels, as well as five painting palettes and a selection of paint brushes.

98. G.F. Watts's painter's palette, 54 × 36 cm (21¼ × 14¼ in), COMWG2007.970.1

99. Letters from G.F. Watts (1882–1929): selections from a recently acquired collection of ninety autograph letters by Watts, his wife Mary and other members of their circle, purchased with grant aid from V&A Purchase Fund from Sotheby's, 2004, COMWG2007.984 – not illustrated

98

100. 'Subject Pictures Volume' of Mary Seton Watts's 'Manuscript Catalogue of Paintings by G.F. Watts O.M. R.A.' in three volumes (MSW/8/2; MSW/8/3; MSW/8/4), *c.*1912, 36 × 52.5 × 8 cm (20¾ × 3¼ in). Compiled by Mary Seton Watts after G.F. Watts's death, the 'Manuscript Catalogue of Paintings by G.F. Watts O.M. R.A.' presents a unique insight into Watts's prolific output and serves as an early attempt at a catalogue raisonné of some 800 paintings. Divided into three volumes – one album of subject pictures (164 pages) and two albums of portraits (175 pages; continuous pagination within the two volumes) – the manuscript catalogue contains detailed entries on each work with information on its full original title, size, provenance, date and exhibitions history, as well an extended catalogue note and a thumbnail photograph by Frederick Hollyer. The manuscript was handwritten by Mary's assistant Miss Sarah Nicol and is unique to the Watts Gallery.

100

100

Medals and honours

Watts was awarded two gold medals at the Paris Universal Exhibitions, one in 1878 (when ten works were exhibited, including the marble *Clytie* and the paintings *Love and Death* and *Judgement of Paris*) and the other in 1889 (eight works exhibited, including *Mammon* and *Hope*), and he won the high regard of the European artistic community. In recognition of his talent the artist was offered the baronetcy twice but turned it down, only to become the first artist recipient of the newly instituted Order of Merit presented by King Edward VII.

101a. Order of Merit medal, 1902, COMWG2008.137a/b

101b. Order of Merit Royal Warrant, GFW/6/14 – not illustrated

101c. Card bearing signatures of all the original recipients of the Order of Merit including G.F. Watts's, 25 July 1902, GFW/6/16 – not illustrated

101d. Gold Exposition Universelle medal, Antwerp, 1885, COMWG2008.139a/b – not illustrated

101e. Gold Exposition Universelle medal, Paris, 1878, COMWG2008.140a/b – not illustrated. Watts was also awarded the honour of 'Chevalier of the Légion d'honneur'.

101f. Gold International Exhibition medal, Melbourne, 1880, COMWG2008.141a/b – not illustrated. Watts received the award for his painting, *Britomart and her Nurse*.

101g. République Française silver medal, 1870, COMWG2008.142a/b – not illustrated

101h. République Française gold medal, 1870, COMWG2008.143a/b

101i. Adelaide Jubilee International Exhibition medal, 1887, COMWG2008.135a/b

101j. Gold Münchener Jahresausstellung medal, 1893, COMWG2008.136a/b

101k. New Gallery letter of congratulations on G.F. Watts's eightieth birthday, GFW/6/4 – not illustrated. Sent from directors and staff of the New Gallery, Regent Street, the letter contains thirteen signatures and a commemorative medal.

102. G.F. Watts Memorial Book, designed and compiled by Christopher Hatton Turnor (architect of the Watts Gallery), 43 × 33 × 6 cm (17 × 13 × 2¼ in). This large album, with an elaborately decorated, metalwork front cover embellished with amber beads and the embossed title '1817 WATTS 1904', bears the handwritten inscription on the inside cover: 'Presented by Mr Christopher Turnor of Stoke Rocheford, Grantham.' The spine and back cover are bound in green leather with embossed gilded borders and black leaf designs. The album contains

101i

101i (reverse)

101j

101j (reverse)

nineteen pages of notes taken by Turnor following his numerous conversations with G.F. Watts. This is one of two copies, the second being made for the architect himself.

The album also features a photograph of a statue of Watts as Edward the Confessor (illustrated p.303; identified and discussed here by Barbara Bryant), which stands on Alfred Gilbert's *Tomb Memorial to the Duke of Clarence*, Albert Memorial Chapel, Windsor Castle (1892–1901, with later additions). Gilbert gave the features of Watts to his small ornamental statue of St Edward, the medieval king and one of the decorative figures of saints adorning the memorial at Windsor. St Edward holds a model of the Albert Memorial Chapel and it seems that Turnor probably used this image in his memorial book to point up his own role as architect of the Watts Gallery, as well as to show his friend Watts as an honoured historical figure.

101a

101a (reverse)

101h

101h (reverse)

Publications

103. *Catalogue to G.F. Watts Solo Exhibition at the Metropolitan Museum of Art, New York* (1 November 1884 to October 1885), reprinted edition dated May to October 1885, GFW/8/2, 22 × 14 cm (8½ × 5½ in) – not illustrated. This is Watts's own copy of the catalogue and bears his annotations.

104a. *G.F. Watts: Reminiscences*, by Mrs Russell Barrington, Macmillan Company, New York, and George Allen, London, 1905 – not illustrated

104b. *George Frederic Watts: Annals of an Artist's Life* (vols I and II) and *George Frederic Watts: His Writings* (vol.III), by Mary Seton Watts, Macmillan and Co., London, 1912 – not illustrated

105. *Catalogue of Pictures by G.F. Watts, O.M., R.A.*, published by 'The Picture Gallery Compton Lane near Guildford, 1904' and printed by 'A. C. Curtis Printer, Guildford' – not illustrated

106. 'The New Gallery at Compton', by David Croal Thomson, *Art Journal*, 1906 – not illustrated

JD

102

102

102

Bibliography

ALSTON 1929   Rowland Alston, *The Mind and Work of G.F. Watts, O.M., R.A.*, London, 1929

BARRINGTON 1905   Mrs Russell (Emilie) Barrington, *G.F. Watts: Reminiscences*, London, 1905

BATEMAN 1901   Charles T. Bateman, *G.F. Watts, R.A.*, London, 1901

BAYES 1907   Walter Bayes, *The Landscapes of George Frederick Watts*, London, 1907

BEATTIE 1983   Susan Beattie, *The New Sculpture*, New Haven and London, 1983

BLUNT 1975   Wilfrid Blunt, *'England's Michelangelo': A Biography of George Frederic Watts, O.M., R.A.*, London, 1975

BROWN 2004   Stephanie Brown, 'Indefinite expansion: Watts and the physicality of sculpture', in Trodd and Brown 2004, pp.83–106

BROWN 2007   Stephanie Brown, *G.F. Watts, Physical Energy, Sculpture and Site*, Compton, 2007

BRYANT 1987   Barbara Bryant, 'G.F. Watts's First *Hope*', *Sotheby's Art at Auction 1986–1987*, London, 1987, pp.62–5

BRYANT 1987–8   Barbara Bryant, 'The Origins of G.F. Watts's "Symbolical" Paintings: A Lost Study Identified', *Porticus: Journal of the Memorial Art Gallery of Rochester*, vols 10–11 (1987–8), pp.52–9

BRYANT 1996   Barbara Bryant, 'G.F. Watts at the Grosvenor Gallery: "Poems Painted on Canvas" and the New Internationalism', in Susan Casteras and Colleen Denney (eds), *The Grosvenor Gallery: A Palace of Art in Victorian England*, New Haven and London, 1996, pp.109–28, 176–9

BRYANT 1997   Barbara Bryant, 'G.F. Watts and the Symbolist Vision' and entries in Watts Symbolism 1997 (Exhibitions), pp.65–81 (essay)

BRYANT 2003   Barbara Bryant, entries on works by Watts, in Stephen Wolohojon (ed.), *A Private Passion: 19th Century Paintings and Drawings from the Grenville L. Winthrop Collection*, exh. cat., Metropolitan Museum of Art, New York (and other venues), 2003

BRYANT 2004   See Watts Portraits 2004 (Exhibitions)

BRYANT ODNB   Barbara Coffey Bryant, 'Watts, George Frederic (1817–1904)', *Oxford Dictionary of National Biography* (http://www.oxforddnb.com/view/article/36781)

CARTWRIGHT 1896   Julia Cartwright, 'George Frederic Watts, R.A.', *Art Journal: Easter Annual*, 1896

CHAPMAN 1945   Ronald Chapman, *The Laurel and the Thorn: A Study of G.F. Watts*, London, 1945

CHESTERTON 1904   G.K. Chesterton, *G.F. Watts*, London, 1904 (and later editions)

COOK AND WEDDERBURN 1903–12   E.T. Cook and Alexander Wedderburn (eds), *The Works of John Ruskin*, 39 vols, London, 1903–12

DAKERS 1999   Caroline Dakers, *The Holland Park Circle: Artists and Victorian Society*, New Haven and London, 1999

DIBDIN 1923   E. Rimbault Dibdin, *George Frederick Watts*, London, 1923

ERSKINE 1906   Mrs Steuart [Beatrice] Erskine, 'The Watts Memorial Gallery at Limnerslease', *The Studio*, August 1906, pp.189–94

FOGG ART MUSEUM 1946   *Paintings of the Pre-Raphaelites and their Circle*, exh. cat., Fogg Art Museum, Harvard University, Cambridge, Mass., 1946

FORD 1998   'The Ford Collection – I, II', 'Drawings by G.F. Watts and other Victorian Artists', with cataloguing by John Christian, *The Sixtieth Volume of the Walpole Society*, II, London, 1998, pp.247–63

FORSYTH 1889   Peter Taylor Forsyth, *Religion in Recent Art: Being Expository Lectures on Rossetti, Burne-Jones, Watts, Holman Hunt and Wagner*, Manchester, 1889

GAJA 1995   Katerine Gaja, *G.F. Watts in Italy: A Portrait of the Artist as a Young Man*, Florence, 1995

GAJA 2005   Katerine Gaja, 'Illustrating Lorenzo the Magnificent from William Roscoe's *The Life of Lorenzo de' Medici called the Magnificent* (1795) to George Frederic Watts's fresco at Careggi (1845)', in *Victorian and Edwardian Responses to the Italian Renaissance*, ed. John E. Law and Lene Østermark-Johansen, Aldershot, 2005, pp.138–9

GOSSE 1894   Edmund Gosse, 'The New Sculpture 1879–1894', *The Art Journal*, 1894

GOULD 2004   Veronica Franklin Gould, *G.F. Watts: The Last Great Victorian*, New Haven and London, 2004

GRIERSON 1959   Edward Grierson, *Storm Bird: The Strange Life of Georgina Weldon*, London, 1959

GUTCH 1968   R.E. Gutch, 'G.F. Watts's Sculpture', *Burlington Magazine*, CX (1968), pp.693–9

HAIGHT 1992   Gordon S. Haight, *George Eliot's Originals and Contemporaries: Essays in Victorian Literary History and Biography*, London, 1992

HUTCHINGS 1994/2000   Elizabeth Hutchings, *Discovering the Sculptures of George Frederick Watts O.M., R.A.*, Newport, 1994 (second edn 2000)

ILCHESTER 1937   The Earl of Ilchester, *Chronicles of Holland House 1820–1900*, London, 1937

IONIDES 1925   Luke Ionides, *Memories*, London, 1925 (reprinted in facsimile with an afterword by Julia Ionides, Ludlow, 1996)

LANGTRY 1925   Lillie Langtry (Lady de Bathe), *The Days I Knew*, London, 1925

LANIGAN 2000   Dennis Lanigan, *A Dream of the Past: Pre-Raphaelite and Aesthetic Movement Paintings, Watercolours and Drawings from the Lanigan Collection*, exh. cat., University of Toronto Art Centre, Toronto, 2000

LOSHAK 1954   See Watts London 1954 (Exhibitions)

LOSHAK 1963   David Loshak, 'G.F. Watts and Ellen Terry', *Burlington Magazine*, CV (1963), pp.476–85

MACLEAN, PELTER AND SHEPHERD 2003   Janet McLean, Richard Pelter and Rupert

Shepherd, ' "Gazing, but not copying": The creation of G.F. Watts's Alfred inciting the Saxons to prevent the landing of the Danes,' *Apollo* CLVIII (2003), pp.35–8

MACMILLAN 1903   Hugh Macmillan, *The Life-Work of George Frederick Watts, R.A.*, London, 1903

MEADE 1894   L.T. Meade, 'The Painter of the Eternal Truths', *Sunday Magazine*, 1894, pp.15–19, 96–100

MONKHOUSE 1882   Cosmo Monkhouse. 'The Watts Exhibition', *Magazine of Art*, 1882, pp.177–82

MORRIS 1996   Edward Morris, *Victorian and Edwardian Paintings in the Walker Art Gallery and at Sudley House*, National Museums and Galleries in Merseyside, London, 1996

MULLEN 1974   See Watts Whitechapel 1974 (Exhibitions)

ORMOND 1975   Richard Ormond, *G.F. Watts: The Hall of Fame: Portraits of his Famous Contemporaries*, London, 1975

Oxford Dictionary of National Biography, Oxford, 2004, online edition (2008) at http://www.oxforddnb.com/view/article/…

PANTAZZI 2006   'Idea and Ideal: The Transformations of *Time, Death, and Judgment* by George Frederic Watts', *National Gallery of Canada Review*, V (2006), pp.45–63

READ 1982   Benedict Read, *Victorian Sculpture*, New Haven and London, 1982

ROSSETTI AND SWINBURNE 1868   W.M. Rossetti and A.C. Swinburne, *Notes on the Royal Academy Exhibition, 1868*, London, 1868

SHORT 1924   Ernest H. Short, *British Artists: Watts*, London, 1924

SHREWSBURY 1918   H.W. Shrewsbury, *The Visions of an Artist: Studies in G.F. Watts, R.A., O.M. with verse interpretations*, London, 1918

SKETCHLEY 1904   R.E.D. Sketchley, *Watts*, London, 1904

SMITH 1996   Alison Smith, *The Victorian Nude: Sexuality, Morality and Art*, Manchester, 1996

SPIELMANN 1886   M[arion] H[arry] Spielmann, 'The Works of Mr. George F. Watts, R.A., with a complete catalogue of his Pictures', *Pall Mall Gazette*, Extra Number, 22 (1886), pp.1–32

SPIELMANN 1902   M[arion] H[arry] Spielmann, 'Mr G.F. Watts, RA', *Review of Reviews*, 10 June 1902, pp.556–79

SPIELMANN 1905   M[arion] H[arry] Spielmann, *G.F. Watts, R.A., O.M., as a Great Painter of Portraits: A Lecture*, Memorial Hall, Manchester, London and Manchester, 1905

STALEY 1978   See Watts Manchester, Minneapolis, Brooklyn 1978 (Exhibitions)

STALEY AND UNDERWOOD 2006   See Watts London and Compton 2006 (Exhibitions)

STEPHENS 1887   F.G. Stephens, 'George Frederick Watts, Esq., R.A., LL.D.', *The Portfolio*, 1887, pp.13–19

STEWART 1993   David Stewart, 'Theosophy and Abstraction in the Victorian Era: The Paintings of G.F. Watts', *Apollo* CXXXVIII (1993), pp.298–302

TENNYSON 1982   Alfred Lord Tennyson, *In Memoriam*, ed. Susan Shatto and Marion Shaw, Oxford, 1982

THOMPSON 1913   Charles Thompson, 'Watts Picture Gallery Curator's Report', 15 November 1913, Watts Archive

THOMPSON 2000   Brian Thompson, *A Monkey among Crocodiles: The Life, Loves and Lawsuits of Mrs. Georgina Weldon*, London, 2000

TRODD AND BROWN 2004   Colin Trodd and Stephanie Brown (eds), *Representations of G.F. Watts: Art Making in Victorian Culture*, Aldershot, 2004

TURNOR 1904   Christopher Turnor, 'Conversations I Had with Mr Watts from 1902 to 1904', Watts Gallery Archive

TWISLETON 1928   *Letters of the Hon. Mrs. Edward Twisleton written to her family, 1852–1862*, London, 1928

VON SCHLEINITZ 1904   Otto von Schleinitz, *George Frederic Watts*, Bielefeld and Leipzig, 1904

WARNER 1996   Malcolm Warner in *The Victorians: British Painting 1837–1901*, National Gallery of Art Washington, Washington, DC, 1996

WATTS 1880   George Frederic Watts, 'The Present Conditions of Art', *Nineteenth Century*, February 1880, pp.235–51

WATTS 1888–9   George Frederic Watts, 'Thoughts on our Art of Today', *Magazine of Art*, 1888, pp.90–2; 'More Thoughts on our Art of Today', *Magazine of Art*, 1888–9, pp.244–56

WATTS 1912   M[ary] S[eton] Watts, *George Frederic Watts: The Annals of an Artist's Life*, 3 vols, London, 1912

WATTS CATALOGUE   'Catalogue of the Works of G.F. Watts, compiled by his widow', three unpublished manuscript volumes by M.S. Watts, begun *c.*1910 and continued thereafter (see also cat.100), Watts Gallery, Compton, Surrey. The first volume contains the Subject Paintings; the second two contain the Portraits. Since the latter two have continuous pagination, these volumes are referred to as volume II

WATTS GALLERY CATALOGUE 1904/1920/1957 *Catalogue of Pictures by G.F. Watts, O.M., R.A.*, The Picture Gallery, Compton Lane, near Guildford, 1904 (and revised editions of 1920 and 1957)

WATTS PAPERS   Watts Papers (formerly Watts Gallery), unpublished, sold at Sotheby's, 14 March 1979, microfiche copies at the National Portrait Gallery (and some originals), the Watts Gallery and Tate

WHEELER 1990   Michael Wheeler, *Death and the Future Life in Victorian Literature and Theology*, Cambridge, 1990

WHEELER 1999   Michael Wheeler, *Ruskin's God*, Cambridge, 1999

WHEELER 2006   Michael Wheeler, *The Old Enemies: Catholic and Protestant in Nineteenth-Century English Culture*, Cambridge, 2006

Exhibitions

WATTS MANCHESTER 1880 *A Collection of Pictures and Sculpture: The Works of G.F. Watts, Esq., R.A.* (the collection of Charles Hilditch Rickards), Royal Institution, Manchester, 1880

WATTS GROSVENOR 1881 *Winter Exhibition: Collection of the Works of G.F. Watts., R.A.*, Grosvenor Gallery, London, 1881

WATTS NEW YORK 1884 *Paintings by G.F. Watts., R.A.* (with catalogue notes compiled in part by Emilie Barrington; reprinted in Barrington 1905, pp.118–38), Metropolitan Museum of Art, New York, 1884–5

WATTS BIRMINGHAM 1885 *Collection of Paintings by G.F. Watts, R.A. and Edward Burne-Jones, A.R.A.*, Museums and Art Gallery, Birmingham, 1885

WATTS NOTTINGHAM 1886 *Collection of Pictures by G.F. Watts, R.A.*, Museum and Art Gallery, Nottingham, 1886

PEOPLE'S PALACE 1888 *Catalogue of the Finest Collection of Modern Paintings ever Seen in East London*, People's Palace for East London, Mile End Road, London, August–September 1888

WATTS NEW GALLERY 1896 *Winter Exhibition: The Works of G.F. Watts*, New Gallery, London, 1896–7

WATTS LEIGHTON HOUSE 1903 *Loan Collection of Works by G.F. Watts RA*, Leighton House, London, March 1903

WATTS GALLERY 1904 See Watts Gallery Compton 1904 (p.305)

MEMORIAL EXHIBITIONS
LONDON 1905 *Winter Exhibition: Works by the Late George Frederick [sic] Watts, R.A., O.M. and the Late Frederick Sandys*, Royal Academy of Arts, London, 1905

MANCHESTER 1905 *G.F. Watts Memorial Exhibition*, City Art Gallery, Manchester, 1905

NEWCASTLE 1905 *Special Loan Collection of Works by the Late G.F. Watts, R.A., O.M.*, Laing Art Gallery, Newcastle, 1905

EDINBURGH 1905 *Memorial Exhibition of Works by the Late G.F. Watts, R.A.*, Royal Scottish Academy, Edinburgh, 1905

DUBLIN 1906 *Watts Memorial Exhibition*, Royal Hibernian Academy, Dublin, 1906

WATTS LONDON 1954 *George Frederic Watts, O.M., R.A., 1817–1904* (exhibition organised by the Arts Council of Great Britain; exh. cat. by David Loshak), Tate Gallery, London, 1954

WATTS ALDEBURGH 1961 *Paintings, Drawings and Sculpture by G.F. Watts (1817–1904)*, Church Hall, Aldeburgh, 1961

WATTS WHITECHAPEL 1974 *G.F. Watts: A Nineteenth-Century Phenomenon* (exh. cat. by Chris Mullen, with an introduction by John Gage), Whitechapel Art Gallery, London, 1974

WATTS MANCHESTER, MINNEAPOLIS, BROOKLYN 1978 *Victorian High Renaisance* (exh. cat. with essay and entries on Watts by Allen Staley), City Art Gallery, Manchester; The Minneapolis Institute of Arts; The Brooklyn Museum, 1978–9

WATTS SYMBOLISM 1997 *The Age of Rossetti, Burne-Jones & Watts: Symbolism in Britain 1860–1910* (exh. cat. with essay, 'G.F. Watts and the Symbolist Vision', and all entries on Watts by Barbara Bryant), Tate Gallery, London, 1997

WATTS COMPTON 2004 *The Vision of G.F. Watts OM RA (1817–1904)* (exh. cat., ed. Veronica Franklin Gould, with contributions from Richard Ormond, Richard Jefferies, Alison Smith, David Stewart and Hilary Underwood), Compton, 2004

WATTS PORTRAITS 2004 *G F Watts Portraits: Fame & Beauty in Victorian Society* (exh. cat. by Barbara Bryant, with an introduction by Andrew Motion), National Portrait Gallery, London, 2004–5

WATTS LONDON AND COMPTON 2006 *Painting the Cosmos: Landscapes by G.F. Watts* (exh. cat. by Allen Staley and Hilary Underwood), Nevill Keating Pictures, London, and Watts Gallery, Compton, 2006

Index